W ILD *at*
H EART

and

Captivating

Christmas 2008

Richard,

May God really bless you
in 2009 and beyond as you
seek Him and His will for you,
with love, your sister in Christ,

Jane x x

Jeremiah 29 v 11-14.

OTHER BOOKS BY JOHN ELDREDGE

The Way of the Wild Heart

Epic

Desire (formerly *The Journey of Desire*)

Waking the Dead

The Sacred Romance (Coauthored with Brent Curtis)

OTHER BOOKS BY STASI ELDREDGE

Your Captivating Heart

WILD at HEART

DISCOVERING THE SECRET *of* A MAN'S SOUL

JOHN ELDREDGE

Captivating

UNVEILING THE MYSTERY *of a* *Woman's Soul*

JOHN AND STASI ELDREDGE

THOMAS NELSON
Since 1798

NASHVILLE   DALLAS   MEXICO CITY   RIO DE JANEIRO   BEIJING

Wild at Heart © 2001 by John Eldredge.
Captivating © 2005 by John Eldredge and Stasi Eldredge.

Published in Nashville, Tennessee, by Thomas Nelson. Thomas Nelson is a trademark of Thomas Nelson, Inc.

Published in association with Yates & Yates, LLP, Attorneys and Counselors, Orange, California

Thomas Nelson, Inc., titles may be purchased in bulk for educational, business, fund-raising, or sales promotional use. For information, please e-mail SpecialMarkets@ThomasNelson.com.

Unless otherwise noted, Scripture quotations are from the HOLY BIBLE: NEW INTERNATIONAL VERSION®. © 1973, 1978, 1984 by International Bible Society. Used by permission of Zondervan Publishing House. All rights reserved.

Scripture quotations noted *Alter* are from *Genesis: Translation and Commentary*. © 1996 by Robert Alter.

Scripture quotations noted NKJV are from THE NEW KING JAMES VERSION. © 1979, 1980, 1982, 1990, 1994 by Thomas Nelson, Inc.

Scripture quotations noted The Message are from *The Message: The New Testament in Contemporary English*. © 1993 by Eugene H. Peterson.

Scripture quotations noted NLT are from the *Holy Bible*, New Living Translation, ©1996. Used by permission of Tyndale House Publishers, Inc., Wheaton, Illinois 60189. All rights reserved.

Scripture taken from the NEW AMERICAN STANDARD BIBLE®, © The Lockman Foundation 1960, 1962, 1963, 1968, 1971, 1972, 1973, 1975, 1977. Used by permission

ISBN 978-1-4002-0205-8 (IE)

Printed in the United States of America

07 08 09 10 QW 5 4 3 2 1

CONTENTS

WILD at HEART

CONTENTS

Captivating

WILD *at* HEART

For Samuel, Blaine, and Luke.

I love your warrior hearts.
You definitely have what it takes.

INTRODUCTION

I know. I almost want to apologize. *Dear Lord—do we really need another book for men?*

Nope. We need something else. We need *permission.*

Permission to be what we are—men made in God's image. Permission to live from the heart and not from the list of "should" and "ought to" that has left so many of us tired and bored.

Most messages for men ultimately fail. The reason is simple: They ignore what is deep and true to a man's *heart,* his real passions, and simply try to shape him up through various forms of pressure. "This is the man you *ought* to be. This is what a good husband/father/Christian/churchgoer *ought* to do." Fill in the blanks from there. He is responsible, sensitive, disciplined, faithful, diligent, dutiful, etc. Many of these are good qualities. That these messengers are well-intentioned I have no doubt. But the road to hell, as we remember, is paved with good intentions. That they are a near total failure should seem obvious by now.

No, men need something else. They need a deeper understanding of why they long for adventures and battles and a Beauty—and why God made them *just like that.* And they need a deeper understanding of why women long to be fought for, to be swept up into adventure, and to *be* the Beauty. For that is how God made them as well.

So I offer this book, not as the seven steps to being a better Christian, but as a safari of the heart to recover a life of freedom, passion, and adventure. I believe it will help men get their heart back—and women as well. Moreover, it will help women to understand their men and help them live the life they both want. That is my prayer for you.

It is not the critic who counts; not the man who points out how the strong man stumbles, or where the doer of deeds could have done them better. The credit belongs to the man in the arena, whose face is marred by dust and sweat and blood; who strives valiantly . . . who knows the great enthusiasms, the great devotions; who spends himself in a worthy cause; who at the best knows in the end the triumph of high achievement, and who at the worst, if he fails, at least fails while daring greatly, so that his place shall never be with those cold and timid souls who have never known neither victory nor defeat.

—TEDDY ROOSEVELT

The kingdom of heaven suffers violence, and violent men take it by force.

—MATTHEW 11:12 NASB

CHAPTER ONE

WILD AT HEART

The heart of a man is like deep water . . .
— PROVERBS 20:5 NKJV

The spiritual life cannot be made suburban. It is always frontier, and we who live in it must accept and even rejoice that it remains untamed.
— HOWARD MACEY

I want to ride to the ridge where the west commences
I can't look at hobbles and I can't stand fences
Don't fence me in.
— COLE PORTER
"Don't Fence Me In"

At last, I am surrounded by wilderness. The wind in the top of the pines behind me sounds like the ocean. Waves are rushing in from the great blue above, cresting upon the ridge of the mountain I have climbed, somewhere in the Sawatch Range of central Colorado. Spreading out below me the landscape is a sea of sagebrush for mile after lonesome mile. Zane Grey immortalized it as the purple sage, but most of the year it's more of a silver gray. This is the kind of country you could ride across for days on horseback without seeing another living soul. Today, I am on foot. Though the sun is shining this afternoon, it will not warm above thirty here near the Continental Divide, and the sweat I worked up scaling this face is now making me shiver. It is late October and winter is coming on. In the distance, nearly a hundred miles south by southwest, the San Juan Mountains are already covered in snow.

The aroma of the pungent sage still clings to my jeans, and it clears my head as I gasp for air—in notably short supply at 10,000 feet. I am forced to rest again, even though I know that each pause broadens the distance between me and my quarry. Still, the advantage has always been his. Though the tracks I found this morning were fresh—only a few hours old—that holds little promise. A bull elk can easily cover miles of rugged country in that amount of time, especially if he is wounded or on the run.

The wapiti, as the Indians called him, is one of the most elusive creatures we have left in the lower forty-eight. They are the ghost kings of the high country, more cautious and wary than deer, and more difficult to track. They live at higher elevations, and travel farther in a day, than nearly any other game. The bulls especially seem to carry a sixth sense to human presence. A few times I've gotten close; the next moment they are gone, vanishing silently into aspen groves so thick you wouldn't have believed a rabbit could get through.

It wasn't always this way. For centuries elk lived out on the prairies, grazing together on the rich grasses in vast numbers. In the spring of 1805 Meriwether Lewis described passing herds lolling about in the thousands as he made his way in search of a Northwest Passage. At times the curious wandered so close he could throw sticks at them, like bucolic dairy cows blocking the road. But by the end of the century westward expansion had pushed the elk high up into the Rocky Mountains. Now they are elusive, hiding out at timberline like outlaws until heavy snows force them down for the winter. If you would seek them now, it is on their terms, in forbidding haunts well beyond the reach of civilization.

And that is why I come.

And why I linger here still, letting the old bull get away. My hunt, you see, actually has little to do with elk. I knew that before I came. There is something else I am after, out here in the wild. I am searching for an even more elusive prey . . . something that can only be found through the help of wilderness.

I am looking for my heart.

WILD AT HEART

Eve was created within the lush beauty of Eden's garden. But Adam, if you'll remember, was created *outside* the Garden, in the wilderness. In the record of our beginnings, the second chapter of Genesis makes it clear: Man was born in the outback, from the untamed part of creation. Only afterward is he brought to Eden. And ever since then boys have never been at home indoors, and men have had an insatiable longing to explore. We long to return; it's when most men come alive. As John Muir said, when a man comes to the mountains, he comes home. The core of a man's heart is undomesticated *and that is good.* "I am not alive in an office," as one Northface ad has it. "I am not alive in a taxi cab. I am not alive on a sidewalk." Amen to that. Their conclusion? "Never stop exploring."

My gender seems to need little encouragement. It comes naturally, like our innate love of maps. In 1260 Marco Polo headed off to find China, and in 1967, when I was seven, I tried to dig a hole straight through from our backyard with my friend Danny Wilson. We gave up at about eight feet, but it made a great fort. Hannibal crosses his famous Alps, and there comes a day in a boy's life when he first crosses the street and enters the company of the great explorers. Scott and Amundsen race for the South Pole, Peary and Cook vie for the North, and when last summer I gave my boys some loose change and permission to ride their bikes down to the store to buy a soda, you'd have thought I'd given them a charter to go find the equator. Magellan sails due west, around the tip of South America—despite warnings that he and his crew will drop off the end of the earth—and Huck Finn heads off down the Mississippi ignoring similar threats. Powell follows the Colorado into the Grand Canyon, even though—no, *because*—no one has done it before and everyone is saying it can't be done.

And so my boys and I stood on the bank of the Snake River in the spring of '98, feeling that ancient urge to shove off. Snow melt was high that year, unusually high, and the river had overflowed its banks and was surging through the trees on both sides. Out in the middle of the river, which is crystal clear in late summer but that day looked like chocolate milk, logs were floating down, large tangles of branches bigger than a car, and who knows what else. High and muddy and fast, the Snake was forbidding. No other rafters could be seen. Did I mention it was raining? But we had a brand-new canoe and the paddles were in hand and, sure, I have never floated the Snake in a canoe, nor any other river for that matter, but what the heck. We jumped in and headed off into the unknown, like Livingstone plunging into the interior of dark Africa.

Adventure, with all its requisite danger and wildness, is a deeply spiritual longing written into the soul of man. The masculine heart needs a place where nothing is prefabricated, modular, nonfat, zip lock, franchised, on-line, microwavable. Where there are no deadlines, cell phones, or committee meetings. Where there is room for the soul. Where, finally, the geography around us corresponds to the geography of our heart. Look at the heroes of the biblical text: Moses does not encounter the living God at the mall. He finds him (or is found by him) somewhere out in the deserts of Sinai, a long way from the comforts of Egypt. The same is true of Jacob, who has his wrestling match with God not on the living room sofa but in a wadi somewhere east of the Jabbok, in Mesopotamia. Where did the great prophet Elijah go to recover his strength? To the wild. As did John the Baptist, and his cousin, Jesus, who is *led by the Spirit* into the wilderness.

Whatever else those explorers were after, they were also searching for themselves. Deep in a man's heart are some fundamental questions that simply cannot be answered at the kitchen table. Who am I? What am I made of? What am I destined for? It is fear that keeps a man at home where things are neat and orderly *and under his control.* But the answers to his deepest questions are not to be found on television or in the refrigerator. Out there on the burning desert sands, lost in a trackless waste, Moses received his life's mission and purpose. He is called out, called up into something much bigger than he ever imagined, much more serious than CEO or "prince of Egypt." Under foreign stars, in the dead of night, Jacob received a new name, his real name. No longer is he a shrewd business negotiator, but now he is one who wrestles with God. The wilderness trial of Christ is, at its core, a test of his *identity*. "If you are who you think you are . . ." If a man is ever to find out who he is and what he's here for, he has got to take that journey for himself.

He has got to get his heart back.

WESTWARD EXPANSION AGAINST THE SOUL

The way a man's life unfolds nowadays tends to drive his heart into remote regions of the soul. Endless hours at a computer screen; selling shoes at the mall; meetings, memos, phone calls. The business world—where the majority of American men live and die—requires a man to be efficient and punctual. Corporate policies and procedures are designed with one aim: to harness a man to the plow and make him produce. But the soul refuses to be harnessed; it knows nothing of Day Timers and deadlines and P&L statements. The soul longs for passion, for freedom, for *life*. As D. H. Lawrence said, "I am not a mechanism." A man needs to feel the rhythms of the earth; he needs to have in hand something real—the tiller of a boat, a set of reins, the roughness of rope, or simply a shovel. Can a man live all his days to keep his fingernails clean and trim? Is that what a boy dreams of?

Society at large can't make up its mind about men. Having spent the last thirty years redefining masculinity into something more sensitive, safe, manageable and, well, feminine, it now berates men for not being men. Boys will be boys, they sigh. As though if a man were to truly grow up he would forsake wilderness and wanderlust and settle down, be at home forever in Aunt Polly's parlor. "Where are all the *real* men?" is regular fare for talk shows and new books. *You asked them to be women,* I want to say. The result is a gender confusion never experienced at such a wide level in the history of the world. How can a man know he is one when his highest aim is minding his manners?

And then, alas, there is the church. Christianity, as it currently exists, has done some terrible things to men. When all is said and done, I think most men in the church believe that God put them on the earth to be a good boy. The problem with men, we are told, is that they don't know how to keep their promises, be spiritual leaders, talk to their wives, or raise their children. But, if they will try real hard they can reach the lofty summit of becoming . . . a nice guy. That's what we hold up as models of Christian maturity: Really Nice Guys. We don't smoke, drink, or swear; that's what makes us *men.* Now let me ask my male readers: In all your boyhood dreams growing up, did you ever dream of becoming a Nice Guy? (Ladies, was the Prince of your dreams dashing . . . or merely nice?)

Really now—do I overstate my case? Walk into most churches in America, have a look around, and ask yourself this question: What is a Christian man? Don't listen to what is said, look at what you find there. There is no doubt about it. You'd have to admit a Christian man is . . . bored. At a recent church retreat I was talking with a guy in his fifties, listening really, about his own journey as a man. "I've pretty much tried for the last twenty years to be a good man as the church defines it." Intrigued, I asked him to say what he thought that was. He paused for a long moment. "Dutiful," he said. "And separated from his heart." *A perfect description,* I thought. *Sadly right on the mark.*

As Robert Bly laments in *Iron John*, "Some women want a passive man if they want a man at all; the church wants a tamed
man—they are called priests; the university wants a domesti-
cated man—they are called tenure-track people; the corporation
wants a . . . sanitized, hairless, shallow man." It all comes
together as a sort of westward expansion against the masculine
soul. And thus the *heart* of a man is driven into the high country,
into remote places, like a wounded animal looking for cover.
Women know this, and lament that they have no access to their
man's heart. Men know it, too, but are often unable to explain
why their heart is missing. They know their heart is on the run,
but they often do not know where to pick up the trail. The
church wags its head and wonders why it can't get more men to
sign up for its programs. The answer is simply this: We have not
invited a man to know and live from his deep heart.

AN INVITATION

But God made the masculine heart, set it within every man, and
thereby offers him an *invitation*: Come, and live out what I meant
you to be. Permit me to bypass the entire nature vs. nurture "is
gender really built-in?" debate with one simple observation: Men
and women are made in the image of God *as men* or *as women*. "So
God created man in his own image, in the image of God he created him; male and female he created them" (Gen. 1:27). Now,
we know God doesn't have a body, so the uniqueness can't be
physical. Gender simply must be at the level of the soul, in the
deep and everlasting places within us. God doesn't make generic
people; he makes something very distinct—a man or a woman.
In other words, there is a masculine heart and a feminine heart,
which in their own ways reflect or portray to the world God's
heart.

God *meant* something when he meant man, and if we are to ever find ourselves we must find that. What has he set in the masculine heart? Instead of asking what you think you ought to do to become a better man (or woman, for my female readers), I want to ask, *What makes you come alive?* What stirs your heart? The journey we face now is into a land foreign to most of us. We must head into country that has no clear trail. This charter for exploration takes us into our own hearts, into our deepest desires. As the playwright Christopher Fry says,

> Life is a hypocrite if I can't live
> The way it moves me!

There are three desires I find written so deeply into my heart I know now I can no longer disregard them without losing my soul. They are core to who and what I am and yearn to be. I gaze into boyhood, I search the pages of literature, I listen carefully to many, many men, and I am convinced these desires are universal, a clue into masculinity itself. They may be misplaced, forgotten, or misdirected, but in the heart of every man is a desperate desire for a battle to fight, an adventure to live, and a beauty to rescue. I want you to think of the films men love, the things they do with their free time, and especially the aspirations of little boys and see if I am not right on this.

A BATTLE TO FIGHT

There's a photo on my wall of a little boy about five years old, with a crew cut, big cheeks, and an impish grin. It's an old photograph, and the color is fading, but the image is timeless. It's Christmas morning, 1964, and I've just opened what may have been the best present any boy received on any Christmas ever—a set of two pearl-handed six-shooters, complete with black leather holsters, a red cowboy shirt with two wild mustangs embroidered on either breast, shiny black boots, red bandanna, and straw hat. I've donned the outfit and won't take it off for weeks because, you see, this is not a "costume" at all; it's an *identity*. Sure, one pant leg is tucked into my boot and the other is hanging out, but that only adds to my "fresh off the trail" persona. My thumbs are tucked inside my gun belt and my chest is out because I am armed and dangerous. Bad guys beware: This town's not big enough for the both of us.

Capes and swords, camouflage, bandannas and six-shooters—these are the *uniforms* of boyhood. Little boys yearn to know they are powerful, they are dangerous, they are someone to be reckoned with. How many parents have tried in vain to prevent little Timmy from playing with guns? Give it up. If you do not supply a boy with weapons, he will make them from whatever materials are at hand. My boys chew their graham crackers into the shape of hand guns at the breakfast table. Every stick or fallen branch is a spear, or better, a bazooka. Despite what many modern educators would say, this is not a psychological disturbance brought on by violent television or chemical imbalance. Aggression is part of the masculine *design;* we are hardwired for it. If we believe that man is made in the image of God, then we would do well to remember that "the LORD is a warrior; the LORD is his name" (Ex. 15:3).

Little girls do not invent games where large numbers of people die, where bloodshed is a prerequisite for having fun. Hockey, for example, was not a feminine creation. Nor was boxing. A boy wants to attack something—and so does a man, even if it's only a little white ball on a tee. He wants to whack it into kingdom come. On the other hand, my boys do not sit down to tea parties. They do not call their friends on the phone to talk about relationships. They grow bored of games that have no element of danger or competition or bloodshed. Cooperative games based on "relational interdependence" are complete nonsense. "No one is killed?" they ask, incredulous. "No one wins? What's the point?" The universal nature of this ought to have convinced us by now: The boy is a warrior; the boy is his name. And those are not boyish antics he is doing. When boys play at war they are rehearsing their part in a much bigger drama. One day, you just might need that boy to defend you.

Those Union soldiers who charged the stone walls at Bloody Angle; the Allied troops that hit the beaches at Normandy or the sands of Iwo Jima—what would they have done without this deep part of their heart? Life *needs* a man to be fierce—and fiercely devoted. The wounds he will take throughout his life will cause him to lose heart if all he has been trained to be is soft. This is especially true in the murky waters of relationships, where a man feels least prepared to advance. As Bly says, "In every relationship something *fierce* is needed once in a while."

Now, this longing may have submerged from years of neglect, and a man may not feel that he is up to the battles he knows await him. Or it may have taken a very dark turn, as it has with inner-city gangs. But the desire is there. Every man wants to play the hero. Every man *needs* to know that he is powerful. Women didn't make *Braveheart* one of the best-selling films of the decade. *Flying Tigers, The Bridge on the River Kwai, The Magnificent Seven, Shane, High Noon, Saving Private Ryan, Top Gun,* the *Die Hard* films, *Gladiator*—the movies a man loves reveal what his heart longs for, what is set inside him from the day of his birth.

Like it or not, there is something fierce in the heart of every man.

AN ADVENTURE TO LIVE

"My mother loves to go to Europe on her vacations." We were talking about our love of the West, a friend and I, and why he moved out here from the East Coast. "And that's okay for her, I guess. There's a lot of culture there. But I need wildness." Our conversation was stirred by the film *Legends of the Fall*, the story of three young men coming of age in the early 1900s on their father's ranch in Montana. Alfred, the eldest, is practical, pragmatic, cautious. He heads off to the Big City to become a businessman and eventually, a politician. Yet something inside him dies. He becomes a hollow man. Samuel, the youngest, is still a boy in many ways, a tender child—literate, sensitive, timid. He is killed early in the film and we know he was not ready for battle.

Then there is Tristan, the middle son. He is wild at heart. It is Tristan who embodies the West—he catches and breaks the wild stallion, fights the grizzly with a knife, and wins the beautiful woman. I have yet to meet a man who wants to be Alfred or Samuel. I've yet to meet a woman who wants to marry one. There's a reason the American cowboy has taken on mythic proportions. He embodies a yearning every man knows from very young—to "go West," to find a place where he can be all he knows he was meant to be. To borrow Walter Brueggeman's description of God: "wild, dangerous, unfettered and free."

Now, let me stop for a moment and make something clear. I am no great white hunter. I have no dead animals adorning the walls of my house. I didn't play college football. In fact, in college I weighed 135 pounds and wasn't much of an athlete. Despite my childhood dreams, I have never been a race car driver or a fighter pilot. I have no interest in televised sports, I don't like cheap beer, and though I do drive an old jeep its tires are not ridiculously large. I say this because I anticipate that many readers—good men and women—will be tempted to dismiss this as some sort of macho-man pep rally. Not at all. I am simply searching, as many men (and hopeful women) are, for an authentic masculinity.

When winter fails to provide an adequate snow base, my boys bring their sleds in the house and ride them down the stairs. Just the other day, my wife found them with a rope out their second-story bedroom window, preparing to rappel down the side of the house. The recipe for fun is pretty simple raising boys: Add to any activity an element of danger, stir in a little exploration, add a dash of destruction, and you've got yourself a winner. The way they ski is a perfect example. Get to the top of the highest run, point your skis straight downhill and go, the faster the better. And this doesn't end with age; the stakes simply get higher.

A judge in his sixties, a real southern gentleman with a pinstriped suit and an elegant manner of speech, pulled me aside during a conference. Quietly, almost apologetically, he spoke of his love for sailing, for the open sea, and how he and a buddy eventually built their own boat. Then came a twinkle in his eye. "We were sailing off the coast of Bermuda a few years ago, when we were hit by a northeaster (a raging storm). Really, it came up out of nowhere. Twenty-foot swells in a thirty-foot homemade boat. I thought we were all going to die." A pause for dramatic effect, and then he confessed, "It was the best time of my life."

Compare your experience watching the latest James Bond or Indiana Jones thriller with, say, going to Bible study. The guaranteed success of each new release makes it clear—adventure is written into the heart of a man. And it's not just about having "fun." Adventure *requires* something of us, puts us to the test. Though we may fear the test, at the same time we yearn to be tested, to discover that we have what it takes. That's why we set off down the Snake River against all sound judgment, why a buddy and I pressed on through grizzly country to find good fishing, why I went off to Washington, D.C., as a young man to see if I could make it in those shark-infested waters. If a man has lost this desire, says he doesn't want it, that's only because he doesn't know he has what it takes, believes that he will fail the test. And so he decides it's better not to try. For reasons I hope to make clear later, most men hate the unknown and, like Cain, want to settle down and build their own city, get on top of their life.

But you can't escape it—there is something wild in the heart of every man.

A BEAUTY TO RESCUE

Romeo has his Juliet, King Arthur fights for Guinevere, Robin rescues Maid Marian, and I will never forget the first time I kissed my grade school sweetheart. It was in the fall of my seventh-grade year. I met Debbie in drama class, and fell absolutely head over heels. It was classic puppy love: I'd wait for her after rehearsals were over, carry her books back to her locker. We passed notes in class, talked on the phone at night. I had never paid girls much attention, really, until now. This desire awakens a bit later in a boy's journey to manhood, but when it does his universe turns on its head. Anyway, I longed to kiss her but just couldn't work up the courage—until the last night of the school play. The next day was summer vacation, she was going away, and I knew it was now or never. Backstage, in the dark, I slipped her a quick kiss and she returned a longer one. Do you remember the scene from the movie *E.T.*, where the boy flies across the moon on his bike? Though I rode my little Schwinn home that night, I'm certain I never touched the ground.

There is nothing so inspiring to a man as a beautiful woman. She'll make you want to charge the castle, slay the giant, leap across the parapets. Or maybe, hit a home run. One day during a Little League game, my son Samuel was so inspired. He likes baseball, but most boys starting out aren't sure they really have it in them to be a great player. Sam's our firstborn, and like so many firstborns he is cautious. He always lets a few pitches go by before he takes a swing, and when he does, it's never a full swing; every one of his hits up till this point were in the infield. Anyway, just as Sam steps up to bat this one afternoon, his friend from down the street, a cute little blonde girl, shows up along the first-base line. Standing up on tiptoe she yells out his name and waves to Sam. Pretending he doesn't notice her, he broadens his stance, grips the bat a little tighter, looks at the pitcher with something fierce in his eye. First one over the plate he knocks into center field.

A man wants to be the hero to the beauty. Young men going off to war carry a photo of their sweetheart in their wallet. Men who fly combat missions will paint a beauty on the side of their aircraft; the crews of the WWII B-17 bomber gave those flying fortresses names like *Me and My Gal* or the *Memphis Belle*. What would Robin Hood or King Arthur be without the woman they love? Lonely men fighting lonely battles. Indiana Jones and James Bond just wouldn't be the same without a beauty at their side, and inevitably they must fight for her. You see, it's not just that a man needs a battle to fight; he needs someone to fight *for*. Remember Nehemiah's words to the few brave souls defending a wall-less Jerusalem? "Don't be afraid . . . fight for your brothers, your sons and your daughters, your wives and your homes." The battle itself is never enough; a man yearns for romance. It's not enough to be a hero; it's that he is a hero *to someone* in particular, to the woman he loves. Adam was given the wind and the sea, the horse and the hawk, but as God himself said, things were just not right until there was Eve.

Yes, there is something passionate in the heart of every man.

THE FEMININE HEART

There are also three desires that I have found essential to a woman's heart, which are not entirely different from a man's and yet they remain distinctly feminine. Not every woman wants a battle to fight, but every woman yearns to be fought *for*. Listen to the longing of a woman's heart: She wants to be more than noticed—she wants to be *wanted*. She wants to be pursued. "I just want to be a priority to someone," a friend in her thirties told me. And her childhood dreams of a knight in shining armor coming to rescue her are not girlish fantasies; they are the core of the feminine heart and the life she knows she was made for. So Zach comes back for Paula in *An Officer and a Gentleman*, Frederick comes back for Jo in *Little Women*, and Edward returns to pledge his undying love for Eleanor in *Sense and Sensibility*.

Every woman also wants an adventure *to share*. One of my wife's favorite films is *The Man from Snowy River*. She loves the scene where Jessica, the beautiful young heroine, is rescued by Jim, her hero, and together they ride on horseback through the wilds of the Australian wilderness. "I want to be Isabo in *Ladyhawk*," confessed another female friend. "To be cherished, pursued, fought for—yes. But also, I want to be strong and a *part* of the adventure." So many men make the mistake of thinking that the woman *is* the adventure. But that is where the relationship immediately goes downhill. A woman doesn't want to be the adventure; she wants to be caught up into something greater than herself. Our friend went on to say, "I know myself and I know I'm not the adventure. So when a man makes me the point,

I grow bored immediately. I know that story. Take me into one I don't know."

And finally, every woman wants to have a beauty to unveil. Not to conjure, but to unveil. Most women feel the pressure to be beautiful from very young, but that is not what I speak of. There is also a deep desire to simply and truly *be* the beauty, and be delighted in. Most little girls will remember playing dress up, or wedding day, or "twirling skirts," those flowing dresses that were perfect for spinning around in. She'll put her pretty dress on, come into the living room and twirl. What she longs for is to capture her daddy's delight. My wife remembers standing on top of the coffee table as a girl of five or six, and singing her heart out. *Do you see me?* asks the heart of every girl. *And are you captivated by what you see?*

The world kills a woman's heart when it tells her to be tough, efficient, and independent. Sadly, Christianity has missed her heart as well. Walk into most churches in America, have a look around, and ask yourself this question: What is a Christian woman? Again, don't listen to what is said, look at what you find there. There is no doubt about it. You'd have to admit a Christian woman is . . . tired. All we've offered the feminine soul is pressure to "be a good servant." No one is fighting for her heart; there is no grand adventure to be swept up in; and every woman doubts very much that she has any beauty to unveil.

BY WAY OF THE HEART

Which would you rather be said of you: "Harry? Sure I know him. He's a real sweet guy." Or, "Yes, I know about Harry. He's a dangerous man . . . in a really good way." Ladies, how about you? Which man would you rather have as your mate? (Some women, hurt by masculinity gone bad, might argue for the "safe" man . . .

and then wonder why, years later, there is no passion in their marriage, why he is distant and cold.) And as for your own femininity, which would you rather have said of you—that you are a "tireless worker," or that you are a "captivating woman"? I rest my case.

What if? What if those deep desires in our hearts are telling us the truth, revealing to us the life we were *meant* to live? God gave us eyes so that we might see; he gave us ears that we might hear; he gave us wills that we might choose, and he gave us hearts that we might *live*. The way we handle the heart is everything. A man must *know* he is powerful; he must *know* he has what it takes. A woman must *know* she is beautiful; she must *know* she is worth fighting for. "But you don't understand," said one woman to me. "I'm living with a hollow man" No, it's in there. His heart is there. It may have evaded you, like a wounded animal, always out of reach, one step beyond your catching. But it's there. "I don't know when I died," said another man. "But I feel like I'm just using up oxygen." I understand. Your heart may feel dead and gone, but it's there. Something wild and strong and valiant, just waiting to be released.

And so this is not a book about the seven things a man ought to do to be a nicer guy. It is a book about the recovery and release of a man's heart, his passions, his true nature, which he has been given by God. It's an invitation to rush the fields at Bannockburn, to go West, to leap from the falls and save the beauty. For if you are going to know who you truly are *as a man*, if you are going to find a life worth living, if you are going to love a woman deeply and not pass on your confusion to your children, you simply must get your heart back. You must head up into the high country of the soul, into wild and uncharted regions and track down that elusive prey.

CHAPTER TWO

THE WILD ONE WHOSE IMAGE WE BEAR

How would telling people to be nice to one another get a man crucified? What government would execute Mister Rogers or Captain Kangaroo?

—PHILIP YANCEY

Safe? Who said anything about safe? 'Course he isn't safe. But he's good.

—C. S. LEWIS

This is a stem
Of that victorious stock, and let us fear
The native mightiness and fate of him.

—HENRY V

Remember that little guy I told you about, with the shiny boots and a pair of six-shooters? The best part of the story is that it wasn't all pretend. I had a place to live out those dreams. My grandfather, my father's father, was a cowboy. He worked his own cattle ranch in eastern Oregon, between the desert sage and the Snake River. And though I was raised in the suburbs, the redemption of my life and the real training grounds for my own masculine journey took place on that ranch, where I spent my boyhood summers. Oh, that every boy should be so lucky. To have your days filled with tractors and pickup trucks, horses and roping steers, running through the fields, fishing in the ponds. I was Huck Finn for three wonderful months every year. How I loved it when my grandfather—"Pop" is what I called him—would look at me, his thumbs tucked in his belt, smile, and say, "Saddle up."

One afternoon Pop took me into town, to my favorite store. It was a combination feed and tack/hardware/ranch supply shop. The classic dry goods store of the Old West, a wonderland of tools and equipment, saddles, bridles and blankets, fishing gear, pocketknives, rifles. It smelled of hay and linseed oil, of leather and gunpowder and kerosene—all the things that thrill a boy's heart. That summer Pop was having a problem with an overrun pigeon population on the ranch. He hated the dirty birds, feared they were carrying diseases to the cattle. "Flying rats," is what he called them. Pop walked straight over to the firearms counter, picked out a BB rifle and a quart-sized milk carton with about a million BBs in it, and handed them to me. The old shopkeeper looked a bit surprised as he stared down at me, squinting over his glasses. "Isn't he a bit young for that?" Pop put his hand on my shoulder and smiled. "This is my grandson, Hal. He's riding shotgun for me."

WHERE DO WE COME FROM?

I may have walked into that feed store a squirrelly little kid, but I walked out as Sheriff Wyatt Earp, the Lone Ranger, Kit Carson. I had an identity and a place in the story. I was invited to be dangerous. If a boy is to become a man, if a man is to know he is one, this is not an option. A man *has* to know where he comes from, and what he's made of. One of the turning points in my good friend Craig's life—maybe *the* turning point—was the day he took back his father's name. Craig's father, Al McConnell, was killed in the Korean War when Craig was only four months old. His mother remarried and Craig was adopted by his stepdad, a sour old navy captain who would call Craig a "seagull" whenever he was angry with him. Talk about an identity, a place in the story. He'd say, "Craig, you're nothing but a seagull—all you're good for is sitting, squawking, and . . ."(you get the idea).

When Craig was a man he learned the truth of his heritage— how his dad was a warrior who had been cut down in battle. How if he had lived, he was planning on going to the mission field, to take the gospel to a place no one else had ever gone before. Craig discovered that his real great-grandfather was William McConnell, the first missionary to Central America, a man who risked his life many times to bring Christ to a lost people. Craig changed his name to McConnell and with it took back a much more noble identity, a much more dangerous place in the story. Would that we were all so fortunate. Many men are ashamed of their fathers. "You're just like your father," is an arrow many a bitter mother fires at her son. Most of the men I know are trying hard *not* to become like their fathers. But who does that leave them to follow after? From whom will they derive their sense of strength?

Maybe it would be better to turn our search to the headwaters, to that mighty root from which these branches grow. Who is this One we allegedly come from, whose image every man bears? What is he like? In a man's search for his strength, telling him that he's made in the image of God may not sound like a whole lot of encouragement at first. To most men, God is either distant or he is weak—the very thing they'd report of their earthly fathers. Be honest now—what is your image of Jesus *as a man?* "Isn't he sort of meek and mild?" a friend remarked. "I mean, the pictures I have of him show a gentle guy with children all around. Kind of like Mother Teresa." Yes, those are the pictures I've seen myself in many churches. In fact, those are the *only* pictures I've seen of Jesus. As I've said before, they leave me with the impression that he was the world's nicest guy. Mister Rogers with a beard. Telling me to be like him feels like telling me to go limp and passive. Be nice. Be swell. Be like Mother Teresa.

I'd much rather be told to be like William Wallace.

BRAVEHEART INDEED

Wallace, if you'll recall, is the hero of the film *Braveheart*. He is the warrior poet who came as the liberator of Scotland in the early 1300s. When Wallace arrives on the scene, Scotland has been under the iron fist of English monarchs for centuries. The latest king is the worst of them all—Edward the Longshanks. A ruthless oppressor, Longshanks has devastated Scotland, killing her sons and raping her daughters. The Scottish nobles, supposed protectors of their flock, have instead piled heavy burdens on the backs of the people while they line their own purses by cutting deals with Longshanks. Wallace is the first to defy the English oppressors. Outraged, Longshanks sends his armies to the field of Sterling to crush the rebellion. The highlanders come down, in groups of hundreds and thousands. It's time for a showdown. But the nobles, cowards all, don't want a fight. They want a treaty with England that will buy them more lands and power. They are typical Pharisees, bureaucrats . . . religious administrators.

Without a leader to follow, the Scots begin to lose heart. One by one, then in larger numbers, they start to flee. At that moment Wallace rides in with his band of warriors, blue warpaint on their faces, ready for battle. Ignoring the nobles—who have gone to parley with the English captains to get another deal—Wallace goes straight for the hearts of the fearful Scots. "Sons of Scotland . . . you have come to fight as free men, and free men you are." he gives them an identity and a reason to fight. He reminds them that a life lived in fear is no life at all, that every last one of them will die some day. "And dying in your beds, many years from now, would you be willing to trade all the days from this day to that to come back here and tell our enemies that they may take our lives, but they'll never take our freedom!" he tells them they have what it takes. At the end of his stirring speech, the men are cheering. They are ready. Then Wallace's friend asks,

> "Fine speech. Now what do we do?"
> "Just be yourselves."
> "Where are you going?"
> "I'm going to pick a fight."

Finally, someone is going to stand up to the English tyrants. While the nobles jockey for position, Wallace rides out and interrupts the parley. He picks a fight with the English overlords and the Battle of Stirling ensues—a battle that begins the liberation of Scotland.

Now—is Jesus more like Mother Teresa or William Wallace? The answer is . . . it depends. If you're a leper, an outcast, a pariah of society whom no one has *ever* touched because you are "unclean," if all you have ever longed for is just one kind word, then Christ is the incarnation of tender mercy. He reaches out and touches you. On the other hand, if you're a Pharisee, one of those self-appointed doctrine police . . . watch out. On more than one occasion Jesus "picks a fight" with those notorious hypocrites. Take the story of the crippled woman in Luke 13. Here's the background: The Pharisees are like the Scottish nobles— they, too, load heavy burdens on the backs of God's people but do not lift a finger to help them. What is more, they are so bound to the Law that they insist it is a sin to heal someone on the Sabbath, for that would be doing "work." They have twisted God's intentions so badly they think that man was made for the Sabbath, rather than the Sabbath for man (Mark 2:27). Christ has already had a number of skirmishes with them, some over this very issue, leaving those quislings "wild with rage" (Luke 6:11 NLT).

Does Jesus tiptoe around the issue next time, so as not to "rock the boat" (the preference of so many of our leaders today)? Does he drop the subject in order to "preserve church unity"? Nope. He walks right into it, he baits them, he picks a fight. Let's pick up the story there:

> One Sabbath day as Jesus was teaching in a synagogue, he saw a woman who had been crippled by an evil spirit. She had been bent double for eighteen years and was unable to stand up straight. When Jesus saw her, he called her over and said,

"Woman, you are healed of your sickness!" Then he touched her, and instantly she could stand straight. How she praised and thanked God! But the leader in charge of the synagogue was indignant that Jesus had healed her on the Sabbath day. "There are six days of the week for working," he said to the crowd. "Come on those days to be healed, not on the Sabbath." (Luke 13:10–14 NLT)

Can you believe this guy? What a weasel. Talk about completely missing the point. Christ is furious:

But the Lord replied, "You hypocrite! You work on the Sabbath day! Don't you untie your ox or your donkey from their stalls on the Sabbath and lead them out for water? Wasn't it necessary for me, even on the Sabbath day, to free this dear woman from the bondage in which Satan has held her for eighteen years?" This shamed his enemies. And all the people rejoiced at the wonderful things he did. (Luke 13:15–17 NLT)

A BATTLE TO FIGHT

Christ draws the enemy out, exposes him for what he is, and shames him in front of everyone. The Lord is a *gentleman???* Not if you're in the service of his enemy. God has a battle to fight, and the battle is for our freedom. As Tremper Longman says, "Virtually every book of the Bible—Old and New Testaments— and almost every page tells us about God's warring activity." I wonder if the Egyptians who kept Israel under the whip would describe Yahweh as a Really Nice Guy? Plagues, pestilence, the death of every firstborn—that doesn't seem very gentlemanly now, does it? What would Miss Manners have to say about taking the promised land? Does wholesale slaughter fit under "Calling on Your New Neighbors"?

You remember that wild man, Samson? He's got a pretty impressive masculine résumé: killed a lion with his bare hands, pummeled and stripped thirty Philistines when they used his wife against him, and finally, after they burned her to death, he killed a thousand men with the jawbone of a donkey. Not a guy to mess with. But did you notice? All those events happened when *"the Spirit of the LORD* came upon him" (Judges 15:14, emphasis added). Now, let me make one thing clear: I am not advocating a sort of "macho man" image. I'm not suggesting we all head off to the gym and then to the beach to kick sand in the faces of wimpy Pharisees. I am attempting to rescue us from a very, very mistaken image we have of God—especially of Jesus—and therefore of men as his image-bearers. Dorothy Sayers wrote that the church has "very efficiently pared the claws of the Lion of Judah," making him "a fitting household pet for pale curates and pious old ladies." Is that the God you find in the Bible? To Job—who has questioned God's strength, he replies:

> Do you give the horse his strength
>> or clothe his neck with a flowing mane?
> Do you make him leap like a locust,
>> striking terror with his proud snorting?
> He paws fiercely, rejoicing in his strength,
>> and charges into the fray.
> He laughs at fear, afraid of nothing;
>> he does not shy away from the sword.
> The quiver rattles against his side,
>> along with the flashing spear and lance.
> In frenzied excitement he eats up the ground;
>> he cannot stand still when the trumpet sounds.

At the blast of the trumpet he snorts, "Aha!"
    He catches the scent of battle from afar,
    the shout of commanders and the battle cry. (Job 39:19–25)

The war horse, the stallion, embodies the fierce heart of his Maker. And so do we; every man is "a stem of that victorious stock." Or at least, he was originally. You can tell what kind of man you've got simply by noting the impact he has on you. Does he make you bored? Does he scare you with his doctrinal nazism? Does he make you want to scream because he's just so very nice? In the Garden of Gesthemane, in the dead of night, a mob of thugs "carrying torches, lanterns and weapons" comes to take Christ away. Note the cowardice of it—why didn't they take him during the light of day, down in the town? Does Jesus shrink back in fear? No, he goes to face them head-on.

> Jesus, knowing all that was going to happen to him, went out and asked them, "Who is it you want?"
>
> "Jesus of Nazareth," they replied.
>
> "I am he," Jesus said. (And Judas the traitor was standing there with them.) When Jesus said, "I am he," *they drew back and fell to the ground.*
>
> Again he asked them, "Who is it you want?"
>
> And they said, "Jesus of Nazareth."
>
> "I told you that I am he," Jesus answered. "If you are looking for me, then let these men go." (John 18:4–8, emphasis added)

Talk about strength. The sheer force of Jesus' bold presence knocks the whole posse over. A few years ago a good man gave me a copy of a poem Ezra Pound wrote about Christ, called "Ballad of the Goodly Fere." It's become my favorite. Written from the perspective of one of the men who followed Christ, perhaps Simon Zelotes, it'll make a lot more sense if you know that *fere* is an Old English word that means *mate*, or *companion*:

> Ha' we lost the goodliest fere o' all
> For the priests and the gallows tree?
> Aye lover he was of brawny men,
> O' ships and the open sea.
>
> When they came wi' a host to take Our Man
> His smile was good to see,
> "First let these go!" quo' our Goodly Fere,
> "Or I'll see ye damned," says he.
>
> Aye he sent us out through the crossed high spears
> And the scorn of his laugh rang free,
> "Why took ye not me when I walked about
> Alone in the town?" says he.
>
> Oh we drunk his "Hale" in the good red wine
> When we last made company,
> No capon priest was the Goodly Fere
> But a man o' men was he.
>
> I ha' seen him drive a hundred men
> Wi' a bundle o' cords swung free,
> That they took the high and holy house
> For their pawn and treasury . . .
>
> I ha' seen him cow a thousand men
> On the hills o' Galilee,
> They whined as he walked out calm between,
> Wi' his eyes like the grey o' the sea,

Like the sea that brooks no voyaging
With the winds unleashed and free,
Like the sea that he cowed at Genseret
Wi' twey words spoke' suddenly.

A master of men was the Goodly Fere,
A mate of the wind and sea,
If they think they ha' slain our Goodly Fere
They are fools eternally.

Jesus is no "capon priest," no pale-faced altar boy with his hair parted in the middle, speaking softly, avoiding confrontation, who at last gets himself killed because he has no way out. He works with wood, commands the loyalty of dockworkers. He is the Lord of hosts, the captain of angel armies. And when Christ returns, he is at the head of a dreadful company, mounted on a white horse, with a double-edged sword, his robe dipped in blood (Rev. 19). Now that sounds a lot more like William Wallace than it does Mother Teresa.

No question about it—there is something fierce in the heart of God.

WHAT ABOUT ADVENTURE?

If you have any doubts as to whether or not God loves wildness, spend a night in the woods . . . alone. Take a walk out in a thunderstorm. Go for a swim with a pod of killer whales. Get a bull moose mad at you. Whose idea was this, anyway? The Great Barrier Reef with its great white sharks, the jungles of India with their tigers, the deserts of the Southwest with all those rattlesnakes—would you describe them as "nice" places? Most of the earth is not safe; but it's good. That struck me a little too late when hiking in to find the upper Kenai River in Alaska. My buddy Craig and I were after the salmon and giant rainbow trout that live in those icy waters. We were warned about bears, but didn't really take it seriously until we were deep into the woods. Grizzly sign was everywhere—salmon strewn about the trail, their heads bitten off. Piles of droppings the size of small dogs. Huge claw marks on the trees, about head-level. *We're dead,* I thought. *What are we doing out here?*

It then occurred to me that after God made all this, he pronounced it *good,* for heaven's sake. It's his way of letting us know he rather prefers adventure, danger, risk, the element of surprise. This whole creation is unapologetically *wild.* God loves it that way. But what about his own life? We know he has a battle to fight—but does God have an *adventure* to live? I mean, he already knows everything that's going to happen, right? How could there be any risk to his life; hasn't he got everything under absolute control?

In an attempt to secure the sovereignty of God, theologians have overstated their case and left us with a chess-player God playing both sides of the board, making all his moves and all ours too. But clearly, this is not so. God is a person who takes immense risks. No doubt the biggest risk of all was when he gave angels and men free will, including the freedom to reject him— not just once, but every single day. Does God cause a person to sin? "Absolutely not!" says Paul (Gal. 2:17). Then he can't be moving all the pieces on the board, because people sin all the time. Fallen angels and men use their powers to commit horrendous daily evil. Does God stop every bullet fired at an innocent victim? Does he prevent teenage liaisons from producing teenage pregnancies? There is something much more risky going on here than we're often willing to admit.

Most of us do everything we can to *reduce* the element of risk in our lives. We wear our seat belts, watch our cholesterol, and practice birth control. I know some couples who have decided against having children altogether; they simply aren't willing to chance the heartache children often bring. What if they are born with a crippling disease? What if they turn their backs on us, and God? What if . . . ? God seems to fly in the face of all caution. Even though he *knew* what would happen, what heartbreak and suffering and devastation would follow upon our disobedience, God chose to have children. And unlike some hyper-controlling parents, who take away every element of choice they can from their children, God gave us a remarkable choice. He did not *make* Adam and Eve obey him. He took a risk. A staggering risk, with staggering consequences. He let others into his story, and he lets their choices shape it profoundly.

This is the world he has made. This is the world that is still going on. And he doesn't walk away from the mess we've made of it. Now he lives, almost cheerfully, certainly heroically, in a dynamic relationship with us and with our world. "Then the Lord intervened" is perhaps the single most common phrase about him in Scripture, in one form or another. Look at the stories he writes. There's the one where the children of Israel are pinned against the Red Sea, no way out, with Pharaoh and his army barreling down on them in murderous fury. Then God shows up. There's Shadrach, Meshach, and Abednego, who get rescued only *after* they're thrown into the fiery furnace. Then God shows up. He lets the mob kill Jesus, bury him . . . then he shows up. Do you know why God loves writing such incredible stories? Because *he loves to come through.* He loves to show us that he has what it takes.

It's not the nature of God to limit his risks and cover his bases. Far from it. Most of the time, he actually lets the odds stack up against him. Against Goliath, a seasoned soldier and a trained killer, he sends . . . a freckle-faced little shepherd kid with a slingshot. Most commanders going into battle want as many infantry as they can get. God cuts Gideon's army from thirty-two thousand to three-hundred. Then he equips the ragtag little band that's left with torches and watering pots. It's not just a battle or two that God takes his chances with, either. Have you thought about his handling of the gospel? God needs to get a message out to the human race, without which they will perish . . . forever. What's the plan? First, he starts with the most unlikely group ever: a couple of prostitutes, a few fishermen with no better than a second-grade education, a tax collector. Then, he passes the ball to us. Unbelievable.

God's relationship with us and with our world is just that: a *relationship*. As with every relationship, there's a certain amount of unpredictability, and the ever-present likelihood that you'll get hurt. The ultimate risk anyone ever takes is to love, for as C. S. Lewis says, "Love anything and your heart will be wrung and possibly broken. If you want to make sure of keeping it intact you must give it to no one, not even an animal." But God does give it, again and again and again, until he is literally bleeding from it all. God's willingness to risk is just astounding—far beyond what any of us would do were we in his position.

Trying to reconcile God's sovereignty and man's free will has stumped the church for ages. We must humbly acknowledge that there's a great deal of mystery involved, but for those aware of the discussion, I am not advocating open theism. Nevertheless, there is definitely something wild in the heart of God.

A BEAUTY TO FIGHT FOR

And all his wildness and all his fierceness are inseparable from his romantic heart. That theologians have missed this says more about theologians than it does about God. Music, wine, poetry, sunsets . . . those were *his* inventions, not ours. We simply discovered what he had already thought of. Lovers and honeymooners choose places like Hawaii, the Bahamas, or Tuscany as a backdrop for their love. But whose idea was Hawaii, the Bahamas, and Tuscany? Let's bring this a little closer to home. Whose idea was it to create the human form in such a way that a kiss could be so delicious? And he didn't stop there, as only lovers know. Starting with her eyes, King Solomon is feasting on his beloved through the course of their wedding night. He loves her hair, her smile, her lips "drop sweetness as the honeycomb" and "milk and honey are under her tongue." You'll notice he's working his way *down*:

> Your neck is like the tower of David,
>   built with elegance . . .
> Your two breasts are like two fawns . . .
>
> Until the day breaks
>   and the shadows flee,
> I will go to the mountain of myrrh
>   and to the hill of incense. (Song 4:4–6)

And his wife responds by saying, "Let my lover come into his garden and taste its choice fruits" (Song 4:16). What kind of God would put the Song of Songs in the canon of Holy Scripture? Really, now, is it conceivable that such an erotic and scandalous book would have been placed in the Bible by the Christians *you* know? And what a delicate, poetic touch, "two fawns." This is no pornography, but there is no way to try to explain it all as "theological metaphor." That's just nonsense. In fact, God himself actually speaks in person in the Songs, once in the entire book. Solomon has taken his beloved to his bedchamber and the two are doing everything that lovers do there. God blesses it all, whispering, "Eat, O friends, and drink; drink your fill, O lovers" (Song 5:1), offering, as if needed, his own encouragement. And then he pulls the shades.

God is a romantic at heart, and he has his own bride to fight for. He is a jealous lover, and his jealousy is for the hearts of his people and for their freedom. As Francis Frangipane so truly states, "Rescue is the constant pattern of God's activity."

> For Zion's sake I will not keep silent,
> > for Jerusalem's sake I will not remain quiet,
> till her righteousness shines out like the dawn,
> > her salvation like a blazing torch . . .
>
> As a bridegroom rejoices over his bride,
> > so will your God rejoice over you. (Isa. 62:1, 5)

And though she has committed adultery against him, though she has fallen captive to his enemy, God is willing to move heaven and earth to win her back. He will stop at nothing to set her free:

> Who is this coming from Edom,
> > from Bozrah, with his garments stained crimson?
> Who is this, robed in splendor,
> > striding forward in the greatness of his strength?
> "It is I, speaking in righteousness,
> > mighty to save."
>
> Why are your garments red,
> > like those of one treading the winepress?
> "I have trodden the winepress alone;
> > from the nations no one was with me.
> I trampled them in my anger
> > and trod them down in my wrath;

their blood spattered my garments,
and I stained all my clothing.
For the day of vengeance was in my heart,
and the year of my redemption has come. (Isa. 63:1–4)

Whoa. Talk about a Braveheart. This is one fierce, wild, and passionate guy. I have never heard Mister Rogers talk like that. Come to think of it, I have never heard anyone in church talk like that, either. But this is the God of heaven and earth. The Lion of Judah.

LITTLE BOYS AND LITTLE GIRLS

And this is our true Father, the stock from which the heart of man is drawn. Strong, courageous love. As George MacDonald wrote,

Thou art my life—I the brook, thou the spring.
Because thine eyes are open, I can see;
Because thou art thyself, 'tis therefore I am me.
(*Diary of an Old Soul*)

I've noticed that so often our word to boys is *don't*. Don't climb on that, don't break anything, don't be so aggressive, don't be so noisy, don't be so messy, don't take such crazy risks. But God's design—which he placed in boys as the picture of himself—is a resounding *yes*. Be fierce, be wild, be passionate. Now, none of this is to diminish the fact that a woman bears God's image as well. The masculine and feminine run throughout all creation. As Lewis says, "Gender is a reality and a more fundamental reality than sex . . . a fundamental polarity which divides all created beings." There is the sun and then there are the moon and stars; there is the rugged mountain and there is the field of wildflowers that grows upon it. A male lion is awesome to behold, but have you ever seen a lioness? There is also something wild in the heart of a woman, but it is feminine to the core, more *seductive* than fierce.

Eve and all her daughters are also "a stem of that victorious stock," but in a wonderfully different way. As a counselor and a friend, and especially as a husband, I've been honored to be welcomed into the deep heart of Eve. Often when I am with a woman, I find myself quietly wondering, *What is she telling me about God? I know he wants to say something to the world through Eve— what is it?* And after years of hearing the heart-cry of women, I am convinced beyond a doubt of this: God wants to be loved. He wants to be a priority to someone. How could we have missed this? From cover to cover, from beginning to end, the cry of God's heart is, "Why won't you choose Me?" It is amazing to me how humble, how *vulnerable* God is on this point. "You will . . . find me," says the Lord, "when you seek me with all your heart" (Jer. 29:13). In other words, "Look for me, pursue me—I want you to pursue me." Amazing. As Tozer says, "God waits to be wanted."

And certainly we see that God wants not merely an adventure, but an adventure to *share*. He didn't have to make us, but he *wanted* to. Though he knows the name of every star and his kingdom spans galaxies, God delights in being a part of our lives. Do you know why he often doesn't answer prayer right away? Because he wants to talk to us, and sometimes that's the only way to get us to stay and *talk* to him. His heart is for relationship, for shared adventure to the core.

And yes, God has a beauty to unveil. There's a reason that a man is captivated by a woman. Eve is the crown of creation. If you follow the Genesis narrative carefully, you'll see that each new stage of creation is better than the one before. First, all is formless, empty and dark. God begins to fashion the raw materials, like an artist working with a rough sketch or a lump of clay. Light and dark, land and sea, earth and sky—it's beginning to take shape. With a word, the whole floral kingdom adorns the earth. Sun, moon, and stars fill the sky. Surely and certainly, his work expresses greater detail and definition. Next come fish and fowl, porpoises and red-tailed hawks. The wild animals are next, all those amazing creatures. A trout is a wonderful creature, but a horse is truly magnificent. Can you hear the crescendo starting to swell, like a great symphony building and surging higher and higher?

Then comes Adam, the triumph of God's handiwork. It is not to any member of the animal kingdom that God says, "You are my very image, the icon of my likeness." Adam bears the likeness of God in his fierce, wild, and passionate heart. And yet, there is one more finishing touch. There is Eve. Creation comes to its high point, its climax with her. She is God's finishing touch. And all Adam can say is, "Wow." Eve embodies the beauty and the mystery and the tender vulnerability of God. As the poet William Blake said, "The naked woman's body is a portion of eternity too great for the eye of man."

The reason a woman wants a beauty to unveil, the reason she asks, *Do you delight in me?* is simply that God does as well. God is captivating beauty. As David prays, "One thing I ask of the LORD, this is what I seek: that I may . . . gaze upon the beauty of the LORD" (Ps. 27:4). Can there be any doubt that God wants to be *worshiped?* That he wants to be seen, and for us to be captivated by what we see? As C. S. Lewis wrote, "The beauty of the female is the root of joy to the female as well as to the male . . . to desire the enjoying of her own beauty is the obedience of Eve, and to both it is in the lover that the beloved tastes of her own delightfulness."

This is far too simple an outline, I admit. There is so much more to say, and these are not hard and rigid categories. A man needs to be tender at times, and a woman will sometimes need to be fierce. But if a man is only tender, we know something is deeply wrong, and if a woman is only fierce, we sense she is not what she was meant to be. If you'll look at the essence of little boys and little girls, I think you'll find I am not far from my mark. Strength and beauty. As the psalmist says,

> One thing God has spoken,
> two things have I heard:
> that you, O God, are strong,
> and that you, O Lord, are loving. (Ps. 62:11–12)

CHAPTER THREE

THE QUESTION THAT HAUNTS EVERY MAN

The tragedy of life is what dies inside a man while he lives.

—ALBERT SCHWEITZER

He begins to die, that quits his desires.

—GEORGE HERBERT

Are you there?
Say a prayer for the Pretender
Who started out so young and strong
Only to surrender.

—JACKSON BROWNE
"The Pretender"
(© 1976 by Swallow Turn Music)

Our local zoo had for years one of the biggest African lions I've ever seen. A huge male, nearly five hundred pounds, with a wonderful mane and absolutely enormous paws. *Panthera leo.* The King of the Beasts. Sure, he was caged, but I'm telling you the bars offered small comfort when you stood within six feet of something that in any other situation saw you as an easy lunch. Honestly, I felt I ought to shepherd my boys past him at a safe distance, as if he could pounce on us if he really wanted to. Yet he was my favorite, and whenever the others would wander on to the monkey house or the tigers, I'd double back just for a few more minutes in the presence of someone so powerful and noble and deadly. Perhaps it was fear mingled with admiration; perhaps it was simply that my heart broke for the big old cat.

This wonderful, terrible creature should have been out roaming the savanna, ruling his pride, striking fear into the heart of every wildebeest, bringing down zebras and gazelles whenever the urge seized him. Instead, he spent every hour of every day and every night of every year alone, in a cage smaller than your bedroom, his food served to him through a little metal door. Sometimes late at night, after the city had gone to sleep, I would hear his roar come down from the hills. It sounded not so much fierce, but rather mournful. During all of my visits, he never looked me in the eye. I desperately wanted him to, wanted for his sake the chance to stare me down, would have loved it if he took a swipe at me. But he just lay there, weary with that deep weariness that comes from boredom, taking shallow breaths, rolling now and then from side to side.

For after years of living in a cage, a lion no longer even believes it is a lion . . . and a man no longer believes he is a man.

THE LION OF JUDAH??

A man is fierce . . . passionate . . . wild at heart? You wouldn't know it from what normally walks around in a pair of trousers. If a man is the image of the Lion of Judah, how come there are so many lonely women, so many fatherless children, so few *men* around? Why is it that the world seems filled with "caricatures" of masculinity? There's the guy who lives behind us. He spends his entire weekend in front of the tube watching sports while his sons play outside—without him. We've lived here nine years and I think I've seen him play with his boys maybe twice. What's with that? Why won't he *engage?* And the guy the next street over, who races motorcycles and drives a huge truck and wears a leather jacket and sort of swaggers when he walks. I thought James Dean died years ago. What's with him? It looks manly, but it seems cartoonish, overdone.

How come when men look in their hearts they don't discover something valiant and dangerous, but instead find anger, lust, and fear? Most of the time, I feel more fearful than I do fierce. Why is that? It was one hundred and fifty years ago that Thoreau wrote, "The mass of men lead lives of quiet desperation," and it seems nothing has changed. As the line from *Braveheart* has it, "All men die; few men ever really live." And so most women lead lives of quiet resignation, having given up on their hope for a true man.

The real life of the average man seems a universe away from the desires of his heart. There is no battle to fight, unless it's traffic and meetings and hassles and bills. The guys who meet for coffee every Thursday morning down at the local coffee shop and share a few Bible verses with each other—where is their great battle? And the guys who hang out down at the bowling alley, smoking and having a few too many—they're in the exact same place. The swords and castles of their boyhood have long been replaced with pencils and cubicles; the six-shooters and cowboy hats laid aside for minivans and mortgages. The poet Edwin Robinson captured the quiet desperation this way:

> Miniver Cheevy, child of scorn,
> Grew lean while he assailed the seasons;
> He wept that he was ever born,
> And he had reasons.

> Miniver loved the days of old
> When swords were bright and steeds were prancing;
> The vision of a warrior bold
> Would set him dancing.

> Miniver Cheevy, born too late,
> Scratched his head and kept on thinking;
> Miniver coughed, and called it fate,
> And kept on drinking. ("Miniver Cheevy")

Without a great battle in which a man can live and die, the fierce part of his nature goes underground and sort of simmers there in a sullen anger that seems to have no reason. A few weeks ago I was on a flight to the West Coast. It was dinnertime, and right in the middle of the meal the guy in front of me drops his seat back as far as it can go, with a couple of hard shoves back at me to make sure. I wanted to knock him into First Class. A friend of mine is having trouble with his toy shop, because the kids who come in "tick him off" and he's snapping at them. Not exactly good for business. So many men, good men, confess to losing it at their own children regularly. Then there's the guy in front of me at a stoplight yesterday. It turned green, but he didn't move; I guess he wasn't paying attention. I gave a little toot on my horn to draw his attention to the fact that now there were twenty-plus cars piling up behind us. The guy was out of his car in a flash, yelling threats, ready for a fight. Truth be told, I wanted desperately to meet him there. Men are angry, and we really don't know why.

And how come there are so many "sports widows," losing their husbands each weekend to the golf course or the TV? Why are so many men addicted to sports? It's the biggest adventure many of them ever taste. Why do so many others lose themselves in their careers? Same reason. I noticed the other day that the *Wall Street Journal* advertises itself to men as "adventures in capitalism." I know guys who spend hours on-line, e-trading stocks. There's a taste of excitement and risk to it, no question. And who's to blame them? The rest of their life is chores and tedious routine. It's no coincidence that many men fall into an affair not for love, not even for sex, but, by their own admission, for adventure. So many guys have been told to put that adventurous spirit behind them and "be responsible," meaning, live only for duty. All that's left are pictures on the wall of days gone by, and maybe some gear piled in the garage. Ed Sissman writes,

> Men past forty
> Get up nights, Look out at city lights
> And wonder

Where they made the wrong turn
And why life is so long.

I hope you're getting the picture by now. If a man does not find those things for which his heart is made, if he is never even invited to live for them from his deep heart, he will look for them in some other way. Why is pornography the number one snare for men? He longs for the beauty, but without his fierce and passionate heart he cannot find her or win her or keep her. Though he is powerfully drawn to the woman, he does not know how to fight for her or even that he *is* to fight for her. Rather, he finds her mostly a mystery that he knows he cannot solve and so at a soul level he keeps his distance. And privately, secretly, he turns to the imitation. What makes pornography so addictive is that more than anything else in a lost man's life, it makes him *feel* like a man without ever requiring a thing of him. The less a guy feels like a real man in the presence of a real woman, the more vulnerable he is to porn.

And so a man's heart, driven into the darker regions of the soul, denied the very things he most deeply desires, comes out in darker places. Now, a man's struggles, his wounds and addictions, are a bit more involved than that, but those are the core reasons. As the poet George Herbert warned, "he begins to die, that quits his desires." And you know what? We all know it. Every man knows that something's happened, something's gone wrong . . . we just don't know what it is.

OUR FEAR

I spent ten years of my life in the theater, as an actor and director. They were, for the most part, joyful years. I was young and energetic and pretty good at what I did. My wife was part of the theater company I managed, and we had many close friends there. I tell you this so that you will understand what I am about to reveal. In spite of the fact that my memories of theater are nearly all happy ones, I keep having this recurring nightmare. This is how it goes: I suddenly find myself in a theater—a large, Broadway-style playhouse, the kind every actor aspires to play. The house lights are low and the stage lights full, so from my position onstage I can barely make out the audience, but I sense it is a full house. Standing room only. So far, so good. Actors love playing to a full house. But I am not loving the moment at all. I am paralyzed with fear. A play is under way and I've got a crucial part. But I have no idea what play it is. I don't know what part I'm supposed to be playing; I don't know my lines; I don't even know my cues.

This is every man's deepest fear: to be exposed, to be found out, to be discovered as an impostor, and not really a man. The dream has nothing to do with acting; that's just the context for my fear. You have yours. A man bears the image of God in his strength, not so much physically but soulfully. Regardless of whether or not he knows the biblical account, if there's one thing a man does know he knows he is made to *come through*. Yet he wonders . . . *Can I? Will I?* When the going gets rough, when it really matters, will he pull it off? For years my soul lived in this turmoil. I'd often wake in the morning with an anxiousness that had no immediate source. My stomach was frequently tied in knots. One day my dear friend Brent asked, "What do you do now that you don't act anymore?" I realized at that moment that my whole life felt like a performance, like I am always "on." I felt in every situation that I must prove myself again. After I spoke or taught a class, I'd hang on what others would say, hoping they would say it went well. Each counseling session felt like a new test: *Can I come through, again? Was my last success all that I had?*

One of my clients got a great promotion and a raise. He came in depressed. *Good grief,* I thought. *Why?* Every man longs to be praised, and paid well on top of it. He confessed that although the applause felt great, he knew it only set him up for a bigger fall. Tomorrow, he'd have to do it all over, hit the ball out of the park again. Every man feels that the world is asking him to be something he doubts very much he has it in him to be. This is universal; I have yet to meet an honest man who won't admit it. Yes, there are many dense men who are wondering what I'm talking about; for them, life is fine and they are doing great. Just wait. Unless it's really and truly a reflection of genuine strength, it's a house of cards, and it'll come down sooner or later. Anger will surface, or an addiction. Headaches, an ulcer, or maybe an affair.

Honestly—how do you see yourself as a man? Are words like *strong, passionate,* and *dangerous* words you would choose? Do you have the courage to ask those in your life what *they* think of you as a man? What words do you fear they would choose? I mentioned the film *Legends of the Fall,* how every man who's seen it wants to be Tristan. But most see themselves as Alfred or Samuel. I've talked to many men about the film *Braveheart* and though every single one of them would love to be William Wallace, the dangerous warrior-hero, most see themselves as Robert the Bruce, the weak, intimidated guy who keeps folding under pressure. I'd love to think of myself as Indiana Jones; I'm afraid I'm more like Woody Allen.

The comedian Garrison Keillor wrote a very funny essay on this in his *The Book of Guys.* Realizing one day that he was not being honest about himself as a man, he sat down to make a list of his strengths and weaknesses:

USEFUL THINGS I CAN DO:

Be nice.

Make a bed.

Dig a hole.

Write books.

Sing alto or bass.

Read a map.

Drive a car.

USEFUL THINGS I CAN'T DO:

Chop down big trees and cut them into lumber or firewood.

Handle a horse, train a dog, or tend a herd of animals.

Handle a boat without panicking the others.

Throw a fastball, curve, or slider.

Load, shoot, and clean a gun. Or bow and arrow. Or use either of them, or a spear, net, snare, boomerang, or blowgun, to obtain meat.

Defend myself with my bare hands.

Keillor confesses: "Maybe it's an okay report card for a *person* but I don't know any persons . . . For a guy, it's not good. A woman would go down the list and say, 'What does it matter if a guy can handle a boat? Throw a curveball? Bag a deer? Throw a left hook? This is 1993.' But that's a womanly view of manhood." Craig and I were joking about this as we hacked our way through grizzly-infested woods in Alaska. The only other guys we met all day were a group of locals on their way out. They looked like something out of *Soldier of Fortune* magazine—sawed-off shotguns, pistols, bandoleers of ammo slung across their chests, huge knives. They were ready. They had what it takes. And we? We had a whistle. I'm serious. That's what we brought for our dangerous trek through the wild: a whistle. Talk about a couple of pansies. Craig confessed, "Me—what can I really do? I mean really? I know how to operate a fax machine."

That's how most men feel about their readiness to fight, to live with risk, to capture the beauty. We have a whistle. You see, even though the *desires* are there for a battle to fight, an adventure to live, and a beauty to rescue, even though our boyhood dreams once were filled with those things, we don't think we're up to it. Why don't men play the man? Why don't they offer their strength to a world desperately in need of it? For two simple reasons: We doubt very much that we have any real strength to offer, and we're pretty certain that if we did offer what we have it wouldn't be enough. Something has gone wrong and we know it. What's happened to us? The answer is partly back in the story of mankind, and partly in the details of each man's story.

WHAT IS A MAN FOR?

Why does God create Adam? What is a man for? If you know what something is designed to do, then you know its purpose in life. A retriever loves the water; a lion loves the hunt; a hawk loves to soar. It's what they're made for. Desire reveals design, and design reveals destiny. In the case of human beings, our design is also revealed by our desires. Let's take adventure. Adam and all his sons after him are given an incredible mission: rule and subdue, be fruitful and multiply. "Here is the entire earth, Adam. Explore it, cultivate it, care for it—it is your kingdom." Whoa . . . talk about an invitation. This is permission to do a heck of a lot more than cross the street. It's a charter to find the equator; it's a commission to build Camelot. Only Eden is a garden at that point; everything else is wild, so far as we know. No river has been charted, no ocean crossed, no mountain climbed. No one's discovered the molecule, or fuel injection, or Beethoven's Fifth. It's a blank page, waiting to be written. A clean canvas, waiting to be painted.

Most men think they are simply here on earth to kill time—and it's killing them. But the truth is precisely the opposite. The secret longing of your heart, whether it's to build a boat and sail it, to write a symphony and play it, to plant a field and care for it—those are the things you were made to do. That's what you're here for. Explore, build, conquer—you don't have to tell a boy to do those things for the simple reason that it *is his purpose*. But it's going to take risk, and danger, and there's the catch. Are we willing to live with the level of risk God invites us to? Something inside us hesitates.

Let's take another desire—why does a man long for a battle to fight? Because when we enter the story in Genesis, we step into a world at war. The lines have already been drawn. Evil is waiting to make its next move. Somewhere back before Eden, in the mystery of eternity past, there was a coup, a rebellion, an assassination attempt. Lucifer, the prince of angels, the captain of the guard, rebelled against the Trinity. He tried to take the throne of heaven by force, assisted by a third of the angelic army, in whom he instilled his own malice. They failed, and were hurled from the presence of the Trinity. But they were not destroyed, and the battle is not over. God now has an enemy . . . and so do we. Man is not born into a sitcom or a soap opera; he is born into a world at war. This is not *Home Improvement*; it's *Saving Private Ryan*. There will be many, many battles to fight on many different battlefields.

And finally, why does Adam long for a beauty to rescue?

Because there is Eve. He is going to need her, and she is going to need him. In fact, Adam's first and greatest battle is just about to break out, as a battle for Eve. But let me set the stage a bit more. Before Eve is drawn from Adam's side and leaves that ache that never goes away until he is with her, God gives Adam some instructions on the care of creation, and his role in the unfolding story. It's pretty basic, and very generous. "You may freely eat any fruit in the garden except fruit from the tree of the knowledge of good and evil" (Gen. 2:16–17 NLT). Okay, most of us have heard about that. But notice what God *doesn't* tell Adam.

There is no warning or instruction over what is about to occur: the Temptation of Eve. This is just staggering. Notably missing from the dialogue between Adam and God is something like this: "Adam, one more thing. A week from Tuesday, about four in the afternoon, you and Eve are going to be down in the orchard and something dangerous is going to happen. Adam, are you listening? The eternal destiny of the human race hangs on this moment. Now, here's what I want you to do . . ." he doesn't tell him. He doesn't even mention it, so far as we know. Good grief—*why not?!* Because God *believes* in Adam. This is what he's designed to do—to come through in a pinch. Adam doesn't need play-by-play instructions because this is what Adam is *for.* It's already there, everything he needs, in his design, in his heart.

Needless to say, the story doesn't go well. Adam fails; he fails Eve, and the rest of humanity. Let me ask you a question: Where is Adam, while the serpent is tempting Eve? He's standing right there: "She also gave some to her husband, who was with her. Then he ate it, too" (Gen. 3:6 NLT). The Hebrew for "with her" means right there, elbow to elbow. Adam isn't away in another part of the forest; he has no alibi. He is standing right there, watching the whole thing unravel. What does he do?

Nothing. Absolutely nothing. He says not a word, doesn't lift a finger.* He won't risk, he won't fight, and he won't rescue Eve. Our first father—the first real man—gave in to paralysis. He denied his very nature and went passive. And every man after him, every son of Adam, carries in his heart now the same failure. Every man repeats the sin of Adam, every day. We won't risk, we won't fight, and we won't rescue Eve. We truly are a chip off the old block.

Lest we neglect Eve, I must point out that she fails her design as well. Eve is given to Adam as his *ezer kenegdo*—or as many translations have it, his "help meet" or "helper." Doesn't sound like much, does it? It makes me think of Hamburger Helper. But Robert Alter says this is "a notoriously difficult word to translate." It means something far more powerful than just "helper"; it means *"lifesaver."* The phrase is only used elsewhere of God, when you need him to come through for you desperately. "There is no one like the God of Jeshurun, who rides on the heavens to help you" (Deut. 33:26). Eve is a life giver; she is Adam's ally. It is to *both* of them that the charter for adventure is given. It will take both of them to sustain life. And they will both need to fight together.

Eve is deceived . . . and rather easily, as my friend Jan Meyers points out. In *The Allure of Hope,* Jan says, "Eve was convinced that God was withholding something from her." Not even the extravagance of Eden could convince her that God's heart is good. "When Eve was [deceived], the artistry of being a woman took a fateful dive into the barren places of control and loneliness." Now every daughter of Eve wants to "control her surrounding, her relationships, her God." No longer is she vulnerable; now she will be grasping. No longer does she want simply to share in the adventure; now, she wants to control it. And as for her beauty,

---

*I'm indebted to Crabb, Hudson, and Andrews for pointing this out in *The Silence of Adam.*

she either hides it in fear and anger, or she uses it to secure her place in the world. "In our fear that no one will speak on our behalf or protect us or fight for us, we start to recreate both ourselves and our role in the story. We manipulate our surroundings so we don't feel so defenseless." Fallen Eve either becomes rigid or clingy. Put simply, Eve is no longer simply *inviting*. She is either hiding in busyness or demanding that Adam come through for her; usually, an odd combination of both.

POSERS

Adam knows now that he has blown it, that something has gone wrong within him, that he is no longer what he was meant to be. Adam doesn't just make a bad decision; he *gives away* something essential to his nature. He is marred now, his strength is fallen, and he knows it. Then what happens? Adam hides. "I was afraid because I was naked; so I hid" (Gen. 3:10). You don't need a course in psychology to understand men. Understand that verse, let its implications sink in, and the men around you will suddenly come into focus. We are hiding, every last one of us. Well aware that we, too, are not what we were meant to be, desperately afraid of exposure, terrified of being seen for what we are and *are not*, we have run off into the bushes. We hide in our office, at the gym, behind the newspaper and mostly *behind our personality*. Most of what you encounter when you meet a man is a facade, an elaborate fig leaf, a brilliant disguise.

Driving back from dinner one night, a friend and I were just sort of shooting the breeze about life and marriage and work. As the conversation deepened, he began to admit some of the struggles he was having. Then he came out with this confession: "The truth is, John, I feel like I'm just [bluffing] my way through life . . . and that someday soon I'll be exposed as an impostor." I was so surprised. This is a popular, successful guy who most people like the moment they meet him. He's bright, articulate, handsome, and athletic. He's married to a beautiful woman, has a great job, drives a new truck, and lives in a big house. There is nothing on the outside that says, "not really a man." But inside, it's another story. It always is.

Before I ever mentioned my nightmare about being onstage with nothing to say, another friend shared with me that he, too, is having a recurring nightmare. It involves a murder, and the FBI. Apparently, in his dream, he has killed someone and buried the body out back of his house. But the authorities are closing in, and he knows that any moment they'll discover the crime scene and he'll be caught. The dream always ends just before he is found out. He wakes in a cold sweat. "Any day now, I'll be found out" is a pretty common theme among us guys. Truth be told, most of us are faking our way through life. We pick only those battles we are sure to win, only those adventures we are sure to handle, only those beauties we are sure to rescue.

Let me ask the guys who don't know much about cars: How do you talk to your mechanic? I know a bit about fixing cars, but not much, and when I'm around my mechanic I feel like a weenie. So what do I do? I fake it; I pose. I assume a sort of casual, laid-back manner I imagine "the guys" use when hanging around the lunch truck, and I wait for him to speak. "Looks like it might be your fuel mixture," he says. "Yeah, I thought it might be that." "When was the last time you had your carb rebuilt?" "Oh, I dunno . . . it's probably been years." (I'm guessing he's talking about my carburetor, and I have no idea if it's ever been rebuilt.) "Well, we'd better do it now or you're going to end up on some country road miles from nowhere and then you'll have to do it yourself." "Yeah," I say casually, as if I don't want to be bothered having to rebuild that thing even though I know I wouldn't have the slightest idea where to begin. All I have is a whistle, remember? I tell him to go ahead, and he sticks out his hand, a big, greasy hand that says *I know tools real well* and what am I supposed to do? I'm dressed in a coat and tie because I'm supposed to give a talk at some women's luncheon, but I can't say, "Gee, I'd rather not get my hands dirty," so I take his hand and pump it extra hard.

Or how about you fellas who work in the corporate world: How do you act in the boardroom, when the heat is on? What do you say when the Big Boss is riding you hard? "Jones, what the devil is going on down there in your division? You guys are three weeks late on that project!!" Do you try to pass the buck? "Actually, sir, we got the plans over to McCormick's department to bid the job weeks ago." Do you feign ignorance? "Really? I had no idea. I'll get right on it." Maybe you just weasel your way out of it: "That job's a slam dunk, sir . . . we'll have it done this week." Years ago I did a tour of duty in the corporate world; the head man was a pretty intimidating guy. Many heads rolled in his office. My plan was basically to try to avoid him at all costs; when I did run into him in the hallway, even in "friendly" conversation, I always felt about ten years old.

How about sports? A few years ago I volunteered to coach for my son's baseball team. There was a mandatory meeting that all coaches needed to attend before the season, to pick up equipment and listen to a "briefing." Our recreation department brought in a retired professional pitcher, a local boy, to give us all a pep talk. The posing that went on was incredible. Here's a bunch of balding dads with beer bellies sort of swaggering around, talking about their own baseball days, throwing out comments about pro players like they knew them personally, and spitting (I kid you not). Their "attitude" (that's a tame word) was so thick I needed waders. It was the biggest bunch of posers I've ever met . . . outside of church.

That same sort of thing goes on Sunday mornings, its just a different set of rules. Dave runs into Bob in the church lobby. Both are wearing their happy faces, though neither is happy at all. "Hey, Bob, how are ya?" Bob is actually furious at his wife and ready to leave her, but he says, "Great, just great, Dave. The Lord is good!" Dave, on the other hand, hasn't believed in the goodness of God for years, ever since his daughter was killed. "Yep – God is good, all the time. I'm just so glad to be here, praising the Lord." "Me too. Well, I'll be praying for you!" I would love to see a tally of the number of prayers actually *prayed* against the number of prayers promised. I bet its about one in a thousand. "And I'll be praying for you too. Well, gotta go! You take care." "Take care" is our way of saying, "I'm done with this conversation and I want to get out of here but I don't want to appear rude so I'll say something that sounds meaningful and caring," but in truth, Dave doesn't give a rip about Bob.

STRENGTH GONE BAD

Adam falls, and all his sons with him. After that, what do you see as the story unfolds? Violent men, or passive men. Strength gone bad. Cain kills Abel; Lamech threatens to kill everybody else. God finally floods the earth because of the violence of men, but it's still going on. Sometimes it gets physical; most of the time, it's verbal. I know Christian men who say the most awful things to their wives. Or they kill them with their silence; a cold, deadly silence. I know pastors, warm and friendly guys in the pulpit, who from the safety of their office send out blistering E-mails to their staff. It's cowardice, all of it. I was intrigued to read in the journals of civil war commanders how the men you thought would be real heroes end up just the opposite. "Roughs that are always ready for street fighting are cowards on the open battlefield," declared one corporal. A sergeant from the same division agreed: "I don't know of a single fist-fighting bully but what he makes a cowardly soldier." The violence, no matter what form, is a cover-up for *fear*.

What about the achievers, the men running hard at life, pressing their way ahead? Most of it is fear-based as well. Not all of it, but most of it. For years, I was a driven, type A, hard-charging perfectionist. I demanded a lot of myself and of those who worked for me. My wife didn't like to call me at work, for as she said, "You have your work voice on." In other words, your fig leaf is showing. All that swaggering and supposed confidence and hard charging came out of fear—the fear that if I did not, I would be revealed to be less than a man. Never let down, never drop your guard, give 150 percent. Achievers are a socially acceptable form of violent men, overdoing it in one way or another. Their casualties tend to be their marriages, their families, and their health. Until a man faces this honestly, and what's really behind it, he'll do great damage.

Then there's the passive men. Abraham is a good example. He's always hiding behind his wife's skirt when the going gets rough. When he and his household are forced by a famine down to Egypt, he tells Pharaoh that Sarah is his sister so that he won't be killed; he jeopardizes her in order to save his own skin. Pharaoh takes Sarah into his harem, but the whole ruse is exposed when God strikes the Egyptians with diseases. You'd think Abraham would have learned his lesson, but no—he does it again years later when he moves to the Negev. In fact, his son Isaac carries on the tradition, jeopardizing Rebekah in the same way. The sins of the father passed along. Abraham is a good man, a friend of God. But he's also a coward. I know many like him. Men who can't commit to the women they've been dragging along for years. Men who won't stand up to the pastor and tell him what they really think. Pastors and Christian leaders who hide behind the fig leaf of niceness and "spirituality" and never, ever confront a difficult situation. Guys who organize their paper clips. Men who hide behind the newspaper or the television and won't really talk to their wives or children.

I'm like him too—a true son of Abraham. I mentioned that the early years of our life in the theater were good ones—but that's not the full story. I also had an affair . . . with my work. I married my wife without ever resolving or even knowing the deeper questions of my own soul. Suddenly, the day after our wedding, I am faced with the reality that I now have this woman as my constant companion and I have no idea what it really means to love her, nor if I have whatever it is she needs from me. *What if I offer her all I have as a man and it's not enough?* That's a risk I was not willing to take. But I knew I had what it took at the theater, and so slowly I began to spend more and more time there. Late nights, weekends, eventually every waking moment. I was hiding, like Adam, running from the fact that my strength was being called for and I really doubted I had any.

The evidence is clear: Adam and Eve's fall sent a tremor through the human race. A fatal flaw entered the original, and it's been passed on to every son and daughter. Thus every little boy and every little girl comes into the world set up for a loss of heart. Even if he can't quite put it into words, every man is haunted by the question, "Am I really a man? Have I got what it takes . . . when it counts?" What follows is the story we are personally much, much more familiar with.

CHAPTER FOUR

THE WOUND

Little Billy's mother was always telling him exactly what he was allowed to do and what he was not allowed to do. All the things he was allowed to do were boring. All the things he was not allowed to do were exciting. One of the things he was NEVER NEVER allowed to do, the most exciting of them all, was to go out through the garden gate all by himself and explore the world beyond.
—ROALD DAHL, *THE MINPINS*

In the clearing stands a boxer
And a fighter by his trade
And he carries the reminders
Of every glove that laid him down
and cut him till he cried out
in his anger and his shame
"I am leaving, I am leaving"
But the fighter still remains.

—PAUL SIMON
"The Boxer"
(© 1968 by Paul Simon)

I believe I was the only one in the entire company to come all the way through Normandy without getting wounded.
—PVT. WILLIAM CRAFT, 314TH INFANTRY REGIMENT

The story of Adam's fall is every man's story. It is simple and straightforward, almost mythic in its brevity and depth. And so every man comes into the world set up for a loss of heart. Then comes the story we are much more aware of—our own story. Where Adam's story seems simple and straightforward, our own seems complex and detailed; many more characters are involved, and the plot is sometimes hard to follow. But the outcome is always the same: a wound in the soul. Every boy, in his journey to become a man, takes an arrow in the center of his heart, in the place of his strength. Because the wound is rarely discussed and even more rarely healed, every man carries a wound. And the wound is nearly always given by his father.

A MAN'S DEEPEST QUESTION

On a warm August afternoon several years ago my boys and I were rock climbing in a place called Garden of the Gods, near our home. The red sandstone spires there look like the dorsal fins of some great beast that has just surfaced from the basement of time. We all love to climb, and our love for it goes beyond the adventure. There's something about facing a wall of rock, accepting its challenge and mastering it that calls you out, tests and affirms what you are made of. Besides, the boys are going to climb everything anyway—the refrigerator, the banister, the neighbor's grape arbor—so we might as well take it outside. And it's an excuse to buy some really cool gear. Anyway, when I climb with the boys we always top-rope, meaning that before the ascent I'll rig protection from the top of the rock down, enabling me to belay from the bottom. That way I can coach them as they go, see their every move, help them through the tough spots. Sam was the first to climb that afternoon, and after he clipped the rope into his harness, he began his attempt.

Things were going well until he hit a bit of an overhang, which even though you're roped in makes you feel exposed and more than a little vulnerable. Sam was unable to get over it and he began to get more and more scared the longer he hung there; tears were soon to follow. So with gentle reassurance I told him to head back down, that we didn't need to climb this rock today, that I knew of another one that might be more fun. "No," he said, "I want to do this." I understood. There comes a time when we simply have to face the challenges in our lives and stop backing down. So I helped him up the overhang with a bit of a boost, and on he went with greater speed and confidence. "Way to go, Sam! You're looking good. That's it . . . now reach up to your right . . . yep, now push off that foothold . . . nice move."

Notice what a crucial part of any male sport this sort of "shop talk" is. It's our way of affirming each other without looking like we're affirming. Men rarely praise each other directly, as women do: "Ted, I absolutely love your shorts. You look terrific today." We praise indirectly, by way of our accomplishments: "Whoa, nice shot, Ted. You've got a wicked swing today." As Sam ascended, I was offering words of advice and exhortation. He came to another challenging spot, but this time sailed right over it. A few more moves and he would be at the top. "Way to go, Sam. You're a *wild man*." He finished the climb, and as he walked down from the back side I began to get Blaine clipped in. Ten or fifteen minutes passed, and the story was forgotten to me. But not Sam. While I was coaching his brother up the rock, Sam sort of sidled up to me and in a quiet voice asked, "Dad . . . did you really think I was a wild man up there?"

Miss that moment and you'll miss a boy's heart forever. It's not a question—it's *the* question, the one every boy and man is longing to ask. Do I have what it takes? Am I powerful? Until a man *knows* he's a man he will forever be trying to prove he is one, while at the same time shrink from anything that might reveal he is not. Most men live their lives haunted by the question, or crippled by the answer they've been given.

WHERE DOES MASCULINITY COME FROM?

In order to understand how a man receives a wound, you must understand the central truth of a boy's journey to manhood: Masculinity is *bestowed*. A boy learns who he is and what he's got from a man, or the company of men. He cannot learn it any other place. He cannot learn it from other boys, and he cannot learn it from the world of women. The plan from the beginning of time was that his father would lay the foundation for a young boy's heart, and pass on to him that essential knowledge and confidence in his strength. Dad would be the first man in his life, and forever the most important man. Above all, he would answer *the question* for his son and give him his name. Throughout the history of man given to us in Scripture, it is the father who gives the blessing and thereby "names" the son.

Adam receives his name from God, and also the power of naming. He names Eve, and I believe it is therefore safe to say he also names their sons. We know Abraham names Isaac, and though Isaac's sons Jacob and Esau are apparently named by their mother, they desperately crave the *blessing* that can only come from their father's hand. Jacob gets the blessing, and nearly a century later, leaning on his staff, he passes it on to his sons—he gives them a name and an identity. "You are a lion's cub, O Judah . . . Issachar is a rawboned donkey . . . Dan will be a serpent . . . Gad will be attacked by a band of raiders, but he will attack them at their heels . . . Joseph is a fruitful vine . . . his bow remained steady" (Gen. 49:9, 14, 17, 19, 22, 24). The Baptist's father names him John, even though the rest of the family was going to name him after his father, Zechariah. Even Jesus needed to hear those words of affirmation from his Father. After he is baptized in the Jordan, before the brutal attack on his identity in the wilderness, his Father speaks: "You are my Son, whom I love; with you I am well pleased" (Luke 3:22). In other words, "Jesus, I am deeply proud of you; you have what it takes."

One father-naming story in particular intrigues me. It centers around Benjamin, the last son born to Jacob. Rachel gives birth to the boy, but she will die as a result. With her last breath she names him Ben-Oni, which means "son of my sorrow." But Jacob intervenes and names him Benjamin—"son of my right hand" (Gen. 35:18). This is the critical move, when a boy draws his identity no longer from the mother, but from the father. Notice that it took an active *intervention* by the man; it always does.

MOTHERS AND SONS

A boy is brought into the world by his mother, and she is the center of his universe in those first tender months and years. She suckles him, nurtures him, protects him; she sings to him, reads to him, watches over him, as the old saying goes, "like a mother hen." She often names him as well, tender names like "my little lamb," or "Mama's little sweetheart," or even "my little boyfriend." But a boy cannot grow to manhood with a name like that, let alone a name like "son of my sorrow," and there comes a time for the shift when he begins to seek out his father's affection and attention. He wants to play catch with Dad, and wrestle with him, spend time outside together, or in his workshop. If Dad works outside the home, as most do, then his return in the evening becomes the biggest event of the boy's day. Stasi can tell you when it happened for each of our boys. This is a very hard time in a mother's life, when the father replaces her as the sun of the boy's universe. It is part of Eve's sorrow, this letting go, this being replaced.

Few mothers do it willingly; very few do it well. Many women ask their sons to fill a void in their soul that their husband has left. But the boy has a question that needs an answer, and he cannot get the answer from his mother. Femininity can never bestow masculinity. My mother would often call me "sweetheart," but my father called me "tiger." Which direction do you think a boy would want to head? He will still turn to his mother for comfort (who does he run to when he skins his knee?), but he turns to Dad for adventure, for the chance to test his strength, and most of all, to get the answer to his question. A classic example of these dueling roles took place the other night. We were driving down the road and the boys were talking about the kind of car they want to get when it comes time for their first set of wheels. "I was thinking about a Humvee, or a motorcycle, maybe even a tank. What do you think, Dad?" "I'd go with the Humvee. We could mount a machine gun on top." "What about you, Mom—what kind of car do you want me to have?" You know what she said . . . "A safe one."

Stasi is a wonderful mother; she has bit her tongue so many times I wonder that she still has one, as she holds her peace while the boys and I rush off to some adventure begging destruction or bloodshed. Her first reaction—"a safe one"—is so natural, so understandable. After all, she is the incarnation of God's tenderness. But if a mother will not allow her son to become dangerous, if she does not let the father take him away, she will emasculate him. I just read a story of a mother, divorced from her husband, who was furious that he wanted to take the boy hunting. She tried to get a restraining order to prevent him from teaching the boy about guns. That is emasculation. "My mom wouldn't let me play with GI Joe," a young man told me. Another said, "We lived back east, near an amusement park. It had a roller coaster—the old wooden kind. But my mom would never let me go." That is emasculation, and the boy needs to be rescued from it by the active intervention of the father, or another man.

This kind of intervention is powerfully portrayed in the movie *A Perfect World*. Kevin Costner plays an escaped convict who takes a young boy hostage and heads for the state line. But as the story unfolds, we see that what looks like the boy's ruin is actually his *redemption*. The boy is in his underpants when Costner abducts him. That is where many mothers want to keep their sons, albeit unconsciously. She wants her little lamb close by. Over the days that follow, days "together on the road" I might add, Costner and the boy—who has no father—grow close. When he learns that the boy's mother has never allowed him to ride a roller coaster, Costner is outraged. The next scene is the boy, arms high in the air, rolling up and down country roads on the roof of the station wagon. That's the invitation into a man's world, a world involving danger. Implicit in the invitation is the *affirmation*, "You can handle it; you belong here."

There comes a moment when Costner buys the boy a pair of pants (the symbolism in the film is amazing), but the boy won't change in front of him. He is a shy, timid boy who has yet to even smile in the story. Costner senses something is up.

"What's the matter—you don't want me to see your pecker?"
"It's . . . puny."

"What?"

"It's puny."

"Who told you that?"

The boy, Phillip, is silent. It is the silence of emasculation and shame. The absence of the father's voice is loud and clear. So Costner intervenes, and speaks. "Lemme see . . . go on, I'll shoot you straight." The boy reluctantly bares himself. "No, Phillip. That's a good size for a boy your age." A smile breaks out on his face, like the sun coming up, and you know a major threshold has been crossed for him.

FROM STRENGTH TO STRENGTH

Masculinity is an *essence* that is hard to articulate but that a boy naturally craves as he craves food and water. It is something passed between men. "The traditional way of raising sons," notes Robert Bly, "which lasted for thousands and thousands of years, amounted to fathers and sons living in close—murderously close—proximity, while the father taught the son a trade: perhaps farming or carpentry or blacksmithing or tailoring." My father taught me to fish. We would spend long days together, out in a boat on a lake, trying to catch fish. I will never, ever forget his delight in me when I'd hook one. But the fish were never really the important thing. It was the delight, the contact, the masculine presence gladly bestowing itself on me. "Atta boy, Tiger! Bring him in! That's it . . . well done!" Listen to men when they talk warmly of their fathers and you'll hear the same. "My father taught me to fix tractors . . . to throw a curveball . . . to hunt quail." And despite the details, what is mostly passed along is the masculine blessing.

"Fathers and sons in most tribal cultures live in an amused

tolerance of each other," says Bly. "The son has a lot to learn, and so the father and son spend hours trying and failing together to make arrowheads or to repair a spear or track a clever animal. When a father and son spend long hours together, which some fathers and sons still do, we could say that a substance almost like food passes from the older body to the younger." This is why my boys love to wrestle with me—why any healthy boy wants the same with his father. They love the physical contact, to brush against my cheek, feel the sandpaper of my whiskers, my strength all around them, and to test theirs on me.

And it's that *testing* that is so essential. As they've gotten older, they love to start punching matches with me. Luke just did it this morning. I'm downstairs fixing breakfast; Luke senses the opportunity, and he sneaks downstairs and silently stalks me; when he's in range, he lets loose a wallop. It hurts, and *they need to see* that it hurts. Do they have a strength like Dad's? Is it growing, real, substantive? I'll never forget the day when Sam gave me a bloody lip, quite by accident, when we were wrestling. At first he drew back in fear, waiting, I'm sorry to admit, for my anger. Thankfully, on this occasion I just wiped the blood away, smiled, and said, "Whoa . . . nice shot." he beamed; no, he *strutted*. Shook his antlers at me. Word quickly spread through the house and his younger brothers were on the scene, eyes wide at the fact that one of them had drawn blood. New possibilities opened up. Maybe young bucks can take on the old bull.

"The ancient societies believed that a boy becomes a man only through ritual and effort—only through the 'active intervention of the older men,'" Bly reminds us. The father or another man must actively intervene, and the mother must let go. Bly tells the story of one tribal ritual, which involves as they all do the men taking the boy away for initiation. But in this case, when he returns, the boy's mother pretends not to know him. She asks to be introduced to "the young man." That is a beautiful picture of how a mother can cooperate in her son's passage to the father's world. If she does not, things get very messy later—especially in marriage. The boy develops a bond with his mother that is like emotional incest. His loyalties are divided. That is why Scripture says, "For this reason *a man will leave* his father and mother and be united to his wife" (Gen. 2:24, emphasis added).

Sometimes, when the mother clings, the boy will try to tear himself away, violently. This typically comes in the teenage years and often involves some ugly behavior, maybe some foul words on the part of the young man. She feels rejected, and he feels guilty, but he knows he *must* get away. This was my story, and my relationship with my mother has never been good since. I've found that many, many adult men resent their mothers but cannot say why. They simply know they do not want to be close to them; they rarely call. As my friend Dave confessed, "I hate calling my mom. She always says something like, 'It's so good to hear your little voice.' I'm twenty-five and she still wants to call me her little lamb." Somehow, he senses that proximity to his mother endangers his masculine journey, as though he might be sucked back in. It is an irrational fear, but it reveals that both essential ingredients in his passage were missing: Mom did not let go, and Dad did not take him away.

Whatever the mother's failure, it can be overcome by the father's engagement. Let's come back to the rock climbing story with Sam. "Did you really think I was a wild man up there?" He did not ask, "Do you think I am a nice boy?" He asked about his strength, his dangerous capacity to really come through. A boy's passage into manhood involves many of those moments. The father's role is to arrange for them, invite his boy into them, keep his eye out for the moment the question arises and then speak into his son's heart *yes, you are*. You have what it takes. And that is why the deepest wound is always given by the father. As Buechner says, "If strangers and strange sights can shake the world of children, it takes the people they know and love best to pull it out from under them like a chair."

THE FATHER-WOUND

Dave remembers the day the wound came. His parents were having an argument in the kitchen, and his father was verbally abusing his mother. Dave took his mom's side, and his father exploded. "I don't remember all that was said, but I do remember his last words: 'You are such a mama's boy,' he yelled at me. Then he walked out." Perhaps if Dave had a strong relationship with his dad most of the time, a wound like this might be lessened, healed later by words of love. But the blow came after years of distance between them. Dave's father was often gone from morning till night with his own business, and so they rarely spent time together. What is more, Dave felt a lingering disappointment from his dad. He wasn't a star athlete, which he knew his dad highly valued. He had a spiritual hunger and often attended church, which his dad did not value. And so those words fell like a final blow, a death sentence.

Leanne Payne says that when the father-son relationship is right, "the quiet tree of masculine strength within the father protects and nurtures the fragile stripling of masculinity within his son." Dave's father took an ax and gave his hardest blow to his young tree. How I wish it were a rare case, but I am deeply sorry to say I've heard countless stories like it. There's a young boy named Charles who loved to play the piano, but his father and brothers were jocks. One day they came back from the gym to find him at the keyboard, and who knows what else had built up years of scorn and contempt in his father's soul, but his son received both barrels: "You are such a faggot." A man my father's age told me of growing up during the depression; times were hard for his family, and his father, an alcoholic rarely employed, hired him out to a nearby farmer. One day while he was in the field he saw his father's car pull up; he hadn't seen him for weeks, and he raced to meet his dad. Before he could get there his father had grabbed the check for his son's wages, and, spying the boy running toward him, he jumped in the car and sped away. The boy was five years old.

In the case of violent fathers, the boy's question is answered in a devastating way. "Do I have what it takes? Am I a man, Papa?" No, you are a mama's boy, an idiot, a faggot, a seagull. Those are defining sentences that shape a man's life. The assault wounds are like a shotgun blast to the chest. This can get unspeakably evil when it involves physical, sexual, or verbal abuse carried on for years. Without some kind of help, many men never recover. One thing about the assault wounds—they are obvious. The passive wounds are not; they are pernicious, like a cancer. Because they are subtle, they often go unrecognized as wounds and therefore are actually more difficult to heal.

My father was in many ways a good man. He introduced me to the West, and taught me to fish and to camp. I still remember the fried egg sandwiches he would make us for dinner. It was his father's ranch that I worked on each summer, and my dad and I saw a lot of the West together as we'd make the long drive from southern California to Oregon, often with fishing detours through Idaho and Montana. But like so many men of his era, my father had never faced the issues of his own wounds, and he fell to drinking when his life began to take a downhill turn. I was about eleven or twelve at the time—a very critical age in the masculine journey, the age when the question really begins to surface. At the very moment when I am desperately wondering what it means to be a man, and do I have what it takes, my father checked out, went silent. He had a workshop out back, attached to the garage, and he would spend his hours out there alone, reading, doing crossword puzzles, and drinking. That is a major wound.

As Bly says, "Not receiving any blessing from your father is an injury . . . Not seeing your father when you are small, never being with him, having a remote father, an absent father, a workaholic father, is an injury." My friend Alex's father died when he was four years old. The sun in his universe set, never to rise again. How is a little boy to understand that? Every after-noon Alex would stand by the front window, waiting for his father to come home. This went on for almost a year. I've had many clients whose fathers simply left and never came back. Stuart's dad did that, just up and left, and his mother, a troubled woman, was unable to raise him. So he was sent to his aunt and uncle. Divorce or abandonment is a wound that lingers because the boy (or girl) believes if they had done things better, Daddy would have stayed.

Some fathers give a wound merely by their silence; they are present, yet absent to their sons. The silence is deafening. I remember as a boy wanting my father to die, and feeling immense guilt for having such a desire. I understand now that I wanted someone to validate the wound. My father was gone, but because he was physically still around, he was not gone. So I lived with a wound no one could see or understand. In the case of silent, passive, or absent fathers, the question goes unan-swered. "Do I have what it takes? Am I a man, Daddy?" Their silence is the answer: "I don't know . . . I doubt it . . . you'll have to find out for yourself . . . probably not."

THE WOUND'S EFFECT

Every man carries a wound. I have never met a man without one. No matter how good your life may have seemed to you, you live in a broken world full of broken people. Your mother and father, no matter how wonderful, couldn't have been perfect. She is a daughter of Eve, and he a son of Adam. So there is no crossing through this country without taking a wound. And every wound, whether it's assaultive or passive, delivers with it a *message*. The message feels final and true, absolutely true, because it is delivered with such force. Our reaction to it shapes our personality in very significant ways. From that flows the false self. Most of the men you meet are living out a false self, a pose, which is directly related to his wound. Let me try to make this clear.

The message delivered with my wound (my father disappearing into his own battles) was simply this: *You are on your own, John. There is no one in your corner, no one to show you the way and above all, no one to tell you if you are or are not a man. The core question of your soul has no answer, and can never get one.* What does a boy do with that? First, I became an unruly teen. I got kicked out of school, had a police record. We often misunderstand that behavior as "adolescent rebellion," but those are cries for involvement, for *engagement.* Even after God's dramatic rescue of me at the age of nineteen, when I became a Christian, the wound remained. As my dear friend Brent said, "Becoming a Christian doesn't necessarily fix things. My arrows were still lodged deep and refused to allow some angry wounds inside to heal."

I mentioned earlier that for years I was a very driven man, a perfectionist, a hard-charger, and a fiercely independent man. The world rewards that kind of drivenness; most of the successful men reading this book are driven. But behind me was a string of casualties—people I had hurt, or dismissed—including my own father. There was the near casualty of my marriage and there was certainly the casualty of my own heart. For to live a driven life you have to literally shove your heart down, or drive it with whips. You can never admit need, never admit brokenness. This is the story of the creation of that false self. And if you had asked my wife during the first ten years of our marriage if we had a good relationship, she probably would have said yes. But if you had asked her if something was missing, if she sensed a fatal flaw, she would have immediately been able to tell you: he doesn't need me. That was my vow, you see. *I won't need anyone.* After all, the wound was deep and unhealed, and the message it brought seemed so final: I am on my own.

Another friend, Stan, is a successful attorney and a genuinely good guy. When he was about fifteen, his father committed suicide—stuck a gun in his mouth and pulled the trigger. His family tried to put it all behind them, sweep it under the rug. They never spoke of it again. The message delivered by that gruesome blow was something like this: *Your background is very dark; the masculine in your family cannot even be spoken of; anything wild is violent and evil.* The effect was another sort of vow: "I will never do anything even remotely dangerous, or risky, or wild. I will never be like my dad (how many men live with that vow?). I won't take one step in that direction. I will be the nicest guy you ever met." You know what? He is. Stan's the nicest guy you could meet—gentle, creative, caring, soft-spoken. And now he hates that about himself; he hates the thought that he's a pushover, that he won't take you on, can't say no, can't stand up for himself.

Those are the two basic options. Men either overcompensate for their wound and become driven (violent men), or they shrink back and go passive (retreating men). Often it's an odd mixture of both. Witness the twin messages sported by young college-age men especially: a goatee, which says, "I'm kind of dangerous," and a baseball hat turned backward, which says, "But really I'm a little boy; don't require anything of me." Which is it? Are you strong, or are you weak? Remember Alex, who stood at the door waiting for a daddy who would never return? You wouldn't in a million years have guessed that was his story if you'd known him in college. He was a man's man, an incredible football player. A hard-drinking, hard-living man every guy looked up to. He drove a truck, chewed tobacco, loved the outdoors. He used to eat glass. I'm serious. It was sort of frat party trick he took on, the ultimate display of dangerous strength. He'd literally take a bite out of a glass, chew it slowly and swallow it. When he worked as a bouncer for a tough bar, it made a pretty impressive show to get the roughnecks in line. But it was a show—the whole macho-man persona.

Charles, the artistic boy, the piano player whose father called him a "faggot"—what do you think happened there? He never played the piano again after that day. Years later, as a man in his late twenties, he does not know what to do with his life. He has no passion, cannot find a career to love. And so he cannot commit to the woman he loves, cannot marry her because he is so uncertain of himself. But of course—his heart was taken out, way back there in his story. Dave is also in his twenties now, drifting, deeply insecure, and loaded with a great deal of self-hatred. He does not feel like a man and he believes he never will. Like so many, he struggles with confidence around women and around men he sees as real men. Stuart, whose father abandoned him, became a man without emotion. His favorite character as a boy was Spock, the alien in *Star Trek* who lives solely from his mind. Stuart is now a scientist and his wife is immensely lonely.

On and on it goes. The wound comes, and with it a message. From that place the boy makes a vow, chooses a way of life that gives rise to the false self. At the core of it all is a deep uncertainty. The man doesn't live from a center. So many men feel stuck—either paralyzed and unable to move, or unable to stop moving. Of course, every little girl has her own story too. But I want to save that for a later chapter, and bring it together with how a man fights for a woman's heart. Let me say a few more words about what happens to a man after the wound is given.

CHAPTER FIVE

THE BATTLE FOR
A MAN'S HEART

Now you're out there God knows where
You're one of the walking wounded.

—JAN KRIST
"Walking Wounded"
by Jan Krist
and Paul Murphy

To give a man back his heart is the hardest mission on earth.
—FROM THE MOVIE *MICHAEL*

Nothing worth having comes without some kind of fight.
—BRUCE COCKBURN
"Lovers in a Dangerous Time"
(written in 1982 for *Stealing Fire*)

A few years ago now my middle son, Blaine, made the big transition to first grade. That's a huge step for any child—leaving the comfort and safety of Mom's side, spending all day at school, being among the "big kids." But Blaine's a very outgoing and winsome boy, a born leader, and we knew he'd handle it swimmingly. Every night at the dinner table he regaled us with tales of the day's adventures. It was fun to recall with him the joys of those early school days—a shiny new lunchbox, brand-new yellow No. 2 pencils, a box of Crayolas with a *built-in sharpener*, a new desk, and new friends. We heard all about his new teacher, gym class, what they played at recess, how he was emerging as a leader in all the games. But then one night he was silent. "What's wrong, Tiger?" I asked. He wouldn't say, wouldn't even look up. "What happened?" He didn't want to talk about it. Finally, the story came out—a bully. Some first-grade poser had pushed him down on the playground in front of all his friends. Tears were streaming down his cheeks as he told us the story.

"Blaine, look at me." He raised his tearful eyes slowly, reluctantly. There was shame written all over his face. "I want you to listen very closely to what I am about to say. The next time that bully pushes you down, here is what I want you to do—are you listening, Blaine?" He nodded, his big wet eyes fixed on mine. "I want you to get up . . . and I want you to hit him . . . as hard as you possibly can." A look of embarrassed delight came over Blaine's face. Then he smiled.

Good Lord—why did I give him such advice? And why was he delighted with it? Why are some of *you* delighted with it, while others are appalled?

Yes, I know that Jesus told us to turn the other cheek. But we have really misused that verse. You cannot teach a boy to use his strength *by stripping him of it*. Jesus was able to retaliate, believe me. But he chose not to. And yet we suggest that a boy who is mocked, shamed before his fellows, stripped of all power and dignity should stay in that beaten place because Jesus wants him there? You will emasculate him for life. From that point on all will be passive and fearful. He will grow up never knowing how to stand his ground, never knowing if he is a man indeed. Oh yes, he will be courteous, sweet even, deferential, minding all his manners. It may look moral, it may look like turning the other cheek, but it is merely *weakness*. You cannot turn a cheek you do not have. Our churches are full of such men.

At that moment, Blaine's soul was hanging in the balance. Then the fire came back into his eyes and the shame disappeared. But for many, many men their souls still hang in the balance because no one, *no one* has ever invited them to be dangerous, to know their own strength, to discover that they have what it takes. "I feel there is this stormy ocean within me, and I keep trying to make those waters calm and placid," confessed a young friend in his early twenties. "I would love to be dangerous," he said, sighing. "You mean . . . it's possible? I feel like I have to ask permission." Why on earth would a young man have to ask permission to be a man? Because the assault continues long after the wound has been given. I don't mean to create a wrong impression—a man is not wounded once, but many, many times in the course of his life. Nearly every blow ends up falling in the same place: against his strength. Life takes it away, one vertebra at a time, until in the end he has no spine at all.

FINISHING HIM OFF

I read a case a few years ago about a baby boy who suffered a terrible blow during surgery: his penis was "accidentally removed." The event took place back in the '70s, and a decision was made that reflected the widely held belief that "sex roles" are not truly part of our design, but merely shaped by culture and therefore interchangeable. His genitalia were reconstructed in female form, and he was raised as a girl. That story is a parable of our times. It is exactly what we've tried to do to boys, starting from when they are very young. As Christina Hoff Sommers says in her book *The War Against Boys*, "It's a bad time to be a boy in America." Our culture has turned against the masculine essence, aiming to cut it off early. As one example she points to the way in which the shootings at Columbine High School in Littleton, Colorado, are being used against boys in general.

Most of you will remember the tragic story from April 1999. Two boys walked into the school library and began shooting; when it was all over, thirteen victims and their two assailants were dead. Sommers is alarmed about the remarks of William Pollack, director of the Center for Men at McLean Hospital, and so am I. Here is what he said: "The boys in Littleton are the tip of the iceberg. And the iceberg is *all* boys." The idea, widely held in our culture, is that the aggressive nature of boys is inherently bad, and we have to make them into something more like girls. The primary tool for that operation is our public school system. The average schoolteacher faces an incredible challenge: to bring order to a room of boys and girls, and promote learning. The main obstacle to that noble goal is getting the boys to sit still, keep quiet, and pay attention . . . for an entire day. You might as well hold back the tide. That's not the way a boy is wired, and it's not the way a boy learns. Rather than changing the way we do male education, we try to change males.

As Lionel Tiger reports in his book *The Decline of Males*, boys are three to four times more likely than girls to be diagnosed as suffering from attention deficit disorder (ADD). But maybe they're not sick; maybe, as Tiger says, "This may simply mean they enjoy large-muscle movements and assertive actions . . . Boys as a group appear to prefer relatively boisterous and mobile activities to the sedate and physically restricted behavior that school systems reward and to which girls seem to be more inclined."

Tell me about it. This guy ought to come over to our house for dinner. With three boys at the table (and one man, but with a boyish heart), things get pretty wild at times. Chairs, for the most part, are an option. The boys use them more like gymnastic equipment than restraints. Just the other night, I look over to see Blaine balancing across his chair on his stomach, like an acrobat. At the same moment Luke, our youngest, is nowhere to be seen. Or rather, in the place at the table where his head should be, we can only see a pair of socks, pointing straight up. My wife rolls her eyes. But not our school systems. As Tiger says,

> At least three to four times as many boys than girls are essentially defined as ill because their preferred patterns of play don't fit easily into the structure of the school. Well-meaning psycho-managers then prescribe tranquilizing drugs for ADD, such as Ritalin . . . The situation is scandalous. The use of drugs so disproportionately among boys betrays the failure of school authorities to understand sex differences . . . The only disease these boys may have is being male.

But it's not just the schools. (Many of them, by the way, are doing a heroic job.) How about our churches? A young man recently came to me very angry and distraught. He was frustrated at the way his father, a church leader, was coaching him in sports. He's a basketball player and his team had made the city finals. The night of the big game, as he was heading out the door, his father literally stopped him and said, "Now don't go out there and 'kick butt'—that's just not a nice thing to do." I am not making this up. What a ridiculous thing to say to a seventeen-year-old athlete. Go out there and give 'em . . . well, don't give 'em anything. Just be nice. Be the nicest guy the opposing team has ever met. In other words, be *soft*. That is a perfect example of what the church tells men. Someone I read said the church may have a masculine exterior, but its soul has turned feminine.

Emasculation happens in marriage as well. Women are often attracted to the wilder side of a man, but once having caught him they settle down to the task of domesticating him. Ironically, if he gives in he'll resent her for it, and she in turn will wonder where the passion has gone. Most marriages wind up there. A weary and lonely woman asked me the other day, "How do I get my husband to come alive?" "Invite him to be dangerous," I said. "You mean, I should let him get the motorcycle, right?" "Yep." She shrank back, disappointment on her face. "I know you're right, but I hate the idea. I've made him tame for years."

Think back to that great big lion in that tiny cage. Why would we put a man in a cage? For the same reason we put a lion there. For the same reason we put God there: he's dangerous. To paraphrase Sayers, we've also pared the claws of the Lion *Cub* of Judah. A man is a dangerous thing. Women don't start wars. Violent crimes aren't for the most part committed by women. Our prisons aren't filled with women. Columbine wasn't the work of two young girls. Obviously, something has gone wrong in the masculine soul, and the way we've decided to handle it is to take that dangerous nature away . . . entirely.

"We know that our society produces a plentiful supply of boys," says Robert Bly, "but seems to produce fewer and fewer men." There are two simple reasons: We don't know how to initiate boys into men; and second, *we're not sure we really want to.* We want to socialize them, to be sure, but *away from* all that is fierce, and wild, and passionate. In other words, away from masculinity and toward something more feminine. But as Sommers says, we have forgotten a simple truth: "The energy, competitiveness, and corporal daring of normal, decent males is responsible for much of what is right in the world." Sommers reminds us that during the Columbine massacre, "Seth Houy threw his body over a terrified girl to shield her from the bullets; fifteen-year-old Daniel Rohrbough paid with his life when, at mortal risk to himself, he held a door open so others could escape."

That strength so essential to men is also what makes them *heroes.* If a neighborhood is safe, it's because of the strength of men. Slavery was stopped by the strength of men, at a terrible price to them and their families. The Nazis were stopped by men. Apartheid wasn't defeated by women. Who gave their seats up on the lifeboats leaving the *Titanic,* so that women and children would be saved? And have we forgotten—it was a Man who let himself be nailed to Calvary's cross. This isn't to say women can't be heroic. I know many heroic women. It's simply to remind us that God made men the way they are because we desperately *need* them to be the way they are. Yes, a man is a dangerous thing. So is a scalpel. It can wound or it can save your life. You don't make it safe by making it dull; you put it in the hands of someone who knows what he's doing.

If you've spent any time around horses, you know a stallion can be a major problem. They're strong, very strong, and they've got a mind of their own. Stallions typically don't like to be bridled, and they can get downright aggressive—especially if there are mares around. A stallion is hard to tame. If you want a safer, quieter animal, there's an easy solution: castrate him. A gelding is much more compliant. You can lead him around by the nose; he'll do what he's told without putting up a fuss. There's only one problem: Geldings don't give life. They can't come through for you the way a stallion can. A stallion is dangerous all right, but if you want the life he offers, you have to have the danger too. They go together.

WHAT'S REALLY GOING ON HERE, ANYWAY?

Let's say it's June 6, 1944, about 0710. You are a soldier in the third wave onto Omaha Beach. Thousands of men have gone before you and now it is your turn. As you jump out of the Higgins boat and wade to the beach, you see the bodies of fallen soldiers everywhere—floating in the water, tossing in the surf, lying on the beach. Moving up the sand you encounter hundreds of wounded men. Some are limping toward the bluffs with you, looking for shelter. Others are barely crawling. Snipers on the cliffs above continue to take them out. Everywhere you look, there are pain and brokenness. The damage is almost overwhelming. When you reach the cliffs, the only point of safety, you find squads of men with no leader. They are shell-shocked, stunned and frightened. Many have lost their weapons; most of them refuse to move. They are paralyzed with fear. Taking all this in, what would you conclude? What would be your assessment of the situation? Whatever else went through your mind, you'd have to admit, *This is one brutal war,* and no one would have disagreed or thought you odd for having said so.

But we do not think so clearly about life and I'm not sure why. Have a look around you—what do you observe? What do you see in the lives of the men that you work with, live by, go to church alongside? Are they full of passionate freedom? Do they fight well? Are their women deeply grateful for how well their men have loved them? Are their children radiant with affirmation? The idea is almost laughable, if it weren't so tragic. Men have been taken out right and left. Scattered across the neighborhood lie the shattered lives of men (and women) who have died at a soul-level from the wounds they've taken. You've heard the expression, "he's a shell of a man?" They have lost heart. Many more are alive, but badly wounded. They are trying to crawl forward, but are having an awful time getting their lives together; they seem to keep taking hits. You know others who are already captives, languishing in prisons of despair, addiction, idleness, or boredom. The place looks like a battlefield, the Omaha Beach of the soul.

And that is precisely what it is. We are now in the late stages of the long and vicious war against the human heart. I know—it sounds overly dramatic. I almost didn't use the term "war" at all, for fear of being dismissed at this point as one more in the group of "Chicken Littles," Christians who run around trying to get everybody worked up over some imaginary fear in order to advance their political or economic or theological cause. But I am not hawking fear at all; I am speaking honestly about the nature of what is unfolding around us . . . *against us*. And until we call the situation what it is, we will not know what to do about it. In fact, this is where many people feel abandoned or betrayed by God. They thought that becoming a Christian would somehow end their troubles, or at least reduce them considerably. No one ever told them they were being moved to the front lines, and they seem genuinely shocked at the fact that they've been shot at.

After the Allies took the beachhead at Normandy, the war wasn't over. In some ways, it had just begun. Stephen Ambrose has given us many unforgettable stories of what followed that famous landing in *Citizen Soldiers*, his record of how the Allies won the war. Many of those stories are almost parables in their meaning. Here is one that followed on the heels of D-Day. It is June 7, 1944:

> Brig. Gen. Norman "Dutch" Cota, assistant division commander of the 29th, came on a group of infantry pinned down by some Germans in a farmhouse. He asked the captain in command why his men were making no effort to take the building. "Sir, the Germans are in there, shooting at us," the captain replied. "Well, I'll tell you what, captain," said Cota, unbuckling two grenades from his jacket. "You and your men start shooting at them. I'll take a squad of men and you and your men watch carefully. I'll show you how to take a house with Germans in it." Cota led his squad around a hedge to get as close as possible to the house. Suddenly, he gave a whoop and raced forward, the squad following, yelling like wild men. As they tossed grenades into the windows, Cota and another man kicked in the front door, tossed a couple of grenades inside, waited for the explosions, then dashed into the house. The surviving Germans inside were streaming out the back door, running for their lives. Cota returned to the captain. "You've seen how to take a house," said the general, still out of breath. "Do you understand? Do you know how to do it now?" "Yes, sir."

What can we learn from the parable? Why were those guys pinned down? First, they seemed almost surprised that they were being shot at. "They're shooting at us, sir." Hello? That's what happens in war—you get shot at. Have you forgotten? We were born into a world at war. This scene we're living in is no sitcom; it's bloody battle. Haven't you noticed with what deadly accuracy the wound was given? Those blows you've taken—they were not random accidents at all. They hit dead center. Charles was meant to be a pianist, but he never touched the piano again. I have a gift and calling to speak into the hearts of men and women. But my wound tempted me to be a loner, live far from my heart and from others. Craig's calling is to preach the gospel, like his father and great-grandfather. His wound was an attempt to take that out. He's a seagull, remember? All he can do is "squawk." I failed to mention Reggie earlier. His dad wounded him when he tried to excel in school. "You are so stupid; you'll never make it through college." He wanted to be a doctor, but he never followed his dream.

On and on it goes. The wound is too well aimed and far too consistent to be accidental. It was an attempt to take you out; to cripple or destroy your strength and get you out of the action. The wounds we've taken were leveled against us with stunning accuracy. Hopefully, you're getting the picture. Do you know why there's been such an assault? The Enemy fears you. You are dangerous big-time. If you ever really got your heart back, lived from it with courage, you would be a huge problem to him. You would do a lot of damage . . . on the side of good. Remember how valiant and effective God has been in the history of the world? You are a stem of that victorious stalk.

Let me come back to the second lesson of the parable from D-Day plus one. The other reason those men were lying there, pinned down, unable to move is because no one had ever shown them how to take a house before. They had been trained, but not for that. Most men have never been initiated into manhood. They have never had anyone show them how to do it, and especially, how to fight for their heart. The failure of so many fathers, the emasculating culture, and the passive church have left men without direction.

That is why I have written this book. I am here to tell you that you *can* get your heart back. But I need to warn you—if you want your heart back, if you want the wound healed and your strength restored and to find your true name, you're going to have to fight for it. Notice your reaction to my words. Does not something in you stir a little, a yearning to live? And doesn't another voice rush in, urging caution, maybe wanting to dismiss me altogether? *He's being melodramatic. What arrogance. Or, maybe some guys could, but not me. Or, I don't know . . . is this really worth it?* That's part of the battle, right there. See? I'm not making this up.

OUR SEARCH FOR AN ANSWER

First and foremost, we still need to know what we never heard, or heard so badly, from our fathers. We *need to know* who we are and if we have what it takes. What do we do now with that ultimate question? Where do we go to find an answer? In order to help you find the answer to The Question, let me ask you another: What *have* you done with your question? Where have you taken it? You see, a man's core question does not go away. He may try for years to shove it out of his awareness, and just "get on with life." But it does not go away. It is a hunger so essential to our souls that it will compel us to find a resolution. In truth, it drives everything we do.

I spent a few days this fall with a very successful man I'll call Peter. He was hosting me for a conference on the East Coast, and when Peter picked me up at the airport he was driving a new Land Rover with all the bells and whistles. *Nice car,* I thought. *This guy is doing well.* The next day we drove around in his BMW 850CSi. Peter lived in the largest house in town, and had a vacation home in Portugal. None of this wealth was inherited; he worked for every dime. He loved Formula One racing, and fly-fishing for salmon in Nova Scotia. I genuinely liked him. *Now here's a man,* I said to myself. And yet, there was something missing. You'd think a guy like this would be confident, self-assured, centered. And of course, he seemed like that at first. But as we spent time together I found him to be . . . hesitant. He had all the appearances of masculinity, but none of it felt like it was coming from a true center.

After several hours of conversation, he admitted he was coming to a revelation. "I lost my father earlier this year to cancer. But I did not cry when he died. You see, we were never really close." Ah yes, I knew what was coming next. "All these years, knocking myself out to get ahead . . . I wasn't even enjoying myself. What was it for? I see now . . . I was trying to win my father's approval." A long, sad silence. Then Peter said quietly, through tears, "It never worked." Of course not; it never does. No matter how much you make, no matter how far you go in life, that will never heal your wound or tell you who you are. But, oh how many men buy into this one.

After years of trying to succeed in the world's eyes, a friend still clings stubbornly to that idea. Sitting in my office, bleeding from all his wounds, he says to me, "Who's the real stud? The guy making money." You understand that he's not making much, so he can still chase the illusion.

Men take their souls' search for validation in all sorts of directions. Brad is a good man who for so many years now has been searching for a sense of significance through belonging. As he said, "Out of my wounds I figured out how to get life: I'll find a group to belong to, do something incredible that others will want, and I'll be somebody." First it was the right gang of kids in school; then it was the wrestling team; years later, it was the right ministry team. It has been a desperate search, by his own admission. And it hasn't gone well. When things didn't work out earlier this year at the ministry he was serving, he knew he had to leave. "My heart has burst and all the wounds and arrows have come pouring out. I have never felt such pain. The sentences scream at me, 'I do not belong. I am wanted by no one. I am alone.'"

Where does a man go for a sense of validation? To what he owns? To who pays attention to him? How attractive his wife is? Where he gets to eat out? How well he plays sports? The world cheers the vain search on: Make a million, run for office, get a promotion, hit a home run . . . *be* somebody. Can you feel the mockery of it all? The wounded crawl up the beach while the snipers fire away. But the deadliest place a man ever takes his search, the place every man seems to wind up no matter what trail he's followed, is the woman.

TAKING IT TO EVE

Remember the story of my first kiss, that little darling I fell in love with in the seventh grade and how she made my bicycle fly? I fell in love with Debbie the very same year my father checked out of my story, the year I took my deepest wound. The timing was no coincidence. In a young boy's development, there comes a crucial time when the father must intervene. It arrives early in adolescence, somewhere between the ages of eleven and fifteen, depending on the boy. If that intervention does not happen, the boy is set up for disaster; the next window that opens in his soul is sexuality. Debbie made me feel like a million bucks. I couldn't have put words to it at the time; I had no idea what was really going on. But in my heart I felt I had found the answer to my question. A pretty girl thinks I'm the greatest. What more can a guy ask for? If I've found Juliet, then I must be Romeo.

When she broke up with me, it began what has been a long and sad story of searching for "the woman that will make me feel like a man." I went from girlfriend to girlfriend trying to get an answer. To be the hero to the beauty—that has been my longing, my image of what it means to really, finally be a man. Bly calls it the search for the Golden-haired Woman.

> He sees a woman across the room, knows immediately that it is "She." He drops the relationship he has, pursues her, feels wild excitement, passion, beating heart, obsession. After a few months, everything collapses; she becomes an ordinary woman. He is confused and puzzled. Then he sees once more a radiant face across the room, and the old certainty comes again. (*Iron John*)

Why is pornography the most addictive thing in the universe for men? Certainly there's the fact that a man is visually wired, that pictures and images arouse men much more than they do women. But the deeper reason is because that seductive beauty reaches down inside and touches your desperate hunger for validation as a man you didn't even know you had, touches it like nothing else most men have ever experienced. You must understand – this is deeper than legs and breasts and good sex. It is mythological. Look at the lengths men will go to find the golden-haired woman. They have fought duels over her beauty; they have fought wars. You see, every man remembers Eve. We are haunted by her. And somehow we believe that if we could find her, get her back, then we'd also recover with her our own lost masculinity.

You'll recall the little boy Philip, from the movie *A Perfect World*? Remember what his fear was? That his penis was puny. That's how many men articulate a sense of emasculation. Later in life a man's worst fear is often impotence. If he can't get an erection, then he hasn't got what it takes. But the opposite is also at work. If a man can feel an erection, well then, he feels powerful. He feels strong. I'm telling you, for many men The Question feels hardwired to his penis. If he can feel like the hero sexually, well, then mister, he's the hero. Pornography is so seductive because what is a wounded, famished man to think when there are literally hundreds of beauties willing to give themselves to him? (Of course, it's not just to him, but when he's alone with the photos, it feels likes it's just for him.)

It's unbelievable—how many movies center around this lie? Get the beauty, win her, bed her, and you are the man. You're James Bond. You're a stud. Look carefully at the lyrics to Bruce Springsteen's song, *Secret Garden* (from his *Greatest Hits* recording, 1995):

> She'll let you in her house
> If you come knockin' late at night
> She'll let you in her mouth
> If the words you say are right
> If you pay the price
> She'll let you deep inside
> But there's a secret garden she hides.
> She'll lead you down a path
> There'll be tenderness in the air
> She'll let you come just far enough
> So you know she's really there
> She'll look at you and smile
> And her eyes will say
> She's got a secret garden
> Where everything you want
> Where everything you need
> Will always stay
> A million miles away.

It's a deep lie wedded to a deep truth. Eve *is* a garden of delight (Song 4:16). But she's not everything you want, everything you need—not even close. Of course it will stay a million miles away. You can't get there from here because it's not there. *It's not there.* The answer to your question can never, ever be found there. Don't get me wrong. A woman is a captivating thing. More captivating than anything else in all creation. "The naked woman's body is a portion of eternity too great for the eye of man." Femininity can *arouse* masculinity. Boy oh boy can it. My wife flashes me a little breast, a little thigh, and I'm ready for action. All systems alert. She tells me in a soft voice that I'm a man and I'll leap tall buildings for her. But femininity can never *bestow* masculinity. It's like asking a pearl to give you a buffalo. It's like asking a field of wildflowers to give you a '57 Chevy. They are different substances entirely.

When a man takes his question to the woman what happens is either addiction or emasculation. Usually both.

Dave, whose father blew a hole in his chest when he called him "mama's boy," took his question to the woman. Recently he confessed to me that younger women are his obsession. You can see why—they're less of a threat. A younger woman isn't half the challenge. He can feel more like a man there. Dave's embarrassed by his obsession, but it doesn't stop him. A younger woman feels like the answer to his question *and he's got to get an answer.* But he knows his search is impossible. He admitted to me just the other day, "Even if I marry a beautiful woman, I will always know there is an even more beautiful woman out there somewhere. So I'll wonder—could I have won her?"

It's a lie. As Bly says, it's a search without an end. "We are looking at the source of a lot of desperation in certain men here, and a lot of suffering in certain women." How often I have seen this. A friend's brother hit rock bottom a few years back when his girlfriend broke up with him. He was a really successful guy, a high school star athlete who became a promising young attorney.

But he was carrying a wound from an alcoholic, workaholic father who never gave him what every boy craves. Like so many of us, he took his heart with its question to the woman. When she dumped him, my friend said, "it blew him out of the water. He went into a major nosedive, started drinking heavily, smoking. He even left the country. His life was shattered."

This is why so many men secretly fear their wives. She sees him as no one else does, sleeps with him, knows what he's made of. If he has given her the power to validate him as a man, then he has also given her the power to *invalidate* him too. That's the deadly catch. A pastor told me that for years he's been trying to please his wife and she keeps giving him an "F." "What if she is not the report card on you?" I suggested. "She sure feels like it . . . and I'm failing." Another man, Richard, became verbally abusive toward his wife in the early years of their marriage. His vision for his life was that he was meant to be Romeo and therefore, she must be Juliet. When she turned out not to be the Golden-haired Woman, he was furious. Because that meant, you see, that he was not the heroic man. I remember seeing a picture of Julia Roberts without costume and makeup; *Oh*, I realized, *she's just an ordinary woman.*

"He was coming to me for his validation," a young woman told me about the man she was dating. Or, had been dating. She was drawn to him at first, and certainly drawn to the way he was taken with her. "That's why I broke up with him." I was amazed at her perceptiveness and her courage. It's very rare to find, especially in younger women. How wonderful it feels at first to be his obsession. To be thought of as a goddess is pretty heady stuff. But eventually, it all turns from romance to immense pressure on her part. "He kept saying, 'I don't know if I have what it takes and you're telling me I don't.' He'll thank me for it some day."

What's fascinating to note is that homosexuals are actually more clear on this point. They know that what is missing in their hearts is *masculine* love. The problem is that they've sexualized it. Joseph Nicolosi says that homosexuality is an attempt to repair the wound by filling it with masculinity, either the masculine love that was missing or the masculine strength many men feel they do not possess. It, too, is a vain search and that is why the overwhelming number of homosexual relationships do not last, why so many gay men move from one man to another and why so many of them suffer from depression and a host of other addictions. What they need can't be found there.

Why have I said all this about our search for validation and the answer to our question? Because we cannot hear the real answer until we see we've got a false one. So long as we chase the illusion, how can we face reality? The hunger is there; it lives in our souls like a famished craving, no matter what we've tried to fill it with. If you take your question to Eve, it will break your heart. I know this now, after many, many hard years. You can't get your answer there. In fact, you can't get your answer from any of the things men chase after to find their sense of self. There is only one source for the answer to your question. And so no matter where you've taken your question, you've got to take it back. You have to walk away. That is the beginning of your journey.

CHAPTER SIX

THE FATHER'S VOICE

No man, for any considerable period of time, can wear one face to himself and another to the multitude without finally getting bewildered as to which may be the truth.

—NATHANIEL HAWTHORNE

Esse quam videri
To be, rather than to appear

Who can give a man this, his own name?

—GEORGE MACDONALD

Summers in the eastern Oregon sagebrush are hot, dry, and dusty. When the sun was high the temperature could soar into the 90s, so whenever possible we saved most of the hard labor on the ranch for the early morning or late afternoon and evening, when the cool air drifted up from the river valley below. Sometimes we'd fix irrigation ditches during the heat of the day, which for me was a great excuse to get really wet. I'd tromp along in the ditch, letting the warm muddy water soak my jeans. But most of the time we'd head back to the ranch house for a glass of iced tea. Pop loved his tea sweetened with a healthy dose of sugar, the way they drink it in the South. We'd sit at the kitchen table and have a glass or two and talk about the events of the morning, or a plan he had to sell some cattle at the auction, or how he thought we'd spend the afternoon.

One day late in the summer of my thirteenth year, Pop and I had just come in for our ritual when he stood up and walked over to the window. The kitchen faced south and from there gave a view over a large alfalfa field and then on toward the pastureland. Like most ranchers Pop grew his own hay, to provide feed for cattle and horses he kept over the winter. I joined him at the window and saw that a steer had gotten out of the range and into the alfalfa. I remembered my grandfather telling me that it's dangerous for a cow to stuff itself on fresh alfalfa; it expands in their stomach like rising bread and could rupture one of their four chambers. Pop was clearly irritated, as only a cowboy can be irritated at cattle. I, on the other hand, was excited. This meant adventure.

"Go saddle up Tony and get that steer," he said, sitting back in his chair and kicking his boots up on the one in front of him. His demeanor made it clear that he was not going with me; he was, in fact, not going anywhere. As he poured himself another glass of tea my mind raced through the implications of what he'd said. It meant I first had to go catch Tony, the biggest horse on the ranch. I was scared of Tony, but we both knew he was the best cattle horse. I had to saddle him up by myself and ride out to get that steer. Alone. Having processed this information I realized I had been standing there for who knows how long and it was time I got going. As I walked out the back porch toward the corral I felt two things and felt them strongly: fear . . . and honor.

Most of our life-changing moments are realized as such later. I couldn't have told you why, but I knew I'd crossed a threshold in my life as a young man. Pop believed in me, and whatever he saw that I did not, the fact that he believed made me believe it too. I got the steer that day . . . and a whole lot more.

DESPERATE FOR INITIATION

A man needs to know his name. He needs to know he's got what it takes. And I don't mean "know" in the modernistic, rationalistic sense. I don't mean that the thought has passed through your cerebral cortex and you've given it intellectual assent, the way you know about the Battle of Waterloo or the ozone layer—the way most men "know" God or the truths of Christianity. I mean a deep knowing, the kind of knowing that comes when you have been there, entered in, experienced firsthand in an unforgettable way. The way "Adam knew his wife" and she gave birth to a child. Adam didn't know *about* Eve; he knew her intimately, through flesh-and-blood experience at a very deep level. There's knowledge *about* and knowledge *of*. When it comes to our question, we need the latter.

In the movie *Gladiator*, set in the second century A.D., the hero is a warrior from Spain called Maximus. He is the commander of the Roman armies, a general loved by his men and by the aging emperor Marcus Aurelius. The emperor's foul son Commodus learns of his father's plan to make Maximus emperor in his place, but before Marcus can pronounce his successor, Commodus strangles his father. He sentences Maximus to immediate execution and his wife and son to crucifixion and burning. Maximus escapes, but too late to save his family. Captured by slave traders, he is sold as a gladiator. That fate is normally a death sentence, but this is Maximus, a valiant fighter. He more than survives; he becomes a champion. Ultimately he is taken to Rome to perform in the Coliseum before the emperor Commodus (who of course believes that Maximus is long dead). After a remarkable display of courage and a stunning upset, the emperor comes down into the arena to meet the valiant gladiator, whose identity remains hidden behind his helmet.

COMMODUS: Your fame is well deserved, Spaniard. I don't believe there's ever been a gladiator that matched you . . . Why doesn't the hero reveal himself and tell us all your real name? (Maximus is silent.) You do have a name?

MAXIMUS: My name is Gladiator. (he turns and walks away.)

COMMODUS: How dare you show your back to me?! Slave! You will remove your helmet and tell me your name.

MAXIMUS: (Slowly, very slowly lifts his helmet and turns to face
            his enemy)
            My name is Maximus Decimus Meridius;
            Commander of the Armies of the North;
            General of the Felix Legions;
            loyal servant to the true emperor, Marcus
            Aurelius;
            father to a murdered son;
            husband to a murdered wife;
            and I will have my vengeance, in this life or in
            the next.

His answer builds like a mighty wave, swelling in size and
strength before it crashes on the shore. Where does a man go to
learn an answer like that—to learn his true name, a name that
can never be taken from him? That deep heart knowledge comes
only through a process of *initiation*. You have to know where
you've come from; you have to have faced a series of trials that
test you; you have to have taken a journey; and you have to have
faced your enemy. But as a young man recently lamented to me,
"I've been a Christian since I was five—no one ever showed me
what it means to really be a man." He's lost now. He moved across
the country to be with his girlfriend, but she's dumped him
because he doesn't know who he is and what he's here for. There
are countless others like him, a world of such men—a world of
uninitiated men.

   The church would like to think it is initiating men, but it's
not. What does the church bring a man into? What does it call
him out to be? Moral. That is pitifully insufficient. Morality is a
good thing, but morality is never the point. Paul says the Law is
given as a tutor to the child, but not to the son. The son is
invited up into something much more. He gets the keys to the

car; he gets to go away with the father on some dangerous mission. I'm struck by the poignancy of the scene at the end of the Civil War, just after Appomattox, where General Robert E. Lee has surrendered to General Ulysses S. Grant. For five years Lee has led the Army of Northern Virginia through some of the most terrible trials men have ever known. You would think they'd be glad to have it over. But Lee's men hang upon the reins of his horse and beg him not to go, plead for one more chance to "whip those Yankees." Lee had become their father, had given those men what most of them had never had before—an identity and a place in a larger story.

Every man needs someone like Robert E. Lee, or that brigadier general from the 29th: "You've seen how to take a house. Do you understand? Do you know how to do it now?" "Yes, sir." We need someone like my grandfather, who can teach us how to "saddle up." But Lee is long gone, brigadier generals are rare, and my grandfather has been dead for many years. Where do we go? To whom can we turn? To a most surprising source.

HOW GOD INITIATES A MAN

A number of years ago, at a point in my own journey when I felt more lost than ever, I heard a talk given by Gordon Dalbey, who had just written *Healing the Masculine Soul*. He raised the idea that despite a man's past and the failures of his own father to initiate him, God could take him on that journey, provide what was missing. A hope rose within me, but I dismissed it with the cynicism I'd learned to use to keep down most things in my soul. Several weeks, perhaps months later, I was downstairs in the early morning to read and pray. As with so many of my "quiet times," I ended up looking out the window toward the east to watch the sun rise. I heard Jesus whisper a question to me: "Will you let me initiate you?" Before my mind ever had a chance to process, dissect, and doubt the whole exchange, my heart leaped up and said *yes*.

"Who can give a man this, his own name?" George MacDonald asks. "God alone. For no one but God sees what the man is." He reflects upon the white stone that Revelation includes among the rewards God will give to those who "overcome." On that white stone there is a new name. It is "new" only in the sense that it is not the name the world gave to us, certainly not the one delivered with the wound. No man will find on that stone "mama's boy" or "fatty" or "seagull." But the new name is really not new at all when you understand that it is your *true* name, the one that belongs to you, "that being whom he had in his thought when he began to make the child, and whom he kept in his thought throughout the long process of creation" and redemption. Psalm 139 makes it clear that we were personally, uniquely planned and created, knit together in our mother's womb by God himself. He had someone in mind and that someone has a name.

That someone has also undergone a terrible assault, and yet God remains committed to the realization of that same someone. The giving of the white stone makes it clear—that is what he is up to. The history of a man's relationship with God is the story of how God calls him out, takes him on a journey and gives him his true name. Most of us have thought it was the story of how God sits on his throne waiting to whack a man broadside when he steps out of line. Not so. He created Adam for adventure, battle and beauty; he created us for a unique place in his story and he is committed to bringing us back to the original design. So God calls Abram out from Ur of the Chaldeas to a land he has never seen, to the frontier, and along the way Abram gets a new name. He becomes Abraham. God takes Jacob off into Mesopotamia somewhere, to learn things he has to learn and cannot learn at his mother's side. When he rides back into town, he has a limp and a new name as well.

Even if your father did his job, he can only take you partway. There comes a time when you have to leave all that is familiar, and go on into the unknown with God. Saul was a guy who really thought he understood the story and very much liked the part he had written for himself. He was the hero of his own little miniseries, "Saul the Avenger." After that little matter on the Damascus road he becomes *Paul*, and rather than heading back into all of the old and familiar ways he is led out into Arabia for three years to learn directly from God. Jesus shows us that initiation can happen even when we've lost our father or grandfather. He's the carpenter's son, which means Joseph was able to help him in the early days of his journey. But when we meet the young man Jesus, Joseph is out of the picture. Jesus has a new teacher—his true Father—and it is from him he must learn who he really is and what he's really made of.

Initiation involves a journey and a series of tests, through which we discover our real name and our true place in the story. Robert Ruark's book *The Old Man and the Boy* is a classic example of this kind of relationship. There's a boy who needs a lot of teaching, and there's an old man who's got a lot of wisdom. But the initiation doesn't take place at a school desk; it takes place *in the field*, where simple lessons about the land and animals and seasons turn into larger lessons about life and self and God. Through each test comes a *revelation*. The boy must keep his eyes open and ask the right questions. Learning to hunt quail helps you learn about yourself: "He's smart as a whip, and every time you go up against him you're proving something about yourself."

Most of us have been misinterpreting life and what God is

doing for a long time. "I think I'm just trying to get God to make my life work easier," a client of mine confessed, but he could have been speaking for most of us. We're asking the wrong questions. Most of us are asking, "God, why did you let this happen to me?" Or, "God, why won't you just . . . (fill in the blank—help me succeed, get my kids to straighten out, fix my marriage—you know what you've been whining about). But to enter into a journey of initiation with God requires a new set of questions: What are you trying to teach me here? What issues in my heart are you trying to raise through this? What is it you want me to see? What are you asking me to let go of? In truth, God has been trying to initiate you for a long time. What is in the way is how you've mishandled your wound and the life you've constructed as a result.

CONTEMPT FOR THE WOUND

"Men are taught over and over when they are boys that a wound that hurts is shameful," notes Bly. "A wound that stops you from continuing to play is a girlish wound. He who is truly a man keeps walking, dragging his guts behind." Like a man who's broken his leg in a marathon, he finishes the race even if he has to crawl and he doesn't say a word about it. That sort of misunderstanding is why for most of us, our wound is an immense source of shame. A man's not supposed to get hurt; he's certainly not supposed to let it really matter. We've seen too many movies where the good guy takes an arrow, just breaks it off, and keeps on fighting; or maybe he gets shot but is still able to leap across a canyon and get the bad guys. And so most men minimize their wound. "It's not a big deal. Lots of people get hurt when they're young. I'm okay." King David (a guy who's hardly a pushover) doesn't act like that at all. "I am poor and needy," he confesses openly, "and my heart is wounded within me" (Ps. 109:22).

Or perhaps they'll admit it happened, but deny it was a wound because they deserved it. After many months of counseling together about his wound, his vow, and how it was impossible to get The Answer from women, I asked Dave a simple question: "What would it take to convince you that you are a man?" "Nothing," he said. "Nothing can convince me." We sat in silence as tears ran down my cheeks. "You've embraced the wound, haven't you, Dave? You've owned its message as final. You think your father was right about you." "Yes," he said, without any sign of emotion at all. I went home and wept—for Dave, and for so many other men I know and for myself because I realized that I, too, had embraced my wound and ever since just tried to get on with life. Suck it up, as the saying goes. The only thing more tragic than the tragedy that happens to us is the way we handle it.

God is fiercely committed to you, to the restoration and release of your masculine heart. But a wound that goes unacknowledged and unwept is a wound that cannot heal. A wound you've embraced is a wound that cannot heal. A wound you think you deserved is a wound that cannot heal. That is why Brennan Manning says, "The spiritual life begins with the acceptance of our wounded self." Really? How can that be? The reason is simple: "Whatever is denied cannot be healed." But that's the problem, you see. Most men deny their wound—deny that it happened, deny that it hurt, certainly deny that it's shaping the way they live today. And so God's initiation of a man must take a very cunning course; a course that feels very odd, even cruel.

He will wound us in the very place where we have been wounded.

THWARTING THE FALSE SELF

From the place of our woundedness we construct a false self. We find a few gifts that work for us, and we try to live off them. Stuart found he was good at math and science. He shut down his heart and spent all his energies perfecting his "Spock" persona. There, in the academy, he was safe; he was also recognized and rewarded. Alex was good at sports and the whole macho image; he became a glass-eating animal. Stan became the nicest guy you could ever meet. "In the story of my life," he admitted, "I want to be seen as the Nice Guy." I became a hard-charging perfectionist; there, in my perfection, I found safety and recognition. "When I was eight," confesses Brennan Manning, "the impostor, or false self, was born as a defense against pain. The impostor within whispered, 'Brennan, don't ever be your real self anymore because nobody likes you as you are. Invent a new self that everybody will admire and nobody will know.'" Notice the key phrase: "as a defense against pain," as a way of saving himself. The impostor is our plan for salvation.

So God must take it all away. This often happens at the start of our initiation journey. He thwarts our plan for salvation; he shatters the false self. In the last chapter I told you of Brad's plan for self-redemption: he would belong to the "inside group." Even after it failed him time and again, breaking his heart over and over, he wouldn't give it up. He simply thought his aim was off; if he found the *right* group, then his plan would work. Our plan for redemption is hard to let go of; it clings to our hearts like an octopus. So what did God do for Brad? He took it all away. God brought Brad to the point where he thought he had found *the* group, and then God prevented him from maneuvering his way in. Brad wrote me a letter to describe what he was going through:

God has taken all that away, stripped me of all the things I used to earn people's admiration. I knew what he was up to. He put me in a place where my heart's deepest wounds and arrows—and sin—came out. As I was weeping all these pictures of what I want to belong to came up—speaker, counselor, in a group—and it was as if Jesus asked me to give them up. What came from my heart was surprising—incredible *fear*. And then the image of never getting them. A sentence arose in my heart: "You want me to die! If I give those up then I'll never belong and be somebody. You are asking me to die." It has been my hope of salvation.

Why would God do something so cruel? Why would he do something so terrible as to wound us in the place of our deepest wound? Jesus warned us that "whoever wants to save his life will lose it" (Luke 9:24). Christ is not using the word *bios* here; he's not talking about our physical life. The passage is not about trying to save your skin by ducking martyrdom or something like that. The word Christ uses for "life" is the word *psyche*—the word for our soul, our inner self, our heart. He says that the things we do to save our psyche, our self, those plans to save and protect our inner life—those are the things that will actually destroy us. "There is a way that seems right to a man but in the end it leads to death" says Proverbs 16:25. The false self, our plan for redemption, seems so right to us. It shields us from pain and secures us a little love and admiration. But the false self is a lie; the whole plan is built on pretense. It's a deadly trap. God loves us too much to leave us there. So he thwarts us, in many, many different ways.

In order to take a man into his wound, so that he can heal it and begin the release of the true self, God will thwart the false self. He will take away all that you've leaned upon to bring you life. In the movie *The Natural*, Robert Redford is a baseball player named Roy Hobbs, perhaps the most gifted baseball player ever. He's a high school wonder boy, a natural who gets a shot at the big leagues. But his dreams of a professional career are cut short when Hobbs is wrongly sentenced to prison for murder. Years later, an aging Hobbs gets a second chance. He's signed by the New York Knights—the worst team in the league. But through his incredible gift, untarnished by the years, Hobbs leads the Knights from ignominy to the play-off game for the National League pennant. He rallies the team, becomes the center of their hopes and dreams.

The climax of the film is the game for the championship. It's the bottom of the ninth; the score is Pittsburgh 2, Knights 0. The Knights have 2 outs; there's a man on first and third when Hobbs steps up to the plate. He's their only chance; this is his moment. Now, there's something you must know, something absolutely crucial to the story. Ever since his high school days, Hobbs has played with a bat he made himself from the heart of a tree felled by lightning in his front yard. Burned into the bat is a lightning bolt and the words "wonder boy." That bat is the symbol of his greatness, his giftedness. He has never, ever played with another. Clutching "wonder boy," Hobbs steps to the plate. His first swing is a miss; his second is a foul ball high and behind. His third is a solid hit along the first-base line; it looks like it's a home run, but it also lands foul. As Hobbs returns to the plate, he sees his bat lying there . . . in pieces. It shattered on that last swing.

This is the critical moment in a man's life, when all he has counted on comes crashing down, when his golden bat breaks into pieces. His investments fail; his company lets him go; the church fires him; he is leveled by an illness; his wife walks out; his daughter turns up pregnant. What is he to do? Will he stay in the game? Will he shrink back to the dugout? Will he scramble to try to put things back together, as so many men do? The true test of a man, the beginning of his redemption, actually starts when he can no longer rely on what he's used all his life. *The real journey begins when the false self fails.* A moment that seems like an eternity passes as Hobbs stands there, holding the broken pieces, surveying the damage. The bat is beyond repair. Then he says to the bat boy, "Go pick me out a winner, Bobby." He stays in the game and hits a home run to win the series.

God will take away our "bat" as well. He will do something to thwart the false self. Stuart "saved" himself by becoming emotionless. Last year his wife walked out on him. She's had it with his two-dimensional existence; what woman wants to be married to Spock? Alex recently suffered a series of panic attacks that left him almost unable to leave his home. The whole macho construct fell to the ground. At first, nobody could believe it; Alex couldn't believe it. He was invincible, the strongest guy you ever met. But it was all built as a defense against the wound. Our loss doesn't necessarily have to be something so dramatic. A man may simply awaken one day to find himself lost, lost as Dante described himself: "In the middle of the road of my life, I awoke in a dark wood, where the true way was wholly lost." That was the turning point in my life.

I went to Washington, D.C., as a young man to try to make something of myself, to prove something, establish credibility. The damnable thing about it was, I succeeded. My giftedness worked against me by coming through for me. I was recognized and rewarded. But the whole experience felt like an act of survival—not something flowing out of a deep center, but something I had to prove, overcome, grasp. As Manning said of his own impostor, "I studied hard, scored excellent grades, won a scholarship in high school, and was stalked every waking moment by the terror of abandonment and the sense that nobody was there for me." At the end of two years I woke one morning and realized I hated my life.

How many helps thou giv'st to those who would learn!
To some sore pain, to others a sinking heart;
To some a weariness worse than any smart;
To some a haunting, fearing, blind concern;
Madness to some; to some the shaking dart
Of hideous death still following as they turn;
To some a hunger that will not depart.

To some thou giv'st a deep unrest—a scorn
Of all they are or see upon the earth;
A gaze, at dusky night and clearing morn,
As on a land of emptiness and dearth;
To some a bitter sorrow; to some the sting
Of love misprized—of sick abandoning;
To some a frozen heart, oh, worse than anything!

The messengers of Satan think to mar,
But make—driving the soul from false to feal—
To thee, the reconciler, the one real,
In whom alone the *would be* and the *is* are met.
(George MacDonald, *Diary of an Old Soul*)

This is a very dangerous moment, when God seems set against everything that has meant life to us. Satan spies his opportunity, and leaps to accuse God in our hearts. *You see,* he says, *God is angry with you. He's disappointed in you. If he loved you he would make things smoother. He's not out for your best, you know.* The Enemy always tempts us back toward control, to recover and rebuild the false self. We must remember that it is out of love that God thwarts our impostor. As Hebrews reminds us, it is the son whom God disciplines, therefore do not lose heart (12:5–6).

God thwarts us to save us. We think it will destroy us, but the opposite is true—we must be saved from what really will destroy us. If we would walk with him in our journey of masculine initiation, we must walk away from the false self—set it down, give it up willingly. It feels crazy; it feels immensely vulnerable. Brad has stopped looking for the group. Stuart has begun to open up his heart to emotion, to relationship, to all that he buried so long ago. Alex stopped "eating glass," stopped the whole macho thing to face what he had never faced inside. I gave up perfectionism, left Washington, and went looking for my heart. We simply accept the invitation to leave all that we've relied on and venture out with God. We can choose to do it ourselves, or we can wait for God to bring it all down.

If you have no clue as to what your false self may be, then a starting point would be to ask those you live with and work with, "What is my effect on you? What am I like to live with (or work with)? What *don't* you feel free to bring up with me?" If you never, ever say a word in a meeting because you fear you might say something stupid, well then, it's time to speak up. If all you ever do is dominate a meeting because your sense of worth comes from being in charge, then you need to shut up for a while. If you've run to sports because you feel best about yourself there, then it's probably time to give it a rest and stay home with your family. If you never play any game with other men, then it's time you go down to the gym with the guys and play some hoops. In other words, you face your fears head-on. Drop the fig leaf; come out from hiding. For how long? Longer than you want to; long enough to raise the deeper issues, let the wound surface from beneath it all.

Losing the false self is painful; though it's a mask, it's one we've worn for years and losing it can feel like losing a close friend. Underneath the mask is all the hurt and fear we've been running from, hiding from. To let it come to the surface can shake us like an earthquake. Brad felt as if he was going to die; you may too. Or you may feel like Andy Gullahorn, who wrote the song "Steel Bars" from *Old Hat* (© 1997 by Andy Gullahorn):

> So this is how it feels at the rock bottom of despair
> When the house I built comes crashing down
> And this is how it feels when I know the man that I say I am
> Is not the man that I am when no one's around

But this is not the end of the road; it's the trailhead. What you are journeying toward is freedom, healing, and authenticity. Listen to the next part of Andy's song:

> This is how it feels to come alive again
> And start fighting back to gain control
> And this is how it feels to let freedom in
> And break the chains that enslave my soul

WALKING AWAY FROM THE WOMAN

As we walk away from the false self, we will feel vulnerable and exposed. We will be sorely tempted to turn to our comforters for some relief, those places that we've found solace and rest. Because so many of us turned to the woman for our sense of masculinity, we must walk away from her as well. *I do not mean you leave your wife.* I mean you stop looking to her to validate you, stop trying to make her come through for you, stop trying to get your answer from her. For some men, this may mean disappointing her. If you've been a passive man, tiptoeing around your wife for years, never doing anything to rock the boat, then it's time to rock it. Stand up to her;

get her mad at you. For those of you violent men (including achievers), it means *you stop abusing her*. You release her as the object of your anger because you release her as the one who was supposed to make you a man. Repentance for a driven man means you become *kind*. Both types are still going to the woman. Repentance depends on which way you've approached her.

But I have counseled many young men to break up with the woman they were *dating* because they had made her their life. She was the sun of his universe, around which he orbited. A man needs a much bigger orbit than a woman. He needs a mission, a life purpose, and he needs to know his name. Only then is he fit for a woman, for only then does he have something to invite her into. A friend tells me that in the Masai tribe in Africa, a young man cannot court a woman until he has killed a lion. That's their way of saying, until he has been initiated. I have seen far too many young men commit a kind of emotional promiscuity with a young woman. He will pursue her, not to offer his strength but to drink from her beauty, to be affirmed by her and feel like a man. They will share deep, intimate conversations. But he will not commit; he is *unable* to commit. This is very unfair to the young lady. After a year of this sort of relationship a dear friend said, "I never felt secure in what I meant to him."

When we feel the pull toward the golden-haired woman, we must recognize that something deeper is at play. As Bly says,

> What does it mean when a man falls in love with a radiant face across the room? It may mean that he has some soul work to do. His soul is the issue. Instead of pursuing the woman and trying to get her alone . . . he needs to go alone himself , perhaps to a mountain cabin, for three months, write poetry, canoe down a river, and dream. That would save some women a lot of trouble. (*Iron John*)

Again, this is not permission to divorce. A man who has married a woman has made her a solemn pledge; he can never heal his wound by delivering another to the one he promised to love. Sometimes she will leave him; that is another story. Too many men run after her, begging her not to go. If she has to go, it is probably because you have some soul work to do. What I am saying is that the masculine journey always takes a man *away* from the woman, in order that he may come back to her with his question answered. A man does not go to a woman to get his strength; he goes to her to *offer* it. You do not need the woman for you to become a great man, and as a great man you do not need the woman. As Augustine said, "Let my soul praise you for all these beauties, but let it not attach itself to them by the trap of love," the trap of addiction because we've taken our soul to her for validation.

But there is an even deeper issue than our question. What else is it we are seeking from the Woman with the Golden Hair? What is that ache we are trying to assuage with her? Mercy, comfort, beauty, ecstasy—in a word, *God*. I'm serious. What we are looking for is God.

There was a time when Adam drank deeply from the source of all Love. He—our first father and archetype—lived in an unbroken communion with the most captivating, beautiful, and intoxicating Source of life in the universe. Adam had God. True, it was not good for man to be alone, and God in his humility gave us Eve, allowed us to need her as well. But something happened at the Fall; something *shifted*. Eve took the place of God in a man's life. Let me explain.

Adam was not deceived by the serpent. Did you know that? Paul makes it clear in 1 Timothy 2:14—Adam did not fall because he was deceived. His sin was different; in some ways, it was more serious in that he did it with open eyes. We do not know how long it lasted, but there was a moment in Eden when Eve was fallen and Adam was not; she had eaten, but he yet had a choice. I believe something took place in his heart that went like this: I have lost my *ezer kenegdo*, my soul mate, the most vital companion I've known. I do not know what life will be like, but I know I cannot live without her.

Adam chose Eve over God.

If you think I exaggerate, simply look around. Look at all the art, poetry, music, drama devoted to the beautiful woman. Listen to the language men use to describe her. Watch the powerful obsession at work. What else can this be but *worship?* Men come into the world without the God who was our deepest joy, our ecstasy. Aching for we know not what, we meet Eve's daughters and we are history. She is the closest thing we've ever encountered, the pinnacle of creation, the very embodiment of God's beauty and mystery and tenderness and allure. And what goes out to her is not just our longing for Eve, but our longing for God as well. A man without his true love, his life, his God, will find another. What better substitute than Eve's daughters? Nothing else in creation even comes close.

To a young man who had never been without a girlfriend since the eighth grade, I gave the advice that he should break up, call off all dating for one year. From the look on his face you'd have thought I told him to cut off his arm . . . or something worse. Do you see what is at work here? Notice that the struggle with pornography or masturbation is most difficult when you are lonely, or beat up, or longing for comfort in some way. This will become more intense as you get closer to your wound. The longing for the ache to go away, and the pull toward other comforters can seem overwhelming. I've watched it in many men. I know it in myself. But if this is the water you are truly thirsty for, then why do you remain thirsty after you've had a drink? It's the wrong well.

We must reverse Adam's choice; we must choose God over Eve. We must take our ache to him. For only in God will we find the healing of our wound.

CHAPTER SEVEN

HEALING THE WOUND

Desperado, why don't you come to your senses
You been out ridin fences for so long now
O you're a hard one, but I know
That you got your reasons . . .
You better let somebody love you
Before it's too late.

—THE EAGLES
"Desperado"
(© 1973 by Glenn Fry
and Don Henley)

The task of healing is to respect oneself as a creature, no more and no
less.

—WENDELL BERRY

The deepest desire of our hearts is for union with God. God created
us for union with himself: This is the original purpose of our lives.
—BRENNAN MANNING

I think I've given a wrong impression of my life with my sons. Rock climbing, canoeing, wrestling, our quest for danger and destruction—you might get the impression we're a sort of military academy of the backwoods or one of those militia cults. So let me tell you of my favorite event of the day. It comes late in the evening, at bedtime, after the boys have brushed their teeth and we've said our family prayers. As I'm tucking them in, one of my boys will ask, "Dad, can we snuggle tonight?" Snuggle time is when I'll cuddle up next to them on a bed that's really not big enough for both of us—and that's the point, to get very close—and there in the dark we'll just sort of talk. Usually we start laughing and then we have to whisper because the others will ask us to "keep it down in there." Sometimes it breaks into tickling, other times it's a chance for them to ask some serious questions about life. But whatever happens, what matters most is what's going on beneath all that: intimacy, closeness, connection.

Yes, my boys want me to guide them into adventure, and they love to test their strength against mine. But all of that takes place in the context of an intimate bond of love that is far deeper than words can express. What they want more than anything, what I love to offer them more than anything, is soul-to-soul oneness. As Tom Wolfe said,

> The deepest search in life, it seemed to me, the thing that in one way or another was central to all living was man's search

to find a father, not merely the father of his flesh, not merely the lost father of his youth, but the image of a strength and wisdom external to his need and superior to his hunger, to which the belief and power of his own life could be united. ("The Story of a Novel")

THE SOURCE OF REAL STRENGTH

Guys are unanimously embarrassed by their emptiness and woundedness; it is for most of us a tremendous source of shame, as I've said. But it need not be. From the very beginning, back before the Fall and the assault, ours was meant to be a desperately dependent existence. It's like a tree and its branches, explains Christ. You are the branches, I am the trunk. From me you draw your life; that's how it was meant to be. In fact, he goes on to say, "Apart from me you can do nothing" (John 15:5). He's not berating us or mocking us or even saying it with a sigh, all the while thinking, *I wish they'd pull it together and stop needing me so much.* Not at all. We are *made* to depend on God; we are made for union with him and nothing about us works right without it. As C. S. Lewis wrote, "A car is made to run on gasoline, and it would not run properly on anything else. Now God designed the human machine to run on himself. He himself is the fuel our spirits were designed to burn, or the food our spirits were designed to feed on. There is no other."

This is where our sin and our culture have come together to keep us in bondage and brokenness, to prevent the healing of our wound. Our sin is that stubborn part inside that wants, above all else, to be independent. There's a part of us fiercely committed to living in a way where we do not have to depend on anyone—especially God. Then culture comes along with figures like John Wayne and James Bond and all those other "real men," and the one thing they have in common is that they are *loners;* they don't need anyone. We come to believe deep in our hearts that needing anyone for anything is a sort of weakness, a handicap. This is why a man never, ever stops to ask for directions. I am notorious for this. I know how to get there; I'll find my own way, thank you very much. Only when I am fully and finally and completely lost will I pull over and get some help, and I'll feel like a wimp for doing it.

Jesus knew nothing of that. The Man who never flinched to take on hypocrites and get in their face, the One who drove "a hundred men wi' a bundle o' cords swung free," the Master of wind and sea, lived in a desperate dependence on his Father. "I assure you, the Son can do nothing by himself. He does only what he sees the Father doing"; "I live by the power of the living Father who sent me"; "The words I say are not my own, but my Father who lives in me does his work through me." This isn't a source of embarrassment to Christ; quite the opposite. He brags about his relationship with his Father. He's happy to tell anyone who will listen, "The Father and I are one" (John 5:19; 6:57; 14:10; 10:30 NLT).

Why is this important? Because so many men I know live with a deep misunderstanding of Christianity. They look at it as a "second chance" to get their act together. They've been forgiven, now they see it as their job to get with the program. They're trying to finish the marathon with a broken leg. But follow this closely now: You'll recall that masculinity is an essence that is passed from father to son. That is a picture, as so many things in life are, of a deeper reality. The *true* essence of strength is passed to us from God *through our union with him.* Notice what a deep and vital part of King David's life this is. Remembering that he is a man's man, a warrior for sure, listen to how he describes his relationship to God in the Psalms:

I love you, O LORD, my strength. (18:1)

But you, O LORD, be not far off;
O my Strength, come quickly to help me. (22:19)

O my Strength, I watch for you;
you, O God, are my fortress, my
loving God. (59:9)

I dare say that David could take on John Wayne or James Bond any day; yet this true man is unashamed to admit his desperate dependence on God. We know we are meant to embody strength, we know we are not what we were meant to be, and so we feel our brokenness as a source of shame. As we spoke of his wound recently, and how he needed to enter into it for healing, Dave protested. "I don't even want to go there. It all feels so true." Men are typically quite harsh with the broken places within them. Many report feeling as though there is a boy inside, and they despise that about themselves. *Quit being such a baby*, they order themselves. But that is not how God feels. He is furious about what's happened to you. "It would be better to be thrown into the sea with a large millstone tied around the neck than to face the punishment in store for harming one of these little ones" (Luke 17:2 NLT). Think of how you would feel if the wounds you were given, the blows dealt to you, were dealt to a boy you loved—your son, perhaps. Would you shame him for it? Would you feel scorn that he couldn't rise above it all? No. You'd feel compassion. As Gerard Manley Hopkins wrote,

My own heart let me more have pity on; let
Me live to my sad self hereafter kind.

In the movie *Good Will Hunting*, there is a beautiful picture of what can happen when a man realizes he has "owned" his wound, and discovers he doesn't have to. Will Hunting (played by Matt Damon) is a brilliant young man, a genius, who works as a janitor at MIT and lives in a rough part of town. No one knows about his gift, because he hides it behind a false self of "tough kid from the wrong side of the tracks." He's a fighter (a violent man). That false self was born out of a father-wound; his original father he does not know, and the man who was his foster father would come home drunk and beat Will mercilessly. After he's arrested for getting into a brawl for the umpteenth time, Will is ordered by the court to see a psychologist, Sean (played by Robin Williams). They form a bond; for the first time in Will's life, an older man cares about him deeply. His initiation has begun. Toward the end of one of their last sessions, Sean and Will are talking about the beatings he endured, now recorded in his case file.

> WILL: So, uh . . . you know, what is it, like "Will has an attachment disorder," is it all that stuff? "Fear of abandonment"? Is that why I broke up with Skyler [his girlfriend]?
>
> SEAN: I didn't know you had.
>
> WILL: I did.
>
> SEAN: You wanna talk about it?
>
> WILL: (Staring at the floor) No.
>
> SEAN: Hey, Will . . . I don't know a lot, but you see this (holding his file) . . . This is not your fault.
>
> WILL: (Dismisses him) Yeah, I know that.
>
> SEAN: Look at me, son. It's not your fault.
>
> WILL: I know.
>
> SEAN: It's not your fault.
>
> WILL: (Beginning to grow defensive) I know.

SEAN: No, no, you don't. It's not your fault.

WILL: (Really defensive) I know.

SEAN: It's not your fault.

WILL: (Trying to end the conversation) All right.

SEAN: It's not your fault . . . it's not your fault.

WILL: (Anger) Don't [mess] with me, Sean, not you.

SEAN: It's not your fault . . . it's not your fault . . . it's not your fault.

WILL: (Collapses into his arms, weeping) I'm so sorry; I'm so sorry.

It is no shame that you need healing; it is no shame to look to another for strength; it is no shame that you feel young and afraid inside. It's not your fault.

ENTERING THE WOUND

Frederick Buechner's father committed suicide when he was ten. He left a note, to his mother: "I adore and love you, and am no good . . . Give Freddie my watch. Give Jaime my pearl pin. I give you all my love," and then he sat in the garage while the running car filled it with carbon monoxide. It happened on a Saturday morning in the fall. He was to have taken Frederick and his brother to a football game that day. Instead, he took himself forever from their lives. What is a ten-year-old boy to do with such an event?

A child takes life as it comes because he has no other way of taking it. The world had come to an end that Saturday morning, but each time we had moved to another place, I had seen a world come to an end, and there had always been another world to replace it. When somebody you love dies, Mark Twain said, it is like when your house burns down; it isn't for years that you realize the full extent of your loss. For me it was longer than for most, if indeed I have realized it fully even yet, and in the meantime the loss came to get buried so deep in me that after a time I scarcely ever took it out to look at it at all, let alone speak of it. (*The Sacred Journey*)

That is the way we are with our wound, especially men. We bury it deep and never take it out again. But take it out we must, or better, enter into it. I entered my wound through the surprising door of my anger. After we moved to Colorado, about eleven years ago, I found myself snapping at my boys for silly things. A spilled glass of milk would elicit a burst of rage. *Whoa, John*, I thought, *there are things going on inside; you'd better have a look under the hood*. As I explored my anger with the help of my dear friend Brent, I realized I was so furious about feeling all alone in a world that constantly demanded more of me than I felt able to give. Something in me felt young—like a ten-year-old boy in a man's world but without a man's ability to come through. There was much fear beneath the surface; fear that I would fail, fear that I would be found out, and finally, fear that I was ultimately on my own. *Where did all this fear come from?* I wondered. *Why do I feel so alone in the world . . . and so young inside? Why does something in my heart feel orphaned?*

My answer came through several movies. As I've written about in other places, I was blindsided by *A River Runs Through It* because through its beautiful retelling of boys who never really had their father except during their fishing trips, and how in the end they lost even that. I realized I had lost my father, and like Buechner the loss got buried so deep in me that after a time I scarcely ever took it out. I was pierced by *A Perfect World* because I saw there just how much a boy's father means to him and how I longed for that intimacy with a source of strength who loved me and could tell me my name. I so identified with Will Hunting because I, too, was a fighter who saw myself as up against the rest of the world and I had also accepted my wound and never grieved it. I thought it was my fault.

In some ways God had to sneak up on me through those stories because I wasn't willing to just skip happily down the path to my heart's deepest pain. We fight this part of the journey. The whole false self, our "lifestyle," is an elaborate defense against entering our wounded heart. It is a chosen blindness. "Our false self stubbornly blinds each of us to the light and the truth of our own emptiness and hollowness," says Manning. There are readers who even now have no idea what their wound is, or even what false self arose from it. Ah, how convenient that blindness is. Blissful ignorance. But a wound unfelt is a wound unhealed. We must go in. The door may be your anger; it may be rejection that you've experienced, perhaps from a girl; it may be failure, or the loss of the golden bat and the way God is thwarting your false self. It may be a simple prayer: Jesus, take me into my wound.

"Behold," he says, "I stand at the door and knock."

HEALING THE WOUND

If you wanted to learn how to heal the blind and you thought that following Christ around and watching how he did it would make things clear, you'd wind up pretty frustrated. He never does it the same way twice. He spits on one guy; for another, he spits on the ground and makes mud and puts that on his eyes. To a third he simply speaks, a fourth he touches, and a fifth he kicks out a demon. There are no formulas with God. The way in which God heals our wound is a deeply personal process. He is a person and he insists on working personally. For some, it comes in a moment of divine touch. For others, it takes place over time and through the help of another, maybe several others. As Agnes Sanford says, "There are in many of us wounds so deep that only the mediation of someone else to whom we may 'bare our grief' can heal us."

So much healing took place in my life simply through my friendship with Brent. We were partners, but far more than that, we were friends. We spent hours together fly-fishing, backpacking, hanging out in pubs. Just spending time with a man I truly respected, a real man who loved and respected me—nothing heals quite like that. At first I feared that I was fooling him, that he'd see through it any day and drop me. But he didn't, and what happened instead was validation. My heart knew that if a man I *know* is a man thinks I'm one, too, well then, maybe I am one after all. Remember—masculinity is bestowed by masculinity. But there have been other significant ways in which God has worked—times of healing prayer, times of grieving the wound and forgiving my father. Most of all, times of deep communion with God. The point is this: Healing never happens outside of intimacy with Christ. The healing of our wound flows out of our union with him.

But there are some common themes that I share with you as you seek the restoration of your heart. The first step seems so simple it's almost hard to believe we overlook it, never ask for it, and when we do, we sometimes struggle for days just to get the words out.

It begins with surrender. As Lewis says, "Until you have given yourself to him you will not have a real self." We return the branch to its trunk; we yield our lives to the One who is our Life. And then *we invite Jesus into the wound;* we ask him to come and meet us there, to enter into the broken and unhealed places of our heart. When the Bible tells us that Christ came to "redeem mankind" it offers a whole lot more than forgiveness. To simply forgive a broken man is like telling someone running a marathon,

"It's okay that you've broken your leg. I won't hold that against you. Now finish the race." That is cruel, to leave him disabled that way. No, there is much more to our redemption. The core of Christ's mission is foretold in Isaiah 61:

> The Spirit of the Sovereign LORD is on me,
> because the LORD has anointed me
> to preach good news to the poor.
> He has sent me to bind up the brokenhearted,
> to proclaim freedom for the captives
> and release for the prisoners. (v. 1)

The Messiah will come, he says, to bind up and heal, to release and set free. What? *Your heart.* Christ comes to restore and release you, your soul, the true you. This is *the* central passage in the entire Bible about Jesus, the one he chooses to quote about himself when he steps into the spotlight in Luke 4 and announces his arrival. So take him at his word—ask him in to heal all the broken places within you and unite them into one whole and healed heart. Ask him to release you from all bondage and captivity, as he promised to do. As MacDonald prayed, "Gather my broken fragments to a whole . . . Let mine be a merry, all-receiving heart, but make it a whole, with light in every part." But you can't do this at a distance; you can't ask Christ to come into your wound while you remain far from it. You have to go there with him.

That is why we must grieve the wound. It was not your fault and it did matter. Oh what a milestone day that was for me when I simply allowed myself to say that the loss of my father *mattered.* The tears that flowed were the first I'd ever granted my wound, and they were deeply healing. All those years of sucking it up melted away in my grief. It is so important for us to grieve our wound; it is the only honest thing to do. For in grieving we admit the truth—that we were hurt by someone we loved, that we lost something very dear, and it hurt us very much. Tears are healing. They help to open and cleanse the wound. As Augustine wrote in his *Confessions,* "The tears . . . streamed down, and I let them flow as freely as they would, making of them a pillow for my heart. On them it rested." Grief is a form of validation; it says the wound *mattered.*

We let God love us; we let him get real close to us. I know, it seems painfully obvious, but I'm telling you few men are ever so vulnerable as to simply let themselves be loved by God. After Brad lost his plan for redemption, I asked him, "Brad, why don't you just let God love you?" He squirmed in his chair. "I have such a hard time with that, just being loved. It feels so naked. I'd rather be in control, be admired for what I bring to the group." Later he wrote this in a letter to me:

> After it all came crashing down, I was overwhelmed by sadness and grief. The pain is incredible. In the midst of that God asked me, "Brad, will you let me love you?" I know what he is asking. I feel anxious that I need to go e-mail all these schools and secure a future. But I'm tired of running away. I want to come home. I flipped through my Bible and came to John 15, "Just as the Father has loved you, I have also loved you; abide in my love." The battle is very intense. At times it is all clear. At others it is a fog. Right now all I can do is cling to Jesus as best I know how and not run from all that is in my heart.

Abiding in the love of God is our only hope, the only true home for our hearts. It's not that we mentally acknowledge that God loves us. It's that we let our hearts come home to him, and stay in his love. MacDonald says it this way:

When our hearts turn to him, that is opening the door to him . . . then he comes in, not by our thought only, not in our idea only, but he comes himself, and of his own will. Thus the Lord, the Spirit, becomes the soul of our souls . . . Then indeed we *are*; then indeed we have life; the life of Jesus has . . . become life in us . . . we are one with God forever and ever. (*The Heart of George MacDonald*)

Or as St. John of the Cross echoes, "O how gently and how lovingly dost thou lie awake in the depth and centre of my soul, where thou in secret and in silence alone, as its sole Lord, abidest, not only as in Thine own house or in Thine own chamber, but also as within my own bosom, in close and intimate union" (*Living Flame of Love*). This deep intimate union with Jesus and with his Father is the source of all our healing and all our strength. It is, as Leanne Payne says, "the central and unique truth of Christianity." After a retreat in which I laid out the masculine journey to a small group of men, I received this E-mail:

> My father never left, he just never had time for me or words of encouragement. He has spent his entire life making himself the center of attention. For the first time I understand why I am highly driven, why I never let anyone get close to me— including my wife—and why I am an impostor to most people. I broke down and cried. I feel the presence of God in my heart like I have never felt him before . . . the beginning of a new heart.

Time has come for us to forgive our fathers. Paul warns us that unforgiveness and bitterness can wreck our lives and the lives of others (Eph. 4:31; Heb. 12:15). I am sorry to think of all the years my wife endured the anger and bitterness that I redirected at her from my father. As someone has said, forgiveness is setting a prisoner free and then discovering the prisoner was you. I found some help in Bly's experience of forgiving his own father, when he said, "I began to think of him not as someone who had deprived me of love or attention or companionship, but as someone who himself had been deprived, by his father and his mother and by the culture." My father had his own wound that no one ever offered to heal. His father was an alcoholic, too, for a time, and there were some hard years for my dad as a young man just as there were for me.

Now you must understand: Forgiveness is a choice. It is not a feeling, but an act of the will. As Neil Anderson has written, "Don't wait to forgive until you feel like forgiving; you will never get there. Feelings take time to heal after the choice to forgive is made." We allow God to bring the hurt up from our past, for "if your forgiveness doesn't visit the emotional core of your life, it will be incomplete." We acknowledge that it hurt, that it mattered, and we choose to extend forgiveness to our father. This is *not* saying, "It didn't really matter"; it is *not* saying, "I probably deserved part of it anyway." Forgiveness says, "It was wrong, it mattered, and I release you."

And then we ask God to father us, and to tell us our true name.

GOD'S NAME FOR US

I noticed a few years ago, a ways into my own masculine journey, that I related well to Jesus and to "God," but not to God as *Father*. It's not hard to figure out why. Father has been a source of pain and disappointment to me . . . to many of us. Then I read this in MacDonald:

In my own childhood and boyhood my father was the refuge from all the ills of life, even sharp pain itself. Therefore I say to son or daughter who has no pleasure in the name *Father*, "You must interpret the word by all that you have missed in life. All that human tenderness can give or desire in the nearness and readiness of love, all and infinitely more must be true of the perfect Father—of the maker of fatherhood." (*The Heart of George MacDonald*)

The gift was perfectly timed, for I knew it was time to allow God to father me. (All along the process of my initiation, God has provided words like that, messages, people, gifts to open the next leg of the journey.) Masculinity is passed from father to son, and then from Father to son. Adam, Abraham, Jacob, David, Jesus—they all learned who they were out of their intimacy with God, with the Father. After all, who can give a man this, his own name? God alone. For no one but God sees what the man is. This is usually thought of with a sense of guilt—*yes, God sees me . . . and what he sees is my sin.* That's wrong on two counts.

First off, your sin has been dealt with. Your Father has removed it from you "as far as the east is from the west" (Ps. 103:12). Your sins have been washed away (1 Cor. 6:11). When God looks at you he does not see your sin. He has not one condemning thought toward you (Rom. 8:1). But that's not all. You have a new heart. That's the promise of the new covenant: "I will give you a new heart and put a new spirit in you; I will remove from you your heart of stone and give you a heart of flesh. And I will put my Spirit in you and move you to follow my decrees and be careful to keep my laws" (Ezek. 36:26–27). There's a reason that it's called good news.

Too many Christians today are living back in the old covenant. They've had Jeremiah 17:9 drilled into them and they walk around believing *my heart is deceitfully wicked*. Not anymore it's not. Read the rest of the book. In Jeremiah 31:33, God announces the cure for all that: "I will put my law in their minds and write it on their hearts. I will be their God, and they will be my people." I will give you a new heart. That's why Paul says in Romans 2:29, "No, a man is a Jew if he is one inwardly; and circumcision is circumcision of the heart, by the Spirit." Sin is not the deepest thing about you. You have a new heart. Did you hear me? Your heart is *good*.

What God sees when he sees you is the *real* you, the true you, the man he had in mind when he made you. How else could he give you the white stone with your true name on it? I've brought you along in Dave's story—how his father dealt him the wound of "mama's boy," how he sought his sense of masculinity through women, how he embraced his wound and its message as final and true. We sat together one day in my office, his life pretty well detailed and unpacked before us, as if we had unpacked a trunk of secrets and laid them all out to the light of day. What else was there to say? "You've only got one hope, Dave . . . that your dad was wrong about you."

You must ask God what he thinks of you, and you must stay with the question until you have an answer. The battle will get fierce here. This is the *last* thing the Evil One wants you to know. He will play the ventriloquist; he'll whisper to you as if he were the voice of God. Remember, he's the accuser of the brethren (Rev. 12:10). After I saw *Gladiator*, I so longed to be a man like Maximus. He reminded me of Henry V, from Shakespeare's play—a courageous, valiant man. Maximus is strong and courageous and he fights so well; yet his heart is given over to eternity. He yearns for heaven but stays to fight so that others might be free. I wept at the end, pierced by a longing to be like him. Satan was all over that, telling me that no, I was really

Commodus—the conniving wretch who plays the villain in the movie. What made that blow so hard to shake is the fact that I once was Commodus; I was a selfish, conniving man who manipulated everything for my own benefit. That was a long time ago, but the accusation stung.

I left for a trip to England where I did four conferences in five days. It was a brutal trip and I was under a great deal of spiritual attack. What a relief it was to slump into my seat and catch my plane home. Tired to the bone, spent and beat up, I needed to hear words from my Father. So I began to pour my heart out to him in my journal.

> What of me, dear Lord? Are you pleased? What did you see? I am sorry that I have to ask, wishing I knew without asking. Fear, I suppose, makes me doubt. Still, I yearn to hear from you—a word, or image, a name or even just a glance from you.

This is what I heard:

> *You are Henry V after Agincourt . . . the man in the arena, whose face is covered with blood and sweat and dust, who strove valiantly . . . a great warrior . . . yes, even Maximus.*

And then

> *You are my friend.*

I cannot tell you how much those words mean to me. In fact, I'm embarrassed to tell them to you; they seem arrogant. But I share them in hopes that they will help you find your own. They are words of life, words that heal my wound and shatter the Enemy's accusations. I am grateful for them; deeply grateful. Oh, what wonderful stories I could tell here of how many times God has spoken to me and to other men since we've been asking the question. My friend Aaron went to a park near our home and found a place of solitude. There he waited for the Father's voice. What he first heard was this: "True masculinity is spiritual." Aaron has for so long felt that spirituality was feminine; it put him in a terrible bind because he is a very spiritual man, and yet longs to be a real man. God spoke exactly what he needed to hear—masculinity is spiritual. Then he heard, "True spirituality is good." And then, "You are a man. You are a man. You are a man."

It's a battle to get to this place, and once words like these have been spoken the Enemy rushes in to steal them. Remember how he assaulted Christ in the wilderness, right on the heels of hearing words from his Father. Another friend and I were talking about these stories and many more like them. He sort of sighed and said, "Yes, I remember a time in church when I heard God say to me, 'You're doing great. I am proud of you, right where you are.' But I could not believe it. It just doesn't seem true." That is why we always rest on propositional truth. We stand on what Scripture says about us. We are forgiven. Our heart is good. The Father's voice is *never* condemning. From that place we ask God to speak personally to us, to break the power of the lie that was delivered with our wound.

He knows your name.

OUT OF OUR WOUND COMES OUR GLORY

I have a favorite painting in my office, a reprint of Charlie Schreyvogel's *My Bunkie*. It's a scene of four cavalry soldiers done in the Western style of Remington. The action is a rescue; one of the riders has apparently been shot off his horse and three men are galloping in to pick him up. In the foreground, the stranded soldier is being swept up onto the back of the horse of his bunk mate (his "bunkie"), while the other two are providing rifle cover. I love this scene because that is what I want to do and be; I want to ride to the rescue of those who have been shot down. But sitting in my office one day, God began to speak to me about the painting and my role in it. *You cannot be the man who rescues, John, until you are the man without a horse, the man who needs rescuing.*

Yes. True strength does not come out of bravado. Until we are broken, our life will be self-centered, self-reliant; our strength will be our own. So long as you think you are really something in and of yourself, what will you need God for? I don't trust a man who hasn't suffered; I don't let a man get close to me who hasn't faced his wound. Think of the posers you know—are they the kind of man you would call at 2:00 A.M., when life is collapsing around you? Not me. I don't want clichés; I want deep, soulful truth, and that only comes when a man has walked the road I've been talking about. As Buechner says,

> To do for yourself the best that you have it in you to do—to grit your teeth and clench your fists in order to survive the world at its harshest and worst—is, by that very act, to be unable to let something be done for you and in you that is more wonderful still. The trouble with steeling yourself against the harshness of reality is that the same steel that secures your life against being destroyed secures your life also against being opened up and transformed. (*The Sacred Journey*)

Only when we enter our wound will we discover our true glory. As Bly says, "Where a man's wound is, that is where his genius will be." There are two reasons for this. First, because the wound was given in the place of your true strength, as an effort to take you out. Until you go there you are still posing, offering something more shallow and insubstantial. And therefore, second, it is out of your brokenness that you discover what you have to offer the community. The false self is never wholly false. Those gifts we've been using are often quite true about us, but we've used them to hide behind. We thought that the power of our life was in the golden bat, but the power is in *us*. When we begin to offer not merely our gifts but our true selves, that is when we become powerful.

That is when we are ready for battle.

CHAPTER EIGHT

A BATTLE TO FIGHT: THE ENEMY

Enemy-occupied territory—that is what this world is.

—C. S. LEWIS

We are but warriors for the working-day;
Our gayness and our gilt are all besmirch'd
With rainy marching in the painful field . . .
But, by the mass, our hearts are in the trim.

—HENRY V

If we would endeavor, like men of courage, to stand in the battle,
surely we would feel the favorable assistance of God from Heaven.
For he who giveth us occasion to fight, to the end we may get the vic-
tory, is ready to succor those that fight manfully, and do trust in his
grace.

—THOMAS À KEMPIS

D ad, are there any castles anymore?" Luke and I were sitting at the breakfast table; actually, he was seated and I was attending his Royal Highness, making him toast with apricot jam. As soon as he asked the question I knew what his young heart was wondering. Are there any great adventures anymore? Are there any great battles? I wanted to explain that indeed there are, but before I could reply he got this gleam in his eye and asked, "And are there any dragons?" O, how deeply this is written into the masculine soul. The boy is a warrior; the boy is his name. A man needs a battle to fight; he needs a place for the warrior in him to come alive and be honed, trained, seasoned. If Bly is right (and I believe he is), that "the early death of a man's warriors keeps the boy in him from growing up," then the opposite is true—if we can reawaken that fierce quality in a man, hook it up to a higher purpose, release the warrior within, then the boy can grow up and become truly masculine.

As I was working on this book a few days ago, Blaine came downstairs and without a word slipped a drawing he had made in front of me. It is a pencil sketch of an angel with broad shoulders and long hair; his wings are sweeping around him as if just unfurled to reveal that he is holding a large two-handed sword like a Scottish claymore. He holds the blade upright, ready for action; his gaze is steady and fierce. Beneath the drawing are the words, written in the hand of a nine-year-old boy, "Every man is a warrior inside. But the choice to fight is his own." And a little child shall lead them. Blaine knows as deeply as he knows anything that every man is a warrior, yet every man must choose to fight. The warrior is not the only role a man must play; there are others we will explore later. But the warrior is crucial in our movement toward any masculine integrity; it is hardwired into every man.

THE WARRIOR HEART

I have in my files a copy of a letter written by Major Sullivan Ballou, a Union officer in the 2nd Rhode Island. He writes to his wife on the eve of the Battle of Bull Run, a battle he senses will be his last. He speaks tenderly to her of his undying love, of "the memories of blissful moments I have spent with you." Ballou mourns the thought that he must give up "the hope of future years, when, God willing, we might still have lived and loved together, and seen our sons grown up to honorable manhood around us." Yet in spite of his love the battle calls and he cannot turn from it. "I have no misgivings about, or lack of confidence in the cause in which I am engaged, and my courage does not halt or falter . . . how great a debt we owe to those who went before us through the blood and sufferings of the Revolution . . . Sarah, my love for you is deathless, it seems to bind me with mighty cables that nothing but Omnipotence could break" and yet a greater cause "comes over me like a strong wind and bears me unresistably on with all these chains to the battle field."

A man must have a battle to fight, a great mission to his life that involves and yet transcends even home and family. He must have a cause to which he is devoted even unto death, for this is written into the fabric of his being. Listen carefully now: *You do.* That is why God created you—to be his intimate *ally,* to join him in the Great Battle. You have a specific place in the line, a mission God made you for. That is why it is so essential to hear from God about your true name, because in that name is the mission of your life. Churchill was called upon to lead the British through the desperate hours of WWII. He said, "I felt as if I were walking with destiny, and that all my past life had been but a preparation for this hour and for this trial." The same is true of you; your whole life has been preparation.

"I'd love to be William Wallace, leading the charge with a big sword in my hand," sighed a friend. "But I feel like I'm the guy back there in the fourth row, with a hoe." That's a lie of the Enemy—that your place is really insignificant, that you aren't really armed for it anyway. In your life you *are* William Wallace—who else could be? There is no other man who can replace you in your life, in the arena you've been called to. If you leave your place in the line, it will remain empty. No one else can be who you are meant to be. You *are* the hero in your story. Not a bit player, not an extra, but the main man. This is the next leg in the initiation journey, when God calls a man forward to the front lines. He wants to develop and release in us the qualities every warrior needs—including a keen awareness of the enemies we will face.

Above all else, a warrior has a *vision*; he has a transcendence to his life, a cause greater than self-preservation. The root of all our woes and our false self was this: We were seeking to save our life and we lost it. Christ calls a man beyond that, "but whoever loses his life for me and for the gospel will save it" (Mark 8:35). Again, this isn't just about being willing to die for Christ; it's much more daily than that. For years all my daily energy was spent trying to beat the trials in my life and arrange for a little pleasure. My weeks were wasted away either striving or indulging. I was a mercenary. A mercenary fights for pay, for his own benefit; his life is devoted to himself. "The quality of a true warrior," says Bly, "is that he is in service to a purpose greater than himself; that is, to a transcendent cause." That is the moving quality in Ballou's letter; that is the secret of the warrior-heart of Jesus.

Second, a warrior is *cunning*. He knows when to fight and when to run; he can sense a trap and never charges blindly ahead; he knows what weapons to carry and how to use them. Whatever specific terrain you are called to—at home, at work, in the realm of the arts or industry or world politics, you will always encounter three enemies: the world, the flesh, and the devil. They make up a sort of unholy trinity. Because they always conspire together it's a bit difficult to talk about them individually; in any battle at least two of them are involved, but usually it's all three. Still, they each have their own personality, so I'll take them one at a time and then try to show how they collude against us. Let's start with the enemy closest at hand.

THE TRAITOR WITHIN

> However strong a castle may be, if a treacherous party resides
> inside (ready to betray at the first opportunity possible), the
> castle cannot be kept safe from the enemy. Traitors occupy
> our own hearts, ready to side with every temptation and to
> surrender to them all. (John Owen, *Sin and Temptation*)

Ever since that fateful day when Adam gave away the essence of his strength, men have struggled with a part of themselves that is ready at the drop of a hat to do the same. We don't want to speak up unless we know it will go well, and we don't want to move unless we're guaranteed success. What the Scriptures call the flesh, the old man, or the sinful nature, is that part of fallen Adam in every man that always wants the easiest way out. It's much easier to masturbate than to make love to your wife, especially if things are not well between you and initiating sex with her feels risky. It's much easier to go down to the driving range and attack a bucket of balls than it is to face the people at work who are angry at you. It's much easier to clean the garage, organize your files, cut the grass, or work on the car than it is to talk to your teenage daughter.

To put it bluntly, your flesh is a weasel, a poser, and a selfish pig. And your flesh is *not you*. Did you know that? Your flesh is not the real you. When Paul gives us his famous passage on what it's like to struggle with sin (Rom. 7), he tells a story we are all too familiar with:

> I decide to do good, but I don't *really* do it; I decide not to do bad, but then I do it anyway. My decisions, such as they are, don't result in actions. Something has gone wrong deep within me and gets the better of me every time. It happens so regularly that it's predictable. The moment I decide to do good, sin is there to trip me up. I truly delight in God's commands, but it's pretty obvious that not all of me joins in that delight. Parts of me covertly rebel, and just when I least expect it, they take charge. (*The Message*)

Okay, we've all been there many times. But what Paul concludes is just astounding: "I am not really the one doing it; the sin within me is doing it" (Rom. 7:20 NLT). Did you notice the distinction he makes? Paul says, "Hey, I know I struggle with sin. But I also know that *my sin is not me*—this is not my true heart." You are not your sin; sin is no longer the truest thing about the man who has come into union with Jesus. Your heart is good. "I will give you a new heart and put a new spirit in you . . ." (Ezek. 36:26). The Big Lie in the church today is that you are nothing more than "a sinner saved by grace." You are a lot more than that. You are a new creation in Christ. The New Testament calls you a saint, a holy one, a son of God. In the core of your being you are a good man. Yes, there is a war within us, but it is a *civil* war. The battle is not between us and God; no, there is a traitor within who wars against our true heart fighting alongside the Spirit of God in us:

> A new power is in operation. The Spirit of life in Christ, like a strong wind, has magnificently cleared the air, freeing you from a fated lifetime of brutal tyranny at the hands of sin and death . . . Anyone, of course, who has not welcomed this invisible but clearly present God, the Spirit of Christ, won't know what we're talking about. But for you who welcome him, in whom he dwells . . . if the alive-and-present God who raised Jesus from the dead moves into your life, he'll do the same thing in you that he did in Jesus . . . When God lives and breathes in you (and he does, as surely as he did in Jesus), you are delivered from that dead life. (Rom. 8:2–3, 9–11 *The Message*)

The *real* you is on the side of God against the false self. Knowing this makes all the difference in the world. The man who wants to live valiantly will lose heart quickly if he believes that his heart is nothing but sin. Why fight? The battle feels lost before it even begins. No, your flesh is your *false self*—the poser, manifest in cowardice and self-preservation—and the only way to deal with it is to crucify it. Now follow me very closely here: We are never, ever told to crucify our heart. We are never told to kill the true man within us, never told to get rid of those deep desires for battle and adventure and beauty. We are told to shoot the traitor. How? Choose against him every time you see him raise his ugly head. Walk right into those situations you normally run from. Speak right to the issues you normally remain silent over. If you want to grow in true masculine strength, then you must stop sabotaging yours.

SABOTAGE

Rich is a deeply passionate young man who is really trying to learn what it means to be a man. A few weeks ago he had plans to go out with some friends. They promised to call him before they left and then come pick him up; they never called. A few days later, when one of them brought it up, Rich said, "Oh, that's okay. It's no big deal." But inside, he was *furious*. That is sabotage. He deliberately chose to push his true strength down and live the false self. Do that enough and you won't believe you have any strength. I've noticed when I deny the anger I am feeling, it turns into fear. If we will not allow what Sam Keen calls "fire in the belly," something weaker will take its place. I had a chance a few years back to tell my boss what I really thought of him; not in sinful anger (there's a difference), not to hurt him but to help him. He actually asked me to, called to see if I was free to chat for a moment. I knew what he was calling for and I ran; I told him I was busy. For days afterward I felt weak; I felt like a poser. I sabotaged my strength by refusing it.

Sabotage also happens when we give our strength away. Taking a bribe, letting yourself be bought off, accepting flattery in exchange for some sort of loyalty, is sabotage. Refusing to confront an issue because if you keep quiet you'll get a promotion or be made an elder or keep your job corrupts you down deep. Masturbation is sabotage. It is an inherently selfish act that tears you down. I've spoken with many men whose addiction to masturbation has eroded their sense of strength. So does sexual involvement with a woman you are not married to. Carl is another young man whom the ladies seem to find especially attractive. I am astounded what young women will offer when they are famished for the love and affirmation they have never had from their fathers. They will throw themselves at a man to get a taste of being wanted, desired. Carl came to me because his sexual activity was out of control. Dozens upon dozens of women offered themselves to him and each time he gave in he felt weakened; his resolve to resist was less the next time around.

Things began to change for Carl when he saw the whole sexual struggle not so much as sin *but as a battle for his strength*. He wants to be strong, wants it desperately, and that began to fuel his choice to resist. As à Kempis said, "A man must strive long and mightily within himself, before he can learn fully to master himself." Carl and I spent hours praying through every one of those relationships, confessing the sin, breaking the bonds sexual liaisons form between two souls, cleansing his strength, asking God to restore him. He did, and I am grateful to say those days are over for Carl. It wasn't easy, but it was real; he is happily married now.

THE REAL THING

Start choosing to live out your strength and you'll discover that it grows each time. Rich was after some brakes for his car; he called the parts store and they quoted him a price of $50 for the pair. But when he got down there, the guy told him it would be $90. He was taking Rich for a fool and something in Rich was provoked. Normally he would have said "Oh, that's okay. It's no big deal," and paid the higher price; but not this time. He told the guy that the price was $50 and stood his ground. The guy backed down and stopped trying to rip him off. "It felt great," Rich told me later. "I felt that I was finally acting like a man." Now that may seem like a simple story, but this is where you will discover your strength, in the daily details of your life. Begin to taste your true strength and you'll want *more*. Something in the center of your chest feels weighty, substantial.

We must let our strength show up. It seems so strange, after all this, that a man would not allow his strength to arrive, but many of us are unnerved by our own masculinity. What will happen if we really let it out? In *Healing the Masculine Soul*, Gordon Dalbey tells a remarkable story about a man who was plagued by a recurring dream, a nightmare "in which a ferocious lion kept chasing the man until he dropped exhausted and awoke screaming." The man was dismayed; he did not know what the dream meant. Was the lion a symbol of fear? Something in his life overwhelming him? One day the man was guided by his pastor (a friend of Dalbey's) to revisit the dream in prayer:

> As they prayed, [the pastor] on impulse invited the man to recall the dream, even in all its fear. Hesitantly, the man agreed, and soon reported that indeed, the lion was in sight and headed his way. [The pastor] then instructed the man, "When the lion comes close to you, try not to run away, but instead, stand there and ask him who or what he is, and what he's doing in your life . . . can you try that?" Shifting uneasily in his chair, the man agreed, then reported what was happening: "The lion is snorting and shaking his head, standing right there in front of me . . . I ask him who he is . . . and—Oh! I can't believe what he's saying! He says, "I'm your courage and your strength. Why are you running away from me?"

I had a recurring dream similar to this one for many years—especially in adolescence. A great wild stallion was standing on the ridge of a hill; I sensed danger but not an evil danger, just something strong and valiant and greater than me. I tried to sneak away; the stallion always turned in time to see me and came charging down the hill. I would wake just as he was upon me. It seems crazy that a man would sneak away from his strength, fear it to show up, but that is why we sabotage. Our strength is wild and fierce, and we are more than unsettled by what may happen if we let it arrive. One thing we know: Nothing will ever be the same. One client said to me, "I'm afraid I'll do something bad if I let all this show up." No, the opposite is true. You'll do something bad if you *don't*. Remember—a man's addictions are the result of his refusing his strength.

Years ago Brent gave me a piece of advice that changed my life: "Let people feel the weight of who you are," he said, "and let them deal with it." That brings us into the arena of our next enemy.

THE WORLD

What is this enemy that the Scripture calls "the world"? Is it drinking and dancing and smoking? Is it going to the movies or playing cards? That is a shallow and ridiculous approach to holiness. It numbs us to the fact that good and evil are much more serious. The Scriptures never prohibit drinking alcohol, only drunkenness; dancing was a vital part of King David's life; and while there are some very godly movies out there, there are also some very ungodly churches. No, "the world" is not a place or a set of behaviors—it is any system built by our collective sin, all our false selves coming together to reward and destroy each other. Take all those posers out there, put them together in an office or a club or a church, and what you get is what the Scriptures mean by the world.

The world is a carnival of counterfeits—counterfeit battles, counterfeit adventures, counterfeit beauties. Men should think of it as a corruption of their strength. Battle your way to the top, says the world, and you are a man. Why is it then that the men who get there are often the emptiest, most frightened, prideful posers around? They are mercenaries, battling only to build their own kingdoms. There is nothing transcendent about their lives. The same holds true of the adventure addicts; no matter how much you spend, no matter how far you take your hobby, it's still merely that—a hobby. And as for the counterfeit beauties, the world is constantly trying to tell us that the Golden-Haired Woman is out there—go for her.

The world offers a man a false sense of power and a false sense of security. Be brutally honest now—where does your own sense of power come from? Is it how pretty your wife is—or your secretary? Is it how many people attend your church? Is it *knowledge*—that you have an expertise and that makes others come to you, bow to you? Is it your position, degree, or title? A white coat, a Ph.D., a podium, or a paneled office can make a man feel like pretty neat stuff. What happens inside you when I suggest you give it up? Put the book down for a few moments and consider what you would think of yourself if tomorrow you lost everything that the world has rewarded you for. "Without Christ a man must fail miserably" says MacDonald, "or succeed even more miserably." Jesus warns us against anything that gives a false sense of power. When you walk into a company dinner or a church function, he said, take a backseat. Choose the path of humility; don't be a self-promoter, a glad-hander, a poser. Climb *down* the ladder; have the mail clerk over for dinner; treat your secretary like she's more important than you; look to be the servant of all. *Where am I deriving my sense of strength and power from?* is a good question to ask yourself . . . often.

If you want to know how the world *really* feels about you, just start living out of your true strength. Say what you think, stand up for the underdog, challenge foolish policies. They'll turn on you like sharks. Remember the film *Jerry McGuire*? Jerry is an agent for professional athletes who comes to a sort of personal epiphany about the corruption of his firm. He issues a memo, a vision statement urging a more humane approach to their work. Let's stop treating people like cattle, he says; stop serving the bottom line and really serve our clients. All his buddies cheer him on; when the firm dumps him (as he knew they would) they rush to seize his clients. I've seen this time and time again. A friend of mine confronted his pastor on some false statements the pastor had made to get his position. This shepherd of the flock started circulating rumors that my friend was gay; he tried to ruin his reputation.

The world of posers is shaken by a real man. They'll do whatever it takes to get you back in line—threaten you, bribe you, seduce you, undermine you. They crucified Jesus. But it didn't work, did it? You must let your strength show up. Remember Christ in the Garden, the sheer force of his presence? Many of us have actually been afraid to let our strength show up because the world doesn't have a place for it. Fine. The world's screwed up. Let people feel the weight of who you are and let them deal with it.

THE DEVIL

My wife and I were driving home the other day from an afternoon out and running a bit late to get to our son's last soccer game of the season. I was in the driver's seat and we were enjoying a lingering conversation about some dreams we have for the future. After several minutes we realized that we were caught in a traffic jam that was going nowhere. Precious moments slipped by as tension mounted in the car. In an effort to be helpful, Stasi suggested an alternate route: "If you take a right here and go up to First Street, we can cut over and take about five minutes off the drive." I was ready to divorce her. I'm serious. In about twenty seconds I was ready for separation. If the judge had been in the car, I'd have signed the papers right there. Good grief—over a comment about my driving? Is that all that was going on in that moment?

I sat at the wheel silent and steaming. On the outside, I looked cool; inside, here is what was happening: *Geez, doesn't she think I know how to get there? I hate it when she does that.* Then another voice says, *She always does that.* And I say (internally—the whole dialogue took place internally, in the blink of an eye), *Yeah, she does . . . she's always saying stuff like that. I hate that about her.* A feeling of accusation and anger and self-righteousness sweeps over me. Then the voice says, *John, this is never going to change,* and I say, *This is never going to change,* and the voice says, *You know, John, there are a lot of women out there who would be deeply grateful to have you as their man,* and I think, *Yeah—there are a lot of women out there . . .* You get the picture. Change the characters and the setting and the very same thing has happened to you. Only, you probably thought the whole thing was your own mess.

The devil no doubt has a place in our theology, but is he a category we even think about in the daily events of our lives? Has it ever crossed your mind that not every thought that crosses your mind comes from you? What I experienced in the midst of traffic that day happens all the time in marriages, in ministries, in any relationship. We are being lied to all the time. Yet we never stop to say, "Wait a minute . . . who else is speaking here? Where are those ideas coming from? Where are those *feelings* coming from?" If you read the saints from every age before the Modern Era—that pride-filled age of reason, science, and technology we all were thoroughly educated in—you'll find that they take the devil very seriously indeed. As Paul says, "We are not unaware of his schemes" (2 Cor. 2:11). But we, the enlightened, have a much more commonsense approach to things. We look for a psychological or physical or even political explanation for every trouble we meet.

Who caused the Chaldeans to steal Job's herds and kill his servants? Satan, clearly (Job 1:12, 17). Yet do we even give him a passing thought when we hear of terrorism today? Who kept that poor woman bent over for eighteen years, the one Jesus healed on the Sabbath? Satan, clearly (Luke 13:16). But do we consider him when we are having a headache that keeps us from praying or reading Scripture? Who moved Ananias and Sapphira to lie to the apostles? Satan again (Acts 5:3). But do we really see his hand behind a fallout or schism in ministry? Who was behind that brutal assault on your own strength, those wounds you've taken? As William Gurnall said, "It is the image of God reflected in you that so enrages hell; it is this at which the demons hurl their mightiest weapons."

There is a whole lot more going on behind the scenes of our lives than most of us have been led to believe. Take Christmas for example.

BEHIND THE SCENES

Most of you probably have a Nativity scene that you take out over the holidays and place on a mantel or coffee table. Most of these scenes share a regular cast of characters: shepherds, wise men, maybe a few barnyard animals, Joseph, Mary, and, of course, the baby Jesus. Yes, ours has an angel or two and I imagine yours does as well. But that's about as far as the supernatural gets. What is the overall *mood* of the scene? Don't they all have a sort of warm, pastoral atmosphere to them, a quiet, intimate feel like the one you get when you sing *Silent Night* or *Away in a Manger*? And while that's all very true, it is also very *deceiving* because it is not a full picture of what's really going on. For that, you have to turn to Revelation 12:

> A great and wondrous sign appeared in heaven: a woman clothed with the sun, with the moon under her feet and a crown of twelve stars on her head. She was pregnant and cried out in pain as she was about to give birth. Then another sign appeared in heaven: an enormous red dragon with seven heads and ten horns and seven crowns on his heads. His tail swept a third of the stars out of the sky and flung them to the earth. The dragon stood in front of the woman who was about to give birth, so that he might devour her child the moment it was born. She gave birth to a son, a male child, who will rule all the nations with an iron scepter . . . And there was war in heaven. Michael and his angels fought against the dragon, and the dragon and his angels fought back. But he was not strong enough, and they lost their place in heaven. The great dragon was hurled down—that ancient serpent called the devil or Satan, who leads the whole world astray. He was hurled to the earth, and his angels with him. (vv. 1–5, 7–9)

As Philip Yancey says, I have never seen this version of the story on a Christmas card. Yet it is the truer story, the rest of the picture of what was going on that fateful night. Yancey calls the birth of Christ the Great Invasion, "a daring raid by the ruler of the forces of good into the universe's seat of evil." Spiritually speaking, this is no silent night. It is D-Day. "It is almost beyond my comprehension too, and yet I accept that this notion is the key to understanding Christmas and is, in fact, the touchstone of my faith. As a Christian I believe that we live in parallel worlds. One world consists of hills and lakes and barns and politicians and shepherds watching their flocks by night. The other consists of angels and sinister forces" and the whole spiritual realm. The child is born, the woman escapes and the story continues like this:

> Then the dragon was enraged at the woman and went off to make war against the rest of her offspring—those who obey God's commandments and hold to the testimony of Jesus. (Rev. 12:17)

Behind the world and the flesh is an even more deadly enemy . . . one we rarely speak of and are even much less ready to resist. Yet this is where we live now—on the front lines of a fierce spiritual war that is to blame for most of the casualties you see around you and most of the assault against you. It's time we prepared ourselves for it. Yes, Luke, there is a dragon. Here is how you slay him.

CHAPTER NINE

A BATTLE TO FIGHT: THE STRATEGY

She was right that reality can be harsh and that you shut your eyes to it only at your peril because if you do not face up to the enemy in all his dark power, then the enemy will come up from behind some dark day and destroy you while you are facing the other way.

—FREDERICK BUECHNER

Gird your sword upon your side, O mighty one;
clothe yourself with splendor and majesty.
In your majesty ride forth victoriously.

—PSALM 45:3–4

As part of Christ's army, you march in the ranks of gallant spirits. Every one of your fellow soldiers is the child of a King. Some, like you, are in the midst of battle, besieged on every side by affliction and temptation. Others, after many assaults, repulses, and rallyings of their faith, are already standing upon the wall of heaven as conquerors. From there they look down and urge you, their comrades on earth, to march up the hill after them. This is their cry: "Fight to the death and the City is your own, as now it is ours!"

—WILLIAM GURNALL

The invasion of France and the end of WWII actually began the night before the Allies hit the beaches at Normandy, when the 82nd and 101st Airborne Divisions were dropped in behind enemy lines to cut off Hitler's reinforcements. If you've seen *The Longest Day* or *Saving Private Ryan*, you remember the dangers those paratroopers were facing. Alone or in small groups, they moved through the dead of night across a country they had never been to in order to fight an enemy they couldn't see or predict. It was a moment of unparalleled bravery . . . and cowardice. For not every trooper played the man that fateful night. Sure, they jumped; but afterward, many hid. One group took cowardice to a new level.

> Too many had hunkered down in hedgerows to await the dawn; a few had even gone to sleep. Pvt. Francis Palys of the 506th saw what was perhaps the worst dereliction of duty. He had gathered a squad near Vierville. Hearing "all kinds of noise and singing from a distance," he and his men sneaked up on a farmhouse. In it was a mixed group from both American divisions. The paratroopers had found [liquor] in the cellar . . . and they were drunker than a bunch of hillbillies on a Saturday night wingding. Unbelievable. (*D-Day*)

Unbelievable indeed. These men *knew* they were at war, yet they refused to act like it. They lived in a dangerous denial—a denial that not only endangered them but countless others who depended on them to do their part. It is a *perfect* picture of the church in the West when it comes to spiritual warfare. During a recent church staff meeting, a friend of mine raised the suggestion that some of the difficulties they were facing might be the work of the Enemy. "What do you think?" he asked. "Well, I suppose that sort of thing does happen," one of the other pastors replied. "In the Third World, perhaps, or maybe to thwart a major crusade. You know . . . places where cutting-edge ministry is going on."

STAGE ONE: "I'M NOT HERE"

Incredible. What a self-indictment. "Nothing dangerous is happening here." Those men have already been taken out because they've swallowed the Enemy's first line of attack: "I'm not here—this is all just you." You can't fight a battle you don't think exists. This is right out of *The Screwtape Letters*, where Lewis has the old devil instruct his apprentice in this very matter:

> My dear Wormwood, I wonder you should ask me whether it is essential to keep the patient in ignorance of your own existence. That question, at least for the present phase of the struggle, has been answered for us by the High Command. Our policy, for the moment, is to conceal ourselves.

As for those who want to be dangerous (cutting-edge), take a close look at 1 Peter 5:8–9: "Be self-controlled and alert. Your enemy the devil prowls around like a roaring lion looking for someone to devour. Resist him, standing firm in the faith, because you know that your brothers throughout the world are undergoing the same kind of sufferings." What is the Holy Spirit, through Peter, assuming about your life? *That you are under spiritual attack.* This is not a passage about nonbelievers; he's talking about "your brethren." Peter takes it for granted that every believer is under some sort of unseen assault. And what does he insist you do? *Resist* the devil. Fight back, take a stand.

A ministry partnership that some dear friends were central to has just dissolved this week, I am deeply sad to say. They had teamed up with another organization to bring the gospel to cities across the U.S. These conferences are very powerful; in fact, I've never seen anything even close to the impact they have. Through grateful tears, the attendees talk about the healing, the freedom, the release they have experienced. They recover their hearts and are drawn into an intimacy with God most have never, ever experienced before. It's beautiful and awe-inspiring. Now, do you think the Enemy just lets that sort of thing go swimmingly along without any interference whatsoever?

The partnership hit some choppy water, nothing much at all really, nothing unusual to any relationship, yet the other members simply decided to end the coalition and walk away mid-season. Were there personal issues involved? You bet; there always are. But they were minor. It was mostly misunderstanding and injured pride. There was not one word, not one thought as far as I could tell about the Enemy and what he might be doing to break up so strategic an alliance. When I brought up the fact that they would do well to interpret things with open eyes, keeping the attacks of the Evil One in mind, I was dismissed. These good people with good hearts wanted to explain everything on a "human" level and let me tell you—when you ignore the Enemy, he wins. He simply loves to blame everything on us, get us feeling hurt, misunderstood, suspicious, and resentful of one another.

Before an effective military strike can be made, you must take out the opposing army's line of communication. The Evil One does this all the time—in ministries and especially between couples. Marriage is a stunning picture of what God offers his

people. Scripture tells us it is a living metaphor, a walking parable, a Rembrandt painting of the gospel. The Enemy knows this,
and he hates it with every ounce of his malicious heart. He has no
intention of just letting that beautiful portrait be lived out before
the world with such deep appeal that no one can resist God's
offer. So just like in the Garden, Satan comes in to divide and
conquer. Often I'll feel this sense of accusation when I'm with my
wife. It's hard to describe and it usually isn't put into words, but
I just receive this message that *I'm blowing it*. I finally brought this
up with Stasi and tears came to her eyes. "You're kidding," she
said. "I've been feeling the very same thing. I thought you were
disappointed with *me*." Wait a minute, I thought. If I'm not sending this message and you're not sending this message . . .

Most of all the Enemy will try to jam communications with
Headquarters. Commit yourself to prayer every morning for two
weeks and just watch what'll happen. You won't want to get up;
an important meeting will be called that interferes; you'll catch a
cold; or, if you do get to your prayers, your mind will wander to
what you'll have for breakfast and how much you should pay for
that water heater repair and what color socks would look best
with your gray suit. Many, many times I've simply come under a
cloak of *confusion* so thick I suddenly find myself wondering why
I ever believed in Jesus in the first place. That sweet communion
I normally enjoy with God is cut off, gone, vanished like the sun
behind a cloud. If you don't know what's up you'll think you
really have lost your faith or been abandoned by God or whatever spin the Enemy puts on it. Oswald Chambers warns us,
"Sometimes there is nothing to obey, the only thing to do is to
maintain a vital connection with Jesus Christ, to see that nothing interferes with that."

Next comes propaganda. Like the infamous Tokyo Rose, the
Enemy is constantly broadcasting messages to try to demoralize

us. As in my episode during the traffic jam, he is constantly *putting his spin* on things. After all, Scripture calls him the "accuser of our brethren" (Rev. 12:10 NKJV). Think of what goes on—what you hear and feel—when you really blow it. *I'm such an idiot; I always do that; I'll never amount to anything.* Sounds like accusation to me. How about when you're really trying to step forward as a man? I can guarantee you what will happen when I'm going to speak. I was driving to the airport for a trip to the West Coast, to give a talk to men about *Wild at Heart.* All the way there I was under this cloud of heaviness; I was nearly overcome by a deep sense of *John, you're such a poser. You have absolutely nothing to say. Just turn the car around, go home, and tell them you can't make it.* Now in my clearer moments I know it's an attack, but you must understand that all this comes on so subtly it seems true at the time. I nearly gave in and went home.

When Christ is assaulted by the Evil One in the wilderness, the attack is ultimately on his identity. *"If you are the Son of God,"* Satan sneers three times, then prove it (Luke 4:1–13). Brad returned from the mission field last year for a sabbatical. After seven years abroad, most of the time without any real companionship, he was pretty beat up; he felt like a failure. He told me that when he woke in the morning he'd "hear" a voice in his thoughts say, *Good morning . . . Loser.* So many men live under a similar accusation. Craig had really been entering into the battle and fighting bravely the past several months. Then he had a nightmare, a very vivid, grisly dream in which he had molested a little girl. He woke up feeling filthy and condemned. That same week I had a dream where I was accused of committing adultery; I really hadn't, but in my dream no one would believe me. Follow this: So long as a man remains no real threat to the Enemy, Satan's line to him is *You're fine.* But after you do take sides, it becomes *Your heart is bad and you know it.*

Finally, he probes the perimeter, looking for a weakness. Here's how this works: Satan will throw a thought or a temptation at us in hopes that we will swallow it. He knows your story, knows what works with you and so the line is tailor-made to your situation. Just this morning in my prayer time it was pride, then worry, then adultery, then greed, then gluttony. If I thought this was all me, my heart, I'd be very discouraged. Knowing that my heart is good allowed me to block it, right then and there. When Satan probes, make no agreements. If we make an agreement, if something in our heart says, *Yeah, you're right*, then he pours it on. You'll see a beautiful woman and something in you will say, *You want her*. That's the Evil One appealing to the traitor within. If the traitor says, *Yes, I do*, then the lust really begins to take hold. Let that go on for years and you've given him a stronghold. This can make a good man feel so awful because he thinks he's a lustful man when he's not; it's an attack through and through.

Please don't misunderstand me. I'm not blaming everything on the devil. In almost every situation there are human issues involved. Every man has his struggles; every marriage has its rough spots; every ministry has personal conflicts. But those issues are like a campfire that the Enemy throws gasoline all over and turns into a bonfire. The flames leap up into a raging inferno and we are suddenly overwhelmed with what we're feeling. Simple misunderstandings become grounds for divorce. All the while we believe that it's us, we are blowing it, we're to blame, and the Enemy is laughing because we've swallowed the lie "I'm not here, it's just you." We've got to be a lot more cunning than that.

HANGING ON TO THE TRUTH

In any hand-to-hand combat, there's a constant back-and-forth of blows, dodges, blocks, counterattacks, and so forth. That's exactly what is going on in the unseen around us. Only it takes place, initially, at the level of our thoughts. When we are under attack, we've got to hang on to the truth. Dodge the blow, block it with a stubborn refusal, slash back with what is true. This is how Christ answered Satan—he didn't get into an argument with him, try to reason his way out. He simply stood on the truth. He answered with Scripture and we've got to do the same. This will not be easy, especially when all hell is breaking loose around you. It will feel like holding on to a rope while you're being dragged behind a truck, like keeping your balance in a hurricane. Satan doesn't just throw a thought at us; he throws *feelings* too. Walk into a dark house late at night and suddenly fear sweeps over you; or just stand in a grocery line with all those tabloids shouting sex at you and suddenly a sense of corruption is yours.

But this is where your strength is revealed and even increased—through exercise. Stand on what is true and do not let go. Period. The traitor within the castle will try to lower the drawbridge but don't let him. When Proverbs 4:23 tells us to guard our hearts, it's not saying, "Lock them up because they're really criminal to the core"; it's saying, "Defend them like a castle, the seat of your strength you do not want to give away." As à Kempis says, "Yet we must be watchful, especially in the beginning of the temptation; for the enemy is then more easily overcome, if he is not suffered to enter the door of our hearts, but is resisted without the gate at his first knock."

Remember the scene in *Braveheart* where Robert the Bruce's evil father is whispering lies to him about treason and compromise? He says to Robert what the Enemy says to us in a thousand ways: "All men betray; all men lose heart." How does Robert answer? He yells back,

I don't want to lose heart!
I want to believe, like [Wallace] does.
I will never be on the wrong side again.

That is the turning point in his life . . . and in ours. The battle shifts to a new level.

STAGE TWO: INTIMIDATION

Stasi lived under a cloud of depression for many years. We had seen her find some healing through counseling, but still the depression remained. We had addressed the physical aspects that we could through medication, yet it lingered still. *Okay, I thought to myself, the Bible tells me that we have a body, a soul, and a spirit. We've addressed the body and soul issues . . . what's left must be spiritual.* Stasi and I began to read a bit on dealing with the Enemy. In the course of our study she came across a passage that referred to different symptoms that sometimes accompany oppression; one of them was dizziness. As she read the passage out loud she sounded surprised. "What about it?" I asked. "Well . . . I get dizzy spells a lot." "Really? How often?" "Oh, every day." "Every day??!!" I had been married to Stasi for ten years and she had never even mentioned this to me. The poor woman had simply thought they were normal for everyone since they were normal for her.

"Stasi, I have never had a dizzy spell in my life. I think we're onto something here." We began to pray against the dizziness, taking authority over any attack in the name of Jesus. You know what happened? It got *worse!* The Enemy, once discovered, usually doesn't just roll over and go away without a fight. Notice that sometimes Jesus rebukes a foul spirit "in a stern voice" (see

Luke 4:35). In fact, when he encounters the guy who lives out in the Gerasenes tombs, tormented by a legion of spirits, the first rebuke by Jesus doesn't work. He had to get more information, really take them on (Luke 8:26–33). Now if Jesus had to get tough with these guys, don't you suppose we'll have to as well? Stasi and I held our ground, resisting the onslaught "firm in the faith," as Peter says, and you know what? The dizzy spells ended. They are history. She hasn't had one for seven years.

That is the next level of our Enemy's strategy. When we begin to question him, to resist his lies, to see his hand in the "ordinary trials" of our lives, then he steps up the attack; he turns to intimidation and fear. In fact, at some point in the last several pages you've probably begun to feel something like *Do I really want to get into all this super-spiritual hocus-pocus? It's kind of creepy anyway.* Satan will try to get you to agree with intimidation *because he fears you.* You are a huge threat to him. He doesn't want you waking up and fighting back because when you do he loses. "Resist the devil," James says, *"and he will flee from you"* (James 4:7, emphasis added). So he's going to try to keep you from taking a stand. He moves from subtle seduction to open assault. The thoughts come crashing in, all sorts of stuff begins to fall apart in your life, your faith seems paper thin.

Why do so many pastors' kids go off the deep end? You think that's a coincidence? So many churches start off with life and vitality only to end in a split, or simply wither away and die. How come? Why did a friend of mine nearly black out when she tried to share her testimony at a meeting? Why are my flights so often thwarted when I'm trying to take the gospel to a city? Why does everything seem to fall apart at work when you're making some advances at home, or vice versa? Because we are at war and the Evil One is trying an old tactic—strike first and maybe the opposition will turn tail and run. He can't win, you know. As Franklin Roosevelt said, "We have nothing to fear but fear itself."

GOD IS WITH US

> Be strong and courageous, because you will lead these people
> to inherit the land I swore to their forefathers to give them.
> Be strong and very courageous . . . Have I not commanded
> you? Be strong and courageous. Do not be terrified; do not be
> discouraged, for the LORD your God will be with you wher-
> ever you go. (Josh. 1:6–7, 9)

Joshua knew what it was to be afraid. For years he had been second in command, Moses' right-hand man. But now it was his turn
to lead. The children of Israel weren't just going to waltz in and
pick up the promised land like a quart of milk; they were going
to have to fight for it. And Moses was not going with them. If
Joshua was completely confident about the situation, why would
God have had to tell him over and over and over again not to be
afraid? In fact, God gives him a special word of encouragement:
"As I was with Moses, so I will be with you; I will never leave you
nor forsake you" (Josh. 1:5). How was God "with Moses"? As a
mighty warrior. Remember the plagues? Remember all those
Egyptian soldiers drowned with their horses and chariots out
there in the Red Sea? It was after that display of God's strength
that the people of Israel sang, "The LORD is a warrior; the LORD
is his name" (Ex. 15:3). God fought for Moses and for Israel; then
he covenanted to Joshua to do the same and they took down
Jericho and every other enemy.

Jeremiah knew what it meant to have God "with him" as
well. "But the Lord is with me like a mighty warrior," he sang.
"so my persecutors will stumble and not prevail" (Jer. 20:11).

Even Jesus walked in this promise when he battled for us here on earth:

> You know what has happened throughout Judea, beginning in Galilee after the baptism that John preached—how God anointed Jesus of Nazareth with the Holy Spirit and power, and how he went around doing good and healing all who were under the power of the devil, *because God was with him*. (Acts 10:37–38, emphasis added)

How did Jesus win the battle against Satan? God was *with him*. This really opens up the riches of the promise Christ gives us when he pledges "I am with you always, even to the end of the age" and "I will never leave you nor forsake you" (Matt. 28:20; Heb. 13:5 NKJV). That doesn't simply mean that he'll be around, or even that he'll comfort us in our afflictions. It means *he will fight for us*, with us, just as he has fought for his people all through the ages. So long as we walk with Christ, stay in him, we haven't a thing to fear.

Satan is trying to appeal to the traitor's commitment to self-preservation when he uses fear and intimidation. So long as we are back in the old story of saving our skin, looking out for Number One, those tactics will work. We'll shrink back. But the opposite is also true. When a man resolves to become a warrior, when his life is given over to a transcendent cause, then he can't be cowed by the Big Bad Wolf threatening to blow his house down. After Revelation describes that war in heaven between the angels and Satan's downfall to the earth, it tells how the saints overcame him:

> They overcame him
> by the blood of the Lamb
> and by the word of their testimony;

> they did not love their lives so much
> as to shrink from death. (12:11)

The most dangerous man on earth is the man who has reckoned with his own death. All men die; few men ever really *live*. Sure, you can create a safe life for yourself . . . and end your days in a rest home babbling on about some forgotten misfortune. I'd rather go down swinging. Besides, the less we are trying to "save ourselves," the more effective a warrior we will be. Listen to G. K. Chesterton on courage:

> Courage is almost a contradiction in terms. It means a strong desire to live taking the form of a readiness to die. "He that will lose his life, the same shall save it," is not a piece of mysticism for saints and heroes. It is a piece of everyday advice for sailors or mountaineers. It might be printed in an Alpine guide or a drill book. The paradox is the whole principle of courage; even of quite earthly or quite brutal courage. A man cut off by the sea may save his life if he will risk it on the precipice. He can only get away from death by continually stepping within an inch of it. A soldier surrounded by enemies, if he is to cut his way out, needs to combine a strong desire for living with a strange carelessness about dying. He must not merely cling to live, for then he will be a coward, and will not escape. He must not merely wait for death, for then he will be a suicide, and will not escape. He must seek his life in a spirit of furious indifference to it; he must desire life like water and yet drink death like wine.

STAGE THREE: CUTTING A DEAL

The third level of attack the Evil One employs, after we have resisted deception and intimidation, is simply to try to get us to cut a deal. So many men have been bought off in one way or another. The phone just rang; a friend called to tell me that yet another Christian leader has fallen into sexual immorality. The church wags its head and says, "You see. He just couldn't keep himself clean." That is naive. Do you think that man, a follower of Christ, in his heart of hearts really *wanted* to fall? What man begins his journey wishing, "I think one day, after twenty years of ministry, I'll torpedo the whole thing with an affair"? He was *picked off;* the whole thing was plotted. In his case it was a long and subtle assignment to wear his defenses down not so much through battle as through *boredom.* I knew that man; he had no great cause to fight for, just the monotony of "professional Christian ministry" that he hated but couldn't get out of because he was being so well paid for it. He was set up for a fall. Unless you are aware that that's what it is, you'll be taken out too.

Notice this—when did King David fall? What were the circumstances of his affair with Bathsheba? "In the spring, at the time when kings go off to war, David sent Joab out with the king's men and the whole Israelite army" (2 Sam. 11:1). David was no longer a warrior; he sent others to do his fighting for him. Bored, sated, and fat, he strolls around on the roof of the palace looking for something to amuse him. The Evil One points out Bathsheba and the rest is history—which, as we all know, repeats itself. William Gurnall warns us,

> Persisting to the end will be the burr under your saddle—the thorn in your flesh—when the road ahead seems endless and your soul begs an early discharge. It weighs down every other difficulty of your calling. We have known many who have joined the army of Christ and like being a soldier for a battle or two, but have soon had enough and ended up deserting. They impulsively enlist for Christian duties . . . and are just as

easily persuaded to lay it down. Like the new moon, they shine a little in the first part of the evening, but go down before the night is over. (*The Christian in Full Armor*)

THE WEAPONS OF WAR

Against the flesh, the traitor within, a warrior uses discipline. We have a two-dimensional version of this now, which we call a "quiet time." But most men have a hard time sustaining any sort of devotional life because it has no vital connection to recovering and protecting their strength; it feels about as important as flossing. But if you saw your life as a great battle and you *knew* you needed time with God for your very survival, you would do it. Maybe not perfectly—nobody ever does and that's not the point anyway—but you would have a reason to seek him. We give a half-hearted attempt at the spiritual disciplines when the only reason we have is that we "ought" to. But we'll find a way to make it work when we are convinced we're history if we don't.

Time with God each day is not about academic study or getting through a certain amount of Scripture or any of that. It's about connecting with God. We've got to keep those lines of communication open, so use whatever helps. Sometimes I'll listen to music; other times I'll read Scripture or a passage from a book; often I will journal; maybe I'll go for a run; then there are days when all I need is silence and solitude and the rising sun. The point is simply to do *whatever brings me back to my heart and the heart of God*. God has spared me many times from an ambush I had no idea was coming; he warned me in my time with him in the early morning about something that was going to happen that day. Just the other day it was a passage from a book about forgiveness. I sensed he was saying something to me personally. *Lord, am I unforgiving? No*, he said. About an hour later I received a very painful phone call—a betrayal. *Oh, you were telling me to be ready to forgive, weren't you? Yes.*

The discipline, by the way, is never the point. The whole point of a "devotional life" is *connecting with God.* This is our primary antidote to the counterfeits the world holds out to us. If you do not have God and have him deeply, you will turn to other lovers. As Maurice Roberts says,

> Ecstasy and delight are essential to the believer's soul and they promote sanctification. We are not meant to live without spiritual exhilaration . . . The believer is in spiritual danger if he allows himself to go for any length of time without tasting the love of Christ . . . When Christ ceases to fill the heart with satisfaction, our souls will go in silent search of other lovers. (*The Thought of God*)

A man will devote long hours to his finances when he has a goal of an early retirement; he'll endure rigorous training when he aims to run a 10k or even a marathon. The ability to discipline himself is there, but dormant for many of us. "When a warrior is in service, however, to a True King—that is, to a transcendent cause," says Bly, "he does well, and his body becomes a hardworking servant, which he requires to endure cold, heat, pain, wounds, scarring, hunger, lack of sleep, hardship of all kinds, do what is necessary."

Against the Evil One we wear the armor of God. That God has provided weapons of war for us sure makes a lot more sense if our days are like a scene from *Saving Private Ryan*. How many Christians have read over those passages about the shield of faith and the helmet of salvation and never really known what to do with them. *What lovely poetic imagery; I wonder what it means.* It means that God has given you armor and you'd better put it on. Every day. This equipment is really there, in the spiritual, unseen realm. We don't see it, but the angels and our enemies do. Start by simply praying through the passage in Ephesians as if suiting up for the arena:

"Therefore put on the full armor of God, so that when the day of evil comes, you may be able to stand your ground, and after you have done everything, to stand. Stand firm then, with the belt of truth buckled around your waist . . ." *Lord, I put on the belt of truth. I choose a lifestyle of honesty and integrity. Show me the truths I so desperately need today. Expose the lies I'm not even aware that I'm believing. ".* . . with the breastplate of righteousness in place . . ." *And yes, Lord, I wear your righteousness today against all condemnation and corruption. Fit me with your holiness and purity—defend me from all assaults against my heart. ".* . . and with your feet fitted with the readiness that comes from the gospel of peace . . ." *I do choose to live for the gospel at any moment. Show me where the larger story is unfolding and keep me from being so lax that I think the most important thing today is the soap operas of this world.*

"In addition to all this, take up the shield of faith, with which you can extinguish all the flaming arrows of the evil one . . ." *Jesus, I lift against every lie and every assault the confidence that you are good, and that you have good in store for me. Nothing is coming today that can overcome me because you are with me. ".* . . Take the helmet of salvation . . ." *Thank you, Lord, for my salvation. I receive it in a new and fresh way from you and I declare that nothing can separate me now from the love of Christ and the place I shall ever have in your kingdom. ".* . . and the sword of the Spirit, which is the word of God . . ." *Holy Spirit, show me specifically today the truths of the Word of*

God that I will need to counter the assaults and the snares of the Enemy. Bring them to mind throughout the day. ". . . . And pray in the Spirit on all occasions with all kinds of prayers and requests. With this in mind, be alert and always keep on praying for all the saints." *Finally, Holy Spirit, I agree to walk in step with you in everything— in all prayer as my spirit communes with you throughout the day.* (6:13-18)

And we walk in the authority of Christ. Do not attack in anger, do not swagger forth in pride. You will get nailed. I love the scene in *The Mask of Zorro* when the old master swordsman saves his young apprentice—who at that moment has had too much to drink—from rushing upon his enemy. "You would have fought bravely," he says, "and died quickly." All authority in heaven and on earth has been given to Jesus Christ (Matt. 28:18). He tells us this before he gives us the Great Commission, the command to advance his kingdom. Why? We've never made the connection. The reason is, if you are going to serve the True King you're going to need his authority. We dare not take on any angel, let alone a fallen one, in our own strength. That is why Christ extends his authority to us, "and you have been given fullness in Christ, who is the head over every power and authority" (Col. 2:10). Rebuke the Enemy in your own name and he laughs; command him in the name of Christ and he flees.

One more thing: Don't even think about going into battle alone. Don't even try to take the masculine journey without at least one man by your side. Yes, there are times a man must face the battle alone, in the wee hours of the morn, and fight with all he's got. But don't make that a lifestyle of isolation. This may be our weakest point, as David Smith points out in *The Friendless American Male:* "One serious problem is the friendless condition of the average American male. Men find it hard to accept that they need the fellowship of other men." Thanks to the men's movement the church understands now that a man needs other men, but what we've offered is another two-dimensional solution: "Accountability" groups or partners. Ugh. That sounds so old covenant: "You're really a fool and you're just waiting to rush into sin, so we'd better post a guard by you to keep you in line."

We don't need accountability groups; we need fellow warriors, someone to fight alongside, someone to watch our back. A young man just stopped me on the street to say, "I feel surrounded by enemies and I'm all alone." The whole crisis in masculinity today has come because we no longer have a warrior culture, a place for men to learn to fight like men. We don't need a meeting of Really Nice Guys; we need a gathering of Really Dangerous Men. *That's* what we need. I think of Henry V at Agincourt. His army has been reduced to a small band of tired and weary men; many of them are wounded. They are outnumbered five to one. But Henry rallies his troops to his side when he reminds them that they are not mercenaries, but a "band of brothers."

> We few, we happy few, we band of brothers;
> For he to-day that sheds his blood with me
> Shall be my brother . . .
> And gentlemen in England, now a-bed
> Shall think themselves accursed they were not here;
> And hold their manhoods cheap whiles any speaks
> That fought with us.

Yes, we need men to whom we can bare our souls. But it isn't going to happen with a group of guys you don't trust, who really aren't willing to go to battle with you. It's a long-standing truth that there is never a more devoted group of men than those who have fought alongside one another, the men of your squadron, the guys in your foxhole. It will never be a large group, but we don't need a large group. We need a band of brothers willing to "shed their blood" with us.

HONOR WOUNDS

A warning before we leave this chapter: You will be wounded. Just because this battle is spiritual doesn't mean it's not real; it is, and the wounds a man can take are in some ways more ugly than those that come in a firefight. To lose a leg is nothing compared to losing heart; to be crippled by shrapnel need not destroy your soul, but to be crippled by shame and guilt may. You will be wounded by the Enemy. He knows the wounds of your past, and he will try to wound you again in the same place. But these wounds are different; these are honor-wounds. As Rick Joyner says, "It is an honor to be wounded in the service of the Lord."

Blaine was showing me his scars the other night at the dinner table. "This one is where Samuel threw a rock and hit me in the forehead. And this one is from the Tetons when I fell into that sharp log. I can't remember what this one was from; oh, here's a good one—this one is from when I fell into the pond while chasing Luke. This one is a really old one when I burned my leg on the stove camping." He's proud of his scars; they are badges of honor to a boy . . . and to a man. We have no equivalent now for a Purple Heart of spiritual warfare, but we will. One of the noblest moments that await us will come at the Wedding Feast of the Lamb. Our Lord will rise and begin to call those forward who were wounded in battle for his name's sake and they will be honored, their courage rewarded. I think of Henry V's line to his men,

> He that outlives this day, and comes safe home,
> Will stand a tip-toe when the day is named,

And rouse him at the name of Crispian . . .
Then will he strip his sleeve and show his scars,
And say, "These wounds I had on Crispin's day."
Old men forget; yet all shall be forgot,
But he'll remember with advantages
What feats he did that day; then shall our names . . .
Be in their flowing cups freshly remember'd.

"The kingdom of heaven suffers violence," said Jesus, "and violent men take it by force" (Matt. 11:12 NASB). Is that a good thing or a bad thing? Hopefully by now you see the deep and holy goodness of masculine aggression and that will help you understand what Christ is saying. Contrast it with this: "The kingdom of heaven is open to passive, wimpy men who enter it by lying on the couch watching TV." If you are going to live in God's kingdom, Jesus says, it's going to take every ounce of passion and forcefulness you've got. Things are going to get fierce; that's why you were given a fierce heart. I love the image of this verse given to us by John Bunyan in *Pilgrim's Progress:*

Then the Interpreter took [Christian] and led him up toward the door of the palace; and behold, at the door stood a great company of men, as desirous to go in, but [dared] not. There also sat a man at a little distance from the door, at a tableside, with a book and his inkhorn before him, to take the names of them that should enter therein; he saw also that in the doorway stood many men in armor to keep it, being resolved to do the men that would enter what hurt and mischief they could. Now was Christian somewhat in amaze. At last, when every man [fell] back for fear of the armed men, Christian saw a man of a very stout countenance come up to the man that sat there to write, saying, "Set down my name, sir," the which when he had done, he saw the man draw his sword, and put a helmet upon his head, and rush toward the door upon the armed men, who laid upon him with deadly force; but the man, not at all discouraged, fell to cutting and hacking most fiercely. So after he had received and given many wounds to those that attempted to keep him out, he cut his way through them all, and pressed forward into the palace.

CHAPTER TEN

A BEAUTY TO RESCUE

Beauty is not only a terrible thing, it is also a mysterious thing. There God and the Devil strive for mastery, and the battleground is the heart of men.

—FYODOR DOSTOYEVSKY

*You'll be glad every night
That you treated her right.*

—GEORGE THOROGOOD
"Treat Her Right"
by Roy Head
and Gene Kurtz

*Cowboy take me away
Closer to heaven and closer to you.*

—DIXIE CHICKS
"Cowboy Take Me Away"
(© 1999 by Martie Seidel
and Marcus Hummon

Once upon a time (as the story goes) there was a beautiful maiden, an absolute enchantress. She might be the daughter of a king or a common servant girl, but we know she is a princess at heart. She is young with a youth that seems eternal. Her flowing hair, her deep eyes, her luscious lips, her sculpted figure—she makes the rose blush for shame; the sun is pale compared to her light. Her heart is golden, her love as true as an arrow. But this lovely maiden is unattainable, the prisoner of an evil power who holds her captive in a dark tower. Only a champion may win her; only the most valiant, daring, and brave warrior has a chance of setting her free. Against all hope he comes; with cunning and raw courage he lays siege to the tower and the sinister one who holds her. Much blood is shed on both sides; three times the knight is thrown back, but three times he rises again. Eventually the sorcerer is defeated; the dragon falls, the giant is slain. The maiden is his; through his valor he has won her heart. On horseback they ride off to his cottage by a stream in the woods for a rendezvous that gives passion and romance new meaning.

Why is this story so deep in our psyche? Every little girl knows the fable without ever being told. She dreams one day her prince will come. Little boys rehearse their part with wooden swords and cardboard shields. And one day the boy, now a young man, realizes that he wants to be the one to win the beauty. Fairy tales, literature, music, and movies all borrow from this mythic theme. Sleeping Beauty, Cinderella, Helen of Troy,

Romeo and Juliet, Antony and Cleopatra, Arthur and Guinevere, Tristan and Isolde. From ancient fables to the latest blockbuster, the theme of a strong man coming to rescue a beautiful woman is universal to human nature. It is written in our hearts, one of the core desires of every man and every woman.

I met Stasi in high school, but it wasn't until late in college that our romance began. Up till that point we were simply friends. When one of us came home for the weekend, we'd give the other a call just to "hang out"—see a movie, go to a party. Then one summer night something shifted. I dropped by to see Stasi; she came sauntering down the hall barefoot, wearing a pair of blue jeans and a white blouse with lace around the collar and the top buttons undone. The sun had lightened her hair and darkened her skin and how is it I never realized she was the beautiful maiden before? We kissed that night, and though I'd kissed a few girls in my time I had never tasted a kiss like that. Needless to say, I was history. Our friendship had turned to love without my really knowing how or why, only that I wanted to be with this woman for the rest of my life. As far as Stasi was concerned, I was her knight.

Why is it that ten years later I wondered if I even wanted to be married to her anymore? Divorce was looking like a pretty decent option for the both of us. So many couples wake one day to find they no longer love each other. Why do most of us get lost somewhere between "once upon a time" and "happily ever after"? Most passionate romances seem to end with evenings in front of the TV. Why does the dream seem so unattainable, fading from view even as we discover it for ourselves? Our culture has grown cynical about the fable. Don Henley says, "We've been poisoned by these fairy tales." There are dozens of books out to refute the myth, books like *Beyond Cinderella* and *The Death of Cinderella*.

No, we have not been poisoned by fairy tales and they are

not merely "myths." Far from it. The truth is, we have not taken them seriously enough. As Roland Hein says, "Myths are stories which confront us with something transcendent and eternal." In the case of our fair maiden, we have overlooked two very crucial aspects to that myth. On the one hand, none of us ever really believed the sorcerer was real. We thought we could have the maiden without a fight. Honestly, most of us guys thought our biggest battle was asking her out. And second, we have not understood the tower and its relation to her wound; the damsel is in distress. If masculinity has come under assault, femininity has been brutalized. Eve is the crown of creation, remember? She embodies the exquisite beauty and the exotic mystery of God in a way that nothing else in all creation even comes close to. And so she is the special target of the Evil One; he turns his most vicious malice against her. If he can destroy her or keep her captive, he can ruin the story.

EVE'S WOUND

Every woman can tell you about her wound; some came with violence, others came with neglect. Just as every little boy is asking one question, every little girl is, as well. But her question isn't so much about her strength. No, the deep cry of a little girl's heart is *am I lovely?* Every woman needs to know that she is exquisite and exotic and *chosen.* This is core to her identity, the way she bears the image of God. *Will you pursue me? Do you delight in me? Will you fight for me?* And like every little boy, she has taken a wound as well. The wound strikes right at the core of her heart of beauty and leaves a devastating message with it: *No. You're not beautiful and no one will really fight for you.* Like your wound, hers almost always comes at the hand of her father.

A little girl looks to her father to know if she is lovely. The power he has to cripple or to bless is just as significant to her as it is to his son. If he's a violent man he may defile her verbally or sexually. The stories I've heard from women who have been abused would tear your heart out. Janet was molested by her father when she was three; around the age of seven he showed her brothers how to do it. The assault continued until she moved away to college. What is a violated woman to think about her beauty? Am I lovely? The message is, *No . . . you are dirty. Anything attractive about you is dark and evil.* The assault continues as she grows up, through violent men and passive men. She may be stalked; she may be ignored. Either way, her heart is violated and the message is driven farther in: *you are not desired; you will not be protected; no one will fight for you.* The tower is built brick by brick, and when she's a grown woman it can be a fortress.

If her father is passive, a little girl will suffer a silent abandonment. Stasi remembers playing hide-and-seek in her house as a girl of five or six. She'd find a perfect place to crawl into, full of excited anticipation of the coming pursuit. Snuggled up in a closet, she would wait for someone to find her. No one ever did; not even after she was missing for an hour. That picture became the defining image of her life. No one noticed; no one pursued. The youngest in her family, Stasi just seemed to get lost in the shuffle. Her dad traveled a lot, and when he was home he spent most of his time in front of the TV. An older brother and sister were trouble in their teens; Stasi got the message, "Just don't be a problem; we've already got too much to handle." So she hid some more—hid her desires, hid her dreams, hid her heart. Sometimes she would pretend to be sick just to get a drop or two of attention.

Like so many unloved young women, Stasi turned to boys to try to hear what she never heard from her father. Her high school boyfriend betrayed her on prom night, told her he had been using her, that he really loved someone else. The man she dated in college became verbally abusive. But when a woman never hears she's worth fighting for, she comes to believe that's the sort of treatment she deserves. It's a form of attention, in a twisted way; maybe it's better than nothing. Then we fell in love on that magical summer night. But Stasi married a frightened, driven man who had an affair with his work because he wouldn't risk engaging a woman he sensed he wasn't enough for. I wasn't mean; I wasn't evil. I was nice. And let me tell you, a hesitant man is the last thing in the world a woman needs. She needs a lover and a warrior, not a Really Nice Guy. Her worst fear was realized—I will never really be loved, never really be fought for. And so she hid some more.

Years into our marriage I found myself blindsided by it all. Where is the beauty I once saw? What happened to the woman I fell in love with? I didn't really expect an answer to my question; it was more a shout of rage than a desperate plea. But Jesus answered me anyway. *She's still in there; but she's captive. Are you willing to go in after her?* I realized that I had—like so many men—married for safety. I married a woman I thought would never challenge me as a man. Stasi adored me; what more did I need to do? I wanted to look like the knight, but I didn't want to bleed like one. I was deeply mistaken about the whole arrangement. I didn't know about the tower, or the dragon, or what my strength was for. The number one problem between men and their women is that we men, when asked to truly fight for her . . . hesitate. We are still seeking to save ourselves; we have forgotten the deep pleasure of spilling our life for another.

OFFERING OUR STRENGTH

There are three things that are too amazing for me,
four that I do not understand:

the way of an eagle in the sky,
the way of a snake on a rock,
the way of a ship on the high seas,
and the way of a man with a maiden. (Prov. 30:18–19)

Agur son of Jakeh is onto something here. There is something mythic in the way a man is with a woman. Our sexuality offers a parable of amazing depth when it comes to being masculine and feminine. The man comes to offer his strength and the woman invites the man into herself, an act that requires courage and vulnerability and selflessness for both of them. Notice first that if the man will not rise to the occasion, nothing will happen. He must move; his strength must swell before he can enter her. But neither will the love consummate unless the woman opens herself in stunning vulnerability. When both are living as they were meant to live, the man enters his woman and offers her his strength. He *spills himself there*, in her, for her; she draws him in, embraces and envelopes him. When all is over he is spent; but ah, what a sweet death it is.

And that is how life is created. The beauty of a woman arouses a man to play the man; the strength of a man, offered tenderly to his woman, allows her to be beautiful; it brings life to her and to many. This is far, far more than sex and orgasm. It is a reality that extends to every aspect of our lives. When a man withholds himself from his woman, he leaves her without the life only he can bring. This is never more true than how a man offers—or does not offer—his words. Life and death are in the power of the tongue says Proverbs (18:21). She is made for and craves words from him. I just went upstairs to get a glass of water from the kitchen; Stasi was in there baking Christmas cookies. The place was a mess; to be honest, so was she, covered with flour and wearing a pair of old slippers. But there was something in her eye, something soft and tender, and I said to her, "You look pretty." The tension in her shoulders gave way; something twinkled in her spirit; she sighed and smiled. "Thank you," she said, almost shyly.

If the man refuses to offer himself, then his wife will remain empty and barren. A violent man destroys with his words; a silent man starves his wife. "She's wilting," a friend confessed to me about his new bride. "If she's wilting then you're withholding something," I said. Actually, it was several things—his words, his touch, but mostly his *delight*. There are so many other ways this plays out in life. A man who leaves his wife with the children and the bills to go and find another, easier life has denied them his strength. He has sacrificed them when he should have sacrificed his strength *for* them. What makes Maximus or William Wallace so heroic is simply this: They are willing to die to set others free.

This sort of heroism is what we see in the life of Joseph, the husband of Mary and the stepfather to Jesus Christ. I don't think we've fully appreciated what he did for them. Mary, an engaged young woman, almost a girl, turns up pregnant with a pretty wild story: "I'm carrying God's child." The situation is scandalous. What is Joseph to think; what is he to feel? Hurt, confused, betrayed no doubt. But he's a good man; he will not have her stoned, he will simply "divorce her quietly" (Matt. 1:19).

An angel comes to him in a dream (which shows you what it sometimes takes to get a good man to do the right thing) to convince him that Mary is telling the truth and he is to follow through with the marriage. This is going to cost him. Do you know what he's going to endure if he marries a woman the whole community thinks is an adulteress? He will be shunned by his business associates and most of his clients; he will certainly lose his standing in society and perhaps even his place in the synagogue. To see the pain he's in for, notice the insult that crowds will later use against Jesus. "Isn't this Joseph and Mary's son?" they say with a sneer and a nudge and a wink. In other words, we know who you are—the bastard child of that slut and her foolish carpenter. Joseph will pay big-time for this move. Does he withhold? No, he offers Mary his strength; he steps right between her and all of that mess and takes it on the chin. He spends himself for her.

"They will be called oaks of righteousness" (Isa. 61:3). There, under the shadow of a man's strength, a woman finds rest. The masculine journey takes a man away from the woman *so that he might return to her.* He goes to find his strength; he returns to offer it. He tears down the walls of the tower that has held her with his words and with his actions. He speaks to her heart's deepest question in a thousand ways. *Yes, you are lovely. Yes, there is one who will fight for you.* But because most men have not yet fought the battle, most women are still in the tower.

USING HER

Most men want the maiden without any sort of cost to themselves. They want all the joys of the beauty without any of the woes of the battle. This is the sinister nature of pornography— enjoying the woman at her expense. Pornography is what happens when a man insists on being energized by a woman; he *uses* her to get a feeling that he is a man. It is a false strength, as I've said, because it depends on an outside source rather than emanating from deep within his center. And it is the paragon of selfishness. He offers nothing and takes everything. We are warned about this sort of man in the story of Judah and Tamar, a story that if it weren't in the Bible you would have thought I drew straight from a television miniseries.

Judah is the fourth son born to Jacob. You might remember

him as the one who came up with the idea to sell his brother Joseph into slavery. Judah has three sons himself. When the eldest becomes a man, Judah finds a wife for him named Tamar. For reasons not fully explained to us, their marriage is short-lived. "But Er, Judah's firstborn, was wicked in the LORD's sight; so the LORD put him to death" (Gen. 38:7). Judah gives his second son to Tamar, as was the law and custom of that time. It is Onan's responsibility to raise up children in his brother's name; but he refuses to do it. He is a proud and self-centered man who angers the Lord, "so he put him to death also" (38:10). You're beginning to get the idea here: selfish men, a woman wronged, and the Lord is mad.

Judah has one son left—Shelah. The boy is the last of his strength and Judah has no intention of spending it on Tamar's behalf. He lies to Tamar, telling her to go back home and when Shelah is old enough he'll give him to her as her husband. He does not. What follows is hard to believe, especially when you consider that Tamar is a righteous woman. She disguises herself as a prostitute and sits by the road Judah is known to use. He has sex with her (uses her), but is unable to pay. Tamar takes his seal and cord and staff as a pledge. Later, word gets out that Tamar is pregnant; Judah is filled with what he insists is righteous indignation. He demands that she be burned to death, at which point Tamar produces the witness against him. "See if you recognize whose seal and cord and staff these are." Judah is nailed. He more than recognizes them—he realizes what he's been doing all along. "She is more righteous than I, since I wouldn't give her to my son Shelah" (38:25–26).

A sobering story of what happens when men selfishly refuse to spend their strength on behalf of the woman. But the same thing happens in all sorts of other ways. Pretty women endure this abuse all the time. They are pursued, but not really; they are wanted, but only superficially. They learn to offer their bodies but never, ever their souls. Most men, you see, marry for safety; they choose a woman who will make them feel like a man but never really challenge them to be one. A young man whom I admire is wrestling between the woman he is dating and one he knew but could not capture years ago. Rachel, the woman he is currently dating, is asking a lot of him; truth be told, he feels in way over his head. Julie, the woman he did not pursue, seems more idyllic; in his imagination she would be the perfect mate. Life with Rachel is tumultuous; life with Julie seems calm and tranquil. "You want the Bahamas," I said. "Rachel is the North Atlantic. Which one requires a true man?" In a brilliant twist of plot, God turns our scheme for safety on us, requiring us to play the man.

Why don't men offer what they have to their women? Because we know down in our guts that it won't be enough. There is an emptiness to Eve after the Fall, and no matter how much you pour into her she will never be filled. This is where so many men falter. Either they refuse to give what they can, or they keep pouring and pouring into her and all the while feel like a failure because she is still needing more. "There are three things that are never satisfied," warns Agur son of Jakeh, "four things that never say, 'Enough!': the grave, the barren womb, land, which is never satisfied with water, and fire, which never says, 'Enough!'" The barrenness of Eve you can never hope to fill. She needs God more than she needs you, just as you need him more than you need her.

So what do you do? Offer what you have. "I'm afraid it won't work," a client said to me when I suggested he move back toward his wife. "She's given up on me coming through for her," he confessed, "and that's good." "No it's not," I said. "That's awful." He was headed to a family reunion back east and I suggested he bring his wife with him, make it a vacation for the two of them. "You need to move toward her." "What if it doesn't work?" he asked. So many men are asking the same question. Work for what? Validate you as a man? Resurrect her heart in a day? Do you see now that you can't bring your question to Eve? No matter how good a man you are you can never be enough. If she's the report card on your strength then you'll ultimately get an F. But that's not why you love her—to get a good grade. You love her because that's what you are made to do; that's what a real man does.

EVE TO ADAM

My friend Jan says that a woman who is living out her true design will be "valiant, vulnerable, and scandalous." That's a far cry from the "church ladies" we hold up as models of Christian femininity, those busy and tired and rigid women who have reduced their hearts to a few mild desires and pretend everything is going just great. Compare their femininity with that of the women named in the genealogy of Jesus. In a list that is nearly all men, Matthew mentions four women: Tamar, Rahab, Ruth, and "Uriah's wife" (1:3, 5–6). That Bathsheba goes unnamed tells you of God's disappointment with her, and of his delight in these three whom he takes a notable exception to name in an otherwise all-male cast. Tamar, Rahab and Ruth . . . whoa; this will open up new horizons of "biblical femininity" for you.

Tamar we now know. Rahab is in the "hall of fame of faith" in Hebrews 11 for committing treason. That's right—she hid the spies who were coming in to scope out Jericho before battle. I've never heard a woman's group study Tamar or Rahab. But what about Ruth? She's often held up as a model at women's studies and retreats—but not in the way God holds her up. The book of Ruth is devoted to one question: How does a good woman help her man to play the man? The answer: She seduces him. She uses all she has as a woman to arouse him to be a man. Ruth, as you'll remember, is the daughter-in-law of a Jewish woman named Naomi. Both women have lost their husbands and are in a pretty bad way; they have no man looking out for them, their financial status is below the poverty line, and they are vulnerable in many other ways as well. Things begin to look up when Ruth catches the eye of a wealthy single man named Boaz. Boaz is a good man, this we know. He offers her some protection and some food. But Boaz is not giving Ruth what she really needs—a ring.

So what does Ruth do? She seduces him. Here's the scene: The men have been working dawn till dusk to bring in the barley harvest; they've just finished and now it's party time. Ruth takes a bubble bath and puts on a knockout dress; then she waits for the right moment. That moment happens to be late in the evening after Boaz has had a little too much to drink: "When Boaz had finished eating and drinking and was in good spirits . . ." (Ruth 3:7). "Good spirits" is in there for the more conservative readers. The man is drunk, which is evident from what he does next: pass out. ". . . He went over to lie down at the far end of the grain pile" (3:7). What happens next is simply scandalous; the verse continues, "Ruth approached quietly, uncovered his feet and lay down."

There is no possible reading of this passage that is "safe" or "nice." This is seduction pure and simple—and God holds it up for all women to follow when he not only gives Ruth her own book in the Bible but also names her in the genealogy. Yes, there are folks that'll try to tell you that it's perfectly common for a beautiful single woman "in that culture" to approach a single man (who's had too much to drink) in the middle of the night with no one else around (the far side of the grain pile) and tuck herself under the covers. They're the same folks who'll tell you that the Song of Solomon is nothing more than a "theological metaphor referring to Christ and his bride." Ask 'em what they do with passages like "Your stature is like that of the palm, and your breasts like clusters of fruit. I said 'I will climb the palm tree; I will take hold of its fruit'" (Song 7:7–8). That's a Bible study, right?

No, I do not think Ruth and Boaz had sex that night; I do not think anything inappropriate happened at all. But this is no fellowship potluck, either. I'm telling you that the church has really crippled women when it tells them that their beauty is vain and they are at their feminine best when they are "serving others." A woman is at her best when she is being a woman. Boaz needs a little help getting going and Ruth has some options. She can badger him: *All you do is work, work, work. Why won't you stand up and be a man?* She can whine about it: *Boaz, pleeease hurry up and marry me.* She can emasculate him: *I thought you were a real man; I guess I was wrong.* Or she can use all she is as a woman to get him to use all he's got as a man. She can arouse, inspire, energize . . . seduce him. Ask your man what he'd prefer.

IT IS A BATTLE

Will you fight for her? That's the question Jesus asked me many years ago, right before our tenth anniversary, right at the time I was wondering what had happened to the woman I married. *You're on the fence, John,* he said. *Get in or get out.* I knew what he was saying—stop being a nice guy and act like a warrior. Play the man. I brought flowers, took her to dinner, and began to move back toward her in my heart. But I knew there was more. That night, before we went to bed, I prayed for Stasi in a way I'd never prayed for her before. Out loud, before all the heavenly hosts, I stepped between her and the forces of darkness that had been coming against her. Honestly, I didn't really know what I was doing, only that I needed to take on the dragon. All hell broke loose. Everything we've learned about spiritual warfare began that night. And you know what happened? Stasi got free; the tower of her depression gave way as I began to truly fight for her.

And it's not just once, but again and again over time. That's where the myth really stumps us. Some men are willing to go in once, twice, even three times. But a warrior is in this for good. Oswald Chambers asks, "God spilt the life of his son that the world might be saved; are we prepared to spill out our lives?" Daniel is in the midst of a very hard, very unpromising battle for his wife. It's been years now without much progress and without much hope. Sitting in a restaurant the other night, tears in his eyes, this is what he said to me: "I'm not going anywhere. This is my place in the battle. This is the hill that I will die on." He has reached a point that we all must come to, sooner or later, when it's no longer about winning or losing. His wife may respond and she may not. That's really no longer the issue. The question is simply this: What kind of man do you want to be? Maximus? Wallace? Or Judah? A young pilot in the RAF wrote just before he went down in 1940, "The universe is so vast and so ageless that the life of one man can only be justified by the measure of his sacrifice."

As I write this chapter, Stasi and I have just returned from a friend's wedding. It was the best nuptials either of us have ever been to; a wonderful, romantic, holy affair. The groom was young and strong and valiant; the bride was seductively beautiful. Which is what made it so excruciating for me. Oh to start over again, to do it all over the right way, marry as a young man knowing what I know now. I could have loved Stasi so much better; she could have loved me so much better as well. We've learned every lesson the hard way over our eighteen years. Any wisdom contained in these pages was paid for . . . dearly. On top of that Stasi and I were in a difficult place over the weekend; that was the campfire. Satan saw his opportunity and turned it into a bonfire *without even one word between us*. By the time we got to the reception, I didn't want to dance with her. I didn't even want to be in the same room. All the hurt and disappointment of the years—hers and mine—seemed to be the only thing that was ever true about our marriage.

It wasn't until later that I heard Stasi's side of the script, but here is how the two fit together. Stasi: *He's disappointed in me. No wonder why. Look at all these beautiful women. I feel fat and ugly.* Me: *I'm so tired of battling for our marriage. How I wish we could start over. It wouldn't be that hard, you know. There are other options. Look at all these beautiful women.* On and on it came, like a wave overwhelming the shore. Sitting at the table with a group of our friends, I felt I was going to suffocate; I had to get out of there, get some fresh air. Truth be told, when I left the reception I had no intention of going back. Either I'd wind up in a bar somewhere or back in our room watching TV. Thankfully, I found a small library off to the side of the reception hall; alone in that sanctuary I wrestled with all I was feeling for what seemed like an hour. (It was probably twenty minutes.) I grabbed a book but could not read; I tried to pray but did not want to. Finally, some words began to arise from my heart:

> *Jesus, come and rescue me. I know what's going on; I know this is assault. But right now it all feels so true. Jesus, deliver me. Get me out from under this waterfall. Speak to me; rescue my heart before I do something stupid. Deliver me, Lord.*

Slowly, almost imperceptibly, the wave began to lift. My thoughts and emotions quieted down to a more normal size. Clarity was returning. The campfire was just a campfire again. *Jesus, you know the pain and disappointment in my heart. What would you have me do?* (The bar was no longer an option, but I was still planning to just go straight to my room for the rest of the night.) *I want you to go back in there and ask your wife to dance.* I knew he was right; I knew that somewhere down deep inside that's what my true heart would want to do. But the desire still seemed so far away. I lingered for five more minutes, hoping he had another option for me. He remained silent, but the assault was over and the bonfire was only embers. Once more I knew the man I wanted to be.

I went back to the reception and asked Stasi to dance; for the next two hours we had one of the best evenings we've had in a long time. We nearly lost to the Evil One; instead, it will go down as a memory we'll share with our friends for a long, long time.

CLOSE

Stasi has given me a number of wonderful presents over the years, but last Christmas was unforgettable. We'd finished with the feeding frenzy the boys call unwrapping presents. Stasi slipped out of the room with the words, "Close your eyes . . . I have a surprise for you." After a good deal of rustling and whispers, she told me I could look. Before me was a long rectangular box on the family room floor. "Open it," she said. I removed the bow and lifted the lid. Inside was a full-size claymore, a Scottish broadsword exactly like the one used by William Wallace. I had been looking for one for several months, but Stasi did not know that. It was not on my Christmas list. She had done this out of the vision of her own heart, as a way of thanking me for fighting for her.

Here is what her note read:

Because you are a Braveheart, fighting for the hearts of so many people . . . and especially for mine. Thanks to you I know a freedom I never thought was possible. Merry Christmas.

CHAPTER ELEVEN

AN ADVENTURE TO LIVE

Dark and cold we may be, but this
Is no winter now. The frozen misery
Of centuries breaks, cracks, begins to move;
The thunder is the thunder of the floes,
The thaw, the flood, the upstart Spring
Thank God our time is now when wrong
Comes up to face us everywhere,
Never to leave us till we take
The longest stride of soul men ever took.

—CHRISTOPHER FRY

The place where God calls you is the place where your deep gladness
and the world's deep hunger meet.

—FREDERICK BUECHNER

There is a river that winds its way through southern Oregon, running down from the Cascades to the coast, which has also wound its way through my childhood, carving a path in the canyons of my memory. As a young boy I spent many summer days on the Rogue, fishing and swimming and picking blackberries; but mostly, fishing. I loved the name given to the river by French trappers; the river Scoundrel. It gave a mischievous benediction to my adventures there—I was a rogue on the Rogue. Those golden days of boyhood are some of my most cherished memories and so last summer I took Stasi and the boys there, to share with them a river and a season from my life. The lower part of the Rogue runs through some hot and dry country in the summer months, especially in late July, and we were looking forward to kayaking as an excuse to get really wet and find a little adventure of our own.

There is a rock that juts out over that river somewhere between Morrison's Lodge and the Foster Bar. The canyon narrows there and the Rogue deepens and pauses for a moment in its rush to the sea. High rock walls rise on either side, and on the north—the side only boaters can reach—is Jumping Rock. Cliff jumping is one of our family favorites, especially when it's hot and dry and the jump is high enough so that it takes your breath away as you plunge beneath the warmer water at the top, down to where it's dark and cold, so cold that it sends you gasping back for the surface and the sun. Jumping Rock is perched above the river at about the height of a two-story house plus some, tall enough that you can slowly count to five before you hit the water (it's barely a two count from the high dive at your local pool). There's a faculty built into the human brain that makes every cliff seem twice the height when you're looking down from the top and everything in you says, *Don't even think about it.*

So you don't think about it, you just hurl yourself off out into the middle of the canyon, and then you free-fall for what feels like enough time to recite the Gettysburg Address and all your senses are on maximum alert as you plunge into the cold water. When you come back up the crowd is cheering and something in you is also cheering because *you did it.* We all jumped that day, first me, then Stasi, Blaine, Sam, and even Luke. Then some big hulking guy who was going to back down once he saw what the view was like from above, but he had to jump because Luke did it and he couldn't live with himself knowing he'd cowered while a six-year-old boy hurled himself off. After that first jump you have to do it again, partly because you can't believe you did it and partly because the fear has given way to the thrill of such freedom. We let the sun heat us up again and then . . . bombs away.

I want to live my whole life like that. I want to love with much more abandon and stop waiting for others to love me first. I want to hurl myself into a creative work worthy of God. I want to charge the fields at Banockburn, follow Peter as he followed Christ out onto the sea, pray from my heart's true *desire.* As the poet George Chapman has said,

> Give me a spirit that on this life's rough sea
> Loves to have his sails fill'd with a lusty wind
> Even till his sail-yards tremble, his masts crack,
> And his rapt ship runs on her side so low
> That she drinks water, and her keel ploughs air.

Life is not a problem to be solved; it is an adventure to be lived. That's the nature of it and has been since the beginning when God set the dangerous stage for this high-stakes drama and called the whole wild enterprise *good*. He rigged the world in such a way that it only works when we embrace *risk* as the theme of our lives, which is to say, only when we live by faith. A man just won't be happy until he's got adventure in his work, in his love and in his spiritual life.

ASKING THE RIGHT QUESTION

Several years ago I was thumbing through the introduction of a book when I ran across a sentence that changed my life. God is intimately personal with us and he speaks in ways that are peculiar to our own quirky hearts—not just through the Bible, but through the whole of creation. To Stasi he speaks through movies. To Craig he speaks through rock and roll (he called me the other day after listening to "Running Through the Jungle" to say he was fired up to go study the Bible). God's word to me comes in many ways—through sunsets and friends and films and music and wilderness and books. But he's got an especially humorous thing going with me and books. I'll be browsing through a secondhand book shop when out of a thousand volumes one will say ,"Pick me up"—just like Augustine in his *Confessions. Tolle legge*—take up and read. Like a master fly fisherman God cast his fly to this cruising trout. In the introduction to the book that I rose to this day, the author (Gil Bailie) shares a piece of advice given to him some years back by a spiritual mentor:

> Don't ask yourself what the world needs. Ask yourself what makes you come alive, and go do that, because what the world needs is people who have come alive.

I was struck dumb. It could have been Balaam's donkey, for all I was concerned. Suddenly my life up till that point made sense in a sickening sort of way; I realized I was living a script written for me by someone else. All my life I had been asking the world to tell me what to do with myself. This is different from seeking counsel or advice; what I wanted was freedom from responsibility and especially freedom from risk. I wanted someone else to tell me who to be. Thank God it didn't work. The scripts they handed me I simply could not bring myself to play for very long. Like Saul's armor, they never fit. Can a world of posers tell you to do anything but pose yourself? As Buechner says, we are in constant danger of being not actors in the drama of our lives but reactors, "to go where the world takes us, to drift with whatever current happens to be running the strongest." Reading the counsel given to Bailie I knew it was God speaking to me. It was an invitation to come out of Ur. I set the volume down without turning another page and walked out of that bookstore to find a life worth living.

I applied to graduate school and got accepted. That program would turn out to be far more than a career move; out of the transformation that took place there I became a writer, counselor, and speaker. The whole trajectory of my life changed and with it the lives of many, many other people. But I almost didn't go. You see, when I applied to school I hadn't a nickel to pay for it. I was married with three children and a mortgage, and that's the season when most men completely abandon their dreams and back down from jumping off anything. The risk just seems too great. On top of it all, I received a call about that time from a firm back in Washington, D.C., offering me a plum job at an incredible salary. I would be in a prestigious company, flying in some very powerful circles, making great money. God was thickening the plot, testing my resolve. Down one road was my dream and desire, which I had no means to pay for, and an absolutely uncertain future after that; down the other was a comfortable step up the ladder of success, a very obvious next career move and the total loss of my soul.

I went to the mountains for the weekend to sort things out. Life makes more sense standing alone by a lake at high elevation with a fly rod in hand. The tentacles of the world and my false self seemed to give way as I climbed up into the Holy Cross Wilderness. On the second day God began to speak. *John, you can take that job if you want to. It's not a sin. But it'll kill you and you know it.* He was right; it had False Self written all over it. *If you want to follow Me,* he continued, *I'm heading that way.* I knew exactly what he meant—"that way" headed into wilderness, frontier. The following week three phone calls came in amazing succession. The first was from the Washington firm; I told them I was not their man, to call somebody else. As I hung up the phone my false self was screaming *what are you doing?!* The next day the phone rang again; it was my wife, telling me that the university had called wanting to know where my first tuition installment was. On the third day a call came from a longtime friend who had been praying for me and my decision. "We think you ought to go to school," he said. "And we want to pay your way."

> Two roads diverged in a wood and I,
> I took the one less traveled by,
> And that has made all the difference.

WHAT ARE YOU WAITING FOR?

Where would we be today if Abraham had carefully weighed the pros and cons of God's invitation and decided that he'd

rather hang on to his medical benefits, three weeks paid vacation and retirement plan in Ur? What would have happened if
Moses had listened to his mother's advice to "never play with
matches" and lived a careful, cautious life steering clear of all
burning bushes? You wouldn't have the gospel if Paul had concluded that the life of a Pharisee, while not everything a man
dreams for, was at least predictable and certainly more stable
than following a voice he heard on the Damascus road. After all,
people hear voices all the time and who really knows whether
it's God or just one's imagination. Where would we be if Jesus
was not fierce and wild and romantic to the core? Come to think
of it, we wouldn't *be* at all if God hadn't taken that enormous risk
of us in the first place.

Most men spend the energy of their lives trying to elimi-
nate risk, or squeezing it down to a more manageable size.
Their children hear "no" far more than they hear "yes"; their
employees feel chained up and their wives are equally bound.
If it works, if a man succeeds in securing his life against all risk,
he'll wind up in a cocoon of self-protection and wonder all the
while why he's suffocating. If it doesn't work, he curses God,
redoubles his efforts and his blood pressure. When you look at
the structure of the false self men tend to create, it always
revolves around two themes: seizing upon some sort of compe-
tence and rejecting anything that cannot be controlled. As
David Whyte says, "The price of our vitality is the sum of all
our fears."

For murdering his brother, God sentences Cain to the life of
a restless wanderer; five verses later Cain is building a city (Gen.
4:12, 17). That sort of commitment—the refusal to trust God
and the reach for control—runs deep in every man. Whyte talks
about the difference between the false self's desire "to have

power *over* experience, to control all events and consequences, and the soul's wish to have power *through* experience, *no matter what that may be.*" You literally sacrifice your soul and your true power when you insist on controlling things, like the guy Jesus talked about who thought he finally pulled it all off, built himself some really nice barns and died the same night. "What will it profit a man if he gains the whole world, and loses his own soul?" (Mark 8:36 NKJV). You can lose your soul, by the way, long before you die.

Canadian biologist Farley Mowat had a dream of studying wolves in their native habitat, out in the wilds of Alaska. The book *Never Cry Wolf* is based on that lonely research expedition. In the film version Mowat's character is a bookworm named Tyler who has never so much as been camping. He hires a crazy old Alaskan bush pilot named Rosie Little to get him and all his equipment into the remote Blackstone Valley in the dead of winter. Flying in Little's single-engine Cessna over some of the most beautiful, rugged, and dangerous wilderness in the world, Little pries Tyler for the secret to his mission:

LITTLE: Tell me, Tyler . . . what's in the valley of the Blackstone? What is it? Manganese? (Silence) Can't be oil. Is it gold?

TYLER: It's kind of hard to say.

LITTLE: You're a smart man, Tyler . . . you keep your own counsel. We're all of us prospectors up here, right, Tyler? Scratchin' for that . . . that one crack in the ground . . . and never have to scratch again.

(After a pause)

I'll let you in on a little secret, Tyler. The gold's not in the ground. The gold is not anywhere up here. The real gold is south at 60, sittin' in living rooms, facing the boob tube bored to death. Bored to death, Tyler.

Suddenly the plane's engine coughs a few times, sputters, gasps . . . and then simply cuts out. The only sound is the wind over the wings.

>   LITTLE: (Groans) Oh, Lord.
>   TYLER: (Panicked) What's wrong?
>   LITTLE: Take the stick.

Little hands over control of the powerless plane to Tyler (who has never flown a plane in his life) and starts frantically rummaging around in an old toolbox between the seats. Unable to find what he's looking for, Little explodes. Screaming, he empties the toolbox all over the plane. Then just as abruptly he stops, calmly rubbing his face with his hands.

>   TYLER: (Still panicked and trying to fly the plane) What's wrong?
>   LITTLE Boredom, Tyler. Boredom . . . that's what's wrong. How do
>   you beat boredom, Tyler? Adventure. ADVENTURE, Tyler!

Little then kicks the door of the plane open and nearly disappears outside, banging on something—a frozen fuel line perhaps. The engine kicks back in just as they are about to fly into the side of a mountain. Little grabs the stick and pulls them into a steep ascent, barely missing the ridge and then easing off into a long, majestic valley below.

Rosie Little may be a madman, but he's also a genius. He knows the secret to a man's heart, the cure for what ails him. Too many men forsake their dreams because they aren't willing to risk, or fear they aren't up to the challenge, or are never told that those desires deep in their heart are *good*. But the soul of a man, the real gold Little refers to, isn't made for controlling things; it's made for adventure. Something in us remembers, however faintly, that when God set man on the earth he gave us an incredible mission—a charter to explore, build, conquer, and care for all creation. It was a blank page waiting to be written; a clean canvas waiting to be painted. Well, sir, God never revoked that charter. It's still there, waiting for a man to seize it.

If you had permission to do what you really want to do, what would you do? Don't ask *how;* that will cut your desire off at the knees. *How* is never the right question; *how* is a faithless question. It means "unless I can see my way clearly I won't believe it, won't venture forth." When the angel told Zechariah that his ancient wife would bear him a son named John, Zechariah asked how and was struck dumb for it. *How* is God's department. He is asking you *what.* What is written in your heart? What makes you come alive? If you could do what you've always wanted to do, what would it be? You see, a man's calling is written on his true heart, and he discovers it when he enters the frontier of his deep desires. To paraphrase Bailie, don't ask yourself what the world needs, ask yourself what makes you come alive because what the world needs are *men* who have come alive.

The invitation in the book shop, I must note, was given to me some years into my Christian life when the transformation of my character was at a point that I could hear it without running off and doing something stupid. I've met men who've used advice like it as permission to leave their wife and run off with their secretary. They are *deceived* about what it is they really want, what they are made for. There is a design God has woven into the fabric of this world, and if we violate it we cannot hope to find life. Because our hearts have strayed so far from home, he's given us the Law as a sort of handrail to help us back from the precipice. But the goal of Christian discipleship is the transformed heart; we move from a boy who needs the Law to the man who is able to live by the Spirit of the law. "My counsel is this: Live freely, animated and motivated by God's Spirit. Then you won't feed the compulsions of selfishness . . . Legalism is helpless in bringing this about; it only gets in the way" (Gal. 5:16, 23 *The Message*).

A man's life becomes an adventure, the whole thing takes on a transcendent purpose when he releases control in exchange for the recovery of the dreams in his heart. Sometimes those dreams are buried deep and it takes some unearthing to get to them. We pay attention to our desire. Often the clues are in our past, in those moments when we found ourselves loving what we were doing. The details and circumstances change as we grow, but the themes remain the same. Dale was the neighborhood ring leader as a boy; in college, he was captain of the tennis team. What makes him come alive is when he is leading men. For Charles it was art; he was always drawing as a child. In high school, what he loved best was ceramics class. He gave up painting after college and finally came alive again when at age fifty-one he got it back.

To recover his heart's desire a man needs to get away from the noise and distraction of his daily life for time with his own soul. He needs to head into the wilderness, to silence and solitude. Alone with himself, he allows whatever is there to come to the surface. Sometimes it is grief for so much lost time. There, beneath the grief, are desires long forsaken. Sometimes it even starts with temptation, when a man thinks that what will really make him come alive is something unholy. At that point he should ask himself, "What is the desire *beneath* this desire? What is it I'm wanting that I think I'll find there?" However the desire begins to surface, we pick up that trail when we allow a cry to rise from the depths of our soul, a cry, as Whyte says, "for a kind of forgotten courage, one difficult to hear, demanding not a raise, but another life."

> I have studied many times
> The marble which was chiseled for me—
> A boat with a furled sail at rest in a harbor.
> In truth it pictures not my destination
> But my life.
> For love was offered me, and I shrank from its disillusionment;
> Sorrow knocked at my door, but I was afraid
> Ambition called to me, but I dreaded the chances.
> Yet all the while I hungered for meaning in my life
> And now I know that we must lift the sail
> And catch the winds of destiny
> Wherever they drive the boat.
> To put meaning in one's life may end in madness,
> But life without meaning is the torture
> Of restlessness and vague desire—
> It is a boat longing for the sea and yet afraid.
>
> (EDGAR LEE MASTERS)

INTO THE UNKNOWN

"The spiritual life cannot be made suburban," said Howard Macey. "It is always frontier and we who live in it must accept and even rejoice that it remains untamed." The greatest obstacle to realizing our dreams is the false self's hatred of mystery. That's a problem, you see, because *mystery is essential to adventure*. More than that, mystery is the heart of the universe and the God who made it. The most important aspects of any man's world—his relationship with his God and with the people in his life, his calling, the spiritual battles he'll face—every one of them is fraught with mystery. But that is not a bad thing; it is a joyful, rich part of reality and essential to our soul's thirst for adventure. As Oswald Chambers says,

> Naturally, we are inclined to be so mathematical and calculating that we look upon uncertainty as a bad thing . . . Certainty is the mark of the common-sense life; gracious uncertainty is the mark of the spiritual life. To be certain of God means that we are uncertain in all our ways, we do not know what a day may bring forth. This is generally said with a sigh of sadness; it should rather be an expression of breathless expectation. (*My Utmost for His Highest*)

There are no formulas with God. Period. So there are no formulas for the man who follows him. God is a Person, not a doctrine. He operates not like a system—not even a theological system—but with all the originality of a truly free and alive person. "The realm of God is dangerous," says Archbishop Anthony Bloom. "You must enter into it and not just seek information about it." Take Joshua and the Battle of Jericho. The Israelites are staged to make their first military strike into the promised land and there's a lot hanging on this moment—the morale of the troops, their confidence in Joshua, not to mention their reputation that will precede them to every other enemy that awaits. This is their D-Day, so to speak, and word is going to get around. How does God get the whole thing off to a good start? He has them march around the city blowing trumpets for a week; on the seventh day he has them do it seven times and then give a big holler. It works marvelously, of course. And you know what? It never happens again. Israel never uses that tactic again.

There's Gideon and his army reduced from thirty-two thousand to three-hundred. What's their plan of attack? Torches and water pots. It also works splendidly and it also never happens again. You recall Jesus healing the blind—he never does it the same way twice. I hope you're getting the idea because the church has really been taken in by the world on this one. The Modern Era hated mystery; we desperately wanted a means of controlling our own lives and we seemed to find the ultimate Tower of Babel in the scientific method. Don't get me wrong—science has given us many wonderful advances in sanitation, medicine, transportation. But we've tried to use those methods to tame the wildness of the spiritual frontier. We take the latest marketing methods, the newest business management fad, and we apply it to ministry. The problem with modern Christianity's obsession with principles is that it removes any real conversation with God. Find the principle, apply the principle—what do you need God for? So Oswald Chambers warns us, "Never make a principle out of your experience; let God be as original with other people as he is with you."

Originality and creativity are essential to personhood and to masculine strength. The adventure begins and our *real* strength is released when we no longer rely on formulas. God is an immensely creative Person and he wants his sons to live that way too. There is a great picture of this in *Raiders of the Lost Ark*, of all places. Of course Indiana Jones is a swashbuckling hero who can handle ancient history, beautiful women, and a forty-five with ease. But the real test of the man comes when all his resources have failed. He's finally found the famous ark, but the Germans have stolen it from him and loaded it onto a truck. They're about to drive off with his dreams under heavy Nazi military protection. Jones and his two companions are watching helplessly as victory slips through their fingers. But Indiana is not finished; oh no, the game has just begun. He says to his friends:

JONES: Get back to Cairo. Get us some transport to England . . . boat, plane, anything. Meet me at Omars. Be ready for me. I'm going after that truck.

SAULACH: How?

JONES: I don't know . . . I'm making this up as I go.

When it comes to living and loving, what's required is a willingness to jump in with both feet and be creative as you go. Here's but one example: A few years ago I got home from a trip on a Sunday afternoon and found the boys playing out on the front yard. It was a cold November day, too cold to be outside, and so I asked them what was up. "Mom kicked us out." Knowing there's often good reason when Stasi banishes them I pressed for a confession, but they maintained their innocence. So, I headed for the door to get the other side of the story. "I wouldn't go in there if I were you, Dad," Sam warned. "She's in a bad mood." I knew exactly what he was describing. The house was shut; inside all was dark and quiet.

Now, let me ask the men reading this: What was everything inside me telling me to do? *Run away. Don't even think about going in. Stay outside.* And you know what? I could have stayed outside and looked like a great dad, playing catch with my sons. But I am tired of being that man; I have run for years. Too many times I've played the coward and I'm sick of it. I opened the door, went inside, climbed the stairs, walked into our bedroom, sat down on the bed and asked my wife the most terrifying question any man ever asks his woman: "What's wrong?" After that it's all mystery. A woman doesn't want to be related to with formulas, and she certainly doesn't want to be treated like a project that has answers to it. She doesn't want to be solved; she wants to be *known*. Mason is absolutely right when he calls marriage the "Wild Frontier."

The same holds true for the spiritual battles that we face. After the Allies landed in France, they encountered something no one had planned or prepared them for: hedgerows. Enclosing every field from the sea to Verdun was a wall of earth, shrubs, and trees. Aerial photographs revealed the existence of the hedgerows, but the Allies assumed they were like the ones found across England, which are two feet high. The Norman hedgerows were ten feet high and impenetrable, a veritable fortress. If the Allies used the solitary gateways into each field, they were mowed down by German machine gunners. If they tried to drive their tanks up and over, the underbelly was exposed to antitank weapons. They had to improvise. American farmboys rigged all sorts of contraptions on the front of the Sherman tanks, which allowed them to punch holes for explosives or break right through the hedgerows. Grease monkeys from the states rebuilt damaged tanks over night. As one captain said,

> I began to realize something about the American Army I had never thought possible before. Although it is highly regimented and bureaucratic under garrison conditions, when the Army gets in the field, it relaxes and the individual initiative comes forward and does what has to be done. This type of flexibility was one of the great strengths of the American Army in World War II. (*Citizen Soldiers*)

It was truly Yankee ingenuity that won the war. This is where we are now—in the midst of battle without the training we really need, and there are few men around to show us how to do it. We are going to have to figure a lot of this out for ourselves. We know how to attend church; we've been taught not to swear or drink or smoke. We know how to be nice. But we don't really know how to fight, and we're going to have to learn as we go. That is where our strength will be crystallized, deepened, and *revealed*. A man is never more a man than when he embraces an adventure beyond his control, or when he walks into a battle he isn't sure of winning. As Antonio Machado wrote,

> Mankind owns four things
> That are no good at sea—
> Rudder, anchor, oars,
> And the fear of going down.

FROM FORMULA TO RELATIONSHIP

I'm not suggesting that the Christian life is chaotic or that a real man is flagrantly irresponsible. The poser who squanders his paycheck at the racetrack or the slot machines is not a man; he's a fool. The sluggard who quits his job and makes his wife go to work so he can stay home to practice his golf swing, thinking he'll make the pro tour, is "worse than an unbeliever" (1 Tim. 5:8). What I *am* saying is that our false self demands a formula before he'll engage; he wants a guarantee of success, and mister, you aren't going to get one. So there comes a time in a man's life when he's got to break away from all that and head off into the unknown with God. This is a vital part of our journey and if we balk here, the journey ends.

Before the moment of Adam's greatest trial God provided no step-by-step plan, gave no formula for how he was to handle the whole mess. That was not abandonment; that was the way God *honored* Adam. *You are a man; you don't need Me to hold you by the hand through this. You have what it takes.* What God *did* offer Adam was friendship. He wasn't left alone to face life; he walked with God in the cool of the day and there they talked about love and marriage and creativity, what lessons he was learning and what adventures were to come. This is what God is offering to us as well. As Chambers says,

> There comes the baffling call of God in our lives also. The call of God can never be stated explicitly; it is implicit. The call of God is like the call of the sea, no one hears it but the one who has the nature of the sea in him. It cannot be stated definitely what the call of God is to, *because his call is to be in comradeship with himself* for his own purposes, and the test is to believe that God knows what he is after. (*My Utmost for His Highest,* emphasis added)

The only way to live in this adventure—with all its danger and unpredictability and immensely high stakes—is in an ongoing, intimate relationship with God. The control we so desperately crave is an illusion. Far better to give it up in exchange for God's offer of companionship, set aside stale formulas so that we might enter into an informal friendship. Abraham knew this; Moses did as well. Read through the first several chapters of Exodus—it's filled with a give-and-take between Moses and God. "Then the Lord said to Moses," "then Moses said to the Lord." The two act like they know each other, like they really are intimate allies. David—a man after God's own heart—also walked and warred and loved his way through life in a conversational intimacy with God.

> When the Philistines heard that David had been anointed king over Israel, they went up in full force to search for him,

but David heard about it and went down to the stronghold. Now the Philistines had come and spread out in the Valley of Rephaim; so David inquired of the LORD, "Shall I go and attack the Philistines? Will you hand them over to me?" The LORD answered him, "Go, for I will surely hand the Philistines over to you." So David went to Baal Perazim, and there he defeated them . . . Once more the Philistines came up and spread out in the Valley of Rephaim; so David inquired of the LORD, and he answered, "Do not go straight up, but circle around behind them and attack them in front of the balsam trees. As soon as you hear the sound of marching in the tops of the balsam trees, move quickly, because that will mean the LORD has gone out in front of you to strike the Philistine army." So David did as the LORD commanded him, and he struck down the Philistines all the way from Gibeon to Gezer. (2 Sam. 5:17–20, 22–25)

Here again there is no rigid formula for David; it changes as he goes, relying on the counsel of God. This is the way every comrade and close companion of God lives. Jesus said, "I no longer call you servants, because a servant does not know his master's business. Instead, I have called you friends, for everything that I learned from my father I have made known to you" (John 15:15). God calls you his friend. He wants to talk to you—personally, frequently. As Dallas Willard writes, "The ideal for divine guidance is . . . a conversational relationship with God: the sort of relationship suited to friends who are mature personalities in a shared enterprise." Our whole journey into authentic masculinity centers around those cool-of-the-day talks with God. Simple questions change hassles to adventures; the events of our lives become opportunities for initiation. "What are you teaching me here, God? What are you asking me to do . . . or to let go of? What in my heart are you speaking to?"

FURTHER UP AND FURTHER IN

For years now I have wanted to climb one of the great peaks— Denali, perhaps, and after that maybe even Everest. Something calls to my heart every time I see a photo or read an account of another attempt. The allure of the wild places we have left haunts me, but there's also the desire for a challenge that requires everything I've got. Yes, even danger; maybe especially danger. Some people think I'm crazy, and I know that this dream may never be realized in my lifetime, but that does not discourage me; there is something symbolic about the desire and I cannot let it go. This is quite crucial for us to understand. We have desires in our hearts that are core to who and what we are; they are almost mythic in their meaning, waking in us something transcendent and eternal. But we can be mistaken about how those desires will be lived out. The way in which God fulfills a desire may be different from what first awakened it.

In the past year or so I've made a number of decisions that make no sense unless there is a God and I am his friend. I left my corporate job and struck out on my own, following a dream I've long feared. I've picked up the shattered pieces of a vision I lost when my best friend and partner Brent was killed in a climbing accident. What feels most crazy of all, I've opened my self to friendship again and a new partner, and we're heading out where Brent and I left off. The battle has been intense; a steep ascent that's taking everything I've got. The stakes I'm playing at now are immense—financially, sure, but more so spiritually, relationally. It's requiring a concentration of body, soul, and spirit I've never before endured.

What is perhaps the hardest part is the misunderstanding I live with from others on a daily basis. Sometimes the winds howl around me; other times I fear I'll fall. The other day I was feeling way out on the end of my rope, cutting a path across a sheer face of risk. Out of my heart rose a question. *What are we doing, God?* *We're climbing Everest.*

CHAPTER TWELVE

WRITING THE NEXT CHAPTER

I am sometimes almost terrified at the scope of the demands made upon me, at the perfection of the self-abandonment required of me; yet outside of such absoluteness can be no salvation.

—GEORGE MACDONALD

Freedom is useless if we don't exercise it as characters making choices . . . We are free to change the stories by which we live. Because we are genuine characters, and not mere puppets, we can choose our defining stories. We can do so because we actively participate in the creation of our stories. We are co-authors as well as characters. Few things are as encouraging as the realization that things can be different and that we have a role in making them so.

—DANIEL TAYLOR

Obey God in the thing he shows you, and instantly the next thing is opened up. God will never reveal more truth about himself until you have obeyed what you know already . . . This chapter brings out the delight of real friendship with God.

—OSWALD CHAMBERS

At once they left their nets and followed him.

—MATTHEW 4:20

N ow, reader, it is your turn to write—venture forth with God. Remember, don't ask yourself what the world needs . . .

Captivating

To the captivating women we
are blessed to call our friends.

Introduction

*N*ow we are on holy ground.

Writing a book for men (*Wild at Heart*) was a fairly straight-forward proposition. Not that men are simpletons. But they *are* the less complicated of the two genders trying to navigate love and life together. Both men and women know this to be true. The mystery of the feminine heart was meant to be a good thing, by the way. A source of joy. Yet it has become a source of shame—women almost universally feel that they are "too much" and "not what they should be." And men tend to pull away from the deeper waters of a woman's soul, unsure of what they will find there or how to handle it. And so we have missed the treasure that is the heart of a woman, missed the richness femininity was meant to bring to our lives, missed the way it speaks to us of the heart of God.

Rest assured—this is not a book about all the things you are fail-ing to do as a woman. We're tired of those books. As a new Christian, the first book I (Stasi) picked up to read on godly femininity I threw across the room. I never picked it up again. In the twenty-five years since, I have only read a few I could wholeheartedly recommend. The rest drive me crazy. Their messages to women make me feel as though, "You are not the woman you ought to be—but if you do the following ten things, you can make the grade." They are, by and large, soul-killing. But femininity cannot be prescribed in a formula.

We have women friends who love tea parties and china, and friends who break out in hives at the thought of them. We have women friends who love to hunt, bow hunt even. Women who love to entertain and women who don't. Women who are professors, moms, doctors, nurses, missionaries, dentists, homemakers, therapists, chefs, artists, poets, rock climbers, triathletes, secretaries, salespeople, and social workers. Beautiful women, all.

So—is a true woman Cinderella or Joan of Arc? Mary Magdalene or Oprah? How do we recover essential femininity without falling into stereotypes, or worse, ushering in more pressure and shame upon our readers? That is the last thing a woman needs. And yet, there *is* an essence that God has given to every woman. We share something deep and true, down in our hearts. So we venture into this exploration of femininity by way of the *heart*. What is at the core of a woman's heart? What are her desires? What did we long for as little girls? What do we still long for as women? And, how does a woman begin to be healed from the wounds and tragedies of her life?

Sometime between the dreams of your youth and yesterday, something precious has been lost. And that treasure is your heart, your priceless feminine heart. God has set within you a femininity that is powerful and tender, fierce and alluring. No doubt it has been misunderstood. Surely it has been assaulted. But it is there, your true heart, and it is worth recovering. You *are* captivating.

So we invite you to take a journey with us, a journey of discovery and healing. For your heart is the prize of God's Kingdom, and Jesus has come to win you back for himself—all of you. To help your journey, we've written *Captivating: A Guided Journal.* You might want to use it as you read this book. And, gather a group of women and go through it together! We pray that God will use this book in your life, in your heart, to bring healing, restoration, joy, and life! And if God does that, it will be cause for a wonderful celebration. With teacups and china. Or paper plates. Whatever. One day, we will all celebrate together. In anticipation and hope, may this little book draw you closer to God's heart—and your own.

CHAPTER ONE

The Heart of a Woman

Sometimes it's hard to be a woman.
—TAMMY WYNETTE

He saw that Fatima's eyes were filled with tears.
"You're crying?"
"I'm a woman of the desert," she said, averting her face.
"But above all, I'm a woman."
—PAULO COELHO

You belong among the wildflowers
You belong in a boat out at sea
You belong with your love on your arm
You belong somewhere you feel free.
—TOM PETTY

Let's do it." Dusk was settling in. The air was cool, fragrant with pine and sage, and the swiftly moving river beckoned. We were camping in the Tetons, and it so happened that our canoe was on top of the car. "Let's put in." John looked at me as if I had lost my mind. In less than twenty minutes night would be upon us and the river and the woods. All would be pitch black. We'd be on the river, alone, with only a general idea of which way to go (down), where to take out (head for the road), and a long walk back to the car. Who knew what dangers lay out there? He looked again at me, looked at our young sons, and then said, "Okay!" We sprang into action.

The evening was stunning. The river's graceful movements caused the water's colors to shift from cobalt to silver to black. No other person was in sight. We had Oxbow Bend to ourselves. In record time we had the canoe in the river; life vests securely fastened, paddles at the ready, boys installed, and off we went, a race to drink as deeply of as much beauty as possible, together.

An old wooden bridge hung low across the river, its broken remains looked as though they would collapse at the next strong breeze. We had to duck to pass underneath. Carefully, we navigated the winding channels of the Snake—John in back, me in front, our three boys in between, full of wonder and delight. As the stars began to come out, we were like the children present at the creation of Narnia—the sky so clear, the stars so close. We held our breath as one fell slowly, slowly across the sky and disappeared.

A beaver slapped the river, the sound like a rifle shot, frightening two ducks into flight, but all we could see between the darkened water and sky were the white ripples of their wake, like synchronized water-skiers. Owls began their nightly calls in the woods above, joined by sandhill cranes along the shore. The sounds were familiar, yet otherworldly. We whispered to one another about each new wonder, as the paddles dipped almost but not quite silently in and out of the water.

Night fell. Time to take out. We planned to go ashore along a cove closest to the road so we wouldn't have to walk too far to find our car. We didn't dare try to take out where we had put in . . . that would require paddling against the current with little ability to see where we were going.

As we drifted toward the bank, a bull moose rose from the tall grasses, exactly where we had planned to come ashore. He was as dark as the night; we could see him only because he was silhouetted against the sky, jagged mountains behind. He was huge. He was gorgeous. He was in the way. Blocking the only exit we had. More people are killed in national parks by moose than by any other animal. Remarkable speed, seventeen hundred pounds of muscle and antlers, and total unpredictability make them dangerous indeed. It would take about two seconds for him to hit the water running and capsize our canoe. We could not pass.

The mood changed. John and I were worried now. There was only one alternative to this way out, now closed to us, and that was paddling back upriver in what had become total darkness. Silently, soberly, we turned the canoe and headed up, searching for the right channel that would keep us out of the main current. We hadn't planned on the adventure taking that turn, but suddenly, everything was required. John must steer with skill; I must paddle with strength. One mistake on our part and the strong current would force the canoe broadside, fill it, and sweep our boys off downriver into the night.

It was glorious.

We did it. He did. I did. We rose to the challenge working together, and the fact that it required all of me, that I was in it with my family and for my family, that I was surrounded by wild, shimmering beauty and it was, well, kind of *dangerous* made the time . . . transcendent. I was no longer Stasi. I was Sacagawea, Indian Princess of the West, a valiant and strong woman.

A Woman's Journey

Then the time came when the risk it took
To remain tight in a bud was more painful
Than the risk it took to blossom.
—Anais Nin

I'm trying to remember when I first knew in my heart that I was no longer a girl, but had become a woman. Was it when I graduated from high school, or college? Did I know it when I married? When I became a mother? I am forty-five years old as I write this, but there remain places in my heart that still feel so very young. As I think back on what would be considered rites of passage in my life, I understand why my journey has felt so unguided, uncertain. The day I started my period, my family embarrassed me at the dinner table by breaking out in song, "This girl is a woman, now . . ." Hmmmm. I didn't *feel* any different. All I felt was mortified that they *knew*. I stared at my plate, suddenly fascinated by corn.

The day I got my first bra, a training bra, the kind with stretchy material over the front, one of my sisters pulled me into the hallway where, to my horror, my father stood at the ready to take my picture. They said I would laugh about it later. (I haven't.) Like so many other women I was left alone to navigate my way through adolescence, through my changing and awakening body, a picture of my changing and awakening heart. No counsel was given for the journey into womanhood. I *was* encouraged, however, to eat less. My father pulled me aside and told me, "No boy will love you if you're fat."

I joined the feminist movement in college, searching, as so many women did in the '70s, for a sense of self. I actually became director of the Women's Resource Center at a liberal state university in California. But no matter how much I asserted my strength and independence as a woman ("hear me roar"), my *heart* as a woman remained empty. To be told when you are young and searching that "you can be anything" is not helpful. It's too vast. It gives no direction. To be told when you are older that "you can do anything a man can do" isn't helpful, either. I didn't want to be a man. What does it mean to be a *woman*?

And as for romance, I stumbled through that mysterious terrain with only movies and music as a guide. Like so many women I know, I struggled alone through the mess of several broken hearts. My last year in college, I fell in love for real, and this young man truly loved me back. John and I dated for two and a half years and then became engaged. As we made wedding plans, my mother gave me a rare bit of counsel, in this case, her marriage advice. It was twofold. First, love flies out the window when there's no pork chop on the table. And second, always keep your kitchen floor clean; it makes the whole house look better. I caught her drift. Namely, that my new position as "wife" centered in the kitchen, making the pork chops and cleaning up after them.

I somehow believed that upon saying, "I do," I would be magically transformed into Betty Crocker. I imagined myself baking fresh bread, looking flushed and beautiful as I removed the steaming loaves from the oven. No matter that I hadn't cooked but five meals in my entire life, I set about preparing dinners, breakfasts even, with determination and zeal. After two weeks of this, I lay on the couch despondent, announcing that I didn't know what was for dinner and that John was on his own. Besides, the kitchen floor was dirty. I had failed.

My story is like most women's stories—we've received all sorts of messages but very little help in what it means to become a woman. As one young woman recently wrote us,

> I remember when I was ten asking myself as well as older females in my life how a woman of God could actually be confident, scandalous and beautiful, yet not portray herself as a feminist Nazi or an insecure I-need-attention emotional whore. How can I become a strong woman without becoming harsh? How can I be vulnerable without drowning myself in my sorrow?

There seems to be a growing number of books on the *masculine* journey—rites of passage, initiations, and the like—many of them helpful. But there has been precious little wisdom offered on the path to becoming a woman. Oh, we know the *expectations* that have been laid upon us by our families, our churches, and our cultures. There are reams of materials on what you *ought* to do to be a good woman. But that is not the same thing as knowing what the journey toward becoming a woman involves, or even what the goal really should be.

The church has not been a big help here. No, that's not quite honest enough. The church has been part of the problem. Its message to women has been primarily "you are here to serve. That's why God created you: to serve. In the nursery, in the kitchen, on the various committees, in your home, in your community." Seriously now—picture the women we hold up as models of femininity in the church. They are sweet, they are helpful, their hair is coiffed; they are busy, they are disciplined, they are composed, and they are *tired.*

Think about the women you meet at church. They're trying to live up to some model of femininity. What do they "teach" you about being a woman? What are they saying to us through their lives? Like we said, you'd have to conclude that a godly woman is . . . tired. And guilty. We're all living in the shadow of that infamous icon, "The Proverbs 31 Woman," whose life is so busy I wonder, when does she have time for friendships, for taking walks, or reading good books? Her light never goes out at night? When *does* she have sex? Somehow she has sanctified the shame most women live under, biblical proof that yet again we don't measure up. Is that supposed to be godly—that sense that you are a failure as a woman?

Unseen, Unsought, and Uncertain

I know I am not alone in this nagging sense of failing to measure up, a feeling of not being good enough *as a woman.* Every woman I've ever met feels it—something deeper than just the sense of failing at what she does. An underlying, gut feeling of failing at who she *is*. *I am not enough*, and, *I am too much* at the same time. Not pretty enough, not thin enough, not kind enough, not gracious enough, not disciplined enough. But too emotional, too needy, too sensitive, too strong, too opinionated, too messy. The result is Shame, the universal companion of women. It haunts us, nipping at our heels, feeding on our deepest fear that we will end up abandoned and alone.

After all, if we were better women—whatever *that* means—life wouldn't be so hard. Right? We wouldn't have so many struggles; there would be less sorrow in our hearts. Why is it so hard to create meaningful friendships and sustain them? Why do our days seem so unimportant, filled not with romance and adventure but with duties and demands? We feel *unseen*, even by those who are closest to us. We feel *unsought*—that no one has the passion or the courage to pursue us, to get past our messiness to find the woman deep inside. And we feel *uncertain*—uncertain what it even means to be a woman; uncertain what it truly means to be feminine; uncertain if we are or ever will be.

Aware of our deep failings, we pour contempt on our own hearts for wanting more. Oh, we long for intimacy and for adventure; we long to be the Beauty of some great story. But the desires set deep in our hearts seem like a luxury, granted only to those women who get their acts together. The message to the rest of us—whether from a driven culture or a driven church—is *try harder*.

The Heart of a Woman

And in all the exhortations we have missed the most important thing of all. We have missed the *heart* of a woman.

And that is not a wise thing to do, for as the Scriptures tell us, the heart is central. "Above all else, guard your heart, for it is the wellspring of life" (Prov. 4:23). Above all else. Why? Because God knows that our heart is core to who we are. It is the source of all our creativity, our courage, and our convictions. It is the fountainhead of our faith, our hope, and of course, our love. This "wellspring of life" within us is the very essence of our existence, the center of our being. Your heart as a woman is the most important thing about you.

Think about it: God created you *as a woman.* "God created man in his own image . . . male and female he created them" (Gen. 1:27). Whatever it means to bear God's image, you do so *as a woman.* Female. That's how and where you bear his image. Your feminine heart has been created with the greatest of all possible dignities—as a reflection of God's own heart. You are a woman to your soul, to the very core of your being. And so the journey to discover what God meant when he created woman in his image—when he created *you* as his woman—that journey begins with your heart. Another way of saying this is that the journey begins with *desire.*

Look at the games that little girls play, and if you can, remember what you dreamed of as a little girl. Look at the movies women love. Listen to your own heart and the hearts of the women you know. What is it that a woman wants? What does she dream of? Think again of women like Tamar, Ruth, Rahab—not very "churchy" women, but women held up for esteem in the Bible. We think you'll find that every woman in her heart of hearts longs for three things: to be romanced, to play an irreplaceable role in a great adventure, and to unveil beauty. That's what makes a woman come alive.

To Be Romanced

I will find you.
No matter how long it takes, no matter how far—I will find you.
—Nathaniel to Cora in *The Last of the Mohicans*

One of my favorite games growing up was "kidnapped and rescued." I know many little girls who played this—or wished they had. To be the beauty, abducted by the bad guys, fought for and rescued by a hero—some version of this had a place in all our dreams. Like Sleeping Beauty, like Cinderella, like Maid Marian, or like Cora in *The Last of the Mohicans*, I wanted to be the heroine and have my hero come for me. Why am I embarrassed to tell you this? I simply loved feeling wanted and fought for. This desire is set deep in the heart of every little girl—and every woman. Yet most of us are ashamed of it. We downplay it. We pretend that it is less than it is. We are women of the twenty-first century after all—strong, independent, and capable, thank you very much. Uh-huh . . . and who is buying all those romance novels?

Think about the movies you once loved, and the movies you love now. Is there a movie for little girls that doesn't have a handsome prince coming to rescue his beloved? *Sleeping Beauty, Snow White, The Little Mermaid.* A little girl longs for romance, to be seen and desired, to be sought after and fought for. So the Beast must win Beauty's heart in *Beauty and the Beast.* So in the gazebo scene in *The Sound of Music*, the Captain finally declares his love to Maria by moonlight and song and then, a kiss. And we sigh.

Isn't something stirred in you when Edward, *finally*, returns at the end of *Sense and Sensibility* to proclaim his love for Elinor? "Then . . . you're not . . . not married?" she asks, nearly holding her breath. "No," he says. "My heart is . . . and always will be . . . yours." Or how about when Friedrich returns for Jo at the end of *Little Women*? Or the sunset scene at the bow of the *Titanic*? And we can't forget *Braveheart*, how William Wallace pursued Murron with flowers and notes and invitations to ride. She is captured by his love, riding off bareback with him in the rain. (Come now. Wouldn't *you* want to ride through the Scottish Highlands with a man like Mel Gibson?)

When John and I began to "date," I had just come out of a three-year relationship that left me wounded, defensive, and gunshy. John and I had been friends for many years, but we never seemed to connect in the romance department. I would like him, and he would want to remain "just friends." He would feel more for me and I would not for him. You get the picture. Until one autumn after he had become a Christian, and I was desperately seeking, our spiritual journeys, and the desires of our hearts, finally met.

John wrote me letters, lots of letters. Each one filled with his love for God and his passion for me, his desire for me. He spent hours carving a beautiful heart out of manzanita wood, then attached it to a delicate chain and surprised me with it. (I still cherish the necklace.) I came out to my car after my waitressing shift ended to find his poetry underneath my windshield. Verses written for me, to me! He loved me. He saw me and knew me and pursued me. I loved being romanced.

When we are young, we want to be precious to someone—especially Daddy. As we grow older, the desire matures into a longing to be pursued, desired, wanted as a woman. "Why am I so embarrassed by the depth of my desire for this?" asked a young friend just the other day. We were talking about her life as a single woman, and how she loves her work but would much rather be married. "I don't want to hang my life on it, but still, I yearn." Of course. You're a woman.

Now, being romanced isn't all that a woman wants, and John and I are certainly not saying that a woman ought to derive the meaning of her existence from whether or not she is being or has been romanced by a man . . . but don't you see that you *want* this? To be desired, to be pursued by one who loves you, to be someone's priority? Most of our addictions as women flare up when we feel that we are not loved or sought after. At some core place, maybe deep within, perhaps hidden or buried in her heart, every woman wants to be seen, wanted, and pursued. We want to be romanced.

An Irreplaceable Role in a Great Adventure

When I was a little girl, I used to love World War II movies. I imagined myself being in them. I dreamed of growing up, braiding my hair, and then tucking it up under my helmet. I planned to disguise my gender so that I could join in. I sensed that the men in these movies were part of something heroic, valiant, and worthy. I longed to be a part of it too. In the depths of my soul, I longed to be a part of something large and good; something that required all of me; something dangerous and worth dying for.

There is something fierce in the heart of a woman. Simply insult her children, her man, or her best friend and you'll get a taste of it. A woman is a warrior too. But she is meant to be a warrior in a uniquely feminine way. Sometime before the sorrows of life did their best to kill it in us, most young women wanted to be a part of something grand, something important. Before doubt and accusation take hold, most little girls sense that they have a vital role to play; they want to believe there is something in them that is needed and needed desperately.

Think of Sarah from *Sarah, Plain and Tall*. A man and his young children need her; their world is not right until she becomes a part of it. She brings her courage and her creativity to the West and helps to tame it. We are awed by the nurses in *Pearl Harbor*, how in the midst of a horrifying assault they bring their courage and strength to rescue the lives of hundreds of men. The women in *The Lord of the Rings* trilogy are valiant and beautiful—women like Arwen, Galadriel, and Éowyn change the fate of Middle Earth. And what about women like Esther and Mary and Ruth? They were biblical characters who had irreplaceable roles in a Great Story. Not "safe" and "nice" women, not merely "sweet," but passionate and powerful women who were beautiful *as* warriors.

Why do I love remembering the story of canoeing in the dark

beauty of the Tetons so much? Because I was needed. *I* was needed. Not only was I needed, but like Arwen, I was irreplaceable. No one else in that canoe could have done what I did.

Women love adventures of all sorts. Whether it be the adventure of horses (most girls go through a horse stage) or white-water rafting, going to a foreign country, performing onstage, having children, starting a business, or diving ever more deeply into the heart of God, we were made to be a part of a great adventure. An adventure that is *shared.* We do not want the adventure merely for adventure's sake but for what it requires of us *for* others. We don't want to be alone in it; we want to be in it *with* others.

Sometimes the idea of living as a hermit appeals to all of us. No demands, no needs, no pain, no disappointments. But that is because we have been hurt, are worn out. In our heart of hearts, that place where we are most *ourselves,* we don't want to run away for very long. Our lives were meant to be lived with others. As echoes of the Trinity, we remember something. Made in the image of a perfect relationship, we are relational to the core of our beings and filled with a desire for transcendent purpose. We long to be an irreplaceable part of a shared adventure.

BEAUTY TO UNVEIL

The King is enthralled by your beauty.
—PSALM 45:11

Lovely little six-year-old Lacey was visiting our ministry outpost the other day, going from office to office, swinging on the doorframe, and asking with a smile, "Would you like to hear my song?" Her faced kissed by the sun with charming freckles, two front teeth missing, and eyes dancing with merriment, who could refuse her? She didn't really care if she was an interruption. I doubt the thought crossed her mind. She sang her newly made-up song about puppies and kitties, fully expecting to be delighted in, then skipped down the hall to grace the occupant of the next office. She was like a ray of summer sun, or, better, a garden fairy, flitting from office to office. She was a little girl in her glory, unashamed in her desire to delight, and be delighted in.

It's why little girls play dress up. Little boys play dress up, too, but in a different way. Our sons were cowboys for years. Or army men. Or Jedi knights. But they never once dressed up as bridegrooms, fairies, or butterflies. Little boys do not paint their toenails. They do not beg to get their ears pierced. (Some teenaged boys do, but that is another story.) Little boys don't play dress up with Mommy's jewelry and high heels. They don't sit for hours and brush each other's hair.

Remember twirling skirts? Most little girls go through a season when they will not wear anything if it does not twirl (and if it sparkles, so much the better). Hours and hours of endless play result from giving little girls a box filled with hats, scarves, necklaces, and clothes. Dime store beads are priceless jewels; hand-me-down pumps are glass slippers. Grandma's nightie, a ballroom gown. Once dressed, they dance around the house or preen in front of a mirror. Their young hearts intuitively want to know they are lovely. Some will ask with words, "Am I lovely?" Others will simply ask with their eyes. Verbal or not, whether wearing a shimmery dress or covered in mud, all little girls want to know. As a young songwriter recently wrote,

> *I want to be beautiful*
> *And make you stand in awe*
> *Look inside my heart*
> *And be amazed*
> *I want to hear you say*

Who I am is quite enough
I just want to be worthy of love
And beautiful.

—BETHANY DILLON, "BEAUTIFUL"

Last summer John and I attended a ball at the beautiful, historic Broadmoor Hotel. It was a stunning affair. Black tie. Candlelight. Dinner. Dancing. You name it. The courtyard where the hors d'oeuvres were served was filled with fresh flowers, flowing fountains, and the music of a gifted pianist. It was an evening long planned for. For weeks—no, *months* ahead of the affair—I, like every other woman who attended, asked the all-important question: "What will I wear?" (As the special night drew closer, I also wondered if it was possible to lose twenty pounds in seven days.)

The evening turned out to be glorious. The weather was perfect. Every detail attended to and lovely. But the highlight by far was the women. Above the sound of the splashing water from the fountains, even above the music that floated through the air, was the sound of delighted exclamations. "You look beautiful!" "You are gorgeous!" "What an amazing dress!" "How lovely you are!" We were delighting in each other's beauty and enjoying our own. We were playing dress up for real and *loving* it.

These women were normal women, women just like you and me. Women you would run into at the bank or the grocery store or the office. Women whose battles against acne have left their faces marked and their souls scarred. Women whose struggle with their weight has been the bane of their lives. Women who always felt their hair was too thin, too thick, too straight, or too curly. Ordinary women, if there is such a thing. But women who, at least for a few hours this night, took the risk of revealing their beauty. Perhaps better, whose beauty was *unveiled*.

Think of your wedding day—or the wedding day you dream

of. How important is your dress as a bride? Would you just grab the first thing in your closet, throw on "any old thing"? A friend of ours is getting married in six months. Now, this young woman has seen her share of boys and heartbreaks. Her tale of beauty has many hurts to it. But as she told us about trying on wedding dresses, and finding just the right dress, the weariness faded away, and she was radiant. "I felt like a princess!" she said, almost shyly. Isn't that what you dreamed of?

One little girl, who is being raised in a home where her feminine heart is welcomed, told her mother about a wonderful dream she had.

My daughter Emma—nearly six years old—came to me all aglow this morning. She lay at my feet on my bed all stretched out as if she hadn't a care in the world. "Mommy," she said, "I had a wonderful dream last night." "What was it about?" I asked. "I was a Queen," she answered. And as she did her cheeks blushed pink. "Really!" I replied. "What happened in your dream?" "I was wearing a long, beautiful dress," she said with hands gesturing downward, flowing. "Was there anything on your head?" I wondered aloud. "Yes, a crown." "Hmmmm, why was that such a wonderful dream?" "I just love feeling that way!" "What way?" And with a sigh she spoke one word . . . "Beauty." (Emma's Dream, as told to her mother)

The desire to be beautiful is an ageless longing. My friend Lilly is in her mideighties. As she descended the stairs of her home one Christmas season, I was captured by her beauty. She was wearing a green corduroy jumper with a white turtleneck that had little candy canes all over it. I said, "Lilly, you look lovely!" Her face lit up, wrinkles and age spots disappearing as she put her hands out at her sides like a ballerina and did a delightful little twirl. She was no longer eighty—she was ageless. God has set eternity in our hearts. The longing to be beautiful is set there as well.

Now, we know that the desire to be beautiful has caused many women untold grief (how many diets have you been on?). Countless tears have been shed and hearts broken in its pursuit. As Janis Ian sang, "I learned the truth at seventeen, that love was meant for beauty queens, and high school girls with clear-skinned smiles." Beauty has been extolled and worshiped and kept just out of reach for most of us. (Do you like having your picture taken? Do you like *seeing* those pictures later? How do you feel when people ask you your age? This issue of beauty runs deep!) For others, beauty has been shamed, used, and abused. Some of you have learned that possessing beauty can be dangerous. And yet—and this is just astounding—*in spite* of all the pain and distress that beauty has caused us as women, the desire remains.

During the midst of a talk I gave on the heart of a woman last year, one of the women in the audience leaned over to a friend and said, "I don't know what this whole thing is about—twirling skirts and all." The words had barely left her mouth when she burst into tears and had to leave the room. Little did she know how deep the desire ran, and how much pain it had caused. Many of us have hardened our hearts to this desire, the desire to be the Beauty. We, too, have been hurt so deeply in this area that we no longer identify with, perhaps even resent, the longing. But it's there.

And it's *not* just the desire for an outward beauty, but more—a desire to be captivating in the depths of *who you are*. Cinderella is beautiful, yes, but she is also good. Her outward beauty would be hollow were it not for the beauty of her heart. That's why we love her. In *The Sound of Music*, the Countess has Maria beat in the looks department, and they both know it. But Maria has a rare and beautiful depth of spirit. She has the capacity to love snowflakes on kittens and mean-spirited children. She sees the handiwork of God in music and laughter and climbing trees. Her soul is Alive. And we are drawn to her.

Ruth may have been a lovely, strong woman, but it is to her unrelenting courage and vulnerability and faith in God that Boaz is drawn. Esther is the most beautiful woman in the land, but it is her bravery and her cunning, good heart that moves the king to spare her people. This isn't about dresses and makeup. Beauty is so important that we'll come back to it again and again in this book. For now, don't you recognize that a woman yearns to be *seen*, and to be thought of as captivating? We desire to possess a beauty that is worth pursuing, worth fighting for, a beauty that is core to who we *truly* are. We want beauty that can be seen; beauty that can be felt; beauty that affects others; a beauty all our own to unveil.

THE HEART OF A MAN

As I (John here) described in *Wild at Heart*, there are three core desires in the heart of every man as well. (If you haven't read that book, you really should. It will open your eyes to the world of men.) But they are uniquely masculine. For starters, every man wants a battle to fight. It's the whole thing with boys and weapons. Over the years our house has become an arsenal—pirate swords, Indian knives, light sabers, six-shooters, paintball markers, "air soft" guns (that name had to have been invented for moms). You name it. Our boys wrestled and hit and slammed one another up against the walls, and that is how they showed *affection!*

And look at the movies men love—*Braveheart, Gladiator, Top Gun, High Noon, Saving Private Ryan.* Men are made for battle. (And ladies, don't you love the heroes of those movies? You might not want to fight in a war, but don't you long for a man who will fight for *you?* To have Daniel Day Lewis look you in the eyes and say, "No matter how long it takes, no matter how far, I will find you"?) Women don't fear a man's strength if he is a good man. In fact, *passivity* might make a man "safe," but it has done untold damage to women in the long run. It certainly did to Eve (more on that later).

Men also long for adventure. Boys love to climb and jump and see how fast they can ride their bikes (with no hands). Just look in your garage—all the gear and go-carts and motorcycles and ropes and boats and stuff. This isn't about "boys and their toys." Adventure is a deeply spiritual longing in the heart of every man. Adventure requires something of us, puts us to the test. Though we may fear the test, at the same time we yearn to be tested, to discover that we have what it takes.

Finally, every man longs for a Beauty to rescue. He really does. Where would Robin Hood be without Marian, or King Arthur without Guinevere? Lonely men fighting lonely battles. You see, it's not just that a man needs a battle to fight. He needs someone to fight *for*. There is nothing that inspires a man to courage so much as the woman he loves. Most of the daring (and okay, sometimes ridiculous) things young men do are to impress the girls. Men go to war carrying photos of their sweethearts in their wallets—that is a metaphor of this deeper longing, to fight for the Beauty. This is not to say that a woman is a "helpless creature" who can't live her life without a man. I'm saying that men long to offer their strength on behalf of a woman.

Now—can you see how the desires of a man's heart and the desires of a woman's heart were at least *meant* to fit beautifully together? A woman in the presence of a good man, a real man, loves being a woman. His strength allows her feminine heart to flourish. His pursuit draws out her beauty. And a man in the presence of a real woman loves being a man. Her beauty arouses him to play the man, it draws out his strength. She inspires him to be a hero. Would that we all were so fortunate.

BY WAY OF THE HEART

The longings God has written deep in your heart are telling you something essential about what it means to be a woman, and the life he meant for you to live. Now we know—many of those desires have gone unmet, or been assaulted, or simply so long neglected, that most women end up living two lives. On the surface we are busy and efficient, professional, even. We are getting by. On the inside women lose themselves in a fantasy world or in cheap novels, or we give ourselves over to food or some other addiction to numb the ache of our hearts. But your heart is still there, crying out to be set free, to find the life your desires tell you of.

You can find that life—if you are willing to embark on
a great adventure.

That is what we are inviting you to. Not to learn one more set of standards you fail to meet. Not toward a new set of rules to live by and things you ought to do. Something far, far better—a journey of the heart. A journey toward the restoration and release of the woman you always longed to be. This book is not about what you ought to do or who you ought to be. It's about discovering who you already are, as a woman. A woman who at her core was made for romance, made to play an irreplaceable role in a shared adventure, and who really does possess a beauty all her own to unveil. The woman God had in mind when he made Eve . . . and when he made *you.* Glorious, powerful, and captivating.

CHAPTER TWO

What Eve Alone Can Tell

Even to see her walk across the room is a liberal education.
—C. S. LEWIS

Suddenly I turned around and she was standing there
With silver bracelets on her wrists and flowers in her hair
She walked up to me so gracefully and took my crown of thorns
Come in, she said I'll give you shelter from the storm.
—BOB DYLAN

My parents named me after St. Anastasia, a woman martyred for her faith in the fifth century, so that every week during Mass, my name would be read aloud when certain saints were commemorated. That's why Stasi is spelled so weirdly. Take off the "Ana" at the beginning and the "a" at the end, and Stasi is what you get. I love it. And there's a deeper reason. I learned about Anastasia while in elementary school. Not St. Anastasia . . . but a princess. The youngest daughter of the last czar of Russia, Anastasia was rumored to have escaped the assassins who murdered the rest of her family. She was a young girl when her family was executed, and it was said that she was still alive, somewhere out there in the world, *incognito*. A true princess in disguise.

Women claimed to be her. One woman in particular was nearly

convincing. Still, Anastasia remained a mystery—a princess lost unto this world, hidden but true. I was intrigued and enamored by Princess Anastasia. I began to read everything I could get my hands on about Russian history. For a reason I could not explain, I felt a kinship with this mysterious princess, a connection to her. I wasn't pretending I was her, but still . . . something deep in my heart whispered that I, too, was more than met the eye. Perhaps I, too, was a part of royalty but my position had been lost. Perhaps I, too, was in disguise. My heart quickened at the thought of being a woman who was once a true princess.

I don't think I'm alone in this. Have you ever wondered why the Cinderella story keeps haunting us? Not only is it a perennial favorite of little girls; women love it too. Think of all the movies made along its themes, movies like *Pretty Woman* and *Ever After* and *A Cinderella Story* and *Maid in Manhattan.* Why is this notion of a hidden princess (and a prince who comes to find her) so enduring? Is there something in our hearts that is trying to speak to us? Is it just fantasy, escapism? Or is there something more?

The desire of a woman's heart and the realities of a woman's life seem an ocean apart. Oh, we long for romance and an irreplaceable role in a great story; we long for beauty. But that's not the life we *have.* The result is a sense of shame. Having listened to the hearts of women for many, many years, both in the context of friendship and in the counseling office, we are struck by how deeply and universally women struggle with their self-worth. "I feel like a household appliance," one woman confessed to us. Now, this is not to say that men don't also wrestle with their sense of worth. But there is something deeper to this struggle for women, and far more universal. And there are reasons for it, reasons unique to Eve and her daughters.

We are reminded of Pascal's metaphor, that our unmet longings and unrequited desires are in fact "the miseries of a dethroned monarch." Mankind is like a king or queen in exile, and we cannot be happy until we have recovered our true state. What would you expect the Queen of a kingdom and the Beauty of the realm to feel when she wakes to find herself a laundress in a foreign land? A woman's struggle with her sense of worth points to something glorious she *was* designed to be. The great emptiness we feel points to the great place we *were* created for. It's true. All those legends and fairy tales of the undiscovered Princess and the Beauty hidden as a maid are more accurate than we thought. There's a *reason* little girls resonate with them so.

Rather than asking, "What should a woman do—what is her role?" it would be far more helpful to ask, "What *is* a woman—what is her design?" and, "Why did God place Woman in our midst?" We must go back to her beginnings, to the story of Eve. Even though we might have heard the story before (we have told it many times), it bears repeating. We clearly haven't learned its lessons—for if we had, men would treat women much, much differently, and women would view themselves in a far better light. So let us start there—with light. With the dawn of the world.

THE CROWN OF CREATION

To understand the creation story you must think of a work of art. Think of the Sistine Chapel, or the Venus de Milo, or Beethoven's Fifth, or of Sarah Brightman and Andre Bocelli singing "Time to Say Good-bye." Creation itself is a great work of art, and all works after it are echoes of the original. How it unfolded and where it reached its climax are mysteries worth unveiling. We will never truly understand women until we understand this. The scene begins in darkness,

Darkness over the deep and God's breath hovering over the waters. (Gen. 1:2 *Alter*)

The breathless moment in the dark before the first notes of a great symphony or concert, a play, or an epic film. All is formless, empty, dark. Then a voice speaks.

"Let there be light." (Gen. 1:3 *Alter*)

And suddenly, there is light, pure light, magnificent light. Its radiance will enable us to see now what is unfolding. The voice speaks again, and again.

"Let there be a vault in the midst of the waters, and let it divide water from water." (Gen. 1:6 *Alter*)

"Let the waters under the heavens be gathered in one place so that the dry land will appear." (Gen. 1:9 *Alter*)

Creation in its early stages begins like any great work of art—with uncut stone or a mass of clay, a rough sketch, a blank sheet of music. "Formless and empty" as Genesis 1:2 has it. Then God begins to fashion the raw materials he has made, like an artist working with the stone or sketch or page before him. Light and dark, heaven and earth, land and sea—it's beginning to take shape. With passion and brilliance the Creator works in large, sweeping movements on a grand scale. Great realms are distinguished from one another and established. Then he moves back over them again for a second pass as he begins to fill in color, detail, finer lines.

"Let the earth grow grass, plants . . . and trees bearing fruit . . ." (Gen. 1:11 *Alter*)

"Let there be lights in the vault of the heavens . . ." (Gen. 1:14 *Alter*)

"Let the waters swarm with the swarm of living creatures and let fowl fly over the earth." (Gen. 1:20 *Alter*)

Forest and meadow burst forth. Tulips and pine trees and moss-covered stones. And notice—the masterpiece is becoming more intricate, more intimate. He fills the night sky with a thousand million stars, and he *names* them, sets them in constellations. Into our world God opens his hand and the animals spring forth. Myriads of birds, in every shape and size and song, take wing—hawks, herons, pelicans. All the creatures of the sea leap into it—whales, dolphins, fish of a thousand colors and designs. Horses, gazelles, buffalo thunder across the plains, running like the wind. It is more astonishing than we could possibly imagine.

From water and stone, to pomegranate and rose, to leopard and nightingale, creation *ascends* in beauty. The plot is thickening, the symphony is building and swelling, higher and higher to a crescendo. No wonder "the morning stars sang together and all the angels shouted for joy" (Job 38:7). A great hurrah goes up from the heavens. The greatest of all masterpieces is emerging. What was once formless and empty is now overflowing with life and color and sound and movement in a thousand variations. Most importantly, notice that each creature is *more* intricate and noble and mysterious than the last. A cricket is amazing, but it cannot compare to a wild horse.

Then something truly astonishing takes place.

God sets his own image on the earth. He creates a being like himself. He creates a son.

The LORD God formed the man from the dust of the ground and breathed into his nostrils the breath of life, and the man became a living being. (Gen. 2:7)

It is nearing the end of the sixth day, the end of the Creator's great labor, as Adam steps forth, the image of God, the triumph of his work. He alone is pronounced the son of God. Nothing in creation even comes close. Picture Michelangelo's *David*. He is . . . magnificent. Truly, the masterpiece seems complete. And yet, the Master says that something is not good, not right. Something is missing . . . and that something is Eve.

> And the Lord God cast a deep slumber on the human, and he
> slept, and He took one of his ribs and closed over the flesh where
> it had been, and the Lord God built the rib He had taken from
> the human into a woman and He brought her to the human.
> (Gen. 2:21–23 *Alter*)

She is the crescendo, the final, astonishing work of God. Woman. In one last flourish creation comes to a finish not with Adam, but with *Eve*. She is the Master's finishing touch. How we wish this were an illustrated book, and we could show you now some painting or sculpture that captures this, like the stunning Greek sculpture of the goddess Nike of Samothrace, the winged beauty, just alighting on the prow of a great ship, her beautiful form revealed through the thin veils that sweep around her. Eve is . . . breathtaking.

Given the way creation unfolds, how it builds to ever higher and higher works of art, can there be any doubt that Eve is the crown of creation? Not an afterthought. Not a nice addition like an ornament on a tree. She is God's final touch, his *pièce de résistance*. She fills a place in the world nothing and no one else can fill. Step to a window, ladies, if you can. Better still, find some place with a view. Look out across the earth and say to yourselves, "The whole, vast world is incomplete without me. Creation reached its zenith in me."

What Does Eve Speak to Us?

The story of Eve holds such rich treasures for us to discover. The essence and purpose of a woman is unveiled here in the story of her creation. These profound, eternal, mythic themes are written not just here in the coming of Eve, but in the soul of every woman after. Woman is the crown of creation—the most intricate, dazzling creature on earth. She has a crucial role to play, a destiny of her own.

And she, too, bears the image of God, but in a way that only the feminine can speak. What can we learn from her? God wanted to reveal something about himself, so he gave us Eve. When you are with a woman, ask yourself, *what is she telling me about God?* It will open up wonders for you.

First, you'll discover that God is relational to his core, that he has a heart for romance. Second, that he longs to share adventures with us—adventures you cannot accomplish without him. And finally, that God has a beauty to unveil. A beauty that is captivating and powerfully redemptive.

Romance and Relationships: The Answer to Loneliness

Man's love is of man's life a thing apart
'Tis a woman's whole existence.

—Byron

Eve is created because things were not right without her. Something was not good. "It is not good for the man to be alone" (Gen. 2:18). This just staggers us. Think of it. The world is young and completely unstained. Adam is yet in his innocence and full of glory. He walks with God. Nothing stands between them. They share something none of us has ever known, only longed for: an unbroken friendship, untouched by sin. Yet something is not good? Something is missing? What could it possibly be? Eve. Woman. Femininity. Wow. Talk about significance.

To be specific, what was "not good" was the fact that the man was "alone." "It is not good for the human to be alone, I shall make him a sustainer beside him" (Gen. 2:18 *Alter*). How true this is. Whatever else we know about women, we know they are relational creatures to their cores. While little boys are killing one another in mock battles on the playground, little girls are negotiating relationships. If you want to know how people are doing, what's going on in our world, don't ask me—ask Stasi. I don't call friends and chat with them on the phone for an hour. I can't tell you who's dating whom, whose feelings have been hurt—ask Stasi.

This is so second nature, so assumed among women, that it goes unnoticed by them. They care more about relationships than just about anything else. Radio talk-show host Dennis Prager reports that when the topic of the day on his show is a "macro issue" like politics or finance, his callers will be Ed, Jack, Bill, and Dave. But when the topic is a "micro issue" involving human relationships, issues like dating or faithfulness or children, his callers will be Jane, Joanne, Susan, and Karen.

We were at a neighborhood Christmas party this past December. It's an annual thing, the only time the neighbors on our street get together. The men pretty quickly became a huddle in the kitchen (near the potato chips), engaged in a passionate debate about . . . concrete. I kid you not. That was our topic of the evening. Concrete driveways. Meanwhile, the women were in the living room talking about sex after menopause.

Most women *define* themselves in terms of their relationships, and the quality they deem those relationships to have. I am a mother, a sister, a daughter, a friend. Or, I am alone. I'm not seeing anyone right now, or my children aren't calling, or my friends seem distant. This is not a weakness in women—it *is* a glory. A glory that reflects the heart of God.

GOD'S HEART FOR RELATIONSHIP

The vast desire and capacity a woman has for intimate relationships tells us of God's vast desire and capacity for intimate relationships. In fact, this may be *the* most important thing we ever learn about God—that he yearns for relationship with us. "Now this is eternal life: that they may know you, the only true God" (John 17:3). The whole story of the Bible is a love story between God and his people. He yearns for us. He *cares*. He has a tender heart.

> But Zion said, "The LORD has forsaken me, the Lord has forgotten me." "Can a mother forget the baby at her breast and have no compassion on the child she has borne? Though she may forget, I will not forget you!" . . . declares the LORD. (Isa. 49:14–15, 18)

> I will give them a heart to know me, that I am the LORD. They will be my people, and I will be their God, for they will return to me with all their heart. (Jer. 24:7)

> O Jerusalem, Jerusalem . . . how often I have longed to gather your children together, as a hen gathers her chicks under her wings, but you were not willing. (Matt. 23:37)

What a comfort to know that this universe we live in is relational at its core, that our God is a tenderhearted God who yearns for relationship with us. If you have any doubt about that, simply look at the message he sent us in Woman. Amazing. Not only does God long *for* us, but he longs to be loved *by* us. Oh, how we've missed this. How many of you see God as longing to be loved by you? We see him as strong and powerful, but not as needing us, vulnerable to us, yearning to be desired. But as I wrote in *Wild at Heart*,

> After years of hearing the heart-cry of women, I am convinced beyond a doubt of this: God wants to be loved. He wants to be a priority to someone. How could we have missed this? From cover to cover, from beginning to end, the cry of God's heart is, "Why won't you choose me?" It is amazing to me how humble, how vulnerable God is on this point. "You will find me," says the Lord, "when you seek me with all your heart" (Jer. 29:13). In other words, "Look for me, pursue me—I want you to pursue me." Amazing. As Tozer says, "God waits to be wanted."

Can there be any doubt that God wants to be sought after? The first and greatest of all commands is to love him (Mark 12:29–30, Matt. 22:36–38). He *wants* us to love him. To seek him with all our hearts. A woman longs to be sought after, too, with the whole heart of her pursuer. God longs to be *desired*. Just as a woman longs to be desired. This is not some weakness or insecurity on the part of a woman, that deep yearning to be desired. "Take me for longing," Alison Krauss sings, "or leave me behind." God feels the same way. Remember the story of Martha and Mary? Mary chose God, and Jesus said that *that* is what he wanted. "Mary has chosen what is better" (Luke 10:42). She chose me.

Life changes dramatically when romance comes into our lives. Christianity changes dramatically when we discover that it, too, is a great romance. That God yearns to share a life of beauty, intimacy, and adventure with us. "I have loved you with an everlasting love" (Jer. 31:3). This whole world was made for romance—the rivers and the glens, the meadows and beaches. Flowers, music, a kiss. But we have a way of forgetting all that, losing ourselves in work and worry. Eve—God's message to the world in feminine form—invites us to romance. Through her, God makes romance a priority of the universe.

So God endows Woman with certain qualities that are essential to relationship, qualities that speak of God. She is inviting. She is vulnerable. She is tender. She embodies mercy. She is also fierce and fiercely devoted. As the old saying goes, "Hell hath no fury like a woman scorned." That's just how God acts when he isn't chosen. "I, the LORD your God, am a jealous God who will not share your affection with any other god!" (Ex. 20:5 NLT). A woman's righteous jealousy speaks of the jealousy of God for us.

Tender and inviting, intimate and alluring, fiercely devoted. Oh yes, our God has a passionate, romantic heart. Just look at Eve.

AN ADVENTURE TO SHARE

While Eve has a glory for relationship, that is *not* all she is essential for. Back in Genesis, when God sets his image bearers on the earth, he gives them their mission:

And God said, "Let us make a human in our image, by our likeness, to hold sway over the fish of the sea and the fowl of the heavens and the cattle and the wild beasts and all the crawling things that crawl upon the earth.

And God created the human in his image,
in the image of God He created him,
male and female He created them.

And God blessed them, and God said to them, "Be fruitful and multiply and fill the earth and conquer it, and hold sway over the fish of the sea and the fowl of the heavens and every beast that crawls upon the earth." (Gen. 1:26–28 *Alter*)

Call it the Human Mission—to be all and do all God sent us here to do. And notice—the mission to be fruitful and conquer and hold sway is given *both* to Adam *and* to Eve. "And God said to *them* . . ." Eve is standing right there when God gives the world over to us. She has a vital role to play; she is a partner in this great adventure. All that human beings were intended to do here on earth—all the creativity and exploration, all the battle and rescue and nurture—we were intended to do *together*. In fact, not only is Eve needed, but she is *desperately* needed.

When God creates Eve, he calls her an *ezer kenegdo*. "It is not good for the man to be alone, I shall make him [an *ezer kenegdo*]" (Gen. 2:18 *Alter*). Hebrew scholar Robert Alter, who has spent years translating the book of Genesis, says that this phrase is "notoriously difficult to translate." The various attempts we have in English are "helper" or "companion" or the notorious "help meet." Why are these translations so incredibly wimpy, boring, flat . . . disappointing? What is a help meet, anyway? What little girl dances through the house singing "One day I shall be a help meet?" Companion? A dog can be a companion. Helper? Sounds like Hamburger Helper. Alter is getting close when he translates it "sustainer beside him."

The word *ezer* is used only twenty other places in the entire Old Testament. And in every other instance the person being described is God himself, when you need him to come through for you *desperately*.

There is no one like the God of Jeshurun, who rides on the heavens to help you . . .

Blessed are you, O Israel! Who is like you, a people saved by the LORD? He is your shield and *helper* and your glorious sword. (Deut. 33:26, 29, emphasis added)

I lift up my eyes to the hills—where does my help come from? My *help* comes from the LORD, the Maker of heaven and earth. (Ps. 121:1–2, emphasis added)

May the LORD answer you when you are in distress; may the name of the God of Jacob protect you. May he send you *help*. (Ps. 20:1–2, emphasis added)

We wait in hope for the LORD, he is our *help* and our shield. (Ps. 33:20, emphasis added)

O house of Israel, trust in the LORD—he is their *help* and shield. O house of Aaron, trust in the LORD—he is their *help* and shield. You who fear him, trust in the LORD—he is their *help* and shield. (Ps. 115:9–11, emphasis added)

Most of the contexts are life and death, by the way, and God is your only hope. Your *ezer*. If he is not there beside you . . . you are dead. A better translation therefore of *ezer* would be "lifesaver." *Kenegdo* means alongside, or opposite to, a counterpart.

You see, the life God calls us to is not a safe life. Ask Joseph, Abraham, Moses, Deborah, Esther—any of the friends of God from the Old Testament. Ask Mary and Lazarus; ask Peter, James, and John; ask Priscilla and Aquila—any of the friends of God in the New Testament. God calls us to a life involving frequent risks and many dangers. Why else would we need him to be our *ezer*? You don't need a lifesaver if your mission is to be a couch potato. You need an *ezer* when your life is in constant danger.

Picture the character Arwen in the mythic motion-picture trilogy, *The Lord of the Rings*. Arwen is a princess, a beautiful and brave elf maiden. She comes into the story in the nick of time to rescue the little hobbit Frodo just as the poisoned wound moving toward his heart is about to claim him.

ARWEN: He's fading. He's not going to last. We must get him to my father. I've been looking for you for two days. There are five wraiths behind you. Where the other four are, I do not know.

ARAGORN: Stay with the hobbits. I'll send horses for you.

ARWEN: I'm the faster rider. I'll take him.

ARAGORN: The road is too dangerous.

ARWEN: I do not fear them.

ARAGORN: (*Relinquishing to her, he takes her hand.*) Arwen, ride hard. Don't look back.

It is she, not the warrior Aragorn, who rides with glory and speed. She is Frodo's only hope. She is the one entrusted with his life and with him, the future of all Middle Earth. She is his *ezer kenegdo*.

That longing in the heart of a woman to share life together as a great adventure—that comes straight from the heart of God, who also longs for this. He does not want to be an option in our lives. He does not want to be an appendage, a tagalong. Neither does any woman. God is essential. He wants us to need him—desperately. Eve is essential. She has an irreplaceable role to play. And so you'll see that women are endowed with fierce devotion, an ability to suffer great hardships, a vision to make the world a better place.

BEAUTY TO UNVEIL

Beauty.

I (John) just let out a deep sigh. That we even need to explain how beauty is so *absolutely essential* to God only shows how dull we have grown to him, to the world in which we live, and to Eve. Far too many years of our own spiritual lives were lived with barely a nod to beauty, to the central role that beauty plays in the life of God, and in our own lives. We held to the importance of truth and goodness. Had you suggested beauty to us, we might have nodded, but not really understood. How could we have missed this?

Beauty is essential to God. No—that's not putting it strongly enough. Beauty is the essence of God.

The first way we know this is through nature, the world God has given us. Scripture says that the created world is filled with the glory of God (Isa. 6:3). In what way? Primarily through its *beauty*. We had a wet spring here in Colorado, and the wildflowers are coming up everywhere—lupine and wild iris and Shasta daisy and a dozen others. The aspens have their heart-shaped leaves again, trembling in the slightest breeze. Massive thunderclouds are rolling in, bringing with them the glorious sunsets they magnify. The earth in summer is brimming with beauty, beauty of such magnificence and variety and unembarrassed lavishness, ripe beauty, lush beauty, beauty given to us with such generosity and abundance it is almost scandalous.

Nature is not primarily functional. It is primarily beautiful. Stop for a moment and let that sink in. We're so used to evaluating everything (and everyone) by their usefulness that this thought will take a minute or two to begin to dawn on us. Nature is not primarily functional. It is primarily *beautiful*. Which is to say, beauty is in and of itself a great and glorious good, something we need in large and daily doses (for our God has seen fit to arrange for this). Nature at the height of its glory shouts, *Beauty is Essential!* revealing that Beauty is the essence of God. The whole world is full of his glory.

Next, there are the visions given to John, who was taken in the Spirit to behold God. As we can only imagine, he finds it hard to put into words what he saw (he keeps using the word *like*, as if grasping to find any comparison that might help us appreciate what he beheld).

> The one sitting on the throne was as brilliant as gemstones—jasper and carnelian. And the glow of an emerald circled his throne like a rainbow . . . In front of the throne was a shiny sea of glass, sparkling like crystal. (Rev. 4:3, 6 NLT)

Is there any doubt that the God John beheld was beautiful *beyond* description? But of course. God must be even more glorious than this glorious creation, for it "foretells" or "displays" the glory that is God's. John describes God as radiant as gemstones, as richly adorned in golds and reds and greens and blues, shimmering as crystal. Why, these are the very things that Cinderella is given—the very things women still prefer to adorn themselves with when they want to look their finest. Hmmm. And isn't that just what a woman longs to hear? "You are radiant this evening. You are absolutely breathtaking."

Saints from ages past would speak of the highest pleasures of heaven as simply beholding the beauty of God, the "beatific vision."

> The reason a woman wants a beauty to unveil, the reason she asks, Do you delight in me? is simply that God does as well. God is captivating beauty. As David prays, "One thing I ask of the LORD, this is what I seek . . . that I may . . . gaze upon the beauty of the LORD" (Ps. 27:4). Can there be any doubt that God wants to be worshipped? That He wants to be seen, and for us to be captivated by what we see? (*Wild at Heart*)

But in order to make the matter perfectly clear, God has given us Eve. The crowning touch of creation. Beauty is the essence of a woman. We want to be perfectly clear that we mean *both* a physical beauty and a soulful/spiritual beauty. The one depends upon and flows out of the other. Yes, the world cheapens and prostitutes beauty, making it all about a perfect figure few women can attain. But Christians minimize it too, or overspiritualize it, making it all about "character." We must recover the prize of Beauty. The church must take it back. Beauty is too vital to lose.

God gave Eve a beautiful form *and* a beautiful spirit. She expresses beauty in both. Better, she expresses beauty simply in who she is. Like God, it is her *essence*.

Stasi and I just spent a weekend together in Santa Fe, New Mexico, which boasts the third largest gathering of art galleries in the world. We love to wander for hours through those galleries and gardens, looking for those works of art that particularly capture us. Toward the afternoon of our second day, Stasi asked me, "Have you seen one painting of a naked man?" The point was startling. After days of looking at maybe a thousand pieces of art, we had not seen one painting devoted to the beauty of the naked masculine form. Not one. (Granted, there are a few examples down through history . . . but only a few.) However, the beauty of Woman was celebrated everywhere, hundreds of times over in paintings and sculptures. There is a reason for this.

For one thing, men look ridiculous lying on a bed buck naked, half-covered with a sheet. It doesn't fit the essence of masculinity. Something in you wants to say, "Get up already and get a job. Cut the grass. Get to work." For Adam is captured best in motion, *doing* something. His essence is *strength in action*. That is what he speaks to the world. He bears the image of God, who is a warrior. On behalf of God, Adam says, "God will come through. God is on the move." That is why a passive man is so disturbing. His passivity defies his very essence. It violates the way he bears God's image. A passive man says, "God will not come through. He is not acting on your behalf."

On the other hand, and bear with us a moment, Eve just doesn't look right in a scene of brutal combat, or chopping a tree down. From time immemorial, when artists have tried to capture the essence of Eve, they have painted her (or photographed her, or sculpted her) *at rest*. There is no agenda here, no social stigmatizing or cultural pressure. This is true across all cultures and down through time. What have the artists seen that we have not? Eve speaks something differently to the world than Adam does. Through her beauty.

Why Beauty Matters

Every experience of beauty points to [eternity].

—Hans Urs von Balthasar

Beauty is powerful. It may be the most powerful thing on earth. It is dangerous. Because it *matters*. Let us try and explain why.

First, beauty *speaks*. Oxford Bishop Richard Harries wrote, "It is the beauty of the created order which gives an answer to our questionings about God." And we do have questions, don't we? Questions born out of our disappointments, our sufferings, our fears. Augustine said he found answers to his questions in the beauty of the world.

> I said to all these things, "Tell me of my God who you are not, tell me something about him." And with a great voice they cried out: "He made us" (Ps. 99:3). My question was the attention I gave to them, and their response was their beauty.

And what does beauty say to us? Think of what it is like to be caught in traffic for more than an hour. Horns blaring, people shouting obscenities. Exhaust pouring in your windows, suffocating you. Then remember what it's like to come into a beautiful place, a garden or a meadow or a quiet beach. There is room for your soul. It expands. You can breathe again. You can rest. It is good. All is well. I sit outside on a summer evening and just listen and behold and drink it all in, and my heart begins to quiet and peace begins to come into my soul. My heart tells me that "All will be well," as Julian of Norwich concluded. "And all manner of things will be well."

That is what beauty says, *All shall be well.*

And this is what it's like to be with a woman at rest, a woman comfortable in her feminine beauty. She is enjoyable to be with. She is lovely. In her presence your heart stops holding its breath. You relax and believe once again that all will be well. And this is also why a woman who is striving is so disturbing, for a woman who is not at rest in her heart says to the world, "All is not well. Things are not going to turn out all right." "Like a fountain troubled," as Shakespeare said, "muddy, ill-seeming, thick, bereft of beauty." We *need* what Beauty speaks. What it says is hard to put into words. But part of its message is that all is well. All will be well.

Beauty also *invites*. Recall what it is like to hear a truly beautiful piece of music. It captures you; you want to sit down and just drink it in. We buy the CD and play it many times over. (This is not visual, showing us that beauty is deeper than looks.) Music like this commands your attention, invites you to come more deeply into it. The same is true of a beautiful garden, or a scene in nature. You want to enter in, explore, partake of it, feast upon it. We describe a great book as "captivating." It draws you in, holds your attention. You can't wait to get back to it, spend time with it. All of the responses that God wants of us. All of the responses a woman wants too. Beauty invites.

Beauty *nourishes*. It is a kind of food our souls crave. A woman's breast is among the loveliest of all God's works, and it is with her breast that she nourishes a baby—a stunning picture of the way in which Beauty itself nourishes us. In fact, a woman's body is one of the most beautiful of all God's creations. "Too much of eternity," as William Blake said, "for the eye of man." It nourishes, offers life. That is such a profound metaphor for Beauty itself. As C. S. Lewis said,

> We do not want merely to see beauty, though, God knows, even that is bounty enough. We want something else which can hardly be put into words—to be united with the beauty we see, to pass into it, to receive it into ourselves. (*The Weight of Glory*)

Beauty *comforts*. There is something profoundly healing about it. Have you ever wondered why we send flowers to the bereaved? In the midst of their suffering and loss, only a gift of beauty says enough, or says it right. After I lost my dearest friend, Brent, there were months when only beauty helped. I could not hear words of counsel. I could not read or even pray. Only beauty helped. There's a touching story told from the hospitals of WWII, where a young and badly wounded soldier was brought in from a hellish week of fighting. After doing what she could for him, the nurse asked if there was anything else she could do. "Yes," he said. "Could you just put on some lipstick while I watch?" Beauty comforts. It soothes the soul.

Beauty *inspires*. After beholding all the marvelous wonders of the creation of Narnia (as told in *The Magician's Nephew* by C. S. Lewis), the cabbie says, "Glory be! I'd have been a better man all my life if I'd known there were things like this!" Or as Jack Nicholson says to Helen Hunt at the end of *As Good As It Gets*, "You make me want to be a better man." Isn't it true? Think of what it might have been like to have been in the presence of a woman like Mother Teresa. Her life was so beautiful, and it called us to something higher. A teacher in the inner city explained to us why he insisted on putting a fountain and flowers in the courtyard of the building. "Because these children need to be inspired. They need to know that life can be better." Beauty inspires.

Beauty is *transcendent*. It is our most immediate experience of the eternal. Think of what it's like to behold a gorgeous sunset, or the ocean at dawn. Remember the ending of a great story. We yearn to linger, to experience it all our days. Sometimes the beauty is so deep it pierces us with longing. For what? For life as it was meant to be. Beauty reminds us of an Eden we have never known, but somehow know our hearts were created for. Beauty speaks of heaven to come, when all shall be beautiful. It haunts us with eternity. Beauty says, *There is a glory calling to you.* And if there is a glory, there is a source of glory. What great goodness could have possibly created this? What generosity gave us this to behold? Beauty draws us to God.

All these things are true for any experience of Beauty. But they are *especially* true when we experience the beauty of a woman—her eyes, her form, her voice, her heart, her spirit, her life. She speaks all of this far more profoundly than anything else in all creation, because she is *incarnate*; she is personal. It flows to us from an immortal being. She is beauty through and through. "For where is any author in the world Teaches such beauty as a woman's eye?" (Shakespeare).

Beauty is, without question, the most *essential* and the most *misunderstood* of all of God's qualities—of all feminine qualities too. We know it has caused untold pain in the lives of women. But even there something is speaking. Why so much heartache over beauty? We don't ache over being geniuses, or fabulous hockey players. Women ache over the issue of beauty—they ache to be beautiful, to believe they are beautiful, and they worry over keeping it if ever they can find it. I was just at Starbucks and overheard the conversation between two women in their late fifties sitting at the table next to mine. The subject? Weight and diets. Their struggle with the issue of beauty.

A woman knows, down in her soul, that she longs to bring beauty to the world. She might be mistaken on how (something every woman struggles with), but she longs for a beauty to unveil. This is not just culture, or the need to "get a man." This is in her heart, part of her design.

BUT WHY A BEAUTY TO UNVEIL?

One of the deepest ways a woman bears the image of God is in her mystery. By "mystery" we don't mean "forever beyond your knowing," but "something to be explored." "It is the glory of God to conceal a matter," says the book of Proverbs, "to search out a matter is the glory of kings" (25:2). God yearns to be known. But he wants to be *sought after* by those who would know him. He says, "You will seek me and find me when you seek me with all your heart" (Jer. 29:13). There is dignity here; God does not throw himself at any passerby. He is no harlot. If you would know him you must love him; you must seek him with your whole heart. This is crucial to any woman's soul, not to mention her sexuality. "You cannot simply have me. You must seek me, pursue me. I won't let you in unless I know you love me."

Is not the Trinity a great mystery? Not something to be solved, but known with ever-deepening pleasure and awe, something to be enjoyed. Just like God, a woman is not a problem to be solved, but a vast wonder to be enjoyed. This is so true of her sexuality. Few women can or even want to "just do it." Foreplay is crucial to her heart, the whispering and loving and exploring of one another that culminates in intercourse. That is a picture of what it means to love her *soul*. She yearns to be known and that takes time and intimacy.

It requires an unveiling. As she is sought after, she reveals more of her beauty. As she unveils her beauty, she draws us to know her more deeply.

Whatever else it means to be feminine, it is depth and mystery and complexity, with beauty as its very essence. Now, lest despair set in, let us say as clearly as we can:

Every woman has a beauty to unveil.

Every woman.

Because she bears the image of God. She doesn't have to conjure it, go get it from a salon, have plastic surgery or breast implants. No, beauty is an *essence* that is given to every woman at her creation.

In Closing

It is very important for you to pause just now and ask yourself, *What did I hear them say?*

We did not say that a woman is prized only for her good looks. We did not say a woman is here merely to complete a man, and therefore a single woman is somehow missing her destiny. What we said was, first, that Eve is the crown of creation. There is something uniquely magnificent and powerful about a woman. We tried to reveal the immeasurable dignity, the holiness of your feminine heart by showing that it is *God* who longs for Romance; it is *God* who longs to be our *ezer*; it is *God* who reveals beauty as essential to life. You are the image bearer of this God. That is why you long for those things too.

There is a radiance hidden in your heart that the world desperately needs.

CHAPTER THREE

Haunted by a Question

She knew treachery,
Rapine, deceit and lust, and ills enow
To be a woman.
—JOHN DONNE

O most pernicious woman!
—WILLIAM SHAKESPEARE

I was standing in line at the grocery store buying a few last-minute items when I heard her. "*That* is the fifteen-item or *less* line, ma'am," she hissed. I looked around wondering who the woman was talking about. My own cart had the required fifteen items. I knew it. I had counted them twice to be sure. When she motioned for her husband to look at the wicked infidel, I saw that she was directing her comments at me! Glancing back I told her that I only had the prescribed fifteen items in my cart. She rolled away in an angry huff.

Soon, she was back in the line next to mine with her husband following. She muttered loudly, accusingly, her voice filled with sarcasm, "She *says* she only has *fifteen* items." At this point, to say I became defensive is a massive understatement. Rage welled up inside me. I felt hot, surprising myself at the intensity of my reaction. Leaning around the candy bars I spoke angrily to her, "I do only have fifteen items, ma'am. Do you want to come over here and *count* them?" Her husband held up his hand signaling me to back off, let it go.

Embarrassed, I quieted and then paid for my order—vindicated that there were indeed only fifteen items in my cart. Oh, how I wanted to show her my receipt. Driving home, still upset, I had to pull over. I mean, I was shaking. I had just gotten into a "fight" with a stranger in the grocery store over the fifteen-item-or-less line. What was going on? What was *that* about?

EVE—WHAT HAPPENED?

Eve was given to the world as the incarnation of a beautiful, captivating God—a life-offering, life-saving lover, a relational specialist, full of tender mercy and hope. Yes, she brought a strength to the world, but not a striving, sharp-edged strength. She was inviting, alluring, captivating.

Is that how you experience the women you know? Is that how people experience you?

Why do so few women have anything close to a life of romance? Loneliness and emptiness are far more common themes—so entirely common that most women buried their longings for romance long ago and are now living merely to survive, get through the week. And it's not just romance—why are most of the relationships of women fraught with hardship? Their friendships, their families, their best friends all seem to have come down with a sort of virus that makes them fundamentally unavailable, leaving a woman lonely at the end of the day. Even when relationships are good, it's never enough. Where does this bottomless pit in us come from?

And women are tired. We are drained. But it's not from a life of shared adventures. No, the weariness of women comes from lives that are crammed with routine, with chores, with hundreds of demands. As Chekov said, "Any idiot can face a crisis. It's the day to day living that wears you out." Somehow, somewhere between our youth and yesterday, *efficiency* has taken the place of adventure. Most women do not feel they are playing an irreplaceable role in a great Story. Oh, no. We struggle to know if we matter at all. If we are at home, we feel ashamed we don't have a "real life" in the outside world. We are swallowed by laundry. If we have a career, we feel as though we are missing out on more important matters like marriage and children. We are swallowed by meetings.

A Woman's Deepest Question

Finally, most women doubt very much that they have any genuine beauty to unveil. It is, in fact, our deepest doubt. When it comes to the issues surrounding beauty, we vacillate between striving and resignation. New diets, new outfits, new hair color. Work out; work on your life; try this discipline or that new program for self-improvement. Oh, forget it. Who cares anyway? Put up a shield and get on with life. Hide. Hide in busyness; hide in church activities; hide in depression. There is nothing captivating about me. Certainly not *inside* me. I'll be lucky to pull it off on the outside.

When I'm going out to a party or gathering, or just to dinner at a friend's house—really, anywhere I am meeting other people—I feel nervous. Often I'm not aware of what I'm truly feeling, but I find myself reapplying lipstick in the car on the way. The more nervous I feel, the more lipstick goes on. Getting close to the destination, I reapply more lipstick. A little closer, on goes some more. Turning into their street, on goes another layer of Sunset Rose or whatever. I clued into this "habit" some time ago when I caught myself putting on another unnecessary layer. What was I doing? *I was afraid*. At least if my makeup looks good, something deep inside me reasoned, maybe I won't be exposed. Found out. Seen.

Every woman is haunted by Eve in the core of her being. She knows, if only when she passes a mirror, that she is not what she was meant to be. We are more keenly aware of our own shortcomings than anyone else. Remembering the glory that was once ours awakens my heart to an ache that has long gone unfulfilled. It's almost too much to hope for, too much to have lost.

You see, every little girl—and every little boy—is asking one fundamental question. But they are very different questions, depending on whether you are a little boy or a little girl. Little boys want to know, *Do I have what it takes?* All that rough and tumble, all that daring and superhero dress up, all of that is a boy seeking to prove that he does have what it takes. He was made in the image of a warrior God. Nearly all a man does is fueled by his search for validation, that longing he carries for an answer to his Question.

Little girls want to know, *Am I lovely?* The twirling skirts, the dress up, the longing to be pretty and to be seen—that is what that's all about. We are seeking an answer to our Question. When I was a girl of maybe five years old, I remember standing on top of the coffee table in my grandparents' living room and singing my heart out. I wanted to capture attention—especially my father's attention. I wanted to be captivating. We all did. But for most of us, the answer to our Question when we were young was "No, there is nothing captivating about you." Get off the coffee table. Nearly all a woman does in her adult life is fueled by her longing to be delighted in, her longing to be beautiful, to be irreplaceable, to have her Question answered, "Yes!"

Why does the Question linger so? Why haven't we been able to find and rest in a wonderful, personal answer for our own hearts?

THE FALL OF EVE

When the world was young and we were innocent—both man and woman—we were naked and unashamed (Gen. 2:25). Nothing to hide. Simply . . . glorious. And while that world was young, and we, too, were young and beautiful and full of life, a corner was turned. Something happened, which we have heard about, but never fully understood, or we would see it playing itself out every day of our lives, and, more important, we would *also* see the chances given to us every day to reverse what happened.

> Now the serpent was the shrewdest of all the creatures the LORD God had made. "Really?" he asked the woman. "Did God really say you must not eat any of the fruit in the garden?"
>
> "Of course we may eat it," the woman told him. "It's only the fruit from the tree at the center of the garden that we are not allowed to eat. God says we must not eat it or even touch it, or we will die."
>
> "You won't die!" the serpent hissed. "God knows that your eyes will be opened when you eat it. You will become just like God, knowing everything, both good and evil."
>
> The woman was convinced. The fruit looked so fresh and delicious, and it would make her so wise! So she ate some of the fruit. She also gave some to her husband, who was with her. Then he ate it, too. (Gen. 3:1–6 NLT)

Alas.

There are no words.

Wail; beat your chest; fall to your knees; let out a long, lonesome howl of bitter remorse.

The woman was convinced. That's it? Just like that? In a matter of moments? Convinced of what? Look in your own heart—you'll see. Convinced that God was holding out on her. Convinced that she could not trust his heart toward her. Convinced that in order to have the best possible life, she must take matters into her own hands. And so she did. She is the first to fall. In disobeying God she also violated her very essence. Eve is supposed to be Adam's *ezer kenegdo*, like one who comes to *save*. She is to bring him life, invite him to life. Instead, she invited him to his death.

Now, to be fair, Adam doesn't exactly ride to her rescue.

> Let me ask you a question: Where is Adam, while the serpent is tempting Eve? He's standing right there: "She also gave some to her husband, who was with her, and he ate it" (3:6). The Hebrew for "with her" means right there, elbow to elbow. Adam isn't away in another part of the forest; he has no alibi. He is standing right there, watching the whole thing unravel. What does he do? Nothing. Absolutely nothing. He says not a word, doesn't lift a finger. [I'm indebted to Crabb, Hudson, and Andrews for pointing this out in *The Silence of Adam*.] He won't risk, he won't fight, and he won't rescue Eve. Our first father—the first real man— gave in to paralysis. He denied his very nature and went passive. And every man after him, every son of Adam, carries in his heart now the same failure. Every man repeats the sin of Adam, every day. We won't risk, we won't fight, and we won't rescue Eve. We truly are a chip off the old block. (*Wild at Heart*)

You can see this play itself out every day. Men, just when we need them to come through for us . . . check out. They disappear, go silent and passive. "He won't talk to me," is many a woman's lament. They won't fight for us.

And women? We tend to be grasping, reaching, controlling. We are often enchanted, like Eve, so easily falling prey to the lies of our Enemy. Having forfeited our confidence in God, we believe that in order to have the life we want, we must take matters into our own hands. And we ache with an emptiness nothing seems able to fill.

THE CURSE

To the woman he said,
> "I will greatly increase your pains in childbearing;
with pain you will give birth to children.
Your desire will be for your husband,
and he will rule over you."

To Adam he said, "Because you listened to your wife and ate from the tree about which I commanded you, 'You must not eat of it,'
> "Cursed is the ground because of you;
through painful toil you will eat of it
all the days of your life.
It will produce thorns and thistles for you." (Gen. 3:16–18)

Now, it would be good for us to give careful attention to all that has unfolded here—especially the curses God pronounced—for the story explains our lives today, east of Eden. For one thing, the curse on Adam cannot be limited *only* to actual thorns and thistles. If that were so, then every man who chooses not to be a farmer gets to escape the curse. Take a white-collar job and you're scot-free. No, the meaning is deeper and the implications are for every son of Adam. Man is cursed with *futility* and *failure*. Life is going to be hard for a man now in the place he will feel it most. Failure is a man's worst fear.

In just the same way, the curse for Eve and all her daughters cannot be limited *only* to babies and marriage, for if that were true then every single woman without children gets to escape the curse. Not so. The meaning is deeper and the implications are for *every* daughter of Eve. Woman is cursed with loneliness (relational heartache), with the urge to control (especially her man), and with the dominance of men (which is not how things were meant to be, and we are not saying it is a good thing—it is the fruit of the Fall and a sad fact of history). [I am also indebted to Dan Allender who first pointed out these insights to me.]

Isn't it true? Aren't your deepest worries and heartaches relational—aren't they connected to some*one*? Even when things are good, is your vast capacity for intimacy ever filled in a lasting way? There *is* an emptiness in us that we continually try to feed. And can't you see how much you need to have things under your control—whether it's a project or a ministry or a marriage? Are you comfortable trusting your well-being to someone else? And haven't you felt "this is a man's world," felt your vulnerability as a woman to be a liability? Most women hate their vulnerability. We are not inviting—we are *guarded.* Most of our energy is spent trying to hide our true selves, and control our worlds to have some sense of security.

When a man goes bad, as every man has in some way gone bad after the Fall, what is most deeply marred is his strength. He either becomes a passive, weak man—strength surrendered—or he becomes a violent, driven man—strength unglued. When a woman falls from grace, what is most deeply marred is her tender vulnerability, beauty that invites to life. She becomes a dominating, controlling woman—or a desolate, needy, mousy woman. Or some odd combination of both, depending on her circumstances.

DOMINATING WOMEN

Think for a moment about the characters of women you dislike—even despise—in movies. (That seems a more charitable place to start—they are, after all, fictional characters.) In *The Horse Whisperer*, Annie MacLean (played by Kristin Scott Thomas) is a sharp, sophisticated New York professional, the editor of a leading women's magazine. She is also an incredibly controlling woman. Annie's daughter is hospitalized in critical condition following a riding accident that takes the life of her best friend, claims her leg, and terribly injures her horse. Understandably, Annie is shaken to the core. The way she handles her crisis is to dominate—the doctors, the nurses, her husband, even her maimed daughter. At one point she notices her daughter's IV bag is running low.

> "You can't leave it to these people."
> (She steps into the hall, apprehends the first nurse coming by.)
> "Excuse me—my daughter needs a new IV."
> "Yes, I know—we have her down . . ."
> "Well I'd like you to take care of it now please."
> ("Please" is a barely veiled threat, more like, "or else." Annie walks back into the room and explains to her embarrassed husband.)
> "You have to stay on top of these people constantly."

She needs no one. She is in charge—"on top of things constantly." She is a woman who knows how to get what she wants. (Some of us might even admire that!) But consider this—there is nothing merciful about her, nothing tender, and certainly nothing vulnerable. She has forsaken essential aspects of her femininity.

There is the despicable Mrs. John Dashwood in *Sense and Sensibility*. John Dashwood's father dies at the beginning of the story, leaving his wife and three daughters to the care of his only son, to whom he has bequeathed his entire estate. But with his dying breath he has commanded that the women be financially provided for through the good will of his son. During the carriage ride home from the funeral, Mrs. Dashwood—the conniving and greedy sister-in-law—spins a web of manipulation around her husband, John, and by the time the ride is over, both mother and sisters are penniless.

Think of Tom Cruise's fiancée at the opening of *Jerry Maguire* (the one who decks him). "I'm not going to let you do this to me, Jerry." Or Rose's mother in *Titanic*. "We have to survive." That line is also said by the horrid mother in *Strictly Ballroom*. And all those villains like Cruella de Ville and Esmeralda ("mirror, mirror on the wall"). Notice also that most of the wicked witches are women. Or stepmothers. Have you ever wondered why it was that for years— until the feminist movement, it might be noted with irony—hurricanes were named after women? Now, sure, a calculating, heartless man makes a frightening villain. But somehow it's even worse when she's a woman.

Fallen Eve controls her relationships. She *refuses* to be vulnerable. And if she cannot secure her relationships, then she kills her heart's longing for intimacy so that she will be safe and in control. She becomes a woman "who doesn't need anyone—especially a man." How this plays out over the course of her life, and how the wounds of her childhood shape her heart's convictions are often a complex story, one worth knowing. But beneath it all, behind it all, is a simple truth: women dominate and control because they fear their vulnerability. Far from God and far from Eden, it seems a perfectly reasonable way to live. But consider also this: "Whatever is not from faith is sin" (Rom. 14:23 NKJV). That self-protective way of relating to others has nothing to do with real loving, and nothing to do with deeply trusting God. It is our gut-level response to a dangerous world.

Now, this is not to say a woman can't be strong. What we are saying is that far too many women forfeit their femininity in order to feel safe and in control. Their strength feels more masculine than feminine. There is nothing inviting or alluring, nothing tender or merciful about them. The archetype would be the infamous Lady

Macbeth, who asks the gods to "unsex her," remove her femininity, so that she can control the fate of the man in her life, and thus secure her own fate.

Controlling women are those of us who don't trust anyone else to drive our cars. Or help in our kitchens. Or speak at our retreats or our meetings. Or carry something for us. Make a decision that is "ours" to make. Suggest a different dress, agenda, restaurant, route. We room alone when we travel. We plan perfect birthday parties for our children. It might look as though we're simply "trying to be a good mom," or a good friend, but what we often do is arrange other people's lives. Controlling women are "the sort of women," as C. S. Lewis said, "who 'live for others.' You can tell the others by their hunted expression."

Controlling women tend to be very well rewarded in this fallen world of ours. We are the ones to receive corporate promotions. We are the ones put in charge of our women's ministries. Can-Do, Bottom-Line, Get-It-Done kinds of women. Women who have never even considered that our Martha Stewart perfectionism might not be a virtue. We have never considered that by living a controlling and domineering life, we are really refusing to trust our God. And it has also never dawned on us that something precious in us is lost. Something the world needs very much from us.

Desolate Women

If on the one side of the spectrum we find that Fallen Eve becomes hard, rigid, and controlling, then on the other side you find women who are desolate, needy, far *too* vulnerable. Women like Ruth Jamison in *Fried Green Tomatoes*. She is naive, lost, bereft of any sense of self. She falls under the abuse of a bad man and hasn't the will to get herself out. Take out the abusive situations and you have a woman like Marianne in *Sense and Sensibility*, who is far too willing to give herself over to an untrustworthy man. She is desperate to be loved. And she ends up heartbroken.

Desolate women are ruled by the aching abyss within them. These are the women who buy books like *Men Who Hate Women and the Women Who Love Them* and *Women Who Love Too Much* and *Co-dependent No More*. They are consumed by a hunger for relationship. A friend of ours, a young man in his twenties, was lamenting how much his mom calls him. "How often does she call?" I asked, thinking he might be exaggerating. "Every day." Whoa. Every day is too often for a mother to call her adult son who has left home.

Sadly, desolate women also tend to hide their true selves. We are certain that if others really knew us, they wouldn't like us—and we can't risk the loss of a relationship. They might be women like Tulah in *My Big Fat Greek Wedding*, who literally hides behind the counter when an attractive man walks in her café. She hides her beauty behind big glasses (in a day of contacts?), baggy outfits, frumpy hair—all chosen because they do *not* draw attention. Because she does not believe she is worth paying attention to. Desolate women might be busy women who hide behind, "There's so much work to do." That's how the women in my (Stasi's) family learned to handle life.

My mother grew up in rural North Dakota. Her parents spent all the long years of their lives in the same house that she was born in. Her father was a cold, detached man. He never spoke the words that little girls long—no, *need*—to hear. She never heard from her father that she was precious or pretty. He never even told her that he loved her. Not once. After one terrible day at school, she ran home with tears streaming down her face. Deeply hurt, sobbing, with her little girl's heart broken, she risked running to her father for comfort. He pushed her away.

Her mother, she knew, loved her. Yet she was not expressive, either. But she was clean . . . and incredibly controlling. My mom was not allowed to have friends over to her house to play because they would mess it up. The living room was not for living in but for looking at. All objects in the house belonged to her mother, and it was not okay to touch them or, heaven forbid, move them. You can imagine, there was no romping in that house. There was no fort building or game playing or dashing about. It was orderly, neat . . . and soul killing.

One day, while her mother was entertaining guests, my own mother was upstairs using the bathroom. A very good girl, she washed her hands in the sink after first closing the drain as she was taught. Then a very bad thing happened. She could not get the water to turn off, or the plug to open. Both were stuck. In a house of rigid rules, one did not interrupt one's parents while they spoke with adults. My mom didn't know what to do. The water ran on. Something was broken. My mom was responsible. She was going to get into trouble. The water was rising. So my mom did what we all do when we are afraid that we have failed and are going to be found out. She hid.

She left the bathroom, went into her bedroom, crawled under her bed, and there she stayed—hiding, cowering, afraid. The water in the sink finally overflowed, spilling onto the floor, soaking through the ceiling, and dripped onto her mother's guests. Oops. Her hiding, like our hiding, only made matters worse.

I was afraid because I was naked; so I hid. (Gen. 3:10)

One of my college roommates was a very pretty young woman, but she didn't know it. She was kind and funny, intelligent and bright. She was also timid and afraid. She spent her evenings camped out in front of her personal television. Declining invitations to go out, she stayed in, night after night, the weeks turning into months. Wounded, heartbroken in ways I could only guess at, she found solace in sitcoms and snacks. Too insecure to enter into the world, she hid from it instead, venturing out only to attend classes and restock her food supply.

Hiding women are those of us who never speak up at a Bible study or PTA council or any kind of meeting. Who, when we pass a beautiful dress in a window, say to ourselves, *I could never wear that.* We stay busy at family gatherings and parties we can't avoid. We'd rather go to a movie than out to dinner with a friend. We don't initiate sex with our husbands ever. We dismiss every compliment. We relinquish major decisions to others.

Like Eve after she tasted the forbidden fruit, we women hide. We hide behind our makeup. We hide behind our humor. We hide with angry silences and punishing withdrawals. We hide our truest selves and offer only what we believe is wanted, what is safe. We act in self-protective ways and refuse to offer what we truly see, believe, and know. We will not risk rejection or looking like a fool. We have spoken in the past and been met with blank stares and mocking guffaws. We will not do it again. We hide because we are afraid. We have been wounded and wounded deeply. People have sinned against us and we have sinned as well. To hide means to remain safe, to hurt less. At least that is what we think. And so by hiding, we take matters into our own hands. We don't return to our God with our broken and desperate hearts. And it has never occurred to us that in all our hiding, something precious is also lost—something the world needs from us so very, very much.

INDULGING

Whether we tend to dominate and control, or withdraw in our desolation and hide, still . . . the ache remains. The deep longings in our hearts as women just won't go away. And so we indulge.

We buy ourselves something nice when we aren't feeling appreciated. We "allow" ourselves a second helping of ice cream or a super-sized something when we are lonely. We move into a fantasy world to find some water for our thirsty hearts. Romance novels (a billion-dollar industry), soap operas, talk shows, gossip, the myriads of women's magazines all feed an inner life of relational dreaming and voyeurism that substitutes—for a while—for the real thing. But none of these really satisfy, and so we find ourselves trying to fill the remaining emptiness with our little indulgences (we call them "bad habits"). Brent Curtis calls them our "little affairs of the heart." They are what we give our hearts away to instead of giving them to the heart of God.

We daydream our way through traffic. We imagine meaningful conversations or difficult ones where we speak brilliantly. We spend our imaginations on cheap novels, picturing ourselves as the beautiful heroine—winsome, pursued, beautiful. We are endlessly creative in our indulgent pursuits, our adulteries of the heart. Certainly, we do not limit ourselves to just one.

Take a moment and consider yours. Where do you go instead of to God when the ache of your heart begins to make itself known? Spending too much money, gambling, bingeing, purging, shopping, drinking, working, cleaning, exercising, too many movies, sitcoms, talk shows, even our negative emotions can become indulgences. When we camp our hearts in self-doubt, condemning thoughts, or even shame because those emotions have become familiar and comfortable, we are faithlessly indulging rather than allowing our deep ache to draw us to God.

Unfortunately, our indulgences make us feel better . . . for a while. They seem to "work," but really only increase our need to indulge again. This is the nightmare of addiction. But it goes far beyond "drugs." We give our hearts to all sorts of other "lovers" that demand our attention, demand we indulge again. We taste something that we think is good, our longings cease to ache, for a minute, but later we find ourselves empty once more, needing to be filled again and again.

The ways we find to numb our aches, our longings, and our pain are not benign. They are malignant. They entangle themselves in our souls like a cancer and, once attached, become addictions that are both cruel and relentless. Though we seek them out for a little relief from the sorrows of life, addictions turn on us and imprison us in chains that separate us from the heart of God and others as well. It is a lonely prison of our own making, each chain forged in the fire of our indulgent choice. Yet, "Our lovers have so intertwined themselves with our identity that to give them up feels like personal death . . . We wonder if it is possible to live without them" *(The Sacred Romance).*

We need not be ashamed that our hearts ache; that we need and thirst and hunger for much more. All of our hearts ache. All of our hearts are at some level unsatisfied and longing. It is our insatiable need for more that drives us to our God. What we need to see is that all our controlling and our hiding, all our indulging, actually serves to separate us from our hearts. We lose touch with those longings that make us women. And the substitutes never, ever resolve the deeper issue of our souls.

EVE'S LINGERING FEAR

Every woman knows now that she is not what she was meant to be. And she fears that soon it will be known—if it hasn't already been discovered—and that she will be abandoned. Left alone to die a death of the heart. That is a woman's worst fear—abandonment. (Isn't it?) Rather than turning back to God, reversing the posture that brought about our crisis in the first place (which Eve set in motion and we have repeated *ad nauseum*), we continue down that path by doing what we can to secure ourselves in a dangerous and unpredictable world.

And down in the depths of our hearts, our Question remains. Unanswered. Or rather, it remains answered in the way it was answered so badly in our youth. "Am I lovely? Do you see me? Do you want to see me? Are you captivated by what you find in me?" We live haunted by that Question, yet unaware that it still needs an answer.

When we were young, we knew nothing about Eve and what she did and how it affected us all. We do not first bring our heart's Question to God, and too often, before we can, we are given answers in a very painful way. We are wounded into believing horrid things about ourselves. And so every woman comes into the world set up for a terrible heartbreak.

CHAPTER FOUR

Wounded

These words are razors to my wounded heart.
—WILLIAM SHAKESPEARE

Ah, Women, that you should be moving
here, among us, grief-filled,
no more protected than we.
— RAINER MARIA RILKE

*C*arrie woke on her sixth birthday to the sound of singing.

She knew instantly that it was her birthday, *her very own day.* She opened her eyes to discover that balloons had been tied all around her bed—a colorful canopy. The celebration had begun. Her mom was standing by her bedside, holding a coffee cake with a lit candle in it, and her dad was there, too, and both of them were singing, "Haaappy Biiirthdaaay tooo youuuu!" Oh, unhindered joy! Squeals of delight, kisses, hugs, and "hoorays!" welcomed her into this day—just as she had been welcomed into the world six years earlier. Her father whispered to his "Little Princess" that he loved her. Her mother reminded her again of how happy she was to have such a wonderful daughter.

There was no doubt about it—this little girl was delighted in.

Life for Carrie was closer to life as God meant it to be for every little girl. She *knew* that her father cherished her. She was his princess. He was her knight in shining armor. He wanted to spend time with her. Carrie *knew* her mother loved her and wanted her. Hers was a world where her father protected her, her mother nurtured her, and she was *enjoyed.* This is the soil a girl's soul was meant to grow in; this was the garden her young heart was meant to flourish within. Every little girl should be so loved, so welcomed—seen, known, treasured. From this place she can become a strong and beautiful and confident woman.

If only that was how it was for all of us.

MOTHERS, FATHERS, AND THEIR DAUGHTERS

For many centuries women lived in close fellowship with other women—gathering at the well, down by the river, preparing meals—many occasions for femininity to just sort of naturally pass from older women to younger women. Our intuition, our keen eye for relationship, our ability to grasp matters of the heart made any sort of formal "passage" into femininity unnecessary. Nowadays those opportunities are nearly gone. When we meet as women, it tends to be in high-stress situations—corporate meetings with deadlines, ministry meetings with agendas, PTA meetings with concerns. The home is the only place left for this vital transmission of feminine identity.

The way you see yourself now, as a grown woman, was shaped early in your life, in the years when you were a little girl. We learned what it meant to be feminine—and *if* we were feminine—while we were very young. Women learn from their mothers what it means to be a woman, and from their fathers the value that a woman has—the value *they* have as a woman. If a woman is comfortable with her own femininity, her beauty, her strength, then the chances are good that her daughter will be too.

From our mothers we receive many, many things, but foremost among them are mercy and tenderness. When my sons were young and got hurt, their dad would say something encouraging like, "Cool wound." I would hold them close and tend their injuries. Our mothers show us the merciful face of God. We are nurtured at their breasts and cradled in their arms. They rock us to sleep and sing us lullabies. Our youngest years are lived within the proximity of their apron strings, and they care for us in all the meanings of the word. When we get hurt, moms kiss us and make it better.

Moms are a bit of a mystery to young girls but also belong to a club that one day they will join. So little girls watch and learn. Little girls learn how to live as women by watching their mothers, their grandmothers, and taking in a myriad of lessons from all the adult women in their lives.

But as for our Question—that is primarily answered by our fathers.

Carrie's father was present to her. He *saw* her, and he made it clear that he enjoyed what he saw. He lavished affection on her with his presence, his protection, his delight. There were names he had for her—secret names only they knew. He called her "Kitten" and "Princess" and "Little Darlin'." Little girls need the tender strength of their fathers. They need to know that their daddies are strong and will protect them; they need to know that their fathers are *for* them. Above all, a little girl learns the answer to her Question from her father.

Remember twirling skirts? We twirled in front of our daddies. We wanted to know, "Daddy, am I lovely? Am I captivating?" From them, we learn that we are delighted in, that we are special . . . or that we are not. How a father relates to his daughter has an enormous effect on her soul—for good or for evil. Numerous studies have shown that women who report a close and caring relationship with their fathers, who received assurance, enjoyment, and approval from them during childhood, suffer less from eating disorders or depression and "developed a strong sense of personal identity and positive self-esteem" (Margo Maine, *Father Hunger*).

But Adam fell, as did Eve, and the fathers and mothers most of us had continued the sad story. They did not provide the things our hearts needed in order to become lovely, vulnerable, strong, adventurous women. No, most of our stories share a different theme.

WOUNDED HEARTS

My friend Sandy was raised in a home with an abusive father and a weak mother. If her dad hit her mother, her mom felt she must have done something to deserve it. When the hitting turned to beating, Sandy came between her father and mother. She tried to stop her dad's cruelty and protect her mom, taking the beating herself. And when her father began to sexually abuse Sandy and her sister, her mother did nothing to protect them; she simply turned away. Sandy's dad began to bring his drunken friends home with him so that they, too, could sexually abuse his daughters. Again and again, her mother did nothing. What do you suppose Sandy learned about masculinity, about femininity, about herself?

Tracey was her parents' second daughter and did not share in the easy intimacy that she saw existed between her father and older sister. She was uncertain about herself, about his feelings for her. On a trip to a water park, she wanted to play with her dad. She asked him to go down the slide with her in the children's area. He didn't want to. Tracey *implored* him to come with her. She was afraid to go alone. She wanted him to catch her at the bottom. She wanted to do it together. He acquiesced. She gleefully walked with him hand in hand to the slide, and he went down first as planned. But it was a children's slide, not made for a grown man, and when he came to the end of it, the water was too shallow for him. The force of his landing broke his foot. He was in pain *and it was her fault.* That's what her young heart believed. What does that teach a girl about her desires, and about the effect of her life upon others?

A woman we'll call Melissa told us, "My wound was delivered at birth. My parents had a three-year-old little girl and desperately wanted to have a little boy." You know what's coming. "They brought me to my father for the first time, and he wouldn't even hold me because he was so disappointed I was a girl. I spent my childhood trying to be a good son and prayed each night before I went to bed that I would grow a penis and turn into a boy. Each morning I would wake and check and cry because I was still a girl." How we wish we could say that stories like this are rare. The nature of the assault might be different, but the reason there are so many struggling women is because there were *so* many wounded girls.

Rachel had a verbally abusive father. "I heard everything I suppose a girl can hear. 'You are so stupid. You are worthless. I wish we never had you. You make me sick.' I grew up believing I was repulsive to my father, and I did everything I could to try and make him like me." Abusive fathers are a too common horror. Accomplices, broken mothers, are a painful reality. Both of them often come from abusive homes where the cycle of pain is ruthlessly repeated and passed down.

You cannot be alive very long without being wounded. The sun rises, the stars follow their courses, the waves roll in crashing against the rocks, and we are wounded. Broken hearts cannot long be avoided in this beautiful yet dangerous world we live in. This is not Eden. Not even close. We are not living in the world our souls were made for. Something's rotten in the state of Denmark and in our own backyards as we journey through the unknown terrain of the moments and months that make up our lives.

Take a deep look into the eyes of anyone and behind the smile or the fear, you will find pain. And most people are in more pain than even they realize. Sorrow is not a stranger to any of us, though only a few have learned that it is not our enemy either. Because we are the ones loved by the God, the King of kings, Jesus himself, who came to heal the brokenhearted and set the captives free, we can take a look back. We can take his hand and remember. We *must* remember if we would not be held prisoner to the wounds and the messages we received growing up.

The horror that abusive fathers inflict on their daughters wounds their souls to their very core. It breaks their hearts, ushers in shame and ambivalence and a host of defensive strategies that shut down our feminine hearts. But at least the assault is obvious. The pain that absent fathers inflict on their daughters is damaging as well, but far harder to see.

Passive Fathers

As I said earlier, fallen men tend to sin in one of two ways. Either they become driven, violent men—their strength gone bad—or they become passive, silent men (like Adam)—their strength gone away. Lori's dad was present physically but absent in every other way. A little girl longs to be delighted in by her father, but Lori's dad wanted nothing to do with her. When her elementary school held a father/daughter dinner, Lori *desperately* wanted to go. She invited her father to go; she begged him to come, but he would have none of it. Lori assumed he did not want to attend because he was ashamed to be seen with her.

As many little girls do, Lori took ballet lessons. She felt so pretty in her pink leotard and tights that she asked her father to please come and watch her dance. He answered her that when she was on a real stage, then he would come and watch her. As you might know, dance classes end with recitals, and so, the day did come for little Lori to dance on a real stage. Pretty in her shimmering costume, she eagerly waited and watched for her father's arrival. He never came. Later that evening, friends of her father had to carry him into the house, as he was too drunk to walk in by himself. Lori's little-girl heart believed her dad had gone to great lengths in order to *not* have to watch her dance.

Debbie's father had an affair when she was young. He was not a violent man. There was nothing abusive about him. In fact, he was kind to her mother, as he was to Debbie and her sister. They shared Sunday dinners, went to church together. Only, he chose another woman. "I guess she wasn't enough to keep him," Debbie said about her mother. Then she paused and said, "I guess *we* weren't enough to keep him." Affairs and divorces strike at a woman's worst fear—abandonment. They wound, not just the mothers, but the daughters as well. The wound is sometimes hard to identify because the transgression seemed to be against his wife. But what does the girl learn?

Laurie's father divorced her mom when she was six. In her heart, *she* was being divorced too. "They tried to talk about it with us, make it all sound mature and like it's going to be okay. But he was leaving." Her father did come for visits, to take her on outings. But she learned to hide her heart from him. "I learned to cry underwater. When we'd go to the pool, I didn't want him to see me crying." So many girls learned something like this. Hide your vulnerability. Hide your heart. You aren't safe.

My (Stasi's) father was absent much of my youth. He was a man raised to be strong and good. In his era, the primary way a man showed his strength was in providing for his family. But like too many men, my dad worked long hours to provide for us financially and yet withheld the thing we needed most: himself. My father was a traveling salesman. He would be gone for two weeks at a time and then be home for a weekend before leaving again. An alcoholic, he often stopped off at the local bar or a neighbor's house to hoist a few before coming in our door. When he was present physically, he was absent emotionally, preferring the company of the television and a glass of scotch to his family. He did not know me. I guess he didn't want to.

MOTHER WOUNDS

My mom was a lonely and busy woman. When I was young I had to pretend to be sick in order to get a morsel of her attention. I remember sitting at the kitchen table as a young girl watching her make dinner when she told me for the first time—but not the last—how devastated she was when she learned that she was pregnant with me. I was the last of four children, too close together, and she wept when she found out that I, the daughter of an overwhelmed mother and an absent father, was coming. You can imagine the effect that has on a little girl's heart.

Chris's dad was not absent. He was, in fact, deeply involved in her life. She loved horses, had a natural gift with them, and he was very proud of her gift. He delighted in her riding abilities and encouraged her to pursue them. He was present and supportive, he enjoyed her immensely, and she knew it. And her mother was jealous. She told Chris that her father was just "using" her. She spewed venom that her father was cruel, selfish, and the attention he paid her was wrong. Chris's mom belittled her love for horses, never came to a class or a show, and told Chris that in her riding clothes she looked manly and unattractive.

Dana's mother locked her and her brother and sisters in the closet for hours on end, day after day growing up. Her mother did not trust them nor trust babysitters, so would put them in the closet while she went "out." They were not a poor family, but her mother bought the cheapest food possible—stale, moldy bread, overripe fruit. Her mother would feed her little, then wake her up at midnight and demand that she eat a piece of bruised, ugly fruit. She was twenty-one years old when she tasted her first perfectly ripe pear and wondered over the flavor.

The stories of these women and the wounds they received as little girls are all different, but the effects of their wounds and the effects of ours are painfully similar. Some of these stories are extreme. The feelings of uncertainty and worthlessness that they breed are not. What was your childhood like? What lessons did you learn as a little girl? What did your parents want from you? Were you delighted in? Did you know to the core of your being that you were loved, special, worth protecting, and wanted? I pray so. But I know that for many of you, the childhood you were meant to have, the childhood you wanted to have, is a far cry from the childhood you *did* have.

THE MESSAGES OF OUR WOUNDS— AND HOW THEY SHAPED US

The wounds that we received as young girls did not come alone. They brought messages with them, messages that struck at the core of our hearts, right in the place of our Question. Our wounds strike at the core of our *femininity*. The damage done to our feminine hearts through the wounds we received is made much worse by the horrible things we believe about ourselves as a result. As children, we didn't have the faculties to process and sort through what was happening to us. Our parents were godlike. We believed them to be right. If we were overwhelmed or belittled or hurt or abused, we believed that somehow it was because of *us*—the problem was with *us*.

Lori's father didn't come to her recital. He went out of his way not to come. That was the wound. The *message* was that she wasn't worth his time. She wasn't worth loving. She felt that there must be something terribly wrong with her. Tracey's father broke his foot.

She invited him into her heart's desire, and the result was disaster. The message? "Your desire for relationship causes pain. You are just 'too much.'" And she has spent the last twenty years trying not to be too much, trying to minimize her desires, trying to find some way to be loved without being too much. She has lopped off huge parts of her wonderful personality as a result.

Debbie's father had an affair. What made it confusing was that in many ways, he was a good man. The message that settled in her heart as a teenage girl was, *You'd better do more than she did or you won't keep your man.* After this came a young man who pursued Debbie, and then left for no apparent reason. We've known this beautiful young woman for several years now, and one thing has puzzled us—why is she always working on her life? Why is she always trying to "improve" herself? Debbie is always looking for something to work on. Prayer, exercise, financial responsibility, a new hair color, more discipline. Why is she trying so hard? Doesn't she know how amazing she is? What makes her search so frustrating is that she doesn't know what *is* wrong with her. She simply fears that somehow she is not enough.

Many women feel that, by the way. We can't put words to it, but down deep we fear there is something terribly wrong with us. If we were the princess, then our prince would have come. If we were the daughter of a king, he would have fought for us. We can't help but believe that if we were different, if we were *better*, then we would have been loved as we so longed to be. It must be us.

Sandy's father abused her, and her mother turned away. It wrought great evil upon her soul. In all that she learned, Sandy came away with two basic things about femininity: To be a woman is to be powerless; there's nothing good about vulnerability; it's just "weakness." And to be feminine is to draw unwanted intimacy to yourself. Does it surprise you that she doesn't want to be feminine? Like so many sexually abused women, Sandy finds herself in the awful bind of longing for intimacy (she was created for that) but fearing to look the least bit alluring to a man. She's settled for the persona of the "competent and efficient professional woman," kind but guarded, never too attractive and never, ever, in need and never "weak."

Some women who were sexually abused choose another path. Or, perhaps more honestly, they find themselves compulsively heading in another direction. They never received love, but they did experience some sort of intimacy through the sexual abuse, and now they give themselves over to one man after another, hoping to somehow heal the wrongful sexual encounters with sex that has love to it.

Melissa's mother was a wicked woman who beat her children with a wooden rod. "I was absolutely terrified of my mother," she confessed. "She seemed psychotic and would play evil mind games. Most of the time we never really knew why we were getting beat. My father did nothing. One thing I did know was that with every blow my hatred for her deepened. She turned my sister into a fragile mush of a person, and I vowed she would never do that to me. I vowed that I would be tough, hard, like a rock." This she became, well into her adult life.

The vows we make as children are very understandable—and very, very damaging. They shut our hearts down. They are essentially a deep-seated agreement with the messages of our wounds. They act as an agreement with the verdict on us. "Fine. If that's how it is, then that's how it is. I'll live my life in the following way . . ."

It's taken a lot of years for me to sort through the wounds and messages that shaped my life. It's been a journey for growing clarity, understanding, and healing. Just last night, as John and I talked about this chapter, I began to realize more clearly what the message of my wounds has been. My mom was overwhelmed with the prospect of having another child—me. The message that landed in my heart was that I was overwhelming; my presence alone caused sorrow and pain. From a father who didn't seem to want to know me or be with me, I got the message, "You don't have a beauty that captivates me. You are a disappointment."

When I was a little girl, I would hide in the closet. No one was looking for me; it was just that I felt safer in there. I began this hiding when I was ten years old—the same year that my family fell apart. We had been living in Kansas in a neighborhood that was everything you would want a neighborhood to be. My sisters, brother, and I played with the neighborhood kids. No one had fences back then, and all was open range. And school was a place we flourished. I was voted "Citizen of the Year." My oldest sister was chosen as a foreign exchange student and was supposed to go to France. My next sister was the star of the school play. My brother was popular and won awards for achievement. You get the picture. It was good.

And then, we moved (the result of a promotion for my father), and it was like an atom bomb went off in our family. We had a huge support system in Kansas, much larger and stronger than we had realized. Friends, neighbors, teachers, all were holding us up. When we moved, we no longer had that support, and my family was not strong enough on its own; we fell down like a house of cards. Though my father no longer traveled as often, he worked long hours, often leaving the house before we arose and coming home long after we had fallen asleep. I would think he was away on a business trip far from home when in reality he was just an hour's drive away. Dad was an alcoholic and was also diagnosed as bipolar, so when he was home, you never knew which father you were going to get. Would it be the happy dad or the raging father?

Our home was no longer a refuge but became a battleground. Meals together often ended with angry words and hot tears. My father's drinking increased, matched only by my mother's escalating pain and resentment. When they were together, barbs flew through the air like poison darts. In an effort to escape, my brother stole a car and tried to drive back to Kansas where life was good. My mother left to stay with her parents for a while, and one of my sisters ran away. Going out to dinner with my father one night, he had too much to drink and began flirting with the waitress, asking for her phone number. It was all too much for my young, lonely heart. Back home, I went to the medicine cabinet and swallowed all the pills I thought necessary to end my life and my pain. I woke the next morning, grateful that I hadn't died, but keenly aware that my world was no longer safe.

And so, I made a vow. Somewhere in my young heart, without even knowing I was doing it or putting words to it, I vowed to protect myself by never causing pain, never requiring attention. My job in the family was to be invisible, to cause no waves. If I upset things at all, surely this ship would sink. So I began to hide. I hid my needs, my desires, my very heart. I hid my true self. And when it was all too much, I hid in the closet.

Fast-forward fourteen years. I am now a newlywed, married to a strong and forthright husband who is not afraid of confrontation, welcomes it even. We would be sitting at the kitchen table and if the conversation became tense, I was out of there. He would come looking for me. "Stasi, where are you?" Where was I? I was hiding in the closet. Literally.

I was embarrassed by my young behavior, felt foolish about my seeming inability to talk maturely through a disagreement. But I had never seen it done, and I didn't know how. John's slightest disappointment in something I had done triggered my unhealed heart. It took many, many months for John's love and reassurance to begin to penetrate my frightened heart. I still remember the first time we were in the middle of a "disagreement," and I was able to stay with him in the room. It took all of my will to keep one foot in the room while the other straddled the doorway of the bathroom, ready to retreat into contrived safety. It was a turning point. I've never hidden *in that way* again.

I did, however, begin to put on weight faster than you would think humanly possible. Unconsciously, I had found a new way to hide. I feared from the start of my marriage that at my core I was—and would always be—a disappointment to John; that it was simply a matter of time before he realized it. (The message of my wound.) The wounded little girl inside thought it would be better to hide. And my hiding, like your hiding, made things much, much worse. John and I have had many years of pain. As Jesus said, she who seeks to save her life will lose it (Matt. 16:25). *The vows we make and the things we do as a result of our wounds only make matters worse.*

WOUNDED FEMININITY

As a result of the wounds we receive growing up, we come to believe that some part of us, maybe every part of us, is marred. Shame enters in and makes its crippling home deep within our hearts. Shame is what makes us look away, so we avoid eye contact with strangers and friends. Shame is that feeling that haunts us, the sense that if someone really knew us, they would shake their heads in disgust and run away. Shame makes us feel, no, *believe*, that we do not measure up—not to the world's standards, the church's standards, or our own.

Others seem to master their lives, but shame grips our hearts and pins them down, ever ready to point out our failures and judge our worth. We are lacking. We know we are not all that we long to be, all that God longs for us to be, but instead of coming up for grace-filled air and asking God what he thinks of us, shame keeps us pinned down and gasping, believing that we deserve to suffocate. If we were not deemed worthy of love as children, it is incredibly difficult to believe we are worth loving as adults. Shame says we are unworthy, broken, and beyond repair.

Shame causes us to hide. We are afraid of being truly seen, and so we hide our truest selves and offer only what we believe is wanted. If we are a dominating kind of woman, we offer our "expertise." If we are a desolate kind of woman, we offer our "service." We are silent and do not say what we see or know when it is different from what others are saying, because we think we must be wrong. We refuse to bring the weight of our lives, who God has made us to be, to bear on others out of a fear of being rejected.

Shame makes us feel very uncomfortable with our beauty. Women are beautiful, every single one of us. It is one of the glorious ways that we bear the image of God. But few of us believe we are beautiful, and fewer still are comfortable with it. We either think we don't have any beauty or if we do, that it's dangerous and bad. So we hide our beauty behind extra weight and layers of unnecessary makeup. Or we neutralize our beauty by putting up protective, defensive walls that warn others to keep their distance.

AN UNHOLY ALLIANCE

Over the years we've come to see that the only thing *more* tragic than the things that have happened to us is what we have done with them.

Words were said, painful words. Things were done, awful things. And they shaped us. Something inside of us *shifted*. We embraced the messages of our wounds. We accepted a twisted view of ourselves. And from that we chose a way of relating to our world. We made a vow never to be in that place again. We adopted strategies to protect ourselves from being hurt again. A woman who is living out of a broken, wounded heart is a woman who is living a self-protective life. She may not be aware of it, but it is true. It's our way of trying to "save ourselves."

We also developed ways of trying to get something of the love our hearts cried out for. The ache is there. Our desperate need for love and affirmation, our thirst for some taste of romance and adventure and beauty is there. So we turned to boys or to food or to romance novels; we lost ourselves in our work or at church or in some sort of service. All this adds up to the women we are today. Much of what we call our "personalities" is actually the mosaic of our choices for self-protection plus our plan to get something of the love we were created for.

The problem is our plan has nothing to do with God.

The wounds we received and the messages they brought formed a sort of unholy alliance with our fallen nature as women. From Eve we received a deep mistrust in the heart of God toward us. Clearly, he's holding out on us. We'll just have to arrange for the life we want. We will control our world. But there is also an ache deep within, an ache for intimacy and for life. We'll have to find a way to fill it. A way that does not require us to trust anyone, especially God. A way that will not require vulnerability.

In some ways, this is every little girl's story, here in this world east of Eden.

But the wounds don't stop once we are grown up. Some of the most crippling and destructive wounds we receive come much later in our lives. The wounds that we have received over our lifetimes have not come to us in a vacuum. There is, in fact, a *theme* to them, a pattern. The wounds you have received have come to you for a purpose from one who knows all you are meant to be and fears you.

CHAPTER FIVE

A Special Hatred

❧

All who hate me whisper about me,
imagining the worst for me.
—PSALM 41:7 NLT

Take away this murdherin' hate, an' give us
Thine own eternal love.
—SEAN O'CASEY

*T*he storm is over now. And Stasi is weeping. She had poured so much love and care into her garden over the years. Many, many hours lovingly given to creating a place of remarkable beauty. Special choices were made; seedlings transplanted with care, fertilizing, mulching, weeding. She pruned and watered and sprayed for aphids. She moved plants, replaced them, looking for the right feel to it all. The result was stunning. People would walk up our path, stop, and just behold—it was so lovely. Wild roses, lavender and delphiniums, fountain grasses, Shasta daisies—more color and texture than I could describe. A place of rest and solace, a refuge from the world. A whiff of Eden.

Until tonight.

The hail began about 6 p.m. At first, it didn't seem that threatening. Summer brings a few hail showers each year in the Rockies, pea-sized balls lasting only about ten minutes. The hail this time began the size of marbles; after fifteen minutes it began to come in the size of golf balls, pouring down like Noah's flood turned to ice. For forty minutes it came, relentlessly, stripping branches off trees, laying waste to all living things like some Old Testament plague. And when it finally passed on over the mountain, Stasi's garden was destroyed.

I stood looking out the window in shock and grief. Summer is so short here; there are just a few months even to enjoy flowers and greenery. But this—this was an *assault*. Beauty ravaged beyond recognition. As we talked about the devastation, both of us turned in our thoughts . . . to Eve. This ruin of a garden is a picture, a terribly fitting metaphor of what has happened to the Crown of Creation. How much more the grief and how much greater the loss when it is the life and heart of a woman.

Yes, women have fallen from grace. Yes, they have been wounded. But in order to understand the lingering doubts in your own heart regarding your femininity, in order to understand why it is so rare to encounter a truly alive and vibrant woman, you must hear more of the story.

FURTHER ASSAULT

By the time I was a teenager—a girl becoming a young woman—I had pretty much divorced myself from my family. My oldest sister had moved to Europe. (She went for a three-month "vacation." She stayed seven years. That tells you something about what life was like in our home.) My brother had moved out, as had my other sister. I was left at home to finish high school. My parents began to give me some of the attention I craved as a girl, but it was too little, too late. My heart had already checked out. It was well hidden. Before them I lived the life of "smart and good student." Out of sight I lived quite another life.

I used alcohol and drugs to numb the pain of my wounds. And, as so many other young women do whose hearts have been badly missed or intentionally wounded by their fathers, I turned to boys, then to men for love. At least, I convinced myself, I was wanted for *something*, if only for a night.

I went to Europe my last summer of college. I was enamored by the ancient beauty I experienced as well as by my boundless freedom. But a young, rebellious, unwise woman set loose with a Eurail Pass and a bleeding heart attracted cruel attention. While traveling through Italy, I was sexually assaulted, and although I was furious at the man, deep in my heart I felt somehow worthy of assault. I believed that I had brought it on myself. I agreed with the enemy of my soul that I was a horrid person, and that I deserved only pain. Later, in the south of France, I unwittingly put myself in a dangerous position. After enjoying a few too many drinks at a local bar, my girlfriend and I accepted a ride back to the hotel from the men we had been drinking with. You must be shaking your head as you read this, knowing what was coming. I am. Their offered ride did not lead us back to the hotel, but instead to a private location where I was raped.

After the assault, I went into a state of shock. I remember discovering new bruises and scrapes with a sense of unbelief. But I was not enraged; I was terrified. I felt indignation toward my violators—but deeper, a sense of shame and self-loathing. I wanted to be a good woman. I wanted to be a valiant woman. I wanted to be a strong woman. But I felt nothing of the kind. I bought and wore a necklace I loved. It was the symbol for woman with a fist in the middle. I wore the necklace as a proud feminist to show my independence and strength—and I hid in my hotel room. I was terrified of men and terrified of my beauty. Beauty was dangerous. I believed it had attracted the assaults; it had caused me unspeakable pain and with it, as too many women know, unrelenting shame.

When I returned to school, I told my boyfriend what had happened to me. His response was, "You probably deserved it." We had, as you can tell, an abusive relationship. He was verbally abusive and angry. I received no compassion from him, no words of comfort. He wasn't even angry at my assailants. The messages from my childhood wounds were painfully reinforced. Hide your heart. You are a disappointment. You are worthless. No one cares. No one wants to care. You are alone.

If you will listen carefully to any woman's story, you will hear a theme: the assault on her heart. It might be obvious as in the stories of physical, verbal, or sexual abuse. Or it might be more subtle, the indifference of a world that cares nothing for her but *uses* her until she is drained. Forty years of being neglected damages a woman's heart, too, dear friends. Either way, the wounds continue to come long after we've "grown up," but they all seem to speak the same message. Our Question is answered again and again throughout our lives, the message driven home into our hearts like a stake.

Melissa was the young girl we told you about whose mother beat her with a two-by-four. She eventually got out of the house, at the age of nineteen.

I married a man who was going to be a youth pastor. I thought I had to marry this man since I was so repulsive and would never get another chance. No one else would want me. I was a virgin when I married and [loved] giving myself to my husband as the ultimate gift. The morning after we were married, I snuggled close to my husband and began to kiss him. He pushed me away and told me he wasn't in the mood. After our wedding night we didn't have sex again for over a week. He didn't touch me or even seem the least bit interested in me. I was devastated! And again my question was answered the exact same way.

As women we tend to feel that "it must be me." That's the effect of our early wounds. "Something is fundamentally wrong with me." So many women feel that way. (Why are we working so hard to improve ourselves? Or why do we keep so busy that the issues of our hearts never have to come to the surface?) We also feel that we are essentially alone. And that somehow the two are related. We believe we are alone because we are not the women we should be.

We don't feel worthy of pursuit. So we hang a "do not disturb" sign on our personalities, send a "back off" message to the world. Or we desperately seek pursuit, losing all self-respect in an emotional and physical promiscuity. We don't feel that we are irreplaceable, so we try and make ourselves useful. We don't believe we are beautiful, so we work hard to be outwardly beautiful *or* we "let ourselves go" and hide behind a persona that has no allure. We try so hard, and in so many ways, to protect our hearts from further pain.

WHAT IS REALLY GOING ON HERE?

> I was sleeping when the attack on Disa started. I was taken away by the attackers, they were all in uniforms. They took dozens of other girls and made us walk for three hours. During the day we were beaten and they were telling us: "You, the black women, we will exterminate you, you have no god." At night we were raped several times. The Arabs guarded us with arms and we were not given food for three days. (Sudanese Woman, quoted in *Amnesty International report*)

The story of the treatment of women down through the ages is not a noble history. It has noble moments in it, to be sure, but taken as a whole, women have endured what seems to be a special hatred ever since we left Eden. The story we just cited is but one of thousands coming not just out of the Sudan, but from many war-torn countries like it. Sexual assault is a far too common theme in these "civil" wars. Now, we don't have a political ax to grind, and Stasi's days as a militant feminist are long past. All that aside, what do you make of the degradation, the abuse, and the open assault that women around the world have endured—are enduring even now?

Up until about seventy years ago, little girls born in China who were not left by the side of the road to die (boys are the preferred child) often had their feet bound to keep them small. Small feet were a sign of feminine beauty and were prized by would-be husbands. They were also crippling, which is quite possibly another reason why men thought them a good thing. Women who had their feet bound as children hobbled in pain throughout their lives, unable to walk freely or quickly. Although the practice was outlawed in the 1930s, it continued long after.

You might know that through the thousands of years of Jewish history recorded in the Old Testament, Jewish women were considered property with no legal rights (as they were and are in many cultures). They were not allowed to study the Law, nor to formally educate their children. They had a segregated place in the synagogue. It was common practice for a Jewish man to add to his morning prayers, "Thank you, God, for not making me a Gentile, a woman, or a slave."

A Chinese proverb says that "a woman should be like water; she should take no form and have no voice." An Indian proverb says, "Educating a woman is like watering your neighbor's garden," meaning, of course, that educating a woman is both foolish and a waste of time. In Hinduism, a woman has less value than a cow. In Islam, a woman requires three men to verify her story in court in order for her testimony to be valid. Her testimony, her worth, is one third of a man's.

The story goes well beyond the denial of education and legal rights. Clitoridectomy is the removal, or circumcision, of the clitoris. A painful, horrible practice, female genital mutilation continues today and is performed on girls when they reach about five years old. Done primarily in Africa, the surgery is often performed in the wilderness with the use of a sharp rock. Infections are common. Sometimes the girl dies. A woman is forever maimed, never able to enjoy sexual pleasure—and that is the point. A sexually aware woman is thought to be dangerous. Femininity must be controlled.

Sexual violence against women is rampant throughout the world. It is also rampant against little girls. More than one million *girls* are sold into the sex trade every year. Dear God—what is to account for the systemic, often brutal, nearly universal assault on femininity? Where does this *come* from? Do not make the mistake of believing that "men are the enemy." Certainly men have had a hand in this, and will have a day of reckoning before their Maker. But you will not understand this story—or *your* story—until you begin to see the actual Forces behind this and get a grip on their motives.

Where does this hatred for women, seen all over the world, come from? Why is it so *diabolical*?

A Special Hatred

> For we are not fighting against people made of flesh and blood,
> but against the evil rulers and authorities of the unseen world,
> against those mighty powers of darkness who rule this world, and
> against wicked spirits in the heavenly realms. (Eph. 6:12 NLT)

The assault on femininity—its long history, its utter viciousness—cannot be understood apart from the spiritual forces of evil we are warned against in the Scriptures. This is not to say that men (and women, for they, too, assault women) have no accountability in their treatment of women. Not at all. It is simply to say that no explanation for the assault upon Eve and her daughters is sufficient unless it opens our eyes to the Prince of Darkness and his special hatred of femininity.

Turn your attention again to the events that took place in the Garden of Eden. Notice—who does the Evil One go after? Who does Satan single out for his move against the human race? He could have chosen Adam . . . but he didn't. Satan went after Eve. He set his sights on *her*. Have you ever wondered why? It might have been that he, like any predator, chose what he believed to be the weaker of the two. There is some truth to that. He is utterly ruthless. But we believe there is more. Why does Satan make Eve the focus of his assault on humanity?

You may know that Satan was first named Lucifer, or Son of the Morning. It infers a glory, a brightness or radiance unique to him. In the days of his former glory he was appointed a guardian angel. Many believe he was the captain of the angel armies of God. The guardian of the glory of the Lord.

> "You were the model of perfection,
> full of wisdom and perfect in beauty.
> You were in Eden,
> the garden of God;
> every precious stone adorned you:
> ruby, topaz and emerald,
> chrysolite, onyx and jasper,
> sapphire, turquoise and beryl.
> Your settings and mountings were made of gold;
> on the day you were created they were prepared.
> You were anointed as a guardian cherub,
> for so I ordained you.
> You were on the holy mount of God;
> you walked among the fiery stones." (Ezek. 28:12–14)

Perfect in beauty. That is the key. Lucifer was gorgeous. He was breathtaking. And it was his ruin. Pride entered Lucifer's heart. The angel came to believe he was being cheated somehow. He craved the worship that was being given to God for himself. He didn't merely want to play a noble role in the Story; he wanted the Story to be about *him*. He wanted to be the star. He wanted the attention, the adoration for himself. ("Mirror, Mirror, on the wall . . .")

> Your heart became proud
>> on account of your beauty,
> and you corrupted your wisdom
>> because of your splendor. (Ezek. 28:17)

Satan fell *because* of his beauty. Now his heart for revenge is to assault beauty. He destroys it in the natural world wherever he can. Strip mines, oil spills, fires, Chernobyl. He wreaks destruction on the glory of God in the earth like a psychopath committed to destroying great works of art.

But *most* especially, he hates Eve.

Because she is captivating, uniquely glorious, and he cannot be. She is the incarnation of the Beauty of God. More than anything else in all creation, she embodies the glory of God. She allures the world to God. He hates it with a jealousy we can only imagine.

And there is more. The Evil One also hates Eve because she gives life. Women give birth, not men. Women nourish life. And they also bring life into the world soulfully, relationally, spiritually—in everything they touch. Satan was a murderer from the beginning (John 8:44). He brings death. His is a kingdom of death. Ritual sacrifices, genocide, the Holocaust, abortion—those are his ideas. And thus Eve is his greatest human threat, for she brings life. She is a lifesaver and a life giver. Eve means "life" or "life producer."

"Adam named his wife Eve, because she would become the mother of all the living" (Gen. 3:20).

Put those two things together—that Eve incarnates the Beauty of God *and* she gives life to the world. Satan's bitter heart cannot bear it. He assaults her with a special hatred. History removes any doubt about this. Do you begin to see it?

Think of the great stories—in nearly all of them, the villain goes after the Hero's true love. He turns his sights on *the Beauty*. Magua goes after Cora in *The Last of the Mohicans*. Longshanks goes after Murron in *Braveheart*. Commodus goes after Maximus's wife in *Gladiator*. The Witch attacks Sleeping Beauty. The stepsisters assault Cinderella. Satan goes after Eve.

This explains an awful lot. It is not meant to scare you. Actually, it will shed so much light on your life's story, if you will let it. Most of you thought the things that have happened to you were somehow *your fault*—that you deserved it. If only you had been prettier or smarter or done more or pleased them, somehow it wouldn't have happened. You would have been loved. They wouldn't have hurt you.

And most of you are living with the guilt that somehow it's your fault you aren't more deeply pursued now. That you do not have an essential role in a great adventure. That you have no beauty to unveil. The message of our wounds nearly always is, "This is because of you. This is what you deserve." It changes things to realize that, no, it is because you are *glorious* that these things happened. It is because you are a major threat to the kingdom of darkness. Because you uniquely carry the glory of God to the world.

You are hated *because* of your beauty and power.

On a Human Level

I (John) have a confession to make: I didn't want to coauthor this book.

Oh, I thought it *ought* to be written. It needed to be written. I just didn't want to be the one to do it. I knew it would require me to enter into the world of women—and into *my* woman's world—in a far deeper way than daily life requires of me. To do any sort of justice to a book for women would require me to go deeper, listen even more carefully, study, delve into the mystery (okay—bloody mess) of a woman's soul. Part of me just didn't want to go there. I had what felt like an allergic reaction. Pull back. Withdraw.

I was keenly aware of this going on inside me, and I felt like a jerk. But I also knew enough about myself and about the battle for a woman's heart that I needed to explore this ambivalence. What is this thing in me—and in most men—that just doesn't want to go deep into a woman's world? *You are too much. Too hard. It's too much work. Men are simpler. Easier.* And isn't that just the message you've lived with all your life as a woman? "You're too much, and not enough. You're just not worth the effort." (And why is it such an effort? There must be something wrong with you.)

Now, part of a man's fundamental reluctance to truly dive into the world of a woman comes from a man's deepest fear, failure. Oh, he may joke about "the differences of men and women," Mars and Venus and all that. But the truth is, he is afraid. He fears that having delved into his woman's world, he won't have what it takes to help her there. That is his sin. That is his cowardice. And because of her shame, most of the time a man gets away with it. Most marriages (and long-term dating relationships) reach this sort of unspoken settlement. "I'm not coming any closer. This is as far as I'm willing to go. But, I won't leave, and that ought to make you happy." And so there is this sort of détente, a cordial agreement to live only so close.

The effect is that most women feel alone.

Some of this is simply selfishness on the part of men. Lord knows men are selfish and self-centered. When Eve was first assaulted, Adam didn't do jack squat. Men sin through violence and through *passivity*. It's that plain and simple . . . and ugly.

But there is something else. There is something even more diabolical at work here. We had an amazing meeting a few months ago that proved to be—for me at least—a surprise unveiling of this mystery.

Stasi and I had gathered with the men and women in our ministry who do the men's and women's retreats. The men's team wanted to offer our counsel and support and prayer to the women's team for their upcoming event. It was a chance for the women—and each of them are really, really amazing women—to just sort of open their hearts to us and process how things were going.

Our gathering moved rather quickly from external kinds of issues—how long the sessions should be and logistical stuff like that—to the internal world of the women's team themselves. As we began to talk more intimately, something started coming over me. Just a sense, an inexplicable but strong impression.

Back off.

That's what I felt. No one said it; nothing they were doing implied it; it wasn't a voice in my head. Just a very strong impression. I wasn't sure where it was coming from, but this strong "reluctance," this sense of *maybe we shouldn't press further into this*, this feeling of just *back off* was growing in me, or over me, every moment we moved more deeply into their lives. With every step we took *toward* their hearts, I felt a stronger impression to end the conversation, withdraw, bail out. Watching this unfold, I knew I was onto something big.

I knew that, as a man, this *wasn't* my heart's true desire toward these women. I love them. I want to fight for them. I have many times. I knew as well it could not be *their* heart's desire. They invite our engagement. So I interrupted the flow of conversation with what seemed like an unrelated question to the women: "Do you feel alone in this?" Silence. Then tears, deep tears, from some deep place within each of them. "Yes," they all said. "We do." But I knew it was more than about the retreats. "Do you feel like that in your lives, too, I mean, just generally, as a woman?" "Yes, absolutely. I feel alone most of the time."

Now, you must understand that each of these women have deep and meaningful relationships in their lives. I knew that if *they* feel alone, my God—what must every other woman feel as well? And this strong message of *back off*—if we feel that after years of fighting for them, what must all the other guys out there feel? I bet they haven't ever identified it, or put words to it, but I'll guarantee they've felt it . . . and probably just thought it was what they, or their woman, or both of them wanted.

Back off, or, *Leave her alone,* or, *You don't really want to go there—she'll be too much for you* is something Satan has set against every woman from the day of her birth. It's the emotional and spiritual equivalent of leaving a little girl by the side of the road to die. And to every woman he has whispered, *You are alone,* or, *When they see who you really are, you will be alone,* or, *No one will ever truly come for you.*

Take a moment. Quiet your heart and ask yourself, "Is this a message I have believed, feared, lived with?" Not only do most women fear they will ultimately be abandoned by the men in their lives—they fear it from other women as well. That they will be abandoned by their friends, and left alone. It's time to reveal this pervasive threat, this crippling fear, this terrible lie.

I'm reminded of a scene from *The Two Towers*, the second film in *The Lord of the Rings* trilogy. It takes place in the land of Rohan, in the hall of the king, in the chambers of the lovely Éowyn. She is the king's niece, the only Lady of the court. Her dearest cousin, Théodred, the son of the king, has just died from wounds he received in battle. She is grieving her loss when Wormtongue—supposed counselor to the king but a treacherous, vile creature—slinks into her chambers and begins to weave his spell around the unprotected maiden.

WORMTONGUE: O . . . he must have died sometime during the night. What a tragedy for the king to lose his only son and heir. I understand his passing is hard to accept. Especially now that your brother has deserted you. [Wormtongue arranged for his banishment.]

ÉOWYN: Leave me alone, snake!

WORMTONGUE: O, but you are alone. Who knows what you have spoken to the darkness in bitter watches of the night when all your life seems to shrink, the walls of your bower closing in about you. A hushed, tremulsome, wild thing. (*He takes her face in his hand.*) So fair . . . and so cold. Like a morning with pale spring, still clinging to winter's chill.

ÉOWYN: (*Finally pulling away from his clutch.*) Your words are poison.

Oh, but you are alone. This is the way of the Evil One toward you. He plays upon a woman's worst fear: Abandonment. He arranges for her to be abandoned, and he puts his spin on every event he can to make it seem like abandonment.

THERE IS HOPE

I am not letting men off the hook. God knows we have a lot more repenting to do. I *am* saying that you won't begin to understand the long and sustained assault on femininity, on women, until you see it as part of something much larger. The most wicked force the world has ever known. The Enemy bears a special hatred for Eve. If you believe he has any role in the history of this world, you cannot help but see it.

The Evil One had a hand in all that has happened to you. If he didn't arrange for the assault directly—and certainly human sin has a large enough role to play—then he made sure he drove the message of the wounds home into your heart. He is the one who has dogged your heels with shame and self-doubt and accusation. He is the one who offers the false comforters to you in order to deepen your bondage. He is the one who has done these things in order to prevent your restoration. For that is what he fears. He fears who you are; what you are; what you might become. He fears your beauty and your life-giving heart.

Now listen to the voice of your King. This is God's heart toward you:

For Zion's sake I will not keep silent,
     for Jerusalem's sake I will not remain quiet,
till her righteousness shines out like the dawn [*until you shimmer*],
     her salvation like a blazing torch.
The nations will see your righteousness,
     and all kings your glory [*your beauty*];
you will be called by a new name
     that the mouth of the LORD will bestow.
You will be a crown of splendor in the LORD's hand [*the crown of creation*],
     a royal diadem in the hand of your God.
No longer will they call you Deserted,
     or name your land Desolate.
But you will be called Hephzibah [*my delight is in her*],
     and your land Beulah [*married*];

for the LORD will take delight in you,
and your land will be married.
As a young man marries a maiden [*he pursues her, romances her*] . . .
as a bridegroom rejoices over his bride [*you are lovely*],
so will your God rejoice over you. (Isa. 62:1–5, emphasis added)

"But all who devour you will be devoured;
all your enemies will go into exile.
Those who plunder you will be plundered;
all who make spoil of you I will despoil.
But I will restore you to health and heal your wounds,"
declares the LORD,
"because you are called an outcast,
Zion for whom no one cares." (Jer. 30:16–17)

You really won't understand your life as a woman until you understand this:

You are passionately loved by the God of the universe.
You are passionately hated by his Enemy.

And so, dear heart, it is time for your restoration. For there is One greater than your Enemy. One who has sought you out from the beginning of time. He has come to heal your broken heart and restore your feminine soul. Let us turn now to him.

CHAPTER SIX

Healing the Wound

I didn't know just what was wrong with me,
Till your love helped me name it.
—ARETHA FRANKLIN

Down those old ancient streets,
Down those old ancient roads,
Baby there together we must go
Till we get the healing done.
—VAN MORRISON

*J*ust an hour ago, a hummingbird was trapped in our garage.

They come here to Colorado in the summer, to mate and nest and to feast upon the flowers that fill our garden. We love to watch them zipping around, hovering, performing acrobatics in the air. First they go straight up, up, up for thirty feet or so, like a helicopter or like those whirligigs we played with as kids, then plunge straight down as fast as they can, pulling out of a nosedive at the last possible moment to race back up and do it again. Then again. They are playfulness squeezed into a tiny size.

If you get a closer look, these delicate little birds shimmer like emeralds, bright green breasts no bigger than your thumb but glittering like the crown jewels. Others have deep brilliant red throats that glisten in the sun like rubies. They are like living rainbows, flying around our backyard—something out of a fairy tale. Carefree, lovely reminders of God. And then, today, one mistook the open garage door for a new passageway, and once she flew in, she couldn't find her way back out. Poor little thing. She became increasingly panicked as she careened against a window, desperately trying to get back to the world she could see before her, blocked by some invisible shield.

My son Blaine went in to rescue her. His brother Sam's been able to get a few other captives to rest on the end of a long stick, which he then takes out the door and, *whoosh,* off they go into life. But this one panicked even further, making a mad dash across the garage toward another window she perceived as a way out. She crashed against the window at full speed and fell to the floor. Blaine picked her up with a pair of gloves on his hands and took her outside to see if he could revive her. For about fifteen minutes things didn't look good, but then she came back to life and flew away.

What struck me was the compassion and concern we all felt for the rescue of this little jewel. The whole family dropped what we were doing and got involved. (Didn't you feel bad for her as I told her tale?) Now, Jesus said, don't you think God cares just a little bit more for you than for the birds of the air? "Are you not much more valuable than they?" (Matt. 6:26). Indeed, you are. You, dear heart, are the crown of creation, his glorious image bearer. And he will do everything it takes to rescue you and set your heart free.

THE OFFER

Stasi and I lived many years of our Christian life in good churches, churches that taught us the place of worship and sacrifice, faith and suffering, and gave us a love for the Word of God. But in all those years the central ministry of Jesus was never explained to us. We understood, as most Christians do, that Christ came to ransom us from sin and death, to pay the price for our transgressions through his blood shed on the cross so that we might be forgiven, might come home to the Father.

It's true. It's so wonderfully true. Only . . . there is *more*.

The purposes of Jesus Christ are not finished when one of his precious ones is forgiven. Not at all. Would a good father feel satisfied when his daughter is rescued from a car accident, but left in ICU? Doesn't he want her to be healed as well? So God has much more in mind for us. Listen to this passage from Isaiah (it might help to read it very slowly, carefully, out loud to yourself) . . .

> The Spirit of the Sovereign LORD is on me,
> because the LORD has anointed me
> to preach good news to the poor.
> He has sent me to bind up the brokenhearted,
> to proclaim freedom for the captives
> and release from darkness for the prisoners,
> to proclaim the year of the LORD's favor
> and the day of vengeance of our God,
> to comfort all who mourn,
> and provide for those who grieve in Zion—
> to bestow on them a crown of beauty instead of ashes,
> the oil of gladness
> instead of mourning,
> and a garment of praise
> instead of a spirit of despair. (61:1–3)

This is the passage that Jesus pointed to when he began his ministry here on earth. Of all the Scriptures he could have chosen, this is the one he picked on the day he first publicly announced his mission. It must be important to him. It must be central. What does it mean? It's supposed to be really good news, that's clear. It has something to do with healing hearts, setting someone free. Let me try and state it in words more familiar to us.

> God has sent me on a mission.
> I have some great news for you.
> God has sent me to restore and release something.
> And that something is *you*.
> I am here to give you back your heart and set you free.
> I am furious at the Enemy who did this to you, and I will fight against him.
> Let me comfort you.
> For, dear one, I will bestow beauty upon you
> where you have known only devastation.
> Joy, in the places of your deep sorrow.
> And I will robe your heart in thankful praise
> in exchange for your resignation and despair.

Now that is an offer worth considering. What if it were true? I mean, what if Jesus really *could* and *would* do this for your broken heart, your wounded feminine soul? Read it again, and ask him, *Jesus—is this true for me? Would you do this for me?*

He can, and he will . . . if you'll let him.

You are the glorious Image Bearer of the Lord Jesus Christ—the crown of his creation. You have been assaulted. You have fallen to your own resources. Your Enemy has seized upon your wounds and your sins to pin your heart down. Now the Son of God has come to ransom you, *and* to heal your broken, wounded, bleeding heart, *and* to set you free from bondage. He came for the brokenhearted captives. That's me. That's you. He came to *restore* the glorious creation that you are. And then set you free . . . to be yourself.

The LORD their God will save them on that day
as the flock of his people.
They will sparkle in his land
like jewels in a crown.
How attractive and beautiful they will be! (Zech. 9:16–17)

Here is the core reason we wrote this book: to let you know that the healing of your feminine heart is available, and to help you find that healing. To help you find the restoration which we long for and which is central to Jesus' mission. Let him take you by the hand now and walk with you through your restoration and release.

HEMMED IN

Why did God curse Eve with loneliness and heartache, an emptiness that nothing would be able to fill? Wasn't her life going to be hard enough out there in the world, banished from the Garden that was her true home, her only home, never able to return? It seems unkind. Cruel, even.

He did it to *save* her. For as we all know personally, something in Eve's heart shifted at the Fall. Something sent its roots down deep into her soul—and ours—that mistrust of God's heart, that resolution to find life on our own terms. So God has to thwart her. In love, he has to block her attempts until, wounded and aching, she turns to him and him alone for her rescue.

Therefore I will block her path with thornbushes;
I will wall her in so she cannot find her way.
She will chase after her lovers but not catch them;
she will look for them but not find them. (Hos. 2:6–7)

Jesus has to thwart us too—thwart our self-redemptive plans, our controlling and our hiding, thwart the ways we are seeking to fill the ache within us. Otherwise, we would never fully turn to him for our rescue. Oh, we might turn to him for our "salvation," for a ticket to heaven when we die. We might turn to him even in the form of Christian service, regular church attendance, a moral life. But *inside*, our hearts remain broken and captive and far from the One who can help us.

And so you will see the gentle, firm hand of God in a woman's life hemming her in. He'll make what once was a great job miserable, if it was in her career that she found shelter. He'll bring hardship into her marriage, even to the breaking point, if it was in marriage she sought her salvation. Wherever it is we have sought life apart from him, he disrupts our plans, our "way of life" which is not life at all. Listen to Susan's story:

Things at work have been hard. It caused me to go to my posture of defensiveness. I wanted to say, "You don't understand—you don't know my story. I have to defend myself because no one else will." I grew up with an alcoholic father and a mother who suffers extreme emotional problems. At a very young age (8 or so) I became the one who when my father beat my mother I would step in to defend her, and when my mother would berate my father I was the one who would step in to defend him. Up until I was 16 I took all the verbal abuse my mother had thrown at me, but there was this day that I decided not to take it anymore. My father told me I needed to go back in there and take it. This arrow pierced my heart so deeply that the walls of my heart became impenetrable. I've not allowed this wound to be touched for many, many years.

God has shown me that because of the defensiveness I buried my truly feminine heart which longs so deeply to be pursued and fought for, to be seen as beautiful, to be tender and kind, to feel deeply. He has shown me that by bringing this into my marriage, I have not allowed Dave the opportunity to fight for me. For this I am grieved. God asked me to repent of this to Dave and take the risk of being vulnerable once again. I stand now in this risky place of vulnerability, with a bleeding heart waiting and praying. Every day I must choose to lay down my defensiveness and allow the healing balm of Jesus to attend to my wound and allow him to be my God, my Strength, and my Defender.

He told me that I didn't need to defend myself anymore, that was his job, he is my Defender and Advocate. Would I let him be that for me? I said yes. There was a huge weight lifted off that I can't fully explain.

TURNING FROM THE WAYS YOU'VE SOUGHT TO SAVE YOURSELF

Change a few of the details and you have my story—and yours. We construct a life of safety (I will not be vulnerable *there*) and find some place to get a taste of being enjoyed or at least of being "needed." Our journey toward healing begins when we repent of those ways, lay them down, let them go. They've been a royal disaster anyway. As Frederick Buechner says,

> To do for yourself the best that you have it in you to do—to grit your teeth and clench your fists in order to survive the world at its harshest and worst—is, by that very act, to be unable to let something be done for you and in you that is more wonderful still. The trouble with steeling yourself against the harshness of reality is that the same steel that secures your life against being destroyed secures your life also against being opened up and transformed. (*The Sacred Journey*)

God comes to us and asks, "Will you let me come for you?" Not only does he thwart, but at the same time he calls to us as he did to our friend Susan, "Set it down. Set it down. Turn from your ways to Me. I want to come for you."

Therefore I am now going to allure her;
I will lead her into the desert
and speak tenderly to her. (Hos. 2:14)

To enter the journey toward the healing of your feminine heart, all it requires is a "Yes. Okay." A simple turning in the heart. Like the Prodigal we wake one day to see that the life we've constructed is no life at all. We let desire speak to us again; we let our hearts have a voice, and what the voice usually says is, *This isn't working. My life is a disaster. Jesus—I'm sorry. Forgive me. Please come for me.*

INVITE HIM IN

There is a famous passage of Scripture that many people have heard in the context of an invitation to know Christ as Savior. "Behold, I stand at the door and knock. If anyone hears My voice and opens the door, I will come in" (Rev. 3:20 NKJV). He does not force himself upon us. He knocks, and waits for us to ask him in. There is an initial step, the first step of this, which we call salvation. We hear Christ knocking and we open our hearts to him as Savior. It is the first turning. But the principle of this "knocking and waiting for permission to come in" remains true well into our Christian life.

You see, we all pretty much handle our brokenness in the same way—we mishandle it. It hurts too much to go there. So we shut the door to that room in our hearts, and we throw away the key— much like Lord Craven locks the Secret Garden upon the death of his wife and buries the key. But that does not bring healing. Not at all. It might bring relief—for a while. But never healing. Usually it orphans the little girl in that room, leaves her to fend for herself. The best thing we can do is to let Jesus come in, open the door and invite him in to find us in those hurting places.

It might come as a surprise that Christ asks our permission to come in and heal, but he is kind, and the door is shut from the inside, and healing never comes *against* our will. In order to experience his healing, we must also give him permission to come in to the places we have so long shut to anyone. *Will you let me heal you?* He knocks through our loneliness. He knocks through our sorrows. He knocks through events that feel too close to what happened to us when we were young—a betrayal, a rejection, a word spoken, a relationship lost. He knocks through many things, waiting for us to give him permission to enter in.

Give him permission. Give him access to your broken heart. Ask him to come to *these* places.

Yes, Jesus, yes. I do invite you in. Come to my heart in these shattered places. [You know what they are—ask him there. Is it the abuse? The loss of your father? The jealousy of your mother? Ask him in.] *Come to me, my Savior. I open this door of my heart. I give you permission to heal my wounds. Come to me here. Come for me here.*

RENOUNCE THE AGREEMENTS YOU'VE MADE

Your wounds brought messages with them. Lots of messages. Somehow they all usually land in the same place. They had a similar theme. "You're worthless." "You're not a woman." "You're too much . . . and not enough." "You're a disappointment." "You are repulsive." On and on they go. Because they were delivered with such pain, they *felt* true. They pierced our hearts, and they seemed so true. So we accepted the message as fact. We embraced it as the verdict on us.

As we said earlier, the vows we made as children act like a deep-seated agreement with the message of our wounds. "Fine. If that's how it is, then that's how it is. I'll live my life in the following way . . ." The vows we made acted like a kind of covenant with the messages that came with our deep wounds. Those childhood vows are very dangerous things. We must renounce them. *Before* we are entirely convinced that they aren't true, we must reject the message of our wounds. It's a way of unlocking the door to Jesus. Agreements lock the door from the inside. Renouncing the agreements unlocks the door to him.

Jesus, forgive me for embracing these lies. This is not what you have said of me. You said I am your daughter, your beloved, your cherished one. I renounce the agreements I made with [name the specific messages you've been living with. "I'm stupid. I'm ugly." You know what they are.] *I renounce the agreements I've been making with these messages all these years. Bring the truth here, oh Spirit of Truth. I reject these lies.*

WE FIND OUR TEARS

Part of the reason women are so tired is because we are spending *so* much energy trying to "keep it together." So much energy devoted to suppressing the pain and keeping a good appearance. "I'm gonna harden my heart," sang Rindy Ross. "I'm gonna swallow my tears." A terrible, costly way to live your life. Part of this is driven by fear that the pain will overwhelm us. That we will be consumed by our sorrow. It's an understandable fear—but it is no more true than the fear we had of the dark as children. Grief, dear sisters, is good. Grief helps to heal our hearts. Why, Jesus himself was a "Man of sorrows and acquainted with grief" (Isa. 53:3 NKJV).

Let the tears come. Get alone, get to your car or your bedroom or the shower and let the tears come. Let the tears come. It is the only kind thing to do for your woundedness. Allow yourself to feel again. And feel you will—many things. Anger. That's okay. Anger's not a sin (Eph. 4:26). Remorse. Of course you feel remorse and regret for so many lost years. Fear. Yes, that makes sense. Jesus can handle the fear as well. In fact, there is no emotion you can bring up that Jesus can't handle. (Look at the psalms—they are a raging sea of emotions.)

Let it all out.

As Augustine wrote in his *Confessions*, "The tears . . . streamed down, and I let them flow as freely as they would, making of them a pillow for my heart. On them it rested." Grief is a form of validation; it says the wound *mattered*. It mattered. You mattered. That's not the way life was supposed to go. There are unwept tears down in there—the tears of a little girl who is lost and frightened. The tears of a teenage girl who's been rejected and has no place to turn. The tears of a woman whose life has been hard and lonely and nothing close to her dreams.

Let the tears come.

FORGIVE

Okay—now for a hard step (as if the others have been easy). A real step of courage and will. We must forgive those who hurt us. The reason is simple: Bitterness and unforgiveness set their hooks deep in our hearts; they are chains that hold us captive to the wounds and the messages of those wounds. Until you forgive, you remain their prisoner. Paul warns us that unforgiveness and bitterness can wreck our lives and the lives of others (Eph. 4:31; Heb. 12:15). We have to let it all go.

Forgive as the Lord forgave you. (Col. 3:13)

Now—listen carefully. Forgiveness is a *choice*. It is not a feeling—don't try and feel forgiving. It is an act of the will. "Don't wait to forgive until you feel like forgiving," wrote Neil Anderson. "You will never get there. Feelings take time to heal after the choice to forgive is made." We allow God to bring the hurt up from our past, for "if your forgiveness doesn't visit the emotional core of your life, it will be incomplete," said Anderson. We acknowledge that it hurt, that it mattered, and we choose to extend forgiveness to our fathers, our mothers, those who hurt us. This is *not* saying, "It didn't really matter"; it is *not* saying, "I probably deserved part of it anyway." Forgiveness says, "It was wrong. Very wrong. It mattered, hurt me deeply. And I release you. I give you to God."

It might help to remember that those who hurt you were also deeply wounded themselves. They were broken hearts, broken when they were young, and they fell captive to the Enemy. They were in fact pawns in his hands. This doesn't absolve them of the choices they made, the things they did. It just helps us to let them go—to realize that they were shattered souls themselves, used by our true Enemy in his war against femininity.

ASK JESUS TO HEAL YOU

We turn from our self-redemptive strategies. We open the door of our hurting heart to Jesus. We renounce the agreements we made with the messages of our wounds, renounce any vows we made. We forgive those who harmed us. And then, with an open heart, we simply ask Jesus to heal us. Melissa was the young girl who "vowed

I would be tough; hard, like a rock," and became so for many years. But that is not the end of her story. She came to the place where Jesus asked to heal her wounded heart. She gave him permission to come in. This is what happened.

> God went back and got the shaking little girl that was hiding under the bed and convinced her to come out. He unclenched her little fists and took her hand and placed it in his and answered her question. He held her and told her it was OK for her not to be tough. He would protect her. She didn't have to be strong. He told her she wasn't a rock but a child. An innocent child. His child. He didn't condemn her for anything but instead understood her and loved her! He told her she was special . . . like no other and that she had special gifts like no other. She knew his voice and trusted him. She could hear the pleasure He had for her in His voice and felt His delight in her as He talked. He was so gentle and loving she couldn't help but melt in His arms.

This is available. This is the offer of our Savior—to heal our broken hearts. To come to the young places within us and find us there, take us in his arms, bring us home. The time has come to let Jesus heal you.

> *Jesus, come to me and heal my heart. Come to the shattered places within me. Come for the little girl that was wounded. Come and hold me in your arms, and heal me. Do for me what you promised to do—heal my broken heart and set me free.*

ASK HIM TO DESTROY YOUR ENEMIES

In the beautiful passage of Isaiah 61, God promises "freedom for the captives and release from darkness for the prisoners" (v. 1). He goes on to proclaim "vengeance" against our enemies (v. 2). Our wounds, our vows, and the agreements we've made with the messages all give ground to the Enemy in our lives. Paul warns about this in Ephesians 4 when he says—writing to Christians—"and do not give the devil a foothold" (v. 27). There are things you've struggled with all your life—self-doubt, anger, depression, shame, addiction, fear. You probably thought that those were your fault, too.

But they are not. They came from the Enemy who wanted to take your heart captive, make you a prisoner of darkness. To be sure, we complied. We allowed those strongholds to form when we mishandled our wounds and made those vows. But Jesus has forgiven us for all of that, and now he wants to set us free.

Ask him to destroy your enemies. He promised to, after all. Ask Jesus to release your heart from captivity to these things.

Jesus, come and rescue me. Set me free from [you know what you need freedom from—name it.] *Release me from darkness. Bring your vengeance on my enemies. I reject them and ask you to take them to judgment. Set my heart free.*

LET HIM FATHER YOU

Then he went with Sara into her little sitting room and they bade each other good-bye. Sara sat on his knee and held the lapels of his coat in her small hands and looked long and hard at his face.

"Are you learning me by heart, little Sara?" he said, stroking her hair.

"No," she answered. "I know you by heart. You are inside my heart." And they put their arms round each other and kissed as if they would never let each other go. (Frances Hodgson Burnett, *A Little Princess*)

This precious story touches something deep in the hearts of little girls—and women. Every little girl was made to live in a world with a father who loves her unconditionally. She first learns who God is, what he is like, and how he feels about her from her earthly dad. God is "Our Father, who art in heaven." He means initially to reveal himself to his daughters and his sons through the love of our dads. We were meant to know a father's love, be kept safe in it, be protected by it, and blossom there.

I (Stasi) have heard many times that what we at first believe about God, the Father, directly comes from what we know of and have experienced from our earthly dads. I first heard this from a pulpit as a young Christian and in my typical, teachable fashion, thought, *How stupid.* Not that the pastor was stupid, but that the idea itself was ludicrous. Of course, my own dad was not God. Everybody knew that. But later, as I heard other women speak of God the Father, I often heard in their voices a softness, a tenderness, perhaps even a childlikeness that was foreign to me. When I began to hear others praying to "Daddy" or "Papa," I knew they were speaking to "Someone" I did not know.

I had never called my own father, "Daddy." "Papa" was what fathers were called in movies. Many of us grew up in homes where the correct term for Dad was "Sir." Intimacy with and dependence on a father who was rarely home—and emotionally absent when he was—was impossible for me. Remember—he didn't want to know me. I was a disappointment to him.

I have come to understand that what that pastor was telling me so many years ago was the truth. I was looking at my heavenly Father through the lenses of my experiences with my own father. And for me, that meant my heavenly Father was distant, aloof, unavailable, hard to please, easily disappointed, quick to anger, and often hard to predict. True, I wanted to please him. But since God the Father was, to me, hard to fathom and not especially inviting, my relationship with God centered on my relationship with his Son. Jesus liked me. I wasn't so sure about his dad.

Years into my Christian life, I began to hunger to know God more deeply as my Father. I asked him to reveal himself to me as my dad. In answer, God invited me to take a journey into my deep heart that took surprising turns and continues still. First, God led me into taking a much closer look at my own father. Who was he really? How did he really feel about me? What did I even remember? God invited me to go with him into the deep places of my heart that were hidden and wounded and bleeding still from heartbreaks and wounds I had received from my father's hand. Places I did not want to go. Memories I did not want to revisit. Emotions I did not want to feel. The only reason I said *yes* to God, the only reason I would travel there, was because I knew he would go with me. Hand in hand. He would hold my heart. And I had come to trust his.

There is a core part of our hearts that was made for Daddy. Made for his strong and tender love. That part is still there, and longing. Open it to Jesus and to your Father God. Ask him to come and love you there. Meet you there. We've all tried so hard to find the fulfillment of this love in other people, and it never, ever works. Let us give this treasure back to the One who can love us best.

Father, I need your love. Come to the core of my heart. Come and bring your love for me. Help me to know you for who you really are—not as I see my earthly father. Reveal yourself to me. Reveal your love for me. Tell me what I mean to you. Come, and father me.

ASK HIM TO ANSWER YOUR QUESTION

Those of you who have read *A Little Princess* by Frances Hodgson Burnett will recall that life did not go well for Sara. In the middle of her eleventh birthday party, word reaches the school that her beloved Papa has died. His fortune has been confiscated, and she is penniless. With no means to pay for her private education, Sara is demeaned, put to work, treated cruelly, and sent to live in the barren attic.

But the love Sara's father poured into her heart has made a lasting impact. Poor, bereft, and ill treated, Sara has a heart of gold. She says to herself, "Whatever comes, cannot alter one thing. If I am a princess in rags and tatters, I can be a princess inside. It would be easy to be a princess if I were dressed in a cloth of gold, but it is a great deal more of a triumph to be one all the time when no one knows it."

How do you come to such a confidence? You take your heart's deepest Question to God. You still have a Question, dear one. We all do. We all still need to know, *Do you see me? Am I captivating? Do I have a beauty all my own?*

I realized last year that this question still needed an answer in Stasi's own heart. We were out to dinner for our anniversary. At one point in the evening I said, "You were a darling little girl." She looked at me with a sort of *Don't lie to me* kind of look. "Didn't you know that?" A long pause. "No." "Oh, Sweetheart—you didn't *know?*" I have seen the photos. I have seen glimpses into what a treasure she was. But life wrote a different message on her heart. And so I urged her, "You must ask God what he saw. Take this to him."

We could tell you so many beautiful stories of women who have received from God the answer to their Question. As a young girl our friend Kim longed to be the princess who was being rescued during childhood games. "But the girl down the street was cuter than me. She was Barbie. So I had to join on the side of the guys, fight the dragon and rescue her. I never got to be the Beauty." Tears came with this story—young tears, tears than had never been cried over this. It was good to finally let them out. "Kim, I tell you what I want you to do. I want you to ask Jesus to show you your beauty." "I can do that?" she said. "I mean, that's okay? He would do that for me?"

She came back after two months, smiling as if she had some great secret to tell. Her face was shining. She told us that Jesus had come. He had shown her beauty—her own—in lots of ways. More than two hundred ways. "It's been amazing. I'm beginning to believe I'm beautiful."

Just a few weeks ago I was talking with our friend Debbie; she's the one whose father had an affair and who has spent so much time and energy trying to "fix" whatever was wrong with her. "What if you have a genuine and captivating beauty that is marred only by your striving?" She leaned back against her chair and sighed at the thought. Something softened. Suddenly she was soft, and beautiful. The veil was parted, and there she was—a beautiful woman. Gone was the resignation; gone were the anxiety and pain. She was, for a moment, at rest. "What does your heart do with that possibility?" A moment's pause. "Two things arise in me," she said. "'Hooray!' and, 'Damn!'" I smiled at her honesty. "*Hooray* that it might be true after all, and *damn* because what have I been doing all these years?"

Let's just start with a thought. What if the message delivered with your wounds simply isn't true about you? Let that sink in. It wasn't true. What does it free you to do? Weep? Rejoice? Let go? Come out? Take your heart back? Here is one woman's experience:

> Even though I've "succeeded" in many areas, I've always been ashamed of the absence of my femininity as defined by the world. Asking God what he thought of me as a woman was beyond agonizing. I wrestled with him right to the end. I knew in my mind he wouldn't be mean, but I was convinced I had failed him miserably in this department . . . When I finally allowed myself to hear God speak a new name, it was Grace. And the lie of "too

much boy and not enough girl" gets shattered in a moment. He crowns me with Grace, He crowns me with love. And I'm satisfied (Ps. 103).

Take your Question to Jesus. Ask him to show you your beauty. And then? Let him Romance you.

CHAPTER SEVEN

Romance∂

I have loved you with an everlasting love.
—GOD (JEREMIAH 31:3)

Romance is the deepest thing in life.
It is deeper even than reality.
—G. K. CHESTERTON

*I*t had been a long, busy day, and I left the boys with John and escaped into the night for some much-needed time alone. It was a beautiful fall Colorado night. I walked along a path toward a park near our home. The air was crisp and clear, the stars winking, glistening. I breathed in the beauty and laid the cares of the day behind me. A cool breeze whispered by, one of the first to speak of the winter to come. As I walked, I was dazzled by the splendor of it all, and I began to compliment God on the great job he had done. "It's beautiful, Lord! The stars are amazing!"

I'm glad you like it, my Darling.

I stopped dead in my tracks. I blushed. Did the God of the universe just call me "Darling"? Was that *okay?* I was warmed to the depths of my soul by the endearment, but I also wondered if I had made it up. And was it sacrilegious to believe God would use such a loving name? For me? I am the one who had lost patience with her

335

children that very day and used an ugly tone of voice that hurt them and mortified me. I am the one who is living her life so imperfectly, disappointing friends and failing family.

Me? *Darling?*

Later that night, I began to read some Scriptures before falling asleep, and my hand turned to the pages of the Song of Songs. My eyes fell to the words, "How beautiful you are, my darling" (1:15). How kind of God, for then I knew. It had been him. The amazing love of God for *me* penetrated my heart in a new and deep way that night. He had spoken to me. This wild God of mine, who knows my every thought and intention, who sees my every failure and sin, loves me. Not in a religious way, not in the way we usually translate when we hear, "God loves us." Which usually sounds like "because he has to" or meaning "he tolerates you." No. He loves me as a *Lover* loves. Whoa.

LONGING FOR ROMANCE

A woman becomes beautiful when she knows she's loved. We've seen this many times—you probably have too. Cut off from love, rejected, no one pursuing her, something in a woman wilts like a flower no one waters anymore. She withers into resignation, duty, and shame. The radiance of her countenance goes out, as if a light has been turned off. But this same woman, who everyone thought was rather plain and unengaging, becomes lovely and inviting when she is *pursued.* Her heart begins to come alive, come to the surface, and her countenance becomes radiant. We wonder, "Where has she been all these years? Why, she really is captivating."

Think of Fran in *Strictly Ballroom*, or Tulah in *My Big Fat Greek Wedding.* Remember Lottie in *Enchanted April*, Adrian in *Rocky*, or Danielle in *Ever After.* Their beauty was always there. What happened to each woman was merely the power of romance *releasing* her true beauty, awakening her heart. She has come alive. As women we long to be loved in a certain way, a way unique to our femininity. We long for romance. We are wired for it; it's what makes our hearts come alive. You know that. Somewhere, down deep inside, you know this. But what you might never have known is this . . .

This doesn't need to wait for a man.

God longs to bring this into your life himself. He wants you to move beyond the childlike "Jesus loves me, this I know, for the Bible tells me so." He wants to heal us through his love to become mature women who actually *know* him. He wants us to *experience* verses like, "Therefore I am now going to allure her; I will lead her into the desert and speak tenderly to her" (Hos. 2:14). And "You have stolen my heart, my sister, my bride" (Song 4:9). Our hearts are desperate for this. What would it be like to experience for yourself that the truest thing about his heart toward yours is not disappointment or disapproval but deep, fiery, passionate love? This is, after all, what a woman was made for.

Faithful obedience to God is vital, but it is not all God draws us to. It is not sufficient for our healing, no more than doing the laundry is sufficient for a marriage. And it will not be enough in the long run to carry us through. The persecuted Church is vast today. More Christians are being martyred in our lifetime than in *any* other time in church history. It is not obedience that is carrying our brothers and sisters—unwavering, steadfast, eyes ablaze—to their deaths. It is holy, fierce *passion*. Hearts afire.

For the root of all holiness is Romance.

God As Lover

Let's go back for a moment to the movies that you love. Think of one of the most romantic scenes you can remember, scenes that made you sigh. Jack with Rose on the bow of the *Titanic*, his arms around her waist, their first kiss. Wallace speaking in French to Murron, then in Italian: "Not as beautiful as you." Aragorn, standing with Arwen in the moonlight on the bridge in Rivendell, declaring his love for her. Edward returning for Elinor in *Sense and Sensibility,* and Professor Behr returning for Jo at the end of *Little Women.*

Now, put yourself in the scene as the Beauty, and Jesus as the Lover.

What does your heart do with that? Is there a bit of a hesitation, "Is that okay?" Is there a bit of longing, "I'd love for that to happen"? Perhaps there might be for some of you a tinge of fear, the wince of your wounded heart, "I don't want to open that up." Then you can see that there is healing for your heart in moving toward this. It's okay. It's quite biblical. Jesus calls himself the Bridegroom (Matt. 9:15, Matt. 25:1–10, John 3:29). Now, you'll need to take the religious drapery and sanctimonious gilding off of this. "Bridegroom" simply means fiancé. Lover. This is the most intimate of all the metaphors Jesus chose to describe his love and longing for us, and the kind of relationship he invites us into.

You might recall that the Scriptures use a number of metaphors to describe our relationship with God. We are portrayed as clay, and he is the potter. We are sheep, and he the shepherd. Each metaphor is beautiful and speaks to the various seasons of our spiritual lives and to the various aspects of God's heart toward us. But have you noticed they *ascend* in a stunning way? From potter and his clay to a shepherd and his sheep, there is a marked difference in intimacy, in the way they relate. It gets even better. From master and servant to father and child, there is a wonderful progression into greater intimacy. It grows more beautiful and rich when he calls us his friends. But what is most breathtaking is when God says he is our Lover (our Bridegroom, our Fiancé), and we his bride. That is the pinnacle, the goal of our redemption (used in the last chapter of the

Bible, when Christ returns for his bride) and the most intimate and romantic of all.

If you'll open your heart to the possibility, you'll find that God has been wooing you ever since you were a little girl. Yes, we said earlier that the story of your life is the story of the long and sustained assault upon your heart by the one who knows what you could be and fears you. But that is only *part* of the story. Every story has a villain. Every story also has a hero. The Great Love Story the Scriptures are telling us about also reveals a Lover who longs for you. The story of your life is *also* the story of the long and passionate pursuit of your heart by the One who knows you best and loves you most.

God has written the Romance not only on our hearts but all over the world around us. What we need is for him to open our eyes, to open our ears that we might recognize his voice calling to us, see his hand wooing us in the beauty that quickens our hearts.

> *Longer than there've been fishes in the ocean*
> *Higher than any bird ever flew*
> *Longer than there've been stars up in the heavens*
> *I've been in love with you.*
>
> *Stronger than any mountain cathedral*
> *Truer than any tree ever grew*
> *Deeper than any forest primeval*
> *I am in love with you.*
> —DAN FOGELBERG, "LONGER"

What were the things that romanced your heart as a girl? Was it horses in a field? Was it the fragrance of the air after a summer rain? Was it a favorite book like *The Secret Garden*? The first snowfall of winter? Those were all whispers from your Lover, notes sent to awaken your heart's longings. And as we journey into a true intimacy with God as women, he often brings those things back into our lives, to remind us he *was* there, to heal and restore things that were lost or stolen.

OPENING OUR HEARTS TO THE ROMANCER

Every song you love, every memory you cherish, every moment that has moved you to holy tears has been given to you from the One who has been pursuing you from your first breath in order to win your heart. God's version of flowers and chocolates and candlelight dinners comes in the form of sunsets and falling stars, moonlight on lakes and cricket symphonies; warm wind, swaying trees, lush gardens, and fierce devotion.

This romancing is immensely personal. It will be as if it has been scripted for *your* heart. He knows what takes your breath away, knows what makes your heart beat faster. We have missed many of his notes simply because we shut our hearts down in order to endure the pain of life. Now, in our healing journey as women, we must open our hearts again, and keep them open. Not foolishly, not to anyone and anything. But yes, we must choose to open our hearts again so that we might hear his whispers, receive his kisses.

It may not come the way we thought, or perhaps even thought we desired it to. A few years ago John was on a business trip to Oregon. He snuck away for some time alone with God, down to the beach where he walked and prayed and finally sat in the sand to watch the waves upon the sea. (His idea of refreshment is "the wilder the better.") Then he saw it. A huge plume of water shot up into the sky, and a massive humpback whale appeared right before him, impossibly close to shore. No one else was near. The time of the whale's annual migration had long passed. John knew immediately that this was a gift from God to his heart alone, a gift from the Lover of his heart.

John told me this story and, as happy as I was for him, I was more hungry for such a kiss for myself. I wanted a whale too. I wanted to experience God's love for me, personally. It wasn't long after this that John and I were in Northern California speaking at a couples' retreat. I, too, snuck away one morning for some much needed time on the beach with God. I sat on the sand, looked out to the sea, and asked God for a whale. "I know you love John, Jesus, but do you love me too? That much? If you do, may I have a whale too?"

I felt a little silly in asking, for I knew the truth—that God had already proven his love for me. He had sent his only Son, Jesus, to die for me (John 3:16). He had rescued me. He had paid the highest price imaginable for me. He had given me all of creation to speak of his great glory and love, and he had given me the Word of God in all its depth and beauty, and here I was, asking for more. And God loved it. God delights in revealing himself to those who will seek him with all their hearts. He is an extravagant, abundant Lover, and he loves to reveal his heart to us again and again.

After a while, with no whale in sight, I got up off the sand and continued to walk. It was early spring, waves crashing, seagulls crying. The northern coast of California is rocky, and as I picked my way through, I rounded a corner and came upon a starfish, a beautiful orange starfish. And I knew at once it was God's gift to me, his kiss. He didn't give me a whale; no, that was for John alone. For me, unique to me, he gave a stunning starfish. He answered my question. Yes. He loved me. I thanked him for it, then rounded the next bend and came upon a sight I will never forget. There before me, behind me, surrounding me, were hundreds of starfish. Zillions of them. There were purple ones and orange ones and blue ones, all sizes. I burst into joyful laughter, my heart exploding inside me.

God didn't just love me. He LOOOOVED me! Intimately, personally, completely.

God gave John a whale. It was huge and strong. God gave me starfish. They were delicate, small, intricate. I could touch them. In being surrounded by them, I felt my heart encompassed by his generous, extravagant love. The amazing starfish were an intimate gift from an intimate God. He has many for you as well. Perhaps it would be good to ask,

Jesus, how are you romancing me now?

We don't always see it. In Chapter 1 we told you of the romantic ball we attended a few years ago. Leslie, a dear friend of ours, was also invited. But she almost missed the invitation. The story is amazing. Several weeks before she received her invitation she had said to God, "I am tired of living in the cellar. I want to come out. I want to go to the ball." She knew nothing of what was in store, knew nothing of the planned ball—she was simply letting her heart express itself in vulnerability to God. She felt like Cinderella in the cellar. And she wanted *out*. (He loves your vulnerability, as any Lover does. He loves it when you share your truest heart's desire with him.) Well, when she got the invitation, she didn't even open it. It sat for a few weeks in the bills pile.

And when she finally did open it—a lovely embossed invitation to a real ball—she didn't think it was for her. Oh, Cinderella. What will it take? A few days later God opened her eyes, and she ran back to the mail, pulled out the invitation, and held her breath. *Really, God? This is really true?* She didn't want to arrange. She waited for her husband to ask her if she'd like to go. He did. The evening was, for her, a deeply healing event, reaching back and addressing old wounds. She was lit up all night, and something has remained lit ever since.

This is not to say that life is one big romantic moment with Jesus. I live a life much like yours—full of demands, pressures, and disappointments. Right now the laundry is going, all the dishes are dirty, there's no food for lunch, and the boys are bored with summer vacation. Like you, there are seasons in my life when Jesus seems very near and seasons where I can't seem to find him at all. Sometimes it feels like we're playing a game of hide-and-seek, but he's got all the best hiding places staked out. All relationships ebb and flow.

The ebbing is to draw our hearts out in deeper longing. In the times of emptiness, an open heart *notices*. What are you feeling? Like a lonely girl missing her daddy? Like a teenage young woman feeling completely invisible, unseen? Often God allows these feelings to surface to help us go back to times when we have felt like this before. Notice also what you want to do—how you handle your heart. Are you shutting down in anger? Turning to food? To others?

What is crucial is that, *this* time, we handle our hearts differently.

We ask our Lover to come for us, and we keep our hearts open to his coming. We choose not to shut down. We let the tears come. We allow the ache to swell into a longing prayer for our God. And he comes, dear hearts. He does come. The times of intimacy—the flowing waters of love—those times then bring healing to places in our hearts that still need his touch.

WHAT DOES GOD WANT FROM YOU?

I am searching through the canyon.
It is your name that I am calling.
Though you're so far away
I know you hear my plea
Why won't you answer me?

Here I am.
Here I am.
—EMMYLOU HARRIS, "HERE I AM"

I was walking through the music store the other day, just sort of browsing, not really after anything in particular, and I sensed the Spirit say *buy this CD.* Just a nudge, not a shout, but I bought it and plugged it into my player on the way home. I wasn't really moved by it. I gave it to Stasi, who came back and told me how incredible it was. She played the song for me, and I "heard" it for what it was. The Romancer calling once again. He has done this for us more times than we could ever count—songs, movies, cards, words from friends, moments in the woods—the Romance is *everywhere.* It is your name that he is calling.

What is it that God wants from you?

He wants the same thing that you want. He wants to be loved. He wants to be known as only lovers can know each other. He wants intimacy with you. Yes, yes, he wants your obedience, but only when it flows out of a heart filled with love for him. "Whoever has my commands and obeys them, he is the one who loves me." (John 14:21). Following hard after Jesus is the heart's natural response when it has been captured and has fallen deeply in love with him.

Reading George MacDonald several years ago, I came across an astounding thought. You've probably heard that there is in every human heart a place that God alone can fill. (Lord knows we've tried to fill it with everything else, to our utter dismay.) But what the old poet was saying was that there is *also* in God's heart a place that you alone can fill. "It follows that there is also a chamber in God himself, into which none can enter but the one, the individual." You. You are meant to fill a place in the heart of God no one and nothing else can fill. Whoa. He longs for *you.*

You are the one that overwhelms his heart with just "one glance of your eyes" (Song 4:9b). You are the one he sings over with delight and longs to dance with across mountaintops and ballroom floors (Zeph. 3:17). You are the one who takes his breath away by your beautiful heart that, against all odds, hopes in him. Let that be true for a moment. Let it be true of *you*.

God wants to live this life together with you, to share in your days and decisions, your desires and disappointments. He wants intimacy with you in the midst of the madness and mundane, the meetings and memos, the laundry and lists, the carpools and conversations and projects and pain. He wants to pour his love into your heart and he longs to have you pour yours into his. He wants your deep heart, that center place within that is the truest *you*. He is not interested in intimacy with the woman you think you are supposed to be. He wants intimacy with the real you.

Here's how the flow goes in Hosea. First, God says that he will thwart our efforts to find life apart from him (we quoted this part earlier).

> Therefore I will block her path with thornbushes;
> I will wall her in so that she cannot find her way.
> She will chase after her lovers but not catch them;
> she will look for them but not find them. (Hos. 2:6–7)

He does this, as we said, in order to wear us out, get us to turn back to him in thirsty longing. Then he begins to woo us. He often takes us aside from every other source of comfort so that he alone can have our heart's attention.

> Therefore I am now going to allure her;
> I will lead her into the desert
> and speak tenderly to her. (Hos. 2:14)

And it is here that we begin to experience him not as the God-way-up-there, not the God-of-Sunday-mornings, but as the pursuer of our hearts. As Lover.

"In that day," declares the LORD,
"you will call me 'my husband';
you will no longer call me 'my master . . .'

I will betroth you to me forever;
I will betroth you in righteousness and justice,
in love and compassion." (Hos. 2:16, 19)

In the spacious love of God, our souls can lie down and rest. This love from him is not something we must struggle for, earn, or fear to lose. It is bestowed. He has bestowed it upon us. He has chosen us. And nothing can separate us from his love. Not even we, ourselves. We are made for such a love. Our hearts yearn to be loved intimately, personally, and yes, romantically. We are created to be the object of desire and affection of one who is totally and completely in love with us.

And we are.

An intimate relationship with Jesus is not only for other women, for women who seem to have their acts together, who appear godly and whose nails are nicely shaped. It is for each and every one of us. God wants intimacy with *you*. In order to have it, you, too, must offer it to him.

ADORING HEARTS

As Jesus and his disciples were on their way, he came to a village where a woman named Martha opened her home to him. She had a sister called Mary, who sat at the Lord's feet listening to what he said. But Martha was distracted by all the preparations that had to be made. She came to him and asked, "Lord, don't you care that my sister has left me to do the work by myself? Tell her to help me!"

"Martha, Martha," the Lord answered, "you are worried and upset about many things, but only one thing is needed. Mary has chosen what is better, and it will not be taken away from her." (Luke 10:38–42)

Okay, we've all heard the story. Martha and Mary. Don't be such a Martha. Got it. But we've often wondered what the "one thing" was that was needed. Some of you might have heard teaching that it was one simple casserole dish, that Martha was busy making a complicated meal when only one simple food was needed. No. That is not what Jesus is saying. Jesus has again spoken straight into the heart of the matter. The one thing that is needed is a captivated, adoring heart, a heart that *responds* to the extravagant love of God with worship.

Our hearts are made to worship. It is what we do; we can't help it. Now, worship is one of those words made sickly by religion. We hear "worship" and we think, *She's talking about going to church. Singing hymns.* Nope. Worship is far more passionate, far more abandoned. Worship is what we give our hearts away to in return for a promise of Life. Some worship fashion; others worship a boyfriend or husband. We really are limitless in what we will give our hearts away to. Movies, food, shopping, gossip, you name it, I've bowed before them all.

But Jesus is the only one worthy of our heart's devotion. Mary recognized who Jesus was—the source of all Life. Love Incarnate. She did what you and I hope we, too, would have done. She dropped everything and sat at his feet, fixing the gaze of her eyes and the gaze of her heart upon him.

Martha here is much like the busy church, a distracted bride. The other day, I was having lunch with an old friend. Telling me about the church she was involved in, she said it was focused on the Great Commission and obeying the first commandment: to love our neighbors as ourselves. I was struck dumb. That is not the First Commandment. Jesus says the first and greatest commandment is "Love the Lord your God with all your heart and with all your soul and with all your mind" (Matt. 22:37). Jesus wants us to love one another, yes. He wants us to serve one another, yes. But first and foremost, he wants our utter devotion and love for him. It is from hearts filled with love for him that all good works and acts of love flow.

Now for one of the most beautiful mysteries of the feminine heart: women minister something to the heart of God that men do not.

Look at the record. There was an event that took place in the life of Jesus that he said should be told whenever the Gospel is proclaimed around the world. It was when Mary of Bethany came and anointed him with the perfume, which cost a year's wages. It was an extravagant act of sacrificial worship, and the aroma of it filled the room. Jesus was profoundly moved by it. The men gathered there were indignant. It was a woman who did this for Christ. Just as it was also a woman who rushed into the Pharisee's house uninvited and washed Jesus' feet with her tears, dried them with her hair, and kissed them in an act of intimate, repentant worship.

It was women who followed Jesus from Galilee to care for his needs. It was women who stayed at the foot of the cross, offering him the comfort of their presence until Jesus breathed his last (only John remained with them). It was to women that Jesus first revealed himself after he rose from the dead, and it was women who first "clasped his feet and worshiped him" (Matt. 28:9) as the Risen, Victorious Lord.

Women hold a special place in the heart of God. A woman's

worship brings Jesus immense pleasure and a deep ministry. You can minister to the heart of God. You impact Him. You matter. Jesus desires you to pour out your love on him in extravagant worship that ministers to his heart. This is not just for women who have the time, women who are really spiritual. You are made for romance, and the only one who can offer it to you consistently and deeply is Jesus.

Offer your heart to him.

CULTIVATING INTIMACY

When I first began to worship Jesus in the privacy of my bedroom, there was one song that I played over and over. It's a simple song made up primarily of the words:

Help us, our God.
We come to you desperately needy.

Yes. That describes *me*. I was then (and remain still) desperately needy for God. My struggle with an addiction to food and a deep loneliness were very real. I needed God to be more tangible, more real in my life. Filled with a deep hunger for his touch within my heart, thirsty for more revelation of who he truly is, and desperate for deeper healing, I began to set aside several hours each week to devote to private worship. I asked him to come.

I made room for it in my life's schedule and fought to protect the time. Whether it required unplugging the phone, arranging childcare for my young boys, or staying up after everyone was asleep, it was worth it. I became captivated by his beauty. It was rich. It was good. And it was *opposed*. To pursue intimacy with Christ, you will have to fight for it. You'll need to fight busyness (Martha's addiction). You'll need to fight accusations. You'll need to fight the Thief that would steal your Lover's gifts to you outright.

That's okay. There is a fierceness in women that was given to us for a purpose. Getting time with your Lover is worth whatever it costs.

Ask his help in making you desperately hungry for him.

Ask his help in creating the time and space you need to draw close to him.

Ask him to come, to reveal himself to you as the Lover that he is.

Go get some worship music that moves you. Not music you'd do aerobics to, but music that speaks of an intimacy with Christ. Music that draws you into intimacy with him. (One friend just told us that her current favorite is "All I Ask of You" from *Phantom of the Opera!*) Get in a private place. Let everyone know it is not a time to interrupt you. Unplug your phone. Bring your Bible and a journal to write down what you hear God say in the depths of your heart. Kneel, sit, or lie down and ask the Holy Spirit to come and help you worship Jesus. Start by telling Jesus how wonderful he is. Remember when he took care of that hard situation? Or that time he answered your prayers for financial help? Recall the times he spoke to you in your loneliness or need. Thank him for being so faithful. Stay. Linger. Worship. Let the music help usher your heart into God.

The first time may not be amazing. You may feel your words and cries are bouncing off the ceiling. We grow in this as we practice. We practice the presence of God, as the old French monk Brother Lawrence knew. We come to God in worship not to *get* from him but to *give* to him. Jesus loves it when we offer our hearts to him in devotion. You are entering the chamber only you can enter. You are bringing something to the heart of Jesus only you can bring. You are his Betrothed, his Beloved, the beat of his heart, and the love of his life. Draw near. He is waiting.

I have always been your Lover.
Here I am.

Here I am.

—EMMYLOU HARRIS, "HERE I AM"

The culture of women in the church today is crippled by some very pervasive lies. "To be spiritual is to be busy. To be spiritual is to be disciplined. To be spiritual is to be dutiful." No, to be spiritual is to be in a Romance with God. The desire to be romanced lies deep in the heart of every woman. It is for such that you were made. And you *are* romanced, and ever will be.

CHAPTER EIGHT

Beauty to Unveil

Beauty is dangerous.
— GERARD MANLEY HOPKINS

Beauty will save the world.
—FYODOR DOSTOYEVSKY

Show me your face, let me hear your voice;
For your voice is sweet and your face is lovely.
—SONG OF SONGS 2:14

*T*he essence of a man is Strength. A man is meant to be the incarnation—our experience in human form—of our Warrior God. A God *who comes through for us.*

> Who is this coming from Edom,
> from Bozrah, with his garments stained crimson?
> Who is this, robed in splendor,
> striding forward in the greatness of his strength?
> "It is I, speaking in righteousness,
> mighty to save." (Isa. 63:1)

Isn't this what makes our hearts beat more quickly, our knees weak when we watch Daniel Day Lewis in *The Last of the Mohicans*, William Wallace in *Braveheart*, Aragorn in *The Lord of the Rings*, or Harrison Ford in nearly any of his movies? Isn't that what we, as women, long to experience from *our* man, and from the men in our lives?

To experience the strength of a man is to have him speak on our behalf. For when men abuse with words, we are pierced. Their strength has wounded us. When they are silent, we are starved. They have offered no strength; they have abandoned us. But when they speak with us, hear us, offer their words to us and on our behalf, something in our hearts is able to rest. "How are you?" is one of the simplest and most loving questions John ever asks me.

We long for the protection masculine strength offers. To have them shield us from physical harm, yes. But also to have them shield us from emotional harm and spiritual attack. To intercede for us in a relationship which has become hurtful. A friend was being verbally abused and manipulated by her mother over the phone, repeatedly. Finally, one night her husband took the phone and spoke to her mother. "You cannot talk to my wife this way. I will not allow it. You may not call again until you are ready to be kind." He did for her what she was, at that time, unable to do for herself. And she was so grateful.

As women we long for someone strong to stand between us and the vicious assaults of our Enemy. One weary night I had gone to bed early, overcome with a sense of despair and hopelessness. I felt pounded down, beyond saving, and worthy of condemnation. I lay still, engulfed in grief. Suddenly, John was at my bedside. He was angry, but not at me. John recognized the hand of our Enemy. He began to take his authority over me as my husband and force-fully commanded the minions of Satan to release me; he com-manded them to be silent, and he sent them to the throne of Jesus for judgment. When he began to pray for me, I was embarrassed. When he continued, I began to feel lighter. When he finished, tears were streaming down my face and my hands were raised to God in holy gratitude and joyful worship. I had gone to bed filled with unrelenting sorrow. I ended the night belting out heartfelt songs of praise.

Strength is what the world longs to experience from a man.

Now—isn't it obvious that we don't mean big muscles?

Of course. A man might like to work out at the gym, but if he is only physically strong, he is a hollow man. Are we satisfied as a woman with that kind of man? On the other hand, our man might prefer to read or play an instrument. Does that in any way diminish the strength of his soul? Not at all. The strength of a man is first a *soulish* strength—a strength of heart. And yes, as he lives it out, owns it, *inhabits* his strength, he does become more handsome. More attractive. As the fruit of an inner reality.

So then you can see that when we speak about the essence of a woman—her beauty—we don't mean "the perfect figure." The beauty of a woman is first a *soulish* beauty. We know—it's a harder jump to make. We've lived so long under the pressure to be beautiful. But stay with the thought for a moment, because it will really help. The beauty of a woman is first a soulful beauty. And yes, as we live it out, own it, *inhabit* our beauty, we do become more lovely. More alluring. As the poet Gerard Manley Hopkins wrote, "Self flashes off frame and face." Our true self becomes reflected in our appearance. But it flows from the inside out.

THE ESSENCE OF A WOMAN

The essence of a woman is Beauty. She is meant to be the incarnation—our experience in human form—of a Captivating God. A God *who invites us.*

"Come, all you who are thirsty, come to the waters . . .
Listen, listen to me, and eat what is good,
and your soul will delight in the richest of fare." (Isa. 55:1–2)

"You have stolen my heart, my sister, my bride;
you have stolen my heart
with one glance of your eyes,
with one jewel of your necklace . . .
You are a garden fountain,
a well of flowing water
streaming down from Lebanon." (Song 4:9,15)

Beauty is what the world longs to experience from a woman.
We know that. Somewhere down deep, we know it to be true. Most
of our shame comes from this knowing and feeling that we have
failed here. So listen to this: beauty is an essence that dwells in *every*
woman. It was given to her by God. It was given to you.

Surely you would agree that God is nothing if not beautiful.

All around us God's creation shouts of his beauty and his goodness. The silhouette of lace on a barren tree draped with ice, the rays
of sun streaming forth from a billowing cloud, the sound of a brook
trickling over smooth stones, the form of a woman's body, and the
face of a child anticipating the arrival of the ice cream truck all
speak of God's good heart if we will have but the eyes to see. The
coming of spring after a hard winter is almost too glorious for a soul
to bear. God's beauty is lavished on the world.

As we tried to illumine in Chapter 2, Beauty is powerful. (You
might want to read that passage again.) Beauty may be the most
powerful thing on earth. Beauty *speaks*. Beauty *invites*. Beauty *nourishes*. Beauty *comforts*. Beauty *inspires*. Beauty is *transcendent*. Beauty
draws us to God. As Simone Weil wrote, "The beauty of the world

is almost the only way by which we can allow God to penetrate us
. . . Beauty captivates the senses in order to obtain permission to
pass straight through to the soul . . . The soul's inclination to love
beauty is the trap God most frequently uses in order to win it."

God has given this Beauty to Eve, to every woman. Beauty is
core to a woman—who she is and what she longs to be—and one
of the most glorious ways we bear the image of God in a broken and
often ugly world. It's messy to talk about. It's mysterious. And that
should not surprise us. Women are creatures of great mystery; not
problems to be solved but mysteries to be enjoyed. And that, too, is
part of her glory.

Women want to impact their world for good. As corulers with
Adam, we are created to do so, and one of the key ways we influence our world is in making it a more beautiful place to live. We
decorate our homes. We put flowers on the table. Pioneer women
brought china teacups into the wilderness, and I bring a pretty
tablecloth to eat on when my family camps. We wear perfume,
paint our toenails, color our hair, and pierce our ears, all in an effort
to be ever more beautiful.

Beauty is the most *essential* and, yes, the most *misunderstood* of
all the feminine qualities. We want you to hear clearly that it is an
essence every woman carries from the moment of her creation. The
only things standing in the way of our beauty are our doubts and
fears, and the hiding and striving we fall to as a result.

BEAUTY FLOWS FROM A HEART AT REST

Janet is twenty-one. She was on the dance team in high school.
Small and petite with a fabulous figure. Unlike so many women in
that world of competitive beauty, she escaped an eating disorder.
But she runs between five and ten miles *a day*. She watches what she
eats. She's able to wear the cutest clothes. And yet . . . when you're

with her, your heart does not rest. Her beauty impresses, but it does not invite. The reason is simple: She is striving. She is a perfectionist (an extra two pounds is a crisis; a pimple is a disaster). Her beauty feels tenuous, shaky. It is not flowing from her heart. It's almost as if it's forced, from the outside, through discipline and fear.

June is one of the most beautiful women we have ever met. We encountered her a few years ago while doing a retreat on the coast of North Carolina. Her hair was long, swept up loosely and held by decorative combs. She wore unique, dangly earrings and pretty flowing skirts. Her eyes sparkled when she laughed, which she did often, and her smile lit up the room. She was clearly in love with her husband, her face adoring as she gazed at him. June was at rest with herself, at home in who she was. Talking with her, just being with her, made us feel more at rest with ourselves as well. Her spacious, beautiful soul invited others to come, to be, to taste and see that the Lord is good, whatever was happening in your life. She wept at the retreat. She laughed at the retreat. She was gloriously alive and in love, both with her husband and with the God of the Universe.

And June was about seventy-five years old.

What is the difference between these two women? Rest. June's beauty flows from a heart at rest.

You see, beauty indwells *every* woman. We've seen it so many times counseling women of all ages. Like a shy doe, it reveals itself for a moment, then fades back into cover. Usually it comes when she doesn't know it, when she isn't trying to make it come. Rather, something is happening that allows her defenses to come down for a moment. For instance, when someone is listening. She knows that she matters. Someone cares about her heart, wants to know her. Her beauty emerges as if from behind a veil.

So the choice a woman makes is not to conjure beauty, but to let her defenses down. To choose to set aside her normal means of survival and just let her heart show up. Beauty comes with it.

Your beauty should not come from outward adornment, such as braided hair and the wearing of gold jewelry and fine clothes. Instead, it should be that of your inner self, the unfading beauty of a gentle and quiet spirit. (1 Peter 3:3–4)

First, Peter is not saying that we shouldn't enjoy wearing pretty things. What he's trying to say is that true beauty *comes from* the inner part of us. Our hearts. A heart at rest. When I first read the part about a gentle and quiet spirit, I gave up having much hope of ever making the grade. I am loud. I make jokes when I am nervous or uncomfortable, and when I am comfortable and at ease. I am not prone to long silences. If no one is talking in a group, I take that as an invitation to share my thoughts. A gentle and quiet spirit? Oh dear.

I began to include in my prayers for sanctification a complete personality transplant. Yes, put an angel at the edge of my tongue to guard my every word. And while you're at it, make me someone else, please. Someone more like Melanie in *Gone with the Wind*. Or Mother Teresa. Someone really *good*. I believed this was not too much to ask. He is the God of miracles, after all.

God, in his faithfulness, is changing me. But I remain an extrovert. In fact, instead of making me into someone else, he is making me more *me*. And that is one of the beautiful things about him. That the more *his* we become, the more ourselves we become; more our true selves. So it is a good thing that I misunderstood the Scripture. Peter doesn't mean that beautiful women rarely speak above a whisper, if they speak at all. No. To have a gentle and quiet spirit is to have a heart of faith, a heart that trusts in God, a spirit that has been quieted by his love and filled with his peace. Not a heart that is striving and restless.

A woman in her glory, a woman of beauty, is a woman who is not striving to become beautiful or worthy or enough. She knows in her quiet center where God dwells that he finds her beautiful, has deemed her worthy, and in him, she is enough. *In fact, the only thing getting in the way of our being fully captivating and enjoyed is our striving.*

"He will quiet you with his love" (Zeph. 3:17). A woman of true beauty is a woman who in the depths of her soul is at rest, trusting God because she has come to know him to be worthy of her trust. She exudes a sense of calm, a sense of rest, and invites those around her to rest as well. She speaks comfort; she knows that we live in a world at war, that we have a vicious enemy, and our journey is through a broken world. But she also knows that because of God all is well, that all will be well. *A woman of true beauty offers others the grace to be and the room to become.* In her presence, we can release the tension and pressure that so often grip our hearts. We can also breathe in the truth that God loves us and he is good.

This is why we must keep asking. Ask Jesus to show you your beauty. Ask him what he thinks of you *as a woman*. His words to us let us rest and unveil our beauty.

BEAUTY IS INVITING

Many years ago, our family was staying with friends at their little cabin in an old mountain town in Colorado. One morning as we drove to a remote area where we planned to take a hike, we passed a home that was surrounded by a garden of stunning beauty. I haven't seen anything like it before or since. Groves of towering delphiniums, profuse foxgloves, oases of dianthus and pansies, clematis and roses caught my eyes and my heart. Later that day, I returned. I needed to get closer to that garden. I needed to get into it. I wanted to immerse myself in its extravagance. Emboldened by my desire, I walked up to the front door and knocked.

A small, elderly woman answered the door and eyed me with

suspicion. I quickly introduced myself as a visitor who had seen her garden, been completely captured by it, and wondered if I could, *please*, walk around in it. Her wariness melted into delight. Enjoy my garden? Enjoy the creative work of my hands? Enjoy the fruit of my labor? You betcha. She came out to show me the garden herself, and we spent a wonderful afternoon together. The next morning I was back, having been invited to bring the whole family.

Beauty beckons us. Beauty invites us. *Come, explore, immerse yourself.* God—Beauty himself—invites us to know him. "Taste and see that the LORD is good" (Ps. 34:8). He delights in alluring us and in revealing himself to those who wholeheartedly seek him. He wants to be known, to be explored. A woman does too. She fears it, but below the fear is a longing to be known, to be seen as beautiful and enjoyed. So the unveiled beauty of a woman entices and invites. The heart of the woman determines *what* it is she is inviting others *to*—to life or to death.

Proverbs speaks about two different women, two archetypes. One is Lady Folly, the other, Lady Wisdom. Both are lovely. Both set their tables with fine food and aged wine and dress in fine linens. Both call to the passersby to come in, taste, eat, linger. Lady Folly's door is the mouth of an open grave. Lady Wisdom's home is the passageway to discernment, holiness, and Life.

A woman who is striving invites others to strive. The message—sometimes implicit in her actions, sometimes explicit through her words—is, "Get your act together. Life is uncertain. There is no time for your heart here. Shape up. Get busy. That's what is important." She does not say, *All is well. All shall be well.* Her fear doesn't allow it. She is withholding the very things her world needs.

By contrast a woman whose heart is at rest invites others to rest. That's what we felt in June's presence—and in the presence of many women we know and have come to love. We are invited to be ourselves. Remember the traffic analogy we used in Chapter 2—the exhaust, the noises, the tension? Compare that to what it's like to come into a beautiful place—a garden or meadow or quiet beach. You find room for your soul. It expands. You can breathe again. You can rest. It is good. That is what it is like to be with a beautiful woman. You are free to be you. It is one of life's greatest gifts.

A woman who is hiding invites others to do the same. "Don't be vulnerable. Hide yourself." A woman who makes herself vulnerable and available for intimacy invites others to do the same. After all, Eve is the incarnation of the heart of God for intimacy. She says to the world, through her invitation to relationship, *You are wanted here. We want to know you. Come in. Share yourself. Be enjoyed. Enjoy me as I share myself.* A woman who is controlling cannot invite others to rest, to be known. They will feel controlled in her presence. It won't feel safe there.

A woman who is unveiling her beauty is inviting others to life. She risks being vulnerable: exposing her true heart and inviting others to share theirs. She is not demanding, but she is hopeful. When our assistant Cherie walks into the room, it feels as if someone has just opened up the windows and let the fresh air in. Cherie is young, but that does not stop her from offering her kindness, her hopefulness, her sincere interest in how you are. She offers her beauty by asking good questions and by bringing something of her times with God—an insight, a glimpse into his heart—to bear. She entices others to the heart of God.

You see, ultimately, a woman invites us to know God. To experience through her that God is merciful. That he is tender and kind. That God longs for us—to be known by us and to know us. She invites us to experience that God is good, deep, lovely, alluring. Captivating.

We know many of you are feeling, *But I'm not there. I'm not that kind of woman.* Here is where we "work out" our salvation as God works in us (Phil. 2:12–13). As you begin to live like this, you discover the places in your heart that still need the healing touch of Jesus. That's how it goes. We don't get to stay in hiding until we are whole; Jesus invites us to live as an inviting woman now, and find our healing along the way.

Beauty overwhelms us, enchants us, fascinates us, and calls us.
—FR. ANDREW GREELEY

For a woman to unveil her beauty means she is offering her heart. Not primarily her works or her usefulness (think Martha in the kitchen). Offering her *presence*. At family gatherings my (Stasi here) mother hid in the kitchen. She cooked and baked and prepared and served and cleaned, and for the life of us, we couldn't get her out of there. We wanted her to share her life with us, her thoughts and her ideas, not just her efforts. She wouldn't come. And we were less because of it.

The gift of presence is a rare and beautiful gift. To come—unguarded, undistracted—and be fully present, fully engaged with whoever we are with at that moment. Have you noticed in reading the Gospels that people enjoyed being around Jesus? They wanted to be near him—to share a meal, take a walk, have a lingering conversation. It was the gift of his presence. When you were with him, you felt he was offering you his heart. When we offer our unguarded presence, we live like Jesus. And we invite others to do the same.

Whenever we are with our friend Jan, there is always an offer and an invitation. She really wants to know how we are, what battles we've been facing, what God is doing in our lives. And she truly offers of herself. Sometimes it's her laughter and a wry joke. Sometimes it's her tears from an old sorrow. She offers herself, her beauty, to us. She invites us to live above the striving of the world. She gives something of God.

Beauty offers mercy. My son Samuel is entering adolescence. My little boy is becoming a man. Sometimes it's hard for me to let go. Sometimes his sullen attitude makes me mad. Boys-becoming-men are hard for a woman to understand. They act as if they don't need us anymore. Sometimes they act rudely in their emerging strength. I want to "come down" on him. (It always backfires when I do.) But that is not what he needs from me. He needs mercy. A kind word, a smile. Grace at the end of the day. He softens toward me, and our relationship is recovered. A woman who is full of tender mercy and soft vulnerability is a powerful, lovely woman.

Beauty isn't demanding. Instead, it speaks from *desire*. When our children were young, John had to travel *a lot* for work. On his days off, he was pursuing a master's degree in counseling. That did not leave much time for our family. It fell to me to pay the bills, run the home, and parent the boys. Two of them were in Little League baseball; our youngest was still in diapers. I was busy. I was tired. I couldn't do it. I still remember the fear I felt when I asked John to sit down and talk. I told him that I couldn't do this family thing without him. I told him that I needed him. I asked for his help. I didn't demand him to come through. I didn't whine. I expressed my need and invited his strength, his presence. To my surprise, John told me that in my vulnerability to him, I had never been more feminine or more beautiful.

To offer your heart is to offer your desire—instead of your demand. Beauty offers desire. Our friend Tammy was in a bad marriage. Her husband was verbally abusive. Rather than becoming hard and cynical, she remained soft. Rather than just giving up, she held on to her desire for something more with him. Instead of demanding, she simply would put her desire before him. "Don't you want more for us?" It was beautiful. Even though he chose not to respond, she retained her feminine beauty and offered it as much as she could.

OF COURSE IT FEELS RISKY

The scariest thing for a man is to offer his strength in situations where he doesn't know if it will make any difference. Or worse, that he will fail. Remember, a man's deepest Question is, *Do I have what it takes?* Failure says, *No.* And that is why most men avoid any situation where they might fail. They fear exposure. They fear it will be discovered that they are not a man.

Given the fact that we live after the Fall, far from Eden, and that a man's life is plagued by "thorns and thistles," *most* situations feel like a test of his strength. There is simply no guarantee of success. That's why some men won't play sports. They fear exposure, fear being seen as weak. That's why other men would rather work late than come home and talk to their wives or their children. They know what to do at work; they don't know what to do in their most important relationships. A man's basic sin is his choice to offer strength only in those situations where he knows things will go well. And so repentance for a man is entering into the very situations that he fears and offering his strength anyway.

If he fears intimacy, then offering strength means offering intimacy. If he fears failing in his career, offering his strength means taking a promotion or accepting a new and risky project. If he fears standing up for his children against an angry school principal, then standing up for them is what he must do. If he fears committing to the woman he's been dating for five years, then offering strength is buying her a ring. If he fears initiating sex with his wife, then offering strength means initiating sexual intimacy.

In the same way, the scariest thing for women is to offer our beauty into situations where we don't know if it will make any difference. Or worse, that we will be rejected. For our Question is, *Am I lovely?* And to be rejected is to hear a resounding, *No.* A woman doesn't want to offer her beauty unless she is guaranteed that it will be well received. But life offers no such guarantees. We, too, must take risks.

A few verses after Peter talks about a quiet heart, he gives us what might be the secret to releasing a woman's heart and her beauty:

Do not give way to fear. (1 Peter 3:6)

Isn't that why we hide, why we strive, why we control, why we do anything *but* offer beauty? We are afraid. We have given way to fear. Just think about your life—why you do the things you do. Have you asked yourself how much you are motivated by fear? Janet's beauty regimen is totally motivated by fear. She doesn't believe she's beautiful. She believes she's ugly. So she strives. June would not let fear in.

That is why God says to us, "In repentance and rest is your salvation, in quietness and trust is your strength" (Isa. 30:15). In repentance and rest. He loves it when we, gripped with doubt and fear that he will not be enough, turn the gaze of our souls to him in hope. He loves to prove himself faithful and more than enough to satisfy our hungry souls. When we do turn to him, our souls rest and we are saved. Again. And again.

We can't wait until we feel safe to love and invite. In fact, if you feel a little scared, then you're probably on the right path. Of course it's scary. It's vulnerable. It's naked. God calls us to stop hiding, to stop dominating, to trust him, and to offer our true selves. He wants us to bring to bear the weight of our lives and all that he has given to us, worked into us, and offer it to our world. To entice, allure, and invite others to Jesus by reflecting his glory in our lives. He will give no guarantee that others will enjoy us and respond well.

In fact, we can be sure that there will be times when they do not. Jesus offered like no other, and many rejected him. In those moments or seasons when that happens to us, God's invitation is to bring our sorrow to him. Not to shut down with, *I'll never try that again.* But to keep our hearts open and alive, and find refuge and healing in his love.

Our friend Melissa is married to a man who is not present; who doesn't "get her." Yet. She has known many lonely years. But Melissa has discovered romance with God, and her heart rests in him. She offers her beauty in so many ways. She works as a teacher of women's Bible studies and Christian literature. When you hear her present her ideas, they don't come across as precepts to believe but invitations to see. She allures others to the heart of God. She invites her husband to come closer. Beauty invites. How he responds—if he responds—is not in her hands. But still, she invites.

Linda is in constant pain. Arthritis in her bones runs throughout her body, from her legs to the back of her neck. Her husband divorced her a few years ago, but Linda's heart has been romanced, awakened by the Lover of her soul. She has chosen to remain alive and present. She offers her beauty in her counseling practice, walking alongside clients into deeper realms of brokenness and ultimately healing. She offers such beauty to her children. And to her friends. She invites others to the heart of God. These women remind us that it can be done—we, too, can risk offering our hearts of beauty despite enormous risk. They happen to be two of the most beautiful women we know. And their beauty has *deepened* as they've chosen this path.

LETTING OUR HEARTS BE DEEPENED

As we increasingly become women of substance, women who offer true beauty, we find that our hearts grow in their capacity to love and be loved, to desire, to live. Our hearts are enlarged by Jesus. And by that, we mean that we must be willing to be honest with him and with ourselves about the true nature of our souls—our sorrows, our desires, our dreams, our fears, our deepest and scariest hopes. To invite Jesus to come and walk with us there, to remove from our hearts the things that are getting in the way of our loving. We do not always get what we want, but that doesn't mean that we no longer want. It means we stay awake to the unmet longing and ache. Wait there. Invite Jesus to come, there.

And he will come. Not always to satisfy us by giving us what we want. But to come himself; to meet us with his very Person and to satisfy us with himself.

To possess true beauty, we must be willing to suffer. I don't like that. Just writing it down makes my heart shrink back. Yet, if Christ himself was perfected through his sufferings, why would I believe God would not do the same with me? Women who are stunningly beautiful are women who have had their hearts enlarged by suffering. By saying, "Yes" when the world says, "No." By paying the high price of loving truly and honestly without demanding that they be loved in return. And by refusing to numb their pain in the myriad of ways available. They have come to know that when everyone and everything has left them, God is there. They have learned, along with David, that those who go through the desolate valley will find it a place of springs (Ps. 84:6).

Living in true beauty can require much waiting, much time, much tenacity of spirit. We must constantly direct our gazes toward the face of God, even in the presence of longing and sorrow. It is in the waiting that our hearts are enlarged. The waiting does not diminish us. As a pregnant woman is enlarged in her waiting, so are our hearts. God does not always rescue us out of a painful season. You know that he does not always give to us what we so desperately want when we want it. He is after something much more valuable than our happiness. Much more substantive than our health. He is restoring and growing in us an eternal weight of glory. And sometimes . . . it hurts.

But the experience of sorrow in no way diminishes the joy of living. Rather, it enhances it. When my (Stasi's) mother was in the last few days of her life, we sat together on a bench in Dana Point, California, overlooking the Pacific Ocean. Watching the powerful blue waves crash over the rocks, feeling the warmth of the sun on our faces, we turned to watch white doves soaring on the wind. We were silenced by the beauty of it all, by sharing in the beauty together, and by knowing that it was the last time we would share it on this side of life.

Knowing the parting that was soon to come did not diminish the beauty nor our delight in being together. No, it heightened it. It made us more alive to the moment. More aware. More present. And so it is with a heart awakened to its sorrow. It is more aware, more present, and more alive, to all of the facets of life.

CULTIVATING BEAUTY

Every woman possesses a captivating beauty. Every woman. But for most of us it has been long buried, wounded, and captive. It takes time for it to emerge into wholeness. It needs to be cultivated, restored, set free.

How do we cultivate beauty? How do we become ever more beautiful? By tending to our hearts with great care, as a master gardener tends to her work.

> My mother's sons were angry with me
> and made me take care of the vineyards;
> my own vineyard I have neglected. (Song of Songs 1:6)

Yes, life is harsh on a woman's heart. It has been hard on your heart. The assault on our beauty is real. But Jesus is urging us now to care for ourselves, watch over our hearts (Prov. 4:23). The world needs your beauty. That is why you are here. Your heart and your beauty are something to be treasured and nourished. And it takes time. Every gardener knows this. In our age of instant makeovers and microwave meals, we don't like to wait. But a newly planted rose's presentation in its first year is nothing compared to its second. If properly cared for, its second year's display doesn't hold a candle to its third. Gardens need to become established; their roots need to go deep through summer rains and winter frosts. A garden's beauty does not diminish with age; rather it takes years for it to become all that it can become.

Our hearts need to feed on beauty to sustain them. We need times of solitude and silence. We need times of refreshment and laughter and rest. We need to listen to the voice of God in our hearts as he tells us what we need. Sometimes it will be a bubble bath. Sometimes it is going for a run or a movie or a nap. Often, Jesus will call us away to spend precious time alone with him. We grow in our intimacy with Jesus as we practice listening to his urging, his nudges within. Pay attention to them and follow. The Holy Spirit is our guide, our counselor, our comforter, our Great Friend, and he will lead us. Abiding in Christ means paying attention to the voice of God within, nourishing our own hearts and nourishing our relationship with him. Over time.

Contrary to what the world claims, Beauty does not diminish with time; Beauty deepens and increases. As with June, gorgeous at seventy-five, we find that our latter glory will be greater than our former (Hag. 2:9). True beauty comes from a depth of soul that can only be attained through living many years well. June was seventy-five and captivating.

I will never forget her because she gave me such hope. I finally understood that it took *that long* to become *that beautiful.* Beauty such as hers is rare because it is a rare woman who chooses to keep her heart alive in this dangerous world. Without striving. Her heart was very much alive. Present. Open. Alluring. She had lived years in the presence of God, with the gaze of her heart fixed on him. As we gaze on Jesus, as we behold his goodness, his glory, we are changed into his likeness, the most beautiful Person of all.

They looked to Him and were radiant. (Ps. 34:5 NKJV)

We have all heard it said that a woman is most beautiful when she is in love. It's true. You've seen it yourself. When a woman knows that she is loved and loved deeply, she glows from the inside. This radiance stems from a heart that has had its deepest questions answered. "Am I lovely? Am I worth fighting for? Have I been and will I continue to be romanced?" When these questions are answered, *Yes*, a restful, quiet spirit settles in a woman's heart.

And every woman can have these questions answered, *Yes*. You have been and you will continue to be romanced all your life. Yes. Our God finds you lovely. Jesus has moved heaven and earth to win you for himself. He will not rest until you are completely his. The King is enthralled by your beauty. He finds you captivating.

Beauty is a quality of the soul that expresses itself in the visible world. You can see it. You can touch it. You are drawn to it. Beauty illuminates. Its essence, says Thomas Aquinas, is its "luminosity." It is bound up with the immortal. Beauty flows from a heart that is alive. We have known women you might describe as "frumpy," who seemed to care nothing for their appearance. We have seen them become women who possessed great beauty. We watched it grow in them as they discovered that they were deeply loved, as their hearts came alive in response to the Great Romancer. We *are* romanced. We *are* loved. When we are at rest in that knowledge, we can offer our hearts to others and invite them to Life.

FAITH, HOPE, AND LOVE

Unveiling our beauty really just means unveiling our feminine hearts.

It's scary, for sure. That is why it is our greatest expression of faith, because we are going to have to trust Jesus—really trust him. We'll have to trust him that we *have* a beauty, that what he has said of us is true. And we'll have to trust him with how it goes when we offer it, because that is out of our control. We'll have to trust him when it hurts, and we'll have to trust him when we are finally seen and enjoyed. That's why unveiling our beauty is *how* we live by faith.

Unveiling our beauty is our greatest expression of hope. We hope that it will matter, that our beauty really does make a difference. We hope there is a greater and higher Beauty, hope we are reflecting that Beauty, and hope it will triumph. Our hope is that all is well because of Jesus and that all will be well because of him. So we unveil beauty in hope. And finally, we unveil beauty in the hope that Jesus is *growing* our beauty. Yes, we are not yet what we long to be. But we are underway. Restoration has begun. To offer beauty now is an expression of hope that it will be completed.

And unveiling beauty is our greatest expression of love, because it is what the world most needs from us. When we choose not to hide, when we choose to offer our hearts, we are choosing to love. Jesus offers; he invites; he is present. That is how he loves. That is how we love—sincerely, as the Scripture says, "from the heart" (1 Pet. 1:22). Our focus shifts from self-protection to the hearts of others. We offer Beauty so that their hearts might come alive, be healed, know God. That is love.

CHAPTER NINE

Arousing Adam

Are you strong enough to be my man?
—SHERYL CROW

Come away, my lover,
and be like a gazelle
or like a young stag
on the spice-laden mountains.
—SONG OF SONGS 8:14

*W*hen it comes to the subject of loving a man—any of the men in your life—we need far more than a chapter. A book would barely feel sufficient. The issues are often murky, and things can get really muddy as time goes by. But we cannot pass over this, either. It's far too important; too many questions linger here for most women. So we will try and lay out in this chapter the deeper issues, and trust the Holy Spirit to help you with the application. (Too many books offer techniques and tips and rules without explaining the issues of the *heart* that lie behind them.) You are a woman, after all, not a child. Your heart can figure this out.

Everything we said about unveiling beauty, about how a woman invites and offers—this is *so* much more true when it comes to loving Adam. (We'll bet you were thinking about the man in your life through most of the last chapter.) True femininity arouses true masculinity. Think about it—all those heroes in all those tales play the hero *because* there is a woman in his life, a true Beauty who is his inspiration. It's that simple and that profound. True femininity calls forth true masculinity. We awaken it, arouse it in a way that nothing else on earth even comes close to.

ADAM'S WOUND

If you watch little boys for any length of time, you'll see how deeply the Hero is written on their hearts. I just saw a mom with a little guy at the grocery store. He must have been all of three. He was dressed in his jammies that had this really cool super-hero cape sewn into the shoulders. I'll wager she doesn't normally let him go out midday still in his jammies. I'll bet what happened was she couldn't get him to take them off. Boys love to dress up as army men, Jedi knights, cowboys, heroes. Their games are filled with battle and courage and testing. Who's brave enough to jump out the second story window onto the trampoline?

When they become teenagers, young boys take on an air of independence and bravado that can really drive moms nuts. It looks arrogant and defiant, but it is their masculine strength emerging in an awkward stage. They race cars and care about what they wear and strut their stuff. As Bruce Springsteen sang, "The girls comb their hair in rearview mirrors and the boys try to look so hard." In all of this, you can see their Question: *Do I have what it takes? Am I the real deal? Am I a man?*

A man's deepest wounds come from the way his Question was answered in his youth. Just like yours. Every man is wounded. As he was growing up, he looked to his father to answer his Question. The result was often devastating.

In the case of violent fathers, the wound is given directly. Dave tried to intervene in an argument between his mom and dad when he was about thirteen. Like a good man should, he stepped in to protect his mom. His father leveled his resentment right at his son's heart: "You are such a mama's boy." He's fought that sentence now for more than a decade. He wants so badly to pursue a woman, but something in him feels young and "not man enough." After all, he was told he wasn't a man; he was a mama's boy. Charles's father was a jock, but Charles was a pianist. One day his father just lost it. Who knows what else had built up in his soul or between them, but he came home to find Charles at the piano, and he said with contempt, "You're a faggot." Charles never played the piano again. And he is finding it hard to commit to the woman in his life. Something in him feels . . . uncertain. Unmanly.

Passive fathers also wound, often leaving the boy's Question *un*answered. His silence leaves a vacuum for fear and doubt to fill. That's where my drivenness came from. My dad was wrestling with some pretty awful battles of his own, especially when I was a teenager, and in many ways he left me to face mine alone. I felt . . . abandoned by him. He left me without an answer to my deepest Question. For the next twenty years I was a frightened, driven perfectionist, running hard to keep from facing my wounds. I was afraid that in fact I was just a boy in a man's world, and I kept overachieving to prove I was a man.

Adam's sin and Adam's woundedness come together to result in the passivity or the drivenness you find in so many men. Why won't he talk to me? Why won't he commit? Why is he so angry? Why is he violent? You won't begin to understand a man until you understand his Question, his wound, and how Adam also fell. His search for validation is the driving force of his life.

Just like yours.

STANDING IN LOVE'S WAY

In *Wild at Heart* I warned men that the greatest obstacle to loving a woman was this: too many men take their Question to Eve. They look to her for the validation of their souls. (Haven't you felt it?) It happens usually around adolescence, this fatal shift. The father has been silent or violent; his chance to redeem his son is nearly gone. The next window that opens in a boy's journey is his sexuality. Suddenly, he is aware of Eve. She looks like life itself to him. She looks like the answer to his Question.

It's a fatal shift. So much of the pornography addiction for men comes from this. It's not about sex—it's about validation. She makes him feel like a man. She offers him her beauty, and it makes him feel strong. This is also the root of most affairs. Some woman comes along and offers to answer his Question. His wife has been giving him an "F," and she comes along and says, "You're an 'A' to me," and he's history. If he hasn't found that deep validation he needs from God, he's a sitting duck.

I've tried in every way to help men understand that no woman can tell you who you are as a man. Masculinity is bestowed by masculinity. It cannot come from any other source. Yes—a woman can offer a man so much. She can be his *ezer*, his companion, his inspiration. But she cannot be the validation of his soul. As men, we have *got* to take our Question to God, to our Father in heaven. Only he knows who we truly are. Only he can pronounce the verdict on us. A man goes to Eve to *offer* his strength. He does not go to her to *get* it.

Now, the same holds true for you, Eve.

You cannot take your Question to Adam. You cannot look to him for the validation of your soul. But *so* many women do. *If I have a man, then I'm okay. Then I'm loved.* It happens around adolescence for women too. The time for her father to speak into her life begins to wane. A new window opens up—boys. And if her father has not been there for her, she is starving for love, and she'll give herself to boys in the hope of finding it. Remember the old maxim, "Girls give sex to get love"? It's true.

Mary Pipher's well-known book *Reviving Ophelia* documents this tragic shift in adolescent girls. This almost total loss of self. Girls who were confident and courageous in their youth become uncertain in their teens. Girls who used to have lots of interests and opinions and dreams suddenly seem depressed, lost, obsessed about their looks and about the attention of boys. The shift, at its root, is simply this: they have taken their Question to Adam. It is a deadly shift.

What makes this seem so natural, especially for women, is that Eve *was* made for Adam. "It is not good for the man to be alone; I will make [an *ezer kenegdo*] for him" (Gen. 2:18). Eve was literally fashioned from the rib taken out of Adam's side. There is an incompleteness that haunts us, makes us yearn for one another. How many of you sighed at the end of *Jerry Maguire*, when he runs through the airport and races across town to get back to his wife, who has separated from him? He says, "You complete me." That is true; it's part of the man-woman design.

And yet.

No man can tell you who you are as a woman. No man is the verdict on your soul. (Dear sister, how many of you have lost yourself in this search?) One woman said to us, "I still feel useless. I am not a woman. I do not have a man. I have failed to captivate someone." The ache is real. But the verdict is false. Only God can tell you who you are. Only God can speak the answer you need to hear. That is why we spoke of the Romance with him first. It comes first. It must. It has to. Adam is a far too unreliable source—amen!

Now, yes, in a loving relationship, we are meant to speak to one another's wounds. In love we can bring such deep joy and healing as we offer to one another our strength and beauty. It means the world for me to have Stasi say, "You are such a man." It means the world to have John say to me, "Stasi, you are a beautiful woman." We can—and should—offer this to one another. This is one way our love helps to heal our mate's wound. But our *core* validation, our *primary* validation has to come from God. And until it does, until we look to him for the healing of our souls, our relationships are really hurt by this looking-to-each-other for something only God can give.

Complicating matters further is the curse upon Eve. "Your desire will be for your husband, and he will rule over you" (Gen. 3:16). There is an ache in Eve now that she tries to get Adam to fill. There is an emptiness given to her to drive her back to God, but she takes it to Adam instead. It makes a mess of many good relationships. You know all about this. No matter how much Adam pours into your aching soul, it's never enough. He cannot fill you. Maybe he's pulled away because he senses you're asking him to fill you. Every woman has to reckon with this—this ache she tries to get her man to fill. In order to learn how to love him, you *must* first stop insisting that he fill you.

We say all this as a sort of prologue because we cannot talk about loving a man well—whoever he might be in your life—until we see that we cannot look to him for things he cannot give. We cannot love Adam while we are looking to him to validate us. It will usher in too much fear. If he's the verdict on us as a woman, we won't be able to truly and freely offer him our beauty. We'll hold it back in fear. Or, we'll give ourselves over to him in inappropriate ways, in a sort of sexual or emotional promiscuity, desperate for his attention. And we won't be able to confront him and stand up to him when he needs *that* from us as well.

Ask Jesus to show you what you've been doing with your Question and how you've related to Adam. Only then can we talk about loving men.

How Does a Woman Love a Man?

Lets start with sex.

Not because "it's all men think about" (as many a cynical woman has said), but because it presents the relationship between femininity and masculinity in such a clear way. It is a beautiful and rich metaphor, a very passionate and heightened picture for a much broader reality. The question before us is, "How does a woman best love a man?" The answer is simple: seduce him.

Think of a woman on her wedding night. She dims the lights and puts on a silky something that accentuates the loveliness of her body, reveals the beauty of her naked form, yet also leaves something yet to be unveiled. She puts on perfume and lipstick and checks her hair. She *allures* her man. She hopes to arouse him and invite him to come to her and enter her. In an act of stunning vulnerability she takes life's greatest risk—offering her unveiled beauty to him, opening herself up to him in every way.

And as for her man, if he does not rise to the occasion, nothing will happen. There will be no consummation of love, no life conceived unless the man is able to offer his strength to his woman. That is how we make love. Femininity is what arouses his masculinity. His strength is what makes a woman yearn to be beautiful.

It's that simple, that beautiful, that mysterious, and incredibly profound.

The beauty of a woman is what arouses the strength of a man. He *wants* to play the man when a woman acts like that. You can't hold him back. He *wants* to come through. And this desire is crucial. Don't you want him to *want* to come through for you? Not to be forced to, not because he "ought to." But because he *wants* to come through. Well, then, arouse his desire. In any facet of life.

Can you imagine what it would be like if a young bride took the approach toward her new husband that so many women take in other matters? Imagine her getting out her Daytimer and asking, "When would you like to have sex this week?" (The Efficient Woman.) Or commenting to her new husband, "I suppose you'll want to have sex tonight. Let's get it over with early—I have a lot to do in the morning." (The Busy Woman.) Or the more direct challenge, "That was a pretty poor performance last night. You wanna try it again?" (The Demanding Woman.)

You get the idea. Your message to your man is either, "Sugar, you have what it takes," or, "I don't think you are much of a man. Want to prove me wrong?" The same is true for a woman. Your heart responds very differently to the *pressure* to be beautiful, "You're going out in *that?*" as opposed to the *assurance* that you *are* beautiful, "Sweetheart, you look so lovely tonight." A woman wants to feel beautiful. The strength of a good man makes her feel so. A man wants to feel strong. The beauty of a good woman makes him feel so. This principle plays out far beyond sex and marriage.

The Holy, Scandalous Women of the Bible

There are five women mentioned in the genealogy of Jesus. Now, that might not strike you as a big deal, until you understand that women are never mentioned in those genealogies. It's *always* men. "The father of so-and-so, the son of so-and-so." They read like baseball scorecards. When Matthew adds a few women to the cast, it is a major and notable exception. These woman are so important to God that he has the writer break all cultural norms and even open himself to criticism and dismissal in order to make a point: "Look here—these are *really* good women."

Of course, Mary the mother of Jesus is mentioned. There is also the Bible-study favorite, Ruth. And two others—Rahab and Tamar. What distinguishes these women? Different situations, different acts of obedience. Yet the common theme is this: *Courage, Cunning,* and *Stunning Vulnerability.* Mary is an amazing young woman. Maybe fifteen or so. She accepts the mission God brings to her even though it will cost her dearly. Really now—a young girl known to be seeing an older man turns up pregnant, claiming she's been impregnated by God? She is virtuous, but her choice will be seen by others as scandalous all her life. She makes herself vulnerable—staggeringly vulnerable (she could be stoned for this; certainly she will be abandoned and ostracized)—in order to follow God.

Tamar's story is difficult and beautiful, one we haven't time for here. But one worth wrestling with. (You can find it in Genesis 38.) She uses cunning in the face of men who are failing her badly in order to expose their sin and invite (not demand) them to come through. Rahab is another scandalous story. She's the woman who committed treason in order to walk with God and save her family. (She hid the spies of Israel when they came to her city, Jericho, on a preinvasion reconnaissance mission—in open defiance of her government.) We haven't heard any Bible studies on that one, either. "When Treason Becomes Essential for a Woman." And there is Ruth. This is how I explained her story in *Wild at Heart*:

> Ruth, as you'll remember, is the daughter-in-law of a Jewish woman named Naomi. Both women have lost their husbands and are in a pretty bad way; they have no man looking out for them, their financial status is below the poverty line, and they are vulnerable in many other ways as well. Things begin to look up when Ruth catches the eye of a wealthy single man named Boaz. Boaz is a good man, this we know. He offers her some protection and some food. But Boaz is not giving Ruth what she really needs—a ring.
>
> So what does Ruth do? She seduces him. Here's the scene: The men have been working dawn till dusk to bring in the barley harvest; they've just finished and now it's party time. Ruth

takes a bubble bath and puts on a knockout dress; then she waits for the right moment. That moment happens to be late in the evening after Boaz has had a little too much to drink: "When Boaz had finished eating and drinking and was in good spirits . . ." (Ruth 3:7). "Good spirits" is in there for the more conservative readers. The man is drunk, which is evident from what he does next: pass out. ". . . he went over to lie down at the far end of the grain pile" (3:7). What happens next is simply scandalous; the verse continues, "Ruth approached quietly, uncovered his feet and lay down."

There is no possible reading of this passage that is "safe" or "nice." This is seduction pure and simple—and God holds it up for all women to follow when He not only gives Ruth her own book in the Bible but also names her in the genealogy. Yes, there are folks that'll try to tell you that it's perfectly common for a beautiful single woman "in that culture" to approach a single man (who's had too much to drink) in the middle of the night with no one else around (the far side of the grain pile) and tuck herself under the covers. They're the same folks who'll tell you that the Song of Solomon is nothing more than a "theological metaphor referring to Christ and his bride." Ask 'em what they do with passages like "Your stature is like that of the palm, and your breasts like clusters of fruit. I said 'I will climb the palm tree; I will take hold of its fruit'" (Song 7:7–8). That's a Bible study, right?

No, I do not think Ruth and Boaz had sex that night; I do not think anything inappropriate happened at all. But this is no fellowship potluck, either. I'm telling you that the church has really crippled women when it tells them that their beauty is vain, and they are at their feminine best when they are "serving others." A woman is at her best when she is being a woman. Boaz needs a little help getting going and Ruth has some options. She can badger him: *All you do is work, work, work. Why won't you stand up and be a man?* She can whine about it: *Boaz, pleeease hurry up and marry me.* She can emasculate him: *I thought you were a real man; I guess I was wrong.* Or she can use all she is as a woman to get him to use all he's got as a man. She can arouse, inspire, energize . . . seduce him. Ask your man what he'd prefer.

Now, am I suggesting that a single woman spend the night at her boyfriend's apartment in order to arouse him to marry her? No. Am I saying that a married woman ought to offer herself sexually to her husband even though he's been abusive to her? No. No more than the story of Peter walking on the water tells us all to get a boat, go out on a lake, and give it a try. The *principle* of the story is what matters here. Ruth takes a risk—a risk every woman knows—when she makes herself vulnerable and alluring to Boaz. She arouses him to play the man. *She awakens his desire to be the Hero.* That's the point.

EMASCULATING WOMEN

Women pretty much fall into one of three categories: Dominating Women, Desolate Women, or Arousing Women. The first two are what happens to Eve as a result of the Fall. The third is a woman whose femininity is being restored by God and who offers it to others.

I mentioned Annie in *The Horse Whisperer* as an example of a dominating, emasculating woman. She needs nothing from her man. She has life under control. She wears the pants in the family. Her message is clear: "You are weak and untrustworthy. I am strong. Let me lead and things will go fine." The effect on a man is not good. When a woman becomes controlling and not in the least vulnerable, her seductiveness is shut down. The message is, "Back off—I'll handle this." Any wonder that he backs off?

So many women fear the wildness God put in their man. They are drawn to his strength but then they set about taming him once they've "caught" him. "I don't want you riding a motorcycle any-more. I don't want you hanging around your friends so much. Why do you need to go off on all those adventures?" Women who make their husbands pee sitting down.

But there are other types of emasculating women. In the movie *Enchanted April*, we meet four women—two who are desolate and two who are emasculating. Caroline is a woman who is beautiful with the kind of beauty most women envy. But hers is a severe beauty. She uses it like a weapon to get what she wants, leaving a trail of broken hearts in her wake. There is nothing soft about her. Softness is key to a woman. Not weakness—softness. Tenderness. Mrs. Fisher, a wealthy widow, is the other emasculating character. She orders everyone around, runs her world like a dictator. She shows no emotion unless it is disgust in someone's apparent weakness. There is nothing alluring about her at all.

Emasculating women send a clear message: "I don't need you. I refuse to be vulnerable and inviting. You have nothing to offer me."

DESOLATE WOMEN

The third character in *Enchanted April* is Lottie. She is not harsh—just shut down from years of living with a selfish, domineering pig of a man. She looks like a whipped puppy, rushing to please him in any way, not out of love but out of fear and some weird idea of submission. She is depressed. Rose is Lottie's friend; they meet at church. She is the Religious Woman. The typical Church Lady. She's actually quite beautiful, but she dresses in such a way as to hide it. Bag-shaped dresses, hair in a bun. Her heart is also shut down. She hides behind her prayers and her "good works of service." She is weary and tired.

Desolate women don't seem at first pass to be all that emasculating. They don't attack or dominate. But neither do they allure. Their message is simply, "There's nothing here for you." The lights are off; they have dimmed their radiance; no one is home. A man in her presence feels . . . uninvited. Unwanted. It's a form of rejection, emasculation to be sure. But it's harder to point out because it's so subtle.

Desolate women can also be those whose ache is what *defines* them. Women who will do whatever it takes to get a man. The Woman at the Well in John 4 would be an example. She moves from lover to lover trying to fill the void within her. She's available—but in a clingy, desperate way. "Groveling," as one friend said, "manipulating, begging for attention." Like the character Catherine Zeta-Jones plays in *The Terminal.* Their message to men is, "I need you too much. Please tell me who I am. Fill me." Men use women like this— but they do not love them. They do not feel challenged to be a Hero. Desolate women do not call the men in their lives to be Heroes.

AROUSING WOMEN

If you would be loved, be loveable.
—OVID

The beautiful story in *Enchanted April* is how each of the women actually becomes a woman indeed. Caroline softens, becomes tender and vulnerable. She no longer resents her beauty, but offers it gently, almost shyly, which for her is repentance. Lottie and Rose gain a sense of self. They become substantive, able to offer their men a real mate, not a doormat. They, too, become alluring; being *less* shy is repentance for them—no longer hiding but coming forward in a gentle way. The effect on the men in their lives is astounding. What severity and domineering and hiding and whining could not do, beauty does. Their men come forth as good men, repentant men. Heroes.

An arousing woman is one who calls forth the best in a man by offering who she is *as* a woman—someone who offers her beauty, her true heart, as we described in the last chapter. Such a stark contrast is set out in the movie *A Walk in the Clouds*. There are two women in Paul Sutton's life (played by Keanu Reeves). His wife is not an arousing woman. She pressures him, "You are not the man I want you to be." She is manipulating and demanding. Eventually she has an affair. The Hispanic woman he meets on the bus, however, is alluring. A strong and self-confident woman, she is also soft and inviting. Her message to him is, "You are an amazing man."

However it is expressed in the uniqueness of your own femininity, arousing Adam comes down to this:

Need him. And believe in him.

That is what a man needs to hear from his woman more than anything else. I need you. I need your strength. I believe in you. You have what it takes.

Loving Fallen Men

Granted, not every man is on the road to redemption. There are men out there who are not safe and good men. Some of you are married to men like this. All of you will encounter them. How do you love them? With great wisdom and cunning. The last three chapters in Dan Allender's book *Bold Love* are, "Loving an Evil Person"; "Loving a Fool"; and "Loving a Normal Sinner." You might find them helpful.

Jesus said, "Do not throw your pearls to pigs," (Matt. 7:6). By this we don't think he was calling some people pigs. He was saying, "Look—be careful that you do not give something precious to someone who, at best, cannot recognize its beauty, or at worst, will trample on it." Consider your feminine heart and beauty your treasure, your pearls. A woman can test and see if a man is willing to move in a good direction by offering a *taste* of what is available with her if he does. She does not give everything in a moment. As God does, she allures and waits to see what he will do. We'll try and offer a few examples.

Janice is married to a dull man. A man whose heart was so far buried she wondered if he was even there. Her anger and disappointment with him only drove him farther underground. He wasn't a violent man; to her knowledge he had no addictions. He was just—absent. Checked out as a human being. He was functioning but not passionate. A roommate but not a Lover, let alone a Hero. She decided to play Ruth.

One night when he came home, he found the children were off for a night at Grandma's. The table was set with a beautiful meal; candles were lit. (This is much like the story of Esther too.) Janice was wearing a beautiful blouse, discreetly *un*buttoned several buttons down. As the evening progressed, she unveiled the lace underwear she was wearing beneath. She invited him to make love. Now, what is important is what followed. The next night he came home, hoping for a similar feast. When he moved toward her, she asked him softly why. He was a bit stunned by the question.

"Why do you want me? Is it only for my body—or are you pursuing my heart?" It was a brilliant trap, well set. He stumbled for an answer, but his intentions were exposed. "I long to give myself to you," she said, "but you need to give yourself to me. I want your heart in this marriage, not just your laundry." She awakened desire in him, but did not give herself to him that second night. She waited for him to move closer emotionally. It began an awkward but hopeful journey toward deeper intimacy.

Betsy was married to a verbally abusive man. An elder in the church, he looked great outside the home. But behind closed doors, he was just plain mean. She chose to keep her heart alive, to try and invite him to see what he was doing to her and how they might share something far better. She asked if he might see a counselor, which he did . . . until things got too close to home for him. Then he bailed.

She finally moved out—not seeking divorce, but as an invitation for him to feel the weight of the consequences of his life and his lack of repentance. She fasted and prayed. He did not choose to change, but laid the blame on her. He villainized her to their children, to his church. She held her ground. We're sad to say that he filed for divorce. She gave him many tastes of what life could be like together, if he would repent of his meanness. He chose not to. Like the story of Jesus with the rich young ruler, she let him walk away.

How generous and lavish God is with his beauty toward us. He sends the sun each day; he sends music and laughter and so many notes to our hearts. But he also says, "You will . . . find me when you seek me with all your heart" (Jer. 29:13). That is a good way for a woman to live as well. Not defiant, not hiding, but alluring and watching to see if he wants to come closer.

SINGLE WOMEN

It might be encouraging to point out that Mary, Rahab, Ruth, and Tamar were all single women when the story of their greatness was told. (True, Mary was engaged, but she had reason to believe it wouldn't last long when she gave her "yes" to God.) They are such powerful reminders that this greatness, this beauty, can be lived out as a single woman. They also stand in stark contrast to some of the messages of "purity" given single women today. As one young woman wrote to us, "I am afraid that I and numerous other women have interpreted womanly purity as 'completely ignore the man you are interested in until he proposes to you.'"

And why, then, *would* he propose to you?

Of course a woman should be alluring to the man she is attracted to. A smile, a tenderness, an interest in him and his life are natural and welcome. To look your best; awaken him to your presence. Yes, you can offer beauty to him—in gently increasing amounts as he pursues and comes closer. And yes, there are parts of you that should be held as mysteries until he fully commits, and you offer yourself to him on your wedding night. Don't offer everything, but don't offer nothing.

How much, and when? That is more than we can say in a chapter. Walk with God. Be a wise and discerning woman. Be aware of the issues that could cause you to hold back or give too much. Be aware of the issues in him that could cause him to look to you for his validation or become paralyzed. Invite, arouse, and maintain your personal integrity.

There is an emotional promiscuity we've noticed among many good young men and women. The young man understands something of the journey of the heart. He wants to talk, to "share the journey." The woman is so grateful to be pursued, she opens up. They share the intimacies of their lives—their wounds, their walks with God. But he never commits. He enjoys her . . . then leaves. And she wonders, *What did I do wrong*? She failed to see his passivity. He really did not ever commit or offer assurances that he would. Like Willoughby to Marianne in *Sense and Sensibility*.

Be careful you do not offer too much of yourself to a man until you have good, solid evidence that he is a strong man willing to commit. Look at his track record with other women. Is there anything to be concerned about there? If so, bring it up. Also, does he have any close male friends—and what are *they* like as men? Can he hold down a job? Is he walking with God in a real and intimate way? Is he facing the wounds of his own life, and is he also demonstrating a desire to repent of Adam's passivity and/or violence? Is he headed somewhere with his life? A lot of questions, but your heart is a treasure and we want you to offer it only to a man who is worthy and ready to handle it well.

GOOD MEN THAT DO NOT BELONG TO YOU

The way femininity can awaken masculine strength—and the way a good man's strength allows a woman to be beautiful—these can be offered in all sorts of holy ways between men and women who are not married to one another. Far too long we have lived in a culture of fear in the Church, fearing that any relationship between men and women will end in an affair. Sadly, we have forsaken so many opportunities to call one another forth with the grace of our genders.

John wasn't able to be present for our recent women's retreat. On the second day I had an encounter with an evil woman that left me shaken and under spiritual attack. I asked our colleague, a young man named Morgan, to pray for me. He did—fiercely. He rose up on my behalf and sent the Enemy packing. His prayers and his kind words to me allowed my heart to rest again and carry on through the day. I made myself vulnerable to him, needed him, in a perfectly innocent way. He came through for me, offered his strength in a perfectly innocent way. My thanks to him was a way of saying, "You have what it takes." Should that not be an encouragement to him?

In the same way, there are women in our fellowship who have offered to me (John) many words of encouragement, many tender kindnesses. They have spoken to me of how I have impacted their lives, touched their hearts, offered my strength on their behalf. And that has brought a great encouragement and inspiration to me— even at times when I felt I was failing Stasi as a man. But their encouragement and inspiration did not make me want to have an affair with them—it actually fueled my fire to go back and offer my strength *to* Stasi. It was a kind of affirmation that said, "You are a good man, a man of strength. As a woman I am grateful."

John has offered his strength and kind heart to many women in our community—listened to their lives, helped them find their way, fought fiercely for many of them. His strong, kind presence awakens their beauty. In some sense it is God saying to them, "This is available—not here, in John—but this kind of man is available. Doesn't that awaken your heart as a woman?"

There are all sorts of opportunities in our lives for this. Truth be told, it will be unavoidable. As a man comes alive, the women in his world will experience and enjoy his strength, the power of his masculine presence. As a woman comes alive, the men in her world will experience and enjoy her beauty, the richness of her feminine presence. Yes—this exchange of strength and beauty will be a test of character. When something is awakened in us by another man or woman, we do have a choice in that moment. We choose to accept the awakening as an invitation to go find that with *our* man or woman. Or to pray, if we are single, that this sort of man or woman will come to us from God's hand. We will *have* to face this kind of test as we relate to members of the opposite sex. The only other option is to veil ourselves—as the Muslims insist their women do. A sad and unbiblical way to live.

Remember our answer to the question "How do I love a man?" Seduce him. The sexual connotation of "seduce" may have some of you struggling still with all those situations in which sexual intimacy is not appropriate. We mean it as a principle, a picture of how femininity can arouse masculinity in many, many ways. Perhaps you have heard the old story, attributed to Aesop, about the argument between the North Wind and the Sun. It might help you get past your concern.

The North Wind and the Sun had an argument one day. They disputed which of them was the stronger. A traveler came along the road at that time, and the Sun suggested a way to resolve the argument. Whoever was able to cause the traveler to remove his coat would be the stronger. The Wind accepted the challenge and the Sun hid himself behind a cloud. The Wind began to blow.

Yet the harder he blew, the more the traveler clutched his coat about himself. The Wind sent rain, even hail. The traveler clung even more desperately to his coat. Finally, in despair, the Wind gave up. The Sun came out and began to shine in all his glory upon the traveler. Quite soon the man had removed his coat. "How did you do that?" asked the Wind. "It was easy," said the Sun, "I lit the day. Through gentleness I got my way." ("The North Wind and the Sun")

CHAPTER TEN

Mothers, Daughters, Sisters

*Adam named his wife Eve, because she would
become the mother of all the living.*
—Genesis 3:20

*How wide and sweet and wild motherhood—
and sisterhood—can be.*
—Rebecca Wells

We have our mother tongue, which is our native language. We have mother earth from which all growing things come, and Mother Nature, the unpredictable source of typhoons and tornadoes. The mother lode is the source of riches and a "mother headache" is one that sends you to bed. The mother of all storms is fierce, and the motherland is the home we left and long for. Mother is the source of life. Mother is powerful. Mother is strong. Mother can nurture, and mother can destroy. Depending on our experiences, the word *mother* can evoke images of a warm, welcoming woman or turn our blood to ice.

Whether good or bad, whether redemptive or destructive, our relationships with our mothers affected us to the core of our beings, helping to shape us into the women we have become. As Dinah says in *The Red Tent*, "If you want to understand any woman you must first ask about her mother and then listen carefully."

We are not all mothers, but we all had one. Or longed for one. The relationship between a mother and daughter is a holy, tender, fierce thing fraught with land mines and umbilical cords that stretch and sometimes strangle. The desire in a daughter to please her mother is matched only by her desire to be separate from her. Most mother/daughter relationships go through a stormy season during the girl's adolescence. Hormones rage and the brunt of the raging often lands on the mom. Words are flung, accusations aimed at the heart. "You're not going to wear *that,* are you?" has been uttered by many a mother in horror as her daughter is getting ready to go out. "You don't even know what you're talking about!" has been slung by many a daughter. The way a mother weathers this stormy season of her daughter's transition from girlhood to woman-hood can affect their relationship for the rest of their lives.

Many a good woman makes the desperate mistake of believing that her daughter is a reflection of herself, an extension of herself, and therefore the verdict on her as a mother and as a woman. She is dumbfounded, disappointed, sometimes wounded deeply when her "little girl" makes choices wholly foreign to what she would have chosen. The result of entangling the verdict on yourself as a woman with your daughter's life is deep wounding and a further twisting of the relationship. The mother will try and set things right; the daughter will pull away even further to establish her own identity.

Mothers rightly teach their daughters how to behave and what to believe. The decision to continue to hold to what has been taught belongs to the daughter when she comes into her own. A mother hopes that her daughter's coming into her own is a passage to cele-brate. But often it takes years for a mother and daughter to recon-cile their differences—let alone enjoy them.

Girls' hearts flourish in homes where they are *seen* and *invited* to become ever more themselves. Parents who enjoy their daughters are giving them and the world a great gift. Mothers in particular have the opportunity to offer encouragement to their daughters by inviting them into their feminine world and by treasuring their daughters' unique beauty.

I don't know what it is like to have a daughter. I missed that. My husband and my sons are outside right now blowing things up. They're taking M-60s apart and combining all the gunpowder to make really big explosions. Tea parties don't happen here. No one lets me brush their hair. But although I don't have a daughter, I am one.

THE LONG ROAD HOME

My relationship with my mother was strained. It was painful. For both of us. Our communication was fraught with hidden meanings and misunderstandings. Remember the messages of the wounds I received? She was grieved to have learned she was having another child, and that child happened to be me. I felt I was a disappointment to her in what I believed, how I dressed, what I thought, and who I was. It wasn't until I was forty-one years old that I realized I made her feel exactly the same way.

You remember my story growing up—how my mother was overwhelmed by my coming along. I was too much for her and so I did my best to hide my true self and be the easy daughter she needed me to be. I longed for her to want to know me, to want to play with me. I loved kissing her cheek good night and inhaling deeply the fragrance of her night cream (something I continued into adulthood). I mentioned earlier that I used to pretend to be sick, because then I got her attention. She'd give me books and read to me and bring me meals in bed. A high fever meant her love was coming along with 7 UP and vanilla ice cream. (It is no fun, by the way, being sick with John. He brings me enormous vitamins and horrible-tasting, good-for-me green drinks.)

In elementary school, my sister ingeniously told my mother that her teacher required my mom to read to her every night to help her with her education. A story she made up but one that brought the desired results of snuggling with my mom and having her undivided attention for a full twenty minutes. We do what we can.

When my mother found out that I was smoking in the fifth grade, she sadly said that I wasn't her little girl anymore. I cried. And I got better at hiding. She didn't know my dreams, my struggles, my gifts, or the treacherous path my life was taking. Throughout junior high, high school, and college, I appeared to be a good student who made no waves. Beneath the surface, I was seeking affirmation and life in all the worldly, destructive ways available. I felt unloved, unwanted, and abandoned—worthless, really. The choices I made from that place brought death to my own soul and death to others as I slid ever more deeply into despair, both hating and hiding myself.

When I came home blasted one night in high school after having been sick all over myself and left my soiled clothes in the tub, neither my mother nor my dad said a word. Nor did they confront me later when I came home too drunk to get into the house without their help. Being arrested for drunk driving cost me driving privileges for two weeks, but that was the end of it. One night, I simply didn't come home. When I finally showed up in the morning, I was met by a hysterical mother who had, during my absence, smashed all the drug paraphernalia I openly kept in my room. In her frantic worry to find me, she had looked through my school notebook to find my friend's phone number. What she found instead was a list of all the drugs I had taken in the last month. It was a very long list.

I loved my mom. I didn't want her to know about the drugs. I did not want to hurt her. Yes, she failed me. All mothers fail their children to varying degrees. But she also loved me. That was what was *most* true. I was shamed by her discovery. But I did not repent. No. Not yet. Instead, I became even better at hiding.

I was sexually promiscuous during my college years . . . searching for the elusive feeling of being wanted, of being thought beautiful. My mother was a strong Catholic and often wondered aloud about people who had done things I had done, seriously questioning if God could ever forgive them, wondering how they could live with themselves. I took in her condemning words as blows while silently hoping God could forgive me, that I could forgive me.

By the grace and to the glory of God, I became a Christian my last year in college. Jesus quite literally saved me. But I wasn't a Catholic anymore. Or at least, I wasn't *pretending* to be a Catholic anymore. (I faked it through high school.) I was now attending a "nondenominational church."

My mom was glad that I stopped doing drugs. (We pretended she didn't know about any of the sexual sin.) She was glad that I was praying again. But she was deeply grieved that I wasn't going to her church. When we would broach the subject of faith, both of our defenses rose like battlements. We couldn't see each other over them, let alone hear what the other was saying. Instead of being a shared joy, our doctrinal differences became a barbed-wire fence we could not cross.

So we talked about the weather. For fifteen years.

I read a story recently about a young woman who had just given birth to her first child, and her own mother had come to help care for her. The baby had kept the new mother up most of the night with his little mysterious noises, so she was going to ask her mom how long it was before you stopped hearing all those sounds. Before she could ask, however, her own mother asked her, "Are you getting a cold, dear? I thought I heard you wheezing last night." No matter how old your children become, they are still your children. Just as it is true that no matter how old you are when your parents die, you are still an orphan.

I don't know exactly when a softening began to occur between my mother and me, but slowly we became more graceful with each other. I do know that it began after I had looked honestly at my childhood and grieved deeply the wounds my parents had dealt me, inflicted by action as well as inaction. I had looked squarely at my youth. I'd been angry. I'd been sorrowful. And after a season, I was able to forgive. I began to see my mother with new eyes.

My mother and I began to enjoy, even celebrate, our shared faith in God, and not debate the differences. From out of the blue one day, my mom apologized to me for missing me, ignoring my questions, and turning a blind eye to my struggles while I was growing up. I began to understand that in those years she had been treading water with all that she had just to stay afloat.

OUR LAST YEAR TOGETHER

In the photograph by my bed my mother is perpetually smiling on me. I guess I have forgiven us both, although sometimes in the night my dreams will take me back to the sadness, and I have to wake up and forgive us again. (Lily in *The Secret Life of Bees* by Sue Monk Kidd)

Years later, as God addressed yet another layer of unhealed wounds, I was grieving that in my mother's presence I still felt "not good enough." I still felt like a failure to her, a deep disappointment. Her words continued to pierce. It was then that God showed me that the way my mother made me feel was exactly the way *I made her feel.* A disappointment. An embarrassment. A failure. And in that moment, I knew with utter clarity that it was true. I felt her sorrow. I saw some of her irritating comments to me in a new light. She wanted me to like her, know her, and enjoy her just as much as I wanted her to feel that way about me. And I had withheld my acceptance from her. I realized for the first time how deeply I had wounded her.

I was compelled by God to see her as soon as possible. I was able to make all the arrangements, get on a plane within days, and fly to see my mother so that I could apologize to her in person. We sat at her kitchen table and I offered her, perhaps for the first time, my true heart. I told her that I knew I had made her feel not good enough. I knew that I made her feel that she was a disappointment to me. I told her that I was deeply sorry, that it simply was not true. I loved who she was. I was proud of her. I was glad she was my mom. And I asked her to forgive me.

She couldn't speak. She didn't have to. But I understood by her eyes, through her shy expression and her tender countenance, that she did forgive me. We embraced then with nothing in between.

How can I relate to you the spacious place in our souls that act of repentance and forgiveness created for us? The walls, the barriers, came down. We could offer and receive each other's love and acceptance and enjoyment for the first time in our lives. We spent the rest of that evening looking over old family albums. Nestled up next to my mother, I heard her say, "Look how precious you are." Pointing at pictures of a very young Stasi, "You were always so adorable!" It was a tender time. A healing time. A time that was true and real and full of love.

It was also the last time we had together before she was diagnosed with multiple myeloma. A short month after our relationship's restoration, Mom felt like she was dying. She told her doctor the same, and he ordered some tests. The tests revealed that her kidneys were failing. The cancer was extremely advanced. She was right. She was dying. My mom and I had four more months together where we loved each other unconditionally and fully. How I wanted to have years together in this new place, and yet, how utterly grateful I am to have had the time at all.

God restored much to us in those months. I am weeping now as I remember. Those times, those memories, are gold to me.

THE COST

It is one thing to suffer. It is something far worse to walk alongside one you love who is suffering intensely and be unable to do anything about it. Many of you have lived this. You know. When I was six years old I nearly cut my finger off in a slamming door. When the doctor was shooting the painkiller directly into my wound, I looked up at my mother through my streaming tears and heard her say that it was hurting her far worse than it was hurting me. I didn't understand her then, but I do now.

During her illness, while I was visiting to take care of her, she looked at me and tenderly said, "I'm sorry. I'm sorry to be putting you through this." Here she is, suffering, dying, in pain, unable to eat or even swallow, and she is sorry for *me*; she is sorry to be the cause of suffering in my heart. She would gladly have borne it herself and spared me the sorrow, spared me the pain of bearing her pain, her loss.

I have heard it said that having a child is like having your heart walk around outside of your body. How a mother aches to protect her child. And yet all the while, from infancy to adulthood, a good mother is training her child to move ever more away from her, to need her less and less. Mothers love and long for their children. Their hearts ache for them, over them. A woman bleeds when she gives birth, but that is only the beginning of the bleeding. A heart enlarged by all a mother endures with and through her child's life, all a mother prays and works and hopes for on her child's behalf bleeds too.

A mother's heart is a vast and glorious thing. My mother's heart was expansive, having been enlarged by suffering and years of clinging to Jesus while being misunderstood, dismissed, and judged by those she loved most. Me included. It had cost her to love, had cost her much to mother. It always does. But she would tell you that it's worth it, that there is no other way.

The last time my mother was able to walk to the bathroom, I helped hold her from the front while her sister held her from behind. On the way back, Mom had to take several stops to rest, walking a few inches at a time. At her last resting stop, I looked down into her eyes and said, "Well, what a great opportunity to hug you!" I hugged her, lingering with her frail frame in my arms and then looked into her sky blue eyes. In those eyes, I saw the depth of my mother's love for me. It was measureless, vast, unconditional, tender, deep, strong, joyful, and clear. You could dive into eyes like that; get lost in that kind of love. Or be found.

Finally I understood. My mother loved me. She had loved me during those years; I just hadn't seen it. There was grace in her eyes and a knowing that all was well, that all would be well. And that nothing was lost. Not in our years of missing one another and not in the years that I am left missing her now.

Both my parents are gone now, off and away and fully alive in heaven. I tell you this story because I want you to know that redemption is possible. Healing is possible. Ask Jesus to bring it to you and yours. Then, if you can, go, call your mother. Tell her you love her.

TO MOTHER

As large as the role is that our mothers play, the word *mother* is more powerful when used as a verb than as a noun. All women are not mothers, but all women are called *to mother*. To mother is to nurture, to train, to educate, to rear. As daughters of Eve, all women are uniquely gifted to help others in their lives become more of who they truly are—*to encourage, nurture, and mother them toward their true selves.* In doing this, women partner with Christ in the vital mission of bringing forth life.

"Train a child in the way he should go, and when he is old he will not depart from it" (Prov. 22:6 NKJV). This verse is not a promise about faith. It is not speaking of training a child to follow Christ or promising that if you do, the grown child will continue to follow him. Sorry. The proverb is about raising a child to know who he is and to guide him in becoming ever more himself. *In the way he should go.* Not in the way you would like him to go in order to validate you as a mother and a woman. It speaks of teaching a child to live from his heart, attuned to it, awake to it, aware of it, and when that child is grown he will continue to live a life from the heart. *It is about seeing who a person really is and calling him out to be that person.*

The impact on a life that has been seen and called out is dramatic and eternal. The nurturing of life is a high and holy calling. And as a woman, it is yours. Yes, it takes many shapes and has a myriad of faces. Yes, men are called to this as well. But uniquely and deeply, this calling makes up part of the very fiber of a woman's soul—the calling to mother.

I am reminded of a courageous African-American woman who was thrilled to purchase her first home. After moving in, she came home from work to find drug dealers doing business on her front steps. It seems her new home was smack dab in the center of their "territory" in Los Angeles. She wouldn't stand for it. Head held high, finger wagging; she "mothered" them to higher aims. She mothered them out of their sin. She mothered them into becoming the young men they were meant to become.

You can mother other people's children. In truth, our world

needs you to. My friend Lori's house was the center of activity while her girls were still in school. Their friends loved to hang out at her house. She offered them life. She counseled them. She encouraged them. She mothered them with love and strength. She also baked them fabulous treats. She has played and continues to play a major role in many young women's lives, impacting them for good, calling them forth to become who they are meant to be. We think of a woman C. S. Lewis describes meeting in heaven in his book *The Great Divorce*. A Teacher is showing him around the place when they encounter a woman of stunning beauty.

"It's someone ye'll never have heard of. Her name on earth was Sarah Smith and she lived at Golders Green."

"She seems to be . . . well, a person of particular importance?"

"Aye. She is one of the great ones. Ye have heard that fame in this country and fame on earth are two quite different things."

". . . And who are all these young men and women on each side?"

"They are her sons and daughters."

"She must have had a very large family, Sir."

"Every young man or boy that met her became her son— even if it was only the boy that brought the meat to her back door. Every girl that met her was her daughter."

"Isn't that a bit hard on their own parents?"

"No. There *are* those that steal other people's children. But her motherhood was of a different kind. Those on whom it fell went back to their natural parents loving them more. Few men looked on her without becoming, in a certain fashion, her lovers. But it was the kind of love that made them not less true, but truer, to their own wives."

We mother each other when we offer our concern, our care, our comfort. We mother each other when we see a need and rise to meet it whether it is a sweater for a friend who is chilly, a meal for a struggling family, or a listening ear for a friend who is hurting.

All women are called to mother. And all women are called to give birth. Women give birth to all kinds of things—to books (it's nearly as hard as a child, believe me), to churches, to movements. Women give birth to ideas, to creative expressions, to ministries. We birth life in others by inviting them into deeper realms of healing, to deeper walks with God, to deeper intimacy with Jesus. A woman is not less of a woman because she is not a wife or has not physically borne a child. The heart and life of a woman is much more vast than that. All women are made in the image of God in that we bring forth life. When we enter into our world and into the lives of those we love and offer our tender and strong feminine hearts, we cannot help but mother them.

MY SISTER, MY FRIEND

I love the way women friends have with each other. When I gather with a group of women friends, inevitably someone begins to rub someone else's back. Hair gets played with. Merciful, tender, caressing, healing touches are given. Men don't do this with each other. It is unique to women. When women gather, they ask meaningful questions. They want to know how you *are*. Recipe swapping is all well and good, gardening hints helpful, but women friends unabashedly dive into matters of the heart.

My mom mothered me. But she isn't the only woman who has. My sisters certainly did. Some of my elementary school teachers did. My neighbors did. These days, I receive it from the gentle, tender acts of kindness offered me from the friends God has given me. The gift of friendship among women is a treasure not to be taken lightly. Women friends become the face of God to one another—the face of grace, of delight, of mercy.

The capacity of a woman's heart for meaningful relationships is vast. There is no way your husband or your children can ever provide the intimacy and relational satisfaction you need. A woman *must* have women friends.

It is here, in the realm of relationship, that women receive the most joy and the profoundest sorrows. The friendships of women inhabit a terrain of great mystery. Movies like *Beaches*, or *Fried Green Tomatoes*, or *Steel Magnolias* try to capture this. In these movies the friendships endure testing and trial; they deepen and they last. The men in the lives of these women may leave, but their girlfriends do not. Although often quoted in weddings, Ruth was speaking to a woman when she said, "Where you go I will go, and where you stay I will stay. Your people will be my people and your God my God" (Ruth 1:16). There is a fierce jealousy, a fiery devotion, and a great loyalty between women friends. Our friendships flow in the deep waters of the heart where God dwells and transformation takes place. It is here, in this holy place, that a woman can partner with God in impacting another and *be impacted* by another for lasting good. It is here that she can mother, nurture, encourage, and call forth Life.

Little girls have best friends. Grown women long for them. To have a woman friend is to relax into another soul and be welcomed in all that you are and all that you are not. To know that as a woman, you are not alone. Friendships between women provide a safe place to share in the experiences of life *as a woman*. Who but another woman can fully understand PAP smears and mammograms, PMS, the longing to bear a child, and living in a world run by men? It is a great gift to know that you see as another sees, an immense pleasure to be understood, to enjoy the easy companionship of one you can let your guard down with.

Friendship is a great gift. One to be prayed for and not taken for granted. If you do not have the kind of friendship you long for, ask God to bring it into your life, to give you eyes to recognize it when he does. When God gives a friend, he is entrusting us with the care of another's heart. It is a chance to mother and to sister, to be a Life giver, to help someone else become the woman she was created to be, to walk alongside her and call her deep heart forth.

Friendships need to be nurtured and guarded and fought for. We need to call one another without waiting to be called first. We need to ask how our friends are doing and really listen to their answers. Listen between the lines. We love our friends by *pursuing* them—calls, little presents, cards, invitations to play, to go for a walk, to go to a movie. We offer our hearts.

My friend Dena realized a few years ago that I liked presents. When I'm out and about, I'll often see a little something that I think a friend would like, so I pick it up and surprise her with it. Small things. Simple things. So Dena started giving me little presents. I loved it! Then I clued in that for Dena, what she liked best wasn't presents at all but the gift of time—the most treasured of all commodities. I still give her little presents every now and again. I can't help it. But when I'm able, I give her hours.

We need to pay attention to each other, really *see* one another. That truly is the greatest gift.

AWKWARD LOVE

And let me say clearly, true friendship is *opposed.*

One woman often feels less important to the other, or accused or needy or misunderstood. Honest communication in love is the only way to live and grow in friendships. There are ebbs and flows. There may be too much dependence. There may be real hurt and disappointment. In fact, it's inevitable in our broken world. But with the grace of God firmly holding us, reminding us that he is the source of our true happiness, it is possible to nurture and sustain deep friendships throughout our lives. We are not made to live our lives alone. We are designed to live in relationship and share in the lives of other women. We need each other. God knows that. He will help us. We have only to ask and surrender, to wait, to hope, and in faith to love. We must also repent.

For a woman to enjoy relationship, she must repent of her need to control and her insistence that people fill her. Fallen Eve demands that people "come through" for her. Redeemed Eve is being met in the depths of her soul by Christ and is free to offer to others, free to desire, and willing to be disappointed. Fallen Eve has been wounded by others and withdraws in order to protect herself from further harm. Redeemed Eve knows that she has something of value to offer; that she is made for relationship. Therefore, being safe and secure in her relationship with her Lord, she can risk being vulnerable with others and offer her true self.

> To love at all is to be vulnerable. Love anything, and your heart will certainly be wrung and possibly broken. If you want to make sure of keeping it intact, you must give your heart to no one, not even to an animal. Wrap it careful round with hobbies and little luxuries; avoid all entanglements; lock it up safe in the casket or coffin of your selfishness. But in that casket—safe, dark, motionless, airless—it will change. It will not be broken; it will become unbreakable, impenetrable, irredeemable . . . The only place outside Heaven where you can be perfectly safe from all the dangers . . . of love is Hell. (C. S. Lewis, *The Four Loves*)

In your friendships, in all your relationships, you will disappoint others and they will disappoint you. That comes with the territory of being human. But it is not the truest thing. In your relationships, you have the opportunity to practice loving; to partner with God in mothering, in bringing forth life in another and having your heart enlarged by caring for another and your life enriched by sharing the adventure that life is.

Perhaps it would be good to say just a few words about circles of intimacy. Jesus had them, and so do we. Jesus had the Twelve, but he also had the three. Peter and the sons of Zebedee were with him at the Mount of Transfiguration and were also invited by him to stay awake and pray in the Garden of Gethsemane. (You remember that they failed him there. Jesus understands well that friends disappoint . . . yet he continues to love.) You can only have one, two, maybe three intimate friends in your life at any given time. That's just the way of the heart.

There is room for more dear friends, but they are a little further out, in the next circle, like Jesus' Twelve. Close, but not the ones you would call in need in the middle of the night. And then there are your acquaintances, loose friendships, as Jesus had in the other disciples. It is natural and good to have circles of friendship. Friends will move from one circle to the other, but you can't possibly sustain intimacy with everyone. That said, you also don't want to have intimacy with no one. Jesus desires it with us, and he understands that we need it with others as well. He made us that way.

God invites us to risk trusting him and enter into redemptive friendships with others—to open ourselves up to the possibility of being hurt as well as to the possibility of tasting the sweet fruit of companionship. Yet, no matter how wonderful a taste of relational fullness you have, you will want more. If you had an amazing connection yesterday with someone, when you wake this morning, you will want it again. Eve possesses a bottomless well of longing. Jesus alone is the never-ending fount, which can slake her thirst. No other source, no other relationship will fully satisfy. God made us that way. On purpose.

Deep longing is part of the grace given to Eve to drive her to the River of Life.

While our hearts drink deeply and rest in God's good heart, he "mothers" us so that we continue to become ever more truly who he intends us and created us to be—the women we truly are. A woman who partners with God in bringing forth life in this damaged world—offering, loving, inviting others to become who they were meant to be—she is a mother indeed. She—like God—offers Freedom and Life.

> *Oh gently lay your head*
> *Upon My chest*
> *And I will comfort you like a Mother while you rest.*
> *The tide can change so fast*
> *But I will stay*
> *The same through Past, the same in Future,*
> *Same Today.*

> *Oh weary, tired and worn*
> *Let out your sighs*
> *And drop that heavy load you hold*
> *Cuz Mine is light.*
> *I know you through and through*
> *There's no need to hide.*
> *I want to show you love that is deep and high and wide.*

> *For I am constant.*
> *I am near.*
> *I am peace that shatters all your secret fears.*
> *I am holy.*
> *I am wise.*
> *I'm the only One, who knows your heart's desires.*

Oh gently lay your head upon My chest
And I will comfort you like a Mother
While you rest.

—JILL PHILLIPS, "I AM"

CHAPTER ELEVEN

Warrior Princesses

> *"Me, a princess?"*
> *"You are the legal heir."*
> *"I never lead anyone."*
> *"We will help you to be a princess, to rule. If you refuse to accept*
> *the throne then the kingdom will cease to exist as we know it."*
> —*THE PRINCESS DIARIES*

> *In God's name, we must fight them!*
> —JOAN OF ARC

*W*omen are often portrayed in stories and tales as the "Damsel in Distress." We are the ones for whom men rise up and slay dragons. We are the "weaker sex," said to faint at the sight of blood, needing to be spared the gory details of battle whether on the field or in the marketplace. We are the ones waiting in our flowing gowns for the knight to come and carry us away on the back of his white horse. And yes, there are days when a knight in shining armor would be most welcome. We do long to be fought for; loved enough to be courageously protected. But there is a mighty fierceness set in the hearts of women by God. This fierceness is true to who we are and what we are created to do.

Women are warriors too.

There is an old tale of an invasion against the Vikings, who were the first Europeans to explore North America and settle here some seven hundred years ago. Gail Collins writes in *America's Women,* "When the Viking camp was attacked by Indians, causing the male defenders to flee, a pregnant Freydis grabbed a handy weapon, took out her swollen breasts, 'and whetted the sword upon them' according to a Viking chronicler. The sight of her so unnerved the war party they 'became afraid and ran away.'" What a woman!

I've already told you that when I was a little girl I used to love World War II movies. How I longed to be a part of them. Not the movies themselves, but the real thing. I wanted to be part of something noble and grand and heroic and good. Didn't you? I am not alone in that deep longing. During the Civil War, more than four hundred women disguised themselves as men so that they, too, could fight alongside their husbands, fathers, and sons. History is laden with stories of women rising up to defend their families, their land, their honor.

In the mythic story *The Return of the King,* Éowyn, battle maiden of the Rohirrim, disguises herself as a man and rides to war, joining her kinsmen in the greatest battle of her time. She rides beautifully, and she handles a sword with deadly skill. In the thick of the battle, she fights heroically. Tragically, her uncle the king is attacked by the leader of the enemy's army, and as he swoops down to finish the king off, Éowyn steps in to block his path. She will not allow her uncle even to be touched by the evil wraith.

"Begone, foul dwimmerlaik, lord of carrion! Leave the dead in peace!"

A cold voice answered: "Come not between the Nazgûl and his prey! Or he will not slay thee in thy turn. He will bear thee away to the houses of lamentation, beyond all darkness, where thy flesh shall be devoured, and thy shriveled mind be left naked to the Lidless Eye."

A sword rang as it was drawn. "Do what you will; but I will hinder it, if I may."

In the battle that follows, the wraith is assured, cocky even. His strength is greater, his weapons more deadly. He boasts of an ancient prophecy, proclaiming, "*Thou fool. No living man may hinder me!*" And it is here that Éowyn is finally and fully victorious.

> It seemed that Dernhelm [Éowyn] laughed, and the clear voice was like the ring of steel. "But no living man am I! You look upon a woman. Éowyn I am, Éomund's daughter . . . Begone, if you be not deathless! For living or dark undead, I will smite you, if you touch him."

Éowyn removes her helmet and lets her hair fall free. She declares herself "no man" and fighting *as a woman*, slays her enemy. Something critically important is revealed in this story. Women are called to join in the Greatest Battle of all time—the battle being waged for the hearts of those around us. The human heart is the battlefield. The war is a deadly one; the results devastating or glorious, but always eternal. We are needed. There is much to be done. The hour is late. But we will only be victorious when we enter in with our feminine hearts—*when we battle as women*.

Redeemed women of God have tender, merciful hearts, backbones of steel, and hands that have been trained for battle. There is something incredibly fierce in the heart of a woman that is to be contended with—not dismissed, not disdained, but recognized, honored, welcomed, and trained.

FIGHTING BACK

"There is a strength in you. I see it."
—WILLIAM WALLACE TO THE PRINCESS IN *BRAVEHEART*

About eleven years ago, John brought home a book by Neil Anderson. I think it was *The Bondage Breaker*. John had begun to encounter spiritual warfare issues in some of the folks he was counseling and wanted to learn a little more about it. Curious, I opened the book and began to read some of the case histories Dr. Anderson writes about. One in particular caught my attention. He described a woman who was often dizzy. The feeling of dizziness would frequently come upon her and throw her off balance both physically and spiritually. *Huh*, I thought. *I get dizzy a lot too.* I mentioned this to John, and he was totally surprised. He never knew this about me. It was something I had lived with or under for years, but it never occurred to me to tell him about it. To me, it was normal.

It's amazing what we will live with because we think it's normal when it is *not*.

So we decided to perform an experiment. The next time a wave of dizziness came over me, I would command it in the name of Jesus to depart from me and see what happened. I didn't have to wait long. The next day I was busy with the activities of my daily life and suddenly, out of nowhere, I got hit with dizziness. I prayed and commanded the dizziness to leave in the authority of Jesus' name. And guess what? It left! Immediately. I was stunned. The next wave came later, and I prayed again. Again it left. Whoa! Something was going on here that was completely foreign to me. A whole new dimension of Christianity opened up for me. The dizziness was a form of spiritual attack. That whole Ephesians passage about putting on the armor of God . . . he meant it. We would need it.

The dizzy spells (interesting phrase) did not cease quickly. In fact, they increased, both in number and intensity. I had to learn to stand and to keep standing, "resist him, standing firm in the faith," as Peter urged (1 Pet. 5:9). I had to learn in a new way to "not grow weary in doing good" (2 Thess. 3:13 NKJV), and to "pray without ceasing"

(1 Thess. 5:17 NKJV). It was as if the assaulting spirit(s) didn't believe I would stand firm against them and so they kept trying.

I got hit a few weeks later with a wave of dizziness that knocked me off my feet. From the ground, I prayed again, commanding it to leave me in the name of Jesus Christ. It did. And I have never been assaulted by dizziness again. Something that I had lived with for decades is now gone, for good. Through the experience of standing firm against the attack of dizziness, God had begun to train my hands and my heart for battle.

EMOTIONAL ATTACKS

I saw, in gradual vision through my tears,
The sweet, sad years, the melancholy years,
Those of my own life, who by turns had flung
A shadow across me.
—ELIZABETH BARRETT BROWNING

I (Stasi) have struggled with depression for most of my life. Even as a child, depression and suicidal thoughts plagued me. You remember, I tried to end my life when I was just ten years old. My spirit was weighed down. After our second child was born, I felt lost at sea. I was filled with self-doubt, anger, shame, and a deep sense of worthlessness. I loved my husband. I loved my sons. But I was keenly aware that I was not able to love them well. I wanted to be happy. But I was not. I was disconnected from my heart and from my God. I had no clue why I felt the way I did, other than believing that there was something deeply wrong with me and there always would be.

When we moved to Colorado Springs, I wanted to volunteer at the local Crisis Pregnancy Center. I wanted to be a counselor who did the pregnancy testing and met with the young women. The issues surrounding an unwanted pregnancy and the choices a girl feels forced to make are something I was and remain passionate about. You see, I had an abortion when I was in high school. I felt as if a part of my soul died along with my unborn child that day, and I wanted to help women not make the same grievous decision.

It turned out, however, that the center didn't allow women who'd had previous abortions to counsel others until they went through a class called "Post Abortion Counseling and Education." They wisely offered this path of healing to women, required it even for their volunteers. Okay. So I went.

It was incredible. I hadn't told many people about my past, and now here I was in a room with ten or so other women, exposing my shame. All of the other women were Christians—repentant and brokenhearted. Most were working in ministry positions. All of them had had at least one abortion, some had had many. And all of us needed the forgiveness and deep healing work of God.

God used that group to lance my heart. The nature of the group was such that we dealt only with the issue of abortion in our lives. If the process caused other painful issues to surface, we needed to seek additional counseling elsewhere. It was not long before I was on the phone to the leader, asking her for a referral. Other issues were not only stirred up, I was reeling in excruciating pain. I began to look at my life and consider for the first time that the sorrows and abuses I had received possibly were not all my fault or merely what I deserved.

Counseling began. God brought me to a wonderful, insightful, lovely Christian woman who honored my soul and invited me to take a deeper look. She walked with me, with God, into the dungeons of my heart and helped me to see that Christ had destroyed the iron gates. I met with Laura for quite a while before I hit a place in my life where I couldn't make any progress. I couldn't think clearly. I didn't have the energy or the hope to go further. It was then that she suggested I begin taking antidepressants.

My father was a manic-depressive. They call it bipolar now. Chemical imbalances get passed down. (Thanks, Dad.) So I started taking the medicine. Within a couple of weeks, I no longer felt the weight over my soul that I had lived with the majority of my life. I wondered, *Is this what other people feel like all the time? Sheesh!* I could now move forward with God into deeper realms of my heart. The sky became blue. Life was no longer altogether too much.

Antidepressants are stigmatized in the church. Some call them "happy pills." Others say that if you are filled with the Holy Spirit and walking with God in faith, you will not need them. They shame those who are responsibly taking them. But we don't shame diabetics who need to take insulin. Why do we shame people with a chemical imbalance who need to take something to help them? Once my father began taking lithium, he no longer had the dramatic mood swings that were the bane of our lives, and he became a much better man, more of the man he truly was. There is no shame in needing to take medicine whether to help in a short, difficult period or for the bulk of your life.

We human beings are made up of three interwoven parts. As Paul says, "May God himself . . . sanctify you through and through. May your whole spirit, soul and body be kept blameless at the coming of our Lord Jesus Christ" (1 Thess. 5:23). We are body, soul, and spirit. Each part affects the others in a mysterious interplay of life. By seeking healing through counseling, God was addressing my soul. God's provision of the help of antidepressants was a tremendous help to my body. I made real progress. But it was not enough. God wanted me to engage my spirit.

A foul spirit of depression had its bloody claws in my life. It often works like that—the Enemy knows our weaknesses, and he preys upon them. Demons smell human brokenness like sharks smell blood in the water, and they move in to take advantage of the weakened soul. Paul warns about this in Ephesians when, *writing to*

Christians, he warns us not to "give the devil a foothold" in our lives through unhealed and mishandled emotions (4:26–27). God had me begin to stand against it.

James and Peter both exhort us to *resist* our Enemy (James 4:7, 1 Peter 5:8–9). Jesus said he has given us his authority to overcome the spiritual attacks against us (Luke 10:18–19). I prayed. John, as my husband, my head, prayed as well. We commanded this foul spirit to leave me by the authority given to believers in Jesus Christ. Deliverance came. Victory. Release. Healing. Restoration. It was the final key. I needed to address all three aspects—my body, soul, and spirit—in order to come more fully into healing. Far too many women will focus only on one or two aspects and not engage in the spiritual warfare that is swirling around us.

But if we would be free, we must.

RELATIONAL ATTACKS

Another common enemy that often is at work in women's relationships is a spirit of accusation. In our friendships, in our relationships with peers at work, and especially in our marriages, we often feel that we are a disappointment to others, that they disapprove of us. We feel in their presence that we are not enough, or that we are too much. After we leave a time with them, we're plagued by a deep sense of failing. We feel frustrated and irritated and ashamed that we feel that way. Our hearts often land in shame and isolation, or we go to resentment . . . and isolation.

Do you know what I am talking about? Do you recognize this in your own life? That replaying of conversations you've had with people, that sense of having blown it, or that other sense of just being really irritated at them? Have you noticed how the feelings grow as you continue to mull it over? Now, who do you suppose would have a vested interest in ruining your relationships? This is exactly what Paul warned the Corinthians about when he said, "For we are not unaware of his schemes" (2 Cor. 2:11).

Well, a spirit of accusation was operating in *our* marriage for the first ten years of our married life. I felt John's disapproval over how I spent my time, my relationship with God, even how I chopped vegetables. I felt as though everything I did disappointed him somehow. I could not live up to his (unspoken) desires. It's hard to offer your heart and love to a person when you feel that way. Our tendency is to withdraw in shame or anger. At least, that's what I do.

Then one night, after an unusually uncomfortable dinner, John wanted to know how he was failing me. He often felt, he said, that I was disappointed in *him*, that he couldn't do anything right, that I disapproved of how he lived and who he was.

What?!

This was unbelievable to me. I felt nothing of the sort toward him. I wanted to be more like him. I told him that I didn't feel that way toward him, but I certainly felt that *from* him—felt that I was a deep disappointment *to him*. He told me that was utterly untrue. He felt nothing of the sort. It was then that John and I realized we were not alone in the room. We were being attacked by a spirit of accusation that had effectively worked between us for ten years, operating to isolate us from one another and ultimately destroy our marriage.

We got mad. Together, we took a stand against it and commanded it to leave. This can feel a little weird at first, talking to the air and saying stuff like, "I bring the cross of Christ against you. In Jesus' name I command you to leave." Sometimes you have to be firm and pray several times. As Peter said, "*firm* in the faith" (1 Pet. 5:9, emphasis added). But leave it does!

What a relief. What a breakthrough for us. To be able to look into my husband's eyes now and not have mine clouded over by false accusation allowed me to see his love for me as true and real and deep. We now could believe that we liked each other, were *for* each other, and that the truest thing in our marriage was committed love.

It changed everything.

A WARRING BRIDE

Ladies, you are the Bride of Christ . . . and the Bride of Christ is a warring bride.

Now, often the hardest person to fight for is . . . yourself. But you must. Your heart is *needed.* You must be present and engaged in order to love well and fight on behalf of others. Without you, much will be lost. It is time to take a stand and to stand firm. We are at war. You are needed.

Yes, men are created in the image of the Warrior King. Men are warriors. But women need to fight too. It is a powerful good when a man battles for a woman's heart and stands between her and her enemies. But often, there is not a man present in a woman's life to fight on her behalf. And even when there is, God desires the woman's spirit to rise up in his strength as well. One day we will be queens—we will rule with Jesus (Rev. 21). We need to grow in our understanding and practice of spiritual warfare not only because we are being attacked but because it is one of the primary ways that we grow in Christ. He uses spiritual warfare in our lives to strengthen our faith, to draw us closer to him, to train us for the roles we are meant to play, to encourage us to play those roles, and to prepare us for our future at his side.

It is *not* that we are abandoned. Christ has not abandoned us.

It is *not* that we are alone. He will never leave us or forsake us.

It is *not* even up to us. The battle is the Lord's.

Jesus came through for us before we were even born. He fought for us before we even knew we needed him. He came, he died, he rose again *for us*. He was given all authority in heaven and on earth *for us* (Eph. 1:22). He has won the decisive victory against our Enemy. *But we must apply it.* Christianity is not a passive religion. It is an invasion of a Kingdom. We who are on the Lord's side must wield his victory. We must learn to enforce it. Women need to grow as warriors because we, too, were created to reign. God said of Eve as well as Adam, "and let them rule" (Gen. 1:26). And one day we will rule again (Matt. 25:21, Rev. 22:5). God allows spiritual warfare and uses it in our lives for our good. It is how we learn to grow in exercising our God-given spiritual authority as women.

There is a fascinating verse in Judges 3. Talking about how hard it was to gain the Promised Land, it explains that the Lord, the God of angel armies, did not drive all the nations out at once "by giving them into the hands of Joshua" (2:23). No, the Lord left some nations to test the Israelites who had not experienced war and to "teach warfare to the descendants of the Israelites who had not had previous battle experience" (3:2). Much of what he allows in your life is not for you to simply accept, *but to get you to rise up!* God wants you to know how to wield the weapons of warfare, how to take a stand, and how to fight.

> *"One day you will be a Queen and you must open your eyes."*
> —WILLIAM WALLACE TO THE PRINCESS IN *BRAVEHEART*

Women are not meant to be helpless creatures. God has given us a fierceness that is holy and is to be used on behalf of others. Chapters 4 and 5 in the book of Judges tells the story of Deborah, a prophetess who led Israel. Through her, God commanded the Israelites to go to war against Sisera and the Canaanite armies. The leader of the Israelite army, a man named Barak, would go to war only if Deborah went with them. He would not go if she did not. So Deborah went. "But because of the way you are going about this," said Deborah, "the honor will not be yours, for the LORD will hand Sisera over to a woman" (Judg. 4:9).

The story of the battle is short. Led by Deborah, the Israelites were victorious. Their enemy Sisera, however, escaped and fled on foot to the tent of Jael, a wife and the "most blessed of [the] tent-dwelling women" (5:24). While Israel's enemy slept in her tent, Jael took a tent peg and hammered it through his temple. He lay dead at her feet. Now, that is a fierce woman! And Deborah led Israel in a victory song:

> So may all your enemies perish, O LORD! But may they who love you be like the sun when it rises in its strength. (Judges 5:31)

WARRIOR PRINCESSES

What does a warrior princess look like? Think Joan of Arc. Think Mother Teresa. Think Esther. Think Mary of Bethany. Think Arwen. Think Éowyn. Think Deborah. Think Mary, Jesus' mother. Women who were wise, cunning, strong, beautiful, courageous, victorious, and very *present*.

I just returned home from a women's retreat where God came for his women. It was stunningly beautiful. My friend Susie was there, and she told me the following story about how Jesus came for her and two of her roommates in one fell swoop and taught them to take their stand against the enemy.

The evening session was on "Healing the Wound," and the women had been released into an hour-long covenant of silence so they could listen to God. They were asking God to reveal the lies they had been living under, the sentences they had agreed with, and the vows they had made as a result. We had prayed God's grace and courage for them that they would renounce the lies, however true they felt, and invite God in to heal their wounded hearts and speak the truth. Women were journaling, praying, weeping, seeking God, and inviting him into the deep places of their hearts to reveal and to heal.

Susie went back to her room to journal, as did two of her roommates. The number one lie of the enemy she realized she had believed and lived with all her life was, "Do not speak. Do not speak. Do not speak." Unbeknownst to her, roommate number one was journaling the key lie she had been living under: "You have nothing of value to offer. Do not offer. Do not offer. Do not offer." Roommate number two was writing down the lie she had lived with and believed: "No one will be there for you. You are too much trouble anyway. Do not ask. Do not ask. Do not ask."

It was then that "Do not ask" began to have a major asthma attack, and "Do not ask" does not have asthma. Has never had asthma. Susie's children do have severe asthma; she has been to the emergency room countless times with them. At once she recognized the attack for what it was. But Susie was in a covenant of silence. She was not supposed to talk. Her lie was screaming at her, "Do not speak!" yet she risked asking the choking, gasping woman, "Are you all right?" The struggling-to-breathe woman shooed Susie off with an "I'm fine," all the while hearing, "Do not ask! Do not ask! Do not ask!"

"Do not offer" was watching and listening and sensing that her roommate was in trouble, but she was frozen, believing she had nothing to offer. She was hearing, "Do not offer; do *not* offer; do *NOT* offer!" The three of them continued this for life-threatening minutes. "Do not speak," "Do not offer," and "Do not ask," a triangle of death until Susie saw that her roommate was turning blue, desperately gasping for breath and in dire need. Susie grabbed "Do not offer" and said, "I need your help!" They both went over to "Do not ask" and began to pray for God's help. Susie spoke loudly in the name of Jesus and commanded this assault on her roommate to cease. "Do not offer" lent her strength, joining in Susie's prayer, and immediately "Do not ask" was freed and breathing deeply. She was saved. Rescued. It was not asthma. It was spiritual attack.

The three women stood in wonder and began to share what their key lies were. They were astounded as they realized that God had come for them and unseated their lies, exposing them for what they were in one dramatic intervention. "Do not speak" needed to speak. "Do not offer" needed to offer. "Do not ask" was in need and was worth fighting for. The three of them became joyous—giddy even—and laughed together until their sides ached as they realized the wild love of Jesus. He had taken them out of the lecture and into the lab, showing them the destructive power of the lies they were living under and calling them to truth and to life.

Women warriors are strong, yes, and they are also tender. There is mercy in them. There is vulnerability. In fact, offering a tender vulnerability can only be done by an incredibly strong woman, a woman rooted in Christ Jesus who knows *whose* she is and therefore knows *who* she is. Offering our hearts wisely, living in the freedom of God's love, inviting others to rest, alluring those in our lives to the heart of God, and responding to the heart of God in worship are some of the most powerful ways that a woman wars for her world. But she also puts on the full armor of God *daily* and takes her immovable stand against the powers of darkness.

Satan is defeated. The prince of this world is cast down (John 12:30–32). The rulers and authorities are disarmed (Col. 2:15). But the demonic realm is a realm of lies, hatred, and murder. Satan and the fallen angels, now demons, have been cast down, but they are not chained. Not yet. Now, "Your enemy the devil prowls around like a roaring lion looking for someone to devour" (1 Pet. 5:8). And he does devour. He assaults and maims and steals and kills and destroys wherever he can, and the brunt of his malice falls on God's image bearers. On you and me. On the Beloved. Satan is a vicious, ruthless bully, and a bully will not back down unless someone stronger stands up to him and exposes him for what he is. That is your job for "greater is He who is in you than he who is in the world" (1 John 4:4 NASB).

> Finally, be strong in the Lord and in his mighty power. Put on the full armor of God so that you can take your stand against the devil's schemes. For our struggle is not against flesh and blood, but against the rulers, against the authorities, against the powers of this dark world and against the spiritual forces of evil in the heavenly realms. Therefore put on the full armor of God, so that when the day of evil comes, you may be able to stand your ground, and after you have done everything, to stand. (Eph. 6:10–13)

There is a Daily Prayer that John and I and our ministry team pray every morning. It is good and true and enormously helpful. You'll find it at the back of this book. It is also gender neutral. A dear friend told us once that while she was praying on the armor of God, she saw it in her spirit's eye, and it was light and lovely. God made you a woman. On purpose. Perhaps it would help you to know that in wearing the armor of God, nothing is diminished—not your beauty, your femininity, or your tender, merciful, mighty heart.

A lovely young woman wrote me and told me that as she takes great care in dressing in the morning, so she takes great care in putting on the armor of God. Listen to the first part of her prayer.

> I now put on with thanks the armor which You have provided for me—girding myself with the belt of truth; binding up all that is vulnerable of my femininity; first my need to be pursued and fought for. Thank You for daily pursuing me and fighting for me as well.

I also gird up my desire to be irreplaceable in a grand scheme of Yours. You have placed this desire within me and I wrap Your truth around it, in hope of what You will do. Grant me eyes to see each day in light of Your activity, to live in the big-ness of Your story.

I gird up my desire to offer life through my gifting, the beauty You have bestowed on me. I ask You to continue to reveal and confirm what You desire to do through me and all You have given to me. I trust that You have called me by name and have given me a love, a beauty, a gift to pour out on my family, my friends, and those You bring to me. May this day be an offering of love poured out before You on the altar of my life."

Let us say it again. Your life is a Love Story set in the midst of a life-and-death battle. The beauty, the adventure, the intimacy—they are what are *most* real. But it is a battle to gain them and a battle to keep them. A battle for your own heart and a battle for the hearts around you. "The LORD is a warrior; the LORD is his name" (Ex. 15:3). Jesus fights on your behalf and on behalf of those you love. He asks you to join him.

CHAPTER TWELVE

An Irreplaceable Role

If there is a real woman—even the trace of one—still there inside the grumbling, it can be brought to life again. If there's one wee spark under all those ashes, we'll blow it till the whole pile is red and clear.
—C. S. LEWIS

Mary responded, "I am the Lord's servant, and I am willing to accept whatever he wants. May everything you have said come true."
—LUKE 1:38 NLT

*T*he story of Cinderella turns upon an invitation.

Up until the moment that the courier from the Palace arrives at her door, Cinderella's life seems set in stone. She will always be a washerwoman, a cellar girl. Her enemies will forever have the upper hand. She will live a life of enduring disappointments, though she will suffer them nobly. No other life seems possible. This is her fate. Then, word from the Prince arrives—an invitation to a ball. It is at this point that all hell breaks loose. Her longings are awakened. Her enemies become enraged. And her life is never the same.

How gracious that it comes by invitation. As a woman, you don't need to strive or arrange; you don't need to make it happen. You only need to respond. Granted—Cinderella's response took immense courage, courage that came only out of a deep desire to find the life her heart knew it was meant for. She *wanted* to go. But it took steadfastness to press through her fears just to get to the ball. It took courage not to abandon all hope even *after* she danced with the Prince. (She ran back to the cellar, as we all do.) But she became the woman she was born to be, and the kingdom was never the same. It is a beautiful parable.

The same holds true for Mary, the mother of Jesus—only it's far, far more weighty. Her life also turned upon an invitation. The angel came as the courier of the King. But still, she needed to say yes. He would not force the whole thing upon her. Her heart needed to be willing. She would *need* her heart through all that followed. Accepting God's invitation required remarkable courage, and once again all hell broke loose. Her Enemy raged. She nearly lost her marriage. She and Joseph certainly lost their standing in the synagogue. Her life became an incredible story. Mary needed a steadfastness of heart to keep saying "Yes" to God. But she became the woman she was born to be, and the Kingdom was never the same. It all started with an *invitation*.

The invitations of our Prince come to us in all sorts of ways. Your heart itself, as a woman, is an invitation. An invitation delivered in the most intimate and personalized way. Your Lover has written something on your heart. It is a call to find a life of Romance and to protect that love affair as your most precious treasure. A call to cultivate the beauty you hold inside, and to unveil your beauty on behalf of others. And it is a call to adventure, to become the *ezer* the world desperately needs you to be.

The Power of a Woman's Life

When the history of the world is finally told rightly—one of the great joys when we reach the Wedding Feast of the Lamb—it will be as clear as day that women have been essential to every great move of God upon this earth.

I wanted to say "*nearly* every great move," not wanting to overstate a crucial point and recognizing that there are moments when men have led the way. But Stasi chimed in and said, "Those men had mothers, didn't they?!" I was thinking of Moses who seemed to lead the Exodus, but it quickly dawned on me that it was his mother who saved his life as a baby (at the risk of her own life and the lives of her entire family). It was his sister who stayed with the babe and suggested a nursemaid when pharaoh's daughter took him for her own. (That nurse would be, of course, his mother.) Okay. I concede. Women have been essential to every great movement of God.

Certainly there are those amazing moments in the Old Testament like the story of Rahab, who secured the Hebrews' successful military launch into the Promised Land. And Esther, who saved her people from genocide and secured the future of Israel . . . and of the world. It's clear that women supported the ministry of Jesus, financially and emotionally, and women were the ones who stayed with him when nearly all the men hightailed it and ran. As we read the story of the spreading Gospel and the birth of the Church in the New Testament, we encounter women like Lydia, whose home became the staging point for the evangelism of Thyatira and Philippi; women like Nympha and Apphia, who hosted the emerging church in their homes—again, at great risk to themselves and their loved ones. There is Priscilla, who risked her life to help Paul spread the Gospel, and Junias, who was with Paul when he was in prison and whom he calls "outstanding among the apostles" (Rom. 16:7).

And of course, the salvation of mankind rested on the courage of a woman, a teenage girl. What if she had said no? What if any of them had said no?

To try and give honor to women in the sweep of history is

impossible here. It would be easier to think of any of the great or small turning points in God's rescue of mankind and try to find one where women were *not* irreplaceable. From the beginning, Eve was God's gift to the world—his *ezer kenegdo* for us. History is still unfolding, and your existence on this earth as a woman is proof that you have an irreplaceable role to play. You are a woman, are you not? An *ezer kenegdo* to your core. Your lingering disbelief (may it be fading away) that anything important hangs on your life is only evidence of the long assault on your heart by the one who knows who you could be and fears you.

There is much life saving that needs to be done yet, and someone needs to do it. Not in a pressure-filled, *You'd better get to it* kind of a way. Rather, an invitation. Your feminine heart is an invitation by your Creator. To what? To play an irreplaceable role in his Story. Isn't that what your Lover wrote there? Some dream, some desire, something so core to who you are it almost hurts to think of it. The very longing is such a part of your being it's scary even to give it a voice. You may not know the dream itself yet. But you know the *longing* to play an irreplaceable part. That is a good beginning.

Ezer is woven into the fabric of your feminine heart. You must live this out. What lives, what destinies are hanging on *your* "Yes" to God?

Your Irreplaceable Role

Our friend Jeanine has been a career missionary with OMS for thirty-two years. For the last fourteen, she has been pouring out her life in Medellín, Colombia—a city and a country infamous for drug cartels, murders, violence—a culture of death. It is not a place friendly to Christianity. "Sixty pastors a year are murdered in Colombia," she told us on a recent visit. Jeanine first followed God's call to teach Hebrew in a seminary there. Then he upped the stakes, asking her to minister in the country's notorious prisons. A single woman, walking into overcrowded, all-male prisons filled with hardened criminals—an incarnation of hell on earth—to bring the love of Jesus.

In Bellavista, a Colombian prison in Medellín, more than 6,000 inmates are crammed into a prison designed to hold 1,500. "Up until (14) years ago when the Bible studies began, Bellavista was known for its violence—there was an average of two murders *a day* within the prison walls . . . As lives are being transformed, the killings are slowing," she said. Only 7 inmates were murdered from 1990 to 1997. Jeanine risks death daily, but she does not keep that from stopping her. For as she says, "Security is not found in the absence of danger, but in the presence of Jesus." More than 500 inmates are currently studying Scripture at the prison, and literally thousands have been saved through the ministry Jeanine started. She is their *ezer*. The *ezer* to many in Colombia.

Our dear friend Carol has a bright mind and a keen intellect. A favorite among her professors, she graduated from an Ivy League university at the top of her class. Her mother is a professional, her father a university professor, her sister a physician, and her brother is finishing a law degree. The sky is the limit for Carol. She reads constantly. She is aware of international events and analyzes world trends. She plans her days so as not to miss National Public Radio broadcasts. And she just gave up what looked like a golden career move to stay at home full time with her newborn son.

There is nothing on earth Carol would rather do—yet it was an incredibly difficult decision to make. Her family doesn't understand; she feels she has let them down. She has hopes and desires to pursue a higher education. There is much that she wants to do, to learn, to experience. She has given up so much of her own life in order to bring life to her little boy. Learning to mother her child is requiring more of her heart and soul than she thought possible.

God called Carol to the high position of mothering, and she is choosing to die a thousand small deaths to her self every single day while at the same time falling ever more in love with her son.

Carol chose to say "yes" to God and followed his lead into the hidden life of a stay-at-home mom. God is meeting her there. In the hiddenness, she is discovering the holy. And she is playing the most irreplaceable, essential, powerful, life-impacting role imaginable. As G. K. Chesterton wrote,

> To be Queen Elizabeth within a definite area, deciding sales, banquets, labors, and holidays; to be Whitely within a certain area, providing toys, boots, cakes, and books; to be Aristotle within a certain area, teaching morals, manners, theology, and hygiene; I can understand how this might exhaust the mind, but I cannot imagine how it could narrow it. How can it be a large career to tell other people's children about the Rule of Three, and a small career to tell one's own children about the universe? How can it be broad to be the same thing to everyone and narrow to be everything to someone? No, a woman's function is laborious, but because it is gigantic, not because it is minute. *(What's Wrong with the World)*

On Ellie Claus's seventeenth birthday, she crossed the finish line as the Junior Iditarod Champion—a 150-mile dogsled race through the Alaskan wilderness. Ellie lives in "the bush," the outback of Alaska, where she has grown up with the untamed wilderness as her backyard. It has been her dream to compete in the full-fledged Iditarod Trail Sled Dog Race, a 1,150-mile cross-country trek from Anchorage to Nome. (You have to be eighteen to run the Iditarod.) Polar bears prowl part of the route. Wolves, too. Mushers are sometimes attacked by moose. Temperatures can dip to seventy degrees below zero. Competitors run the nine- to twelve-day race alone, without any outside assistance, on just a couple of hours' sleep a day.

Ellie is a petite, darling young woman you'd picture more at home at a prep school or on a dance team than running the dangerous Iditarod. But Ellie's heart is alive and passionate, thanks to her love of God. She is willing to take enormous risks to become the woman that she is meant to be. In 2004, twelve days after she turned eighteen, Ellie became the youngest person (man or woman) to run the Iditarod. She crossed the finish line after eleven days, nineteen hours, and twenty-four minutes, finishing forty-fifth out of a field of eighty-seven. Her grandmother runs marathons (twenty to date) and her mom guides backcountry skiing in Alaska. Women of adventure, each of them!

My friend Tammy has been a leader in women's ministry for decades. She is a gifted woman, totally sold out to God. And a few years ago, God invited her to come away with him and sit at his feet. Alone. He called her to leave her position on the church staff. He called her to quit leading her small group, her Bible study, her accountability group. He asked her to become a woman of "one thing"—to become a Mary, a woman devoted to worship. To minister to the heart of God.

Tammy chose to say "yes" to God and followed his lead into the secret realm of his heart. Her friends thought she was nuts. The church leaders chastised her publicly for abandoning the Great Commission. She was accused and misunderstood. It hurt. But God had captured Tammy's heart and has been capturing it ever more deeply since. She has been captivated by his beauty. And his radiant beauty shines forth from her countenance.

Tammy became a worshiper, and her life of pouring her adoring devotion onto Jesus has become a beacon and a call to countless women to do the same—to attain to the high and holy calling of ministering to the heart of God and to discover ever more the treasure of who he is. I am one of those women who have been changed by her life. Tammy is playing her amazing, irreplaceable role very well.

Kathleen felt the call of God to become a doctor early in her life. As the daughter of an OB-GYN, she was exposed early and often to the cost paid by doctors and their families—the long hours, the sleepless nights, the inconvenient emergencies. Kathleen has also been captured by the call of Christ to third world countries. She is pursuing her medical degree overseas so that she can play her irreplaceable role as a missionary doctor, bringing physical healing through her expertise and spiritual healing through her God.

You see, our true places as women in God's Story are as diverse and unique as wildflowers in a field. No two look quite the same. But we all share certain spheres of influence to which we are called to be an *ezer*.

In Your Relationships

Eve is God's relational specialist given to the world *to keep relationship a priority*.

Men have a way of letting these things slip. They'll go months without checking in on the health of their relationships. Years, even. And the World simply uses people, then spits them out when they are worn out and no longer "on top of their game." Our Enemy despises relationship, hates love in any form, fears its redemptive power. This is why God sent Eve. Women are *needed* to protect relationships, bring them back to center stage where they belong. You might at times feel like the only one who cares. But as women we must hang onto this—that because of the Trinity, relationship is *the* most important thing in the universe. Let us not give way or yield our intuitive sense of the importance of relationship for anything.

It is here, *starting* in our circles of intimacy, that we are first and foremost women. It is here that we must first turn our gaze to ask,

"What does it look like to offer my Beauty, my fierce devotion, my love? How do they need me to be their *ezer*?" You have an irreplaceable role in your relationships. No one can be to the people in your life who you can be to them. No one can offer what you can offer. There are many things God calls us to do, but loving well always comes first. And don't your relationships feel *opposed*? Of course. They must be fought for.

Satan knew that to take out Adam, all he had to do was take out Eve—his *ezer kenegdo*. It worked rather well, and he has not abandoned the basic plan ever since. Your place in the world as God's heart for relationship is vital. All the Enemy has to do to destroy people's lives is to get them isolated, a lamb separated from the flock. To do this he removes the *ezers* in their life. He makes a woman feel like, "What do I have to offer, really? They're probably doing fine." Don't you believe it for a moment. You have been sent by the Trinity on behalf of love, of relationships. Fight for them.

IN THE BODY OF CHRIST

Your life is also part of a larger movement, a mystical fellowship, the Kingdom of God advancing here on earth. That fellowship of the Ransomed being Restored—that is an amazing fellowship to be a part of. To be sure, it's messy. Have you noticed in Paul's letters to the young church how often he has to intervene in relationships? "I plead with Euodia and I plead with Syntyche to agree with each other in the Lord" (Phil. 4:2). He's addressing two women there, by the way. The fellowship of Christ is *messy* because it, too, is *opposed*. And here you have an irreplaceable role to play.

Yes, we know—women haven't always felt welcomed to bring their gifts to their churches, unless those gifts fall within certain narrow parameters (the nursery, the bake sale, etc.). We haven't time here to address the issues surrounding "the proper role of women" in the church. That would also take a book in itself. However, we do believe it is far more helpful to start with *Design*—with what God designed a woman to be and to offer. That comes first. Understand Design and you can then interpret roles. A woman is *not* the same as a man (thank God!). She is designed differently. We hope that's clear by now. Doesn't it follow that her contributions will be uniquely feminine? And therefore the roles she plays will best fit her feminine heart? (Not as Fallen Eve, but as Redeemed and Restored Eve.)

Furthermore, many of the Scriptures on the *Role* of women in the church are a reflection of God's concern for a woman's protection and spiritual covering. We live in a dangerous world. Satan's opposition of the Church is vicious. He bears a special hatred for Eve. It follows that God would want to ensure that a woman helping to advance his Kingdom would be offered the covering and protection of good men. Issues of headship and authority are intended for the *benefit* of women, not their suppression. You know how dangerous it can be to try and come alive as a truly feminine woman. Right?

God desires that wherever and however you offer yourself to the Body of Christ, you'll have the protection of good men over you. Not to hold you back, but to set you free as a woman. Christ has made man as his warrior, to offer his strength on behalf of Eve *so that she might flourish*. If that's not the context you've found yourself in, find one that is. After all, when we speak of your irreplaceable role within the Body of Christ, we're talking about the true fellowship of those whose hearts are captured for Jesus, who have become his intimate allies. You want to offer yourself to those who thirst for what you have. If it's not wanted where you are, ask Jesus what he wants you to do.

If you are called, God will make a way. Either where you are or through a change of circumstances. Follow your Lover; respond to his invitations. With him, there is no stopping you.

IN THE WORLD

Stepping further out into your farthest sphere of influence, you have something essential to offer the World. It may be in the form of a notable career. It may be a hidden life, well lived. Some women are called to the marketplace. Lydia was an entrepreneur when Paul met her, "a dealer in purple cloth from the city of Thyatira, who was a worshiper of God" (Acts 16:14). Deborah was an advisor to Israel on matters of justice, economics, and warfare (Judg. 4–5). Some women find themselves in the marketplace of the World because they want to be there. It is their calling. Others are there because at this time in their lives they have no choice.

Either way, the crucial issue is this: It is *as a woman* you must live there. Do not be naive. The World is still deeply marred by the Fall. Men still dominate in many sinful ways (remember the curse). Women who "make it" there tend to be dominating and controlling (remember Fallen Eve). The Evil One holds sway over the World and its systems (1 John 5:19). In the World you *must* be as cunning as a Rahab, an Esther, a Tamar. You must walk wisely. You must not let them shape you into their view of what a woman is. You'll end up a man. What you have to offer is *as a woman*. Uniquely feminine.

Above all, you must live in that World as a response to the invitation of Jesus, for you will be hurt if he has not called you there. You will be covered if he has.

WHAT IS WRITTEN ON YOUR HEART?

As I said earlier, the invitations of Jesus come to us in many ways. Sometimes they come through a circumstance, an opportunity that opens before us. Sometimes they come through other people who see something in us that we may not yet see, and they invite us to step forth in some way. But God's invitations ultimately are matters of the heart. They come through our passions, those desires set deep within us. What is it you yearn to see happen—how do *you* long for the world to be a better place? What makes you so angry you nearly see red? What brings you to tears?

You will find that as God restores your heart and sets you free, you will recover long-lost passions, long-forsaken dreams. You'll find yourself drawn to some vision for making the world a better place. Those emerging desires are invitations—not to rush out and attempt them immediately. That also is naive. They are invitations to bring your heart to your Lover and ask him to clarify, to deepen, to speak to you about how and when and with whom. We love Frederick Buechner's description when he writes, "The place that God calls us is that place where the world's deep hunger and our deep desire meet."

Do Not Give Way to Fear

Of course this is scary.

Responding to the invitations of Jesus often feels like the riskiest thing we've ever done. Just ask Rahab, Esther, Ruth, and Mary. Ask Jeanine, Ellie, Tammy, Carol, and Kathleen. Webster defines "risk" as exposing one's life to the possibility of injury, damage, or loss. The life of the friends of God is a life of profound risk. The risk of loving others. The risk of stepping out and offering, speaking up and following our God-given dreams. The risk of playing the irreplaceable role that is ours to play. Of course it is hard. If it were easy, you'd see lots of women living this way.

So let's come back then to what Peter said when he urged women to offer their beauty to others in love. This is the secret of femininity unleashed:

Do not give way to fear. (1 Pet. 3:6)

The reason we fear to step out is because we know that it might not go well (is that an understatement?). We have a history of wounds screaming at us to play it safe. We feel so deeply that if it doesn't go well, if we are not received well, their reaction becomes the verdict on our lives, on our very beings, on our hearts. We fear that our deepest doubts about ourselves as women will be confirmed. Again. That we will hear yet again the message of our wounds, the piercing negative answers to our Question. That is why we can *only* risk stepping out when we are resting in the love of God. When we have received his verdict on our lives—that we are chosen and dearly loved. That he finds us captivating. Then we are free to offer.

You could say that people did not respond very well to Jesus' love, to his stepping out in faith and playing the role that was his alone to play. And that would be a ridiculous understatement. The very people that Jesus died for hurled insults at him, mocked him, spat at him, crucified him. Jesus had to trust his Father *profoundly*, with his very being. Peter uses him as our example saying, "Follow in his steps . . . He did not retaliate when he was insulted. When he suffered, he did not threaten to get even. He left his case in the hands of God" (1 Pet. 2:21–23 NLT). Or, as another translation has it, "he entrusted himself" to God. He was okay. He entrusted himself to God.

A few verses later Peter, writing to women, says, "in the same way . . . do not give way to fear" (3:1, 6). Jesus lived a life of love and he invites us to do the same. Regardless of the response.

It was very hard and immensely risky for me to begin to speak and offer from my heart at our women's retreats. Terrifying, really. You see, when I first began to speak, I was severely overweight. My sin, my addiction, was plain for all to see. To stand in front of a group of women and be clearly failing in the outward beauty department was humbling and hard. It has felt risky for me to write this book with John. Risky to share so much of my story. Risky because I'm a first-time author and he is so well-known, so good at it.

But we don't get to wait to offer our lives until we have our acts together. We don't get that luxury. If we did, would anyone *ever* feel like offering *anything*? God asks us to be vulnerable. He invites us to share and give in our weaknesses. He wants us to offer the beauty that he has given us even when we are keenly aware that it is not all that we wish it were. He wants us to *trust* him.

How it turns out is no longer the point. Living in this way, as a woman alive, is a choice we make because it is the woman we want to be. It is our loving response to our Lover's invitation.

Be Present

John and I were at a newcomers' dessert-type thing, a get-acquainted deal where, as part of our introductions to each other, we were to share what our "family motto" was. In our little group was an older couple we had been drawn to. The gentleman had a twinkle in his eye, a spark, as if he had discovered the secret to life and it brought him much joy. His wife was a tiny woman who I can best describe as being very *present*. She was not a woman hiding, nor a woman afraid. She was a woman at rest, at home with herself and with all pistons firing. She was alive and beautiful.

The gentleman looked to his wife and asked, "Do we have a family motto?" She answered, "Well, it's been on the refrigerator for the past thirty years." He asked, "What? Amana?" After some laughter, this is what she shared. This is what she lived by. This is what she invited others into.

Now we should live when the pulse of life is strong. Life is a tenuous thing . . . fragile, fleeting. Don't wait for tomorrow. Be here now! Be here now! Be here now!

Be here now.

To live as an authentic, ransomed, and redeemed woman means to be real and present in this moment. If we continue to hide, much will be lost. We cannot have intimacy with God or anyone else if we stay hidden and offer only who we think we ought to be or what we believe is wanted. We cannot play the *ezer* role we were meant to play if we remain bound by shame and fear, presenting only to the world the face we have learned is safe. *You have only one life to live. It would be best to live your own.*

What have we to offer, really, other than who we are and what God has been pouring into our lives? It was not by accident that you were born; it was not by chance that you have the desires you do. The Victorious Trinity has planned on your being here now, "for such a time as this" (Esther 4:14). We need you.

> Jesus knew that the Father had put all things under his power, *and that he had come from God and was returning to God;* so he got up from the meal, took off his outer clothing, and wrapped a towel around his waist. After that, he poured water into a basin and began to wash his disciples' feet, drying them with the towel that was wrapped around him. (John 13:3–5, emphasis added)

Jesus knew who he was. He knew where he had come from and where he was going. He knew why he was here. And so, in power and strength, in humility and complete freedom, he offers. He ministers to and ultimately he pours out his life as an offering for ours. Pleasing and holy and acceptable. Jesus does this, he says, as "an example that you should do as I have done for you" (v. 15).

God really does want you to know who *you* are. He wants you to be able to understand the story of your life, to know where you have come from, and to know where you are going. There is freedom there. Freedom to be and to offer and to love. So, may we take a moment and remind you who you truly are?

You are a woman. An image bearer of God. The Crown of Creation. You were chosen before time and space, and you are wholly and dearly loved. You are sought after, pursued, romanced, the passionate desire of your Fiancé, Jesus. You are dangerous in your beauty and your life-giving power. And you are needed.

As a woman who has been ransomed and redeemed, you can be strong and tender. You speak to the world of God's mercy, mystery, beauty, and his desire for intimate relationship. You are inviting; you can risk being vulnerable, offering the weight of your life as well as your need for more because you are safe in God's love. You labor with God to bring forth life—in creativity, in work, in others. Your aching, awakened heart leads you to the feet of Jesus, where you wait on him and wait for him. The eyes of his heart are ever upon you. The King is captivated by your beauty.

We need you. We need you to awaken to God more fully and to awaken to the desires of the heart that he placed within you so that you will come alive to him and to the role that is yours to play. Perhaps you are meant to be a concert musician or a teacher. Perhaps you are meant to be a neurologist or a horse trainer. Perhaps you are to be an activist for ecology or the poor or the aged or the ill. You are certainly called to be a woman, wherever else he leads you.

And that is crucial, dear heart. Whatever your particular calling, you are meant to grace the world with your dance, to follow the lead of Jesus wherever he leads you. He will lead you first into himself; and then, with him, he will lead you into the world that he loves and needs you to love.

It is by Invitation.

Take My Hand

There is a scene near the end of the film *Anna and the King* I wish I could now play for you. Let me describe it.

The setting is nineteenth-century Siam, a tiny but beautiful Asian country still in the grips of its ancient past. Anna, an English woman living in Siam as a tutor to the king's many offspring, has helped King Mangkut prepare for a state dinner. He wants to show the British that his country is ready to enter into the affairs of the world, so the dinner is given in the English style—silverware, table-cloths, candlelight, and, at the end of the meal, ballroom dancing.

When the feast is over and it comes time for the first dance, the king stands and extends his hand to Anna. He invites her to dance with him. He fixes his gaze upon her and is distracted by nothing and no one else. He waits for her response. She is clearly surprised, taken aback, but has the grace to respond and stand. As they walk past the long table, the king's eyes never stray from hers, a smile playing on his lips. Others are upset that he has chosen her. Some watch with contempt, others with pleasure. It is of no consequence to the king or to Anna.

Anna came to the ball prepared. She was beautiful in a striking gown that shimmered like starlight. She spent hours getting herself ready—her hair, her dress, her heart. As they reach the dance floor, Anna expresses her fear of dancing with the King before the eyes of others. "We wouldn't want to end up in a heap," she says. His answer to her questioning heart? "I am King. I will lead."

Jesus is extending his hand to you. He is inviting you to dance with him. He asks, "May I have this dance . . . every day of your life?" His gaze is fixed on you. He is captivated by your beauty. He is smiling. He cares nothing of the opinion of others. He is standing. He will lead. He waits for your response.

> My lover spoke and said to me,
> "Arise, my darling,
> my beautiful one, and come with me." (Song 2:10)

A Daily Prayer for Freedom

$\mathscr{M}$y dear Lord Jesus, I come to you now to be restored in you—to renew my place in you, my allegiance to you, and to receive from you all the grace and mercy I so desperately need this day. I honor you as my sovereign Lord, and I surrender every aspect of my life totally and completely to you. I give you my body as a living sacrifice; I give you my heart, soul, mind, and strength; and I give you my spirit as well. I cover myself with your blood—my spirit, my soul, and my body. And I ask your Holy Spirit to restore my union with you, seal me in you, and guide me in this time of prayer.

Dear God, holy and victorious Trinity, you alone are worthy of all my worship, my heart's devotion, all my praise and all my trust and all the glory of my life. I worship you, bow to you, and give myself over to you in my heart's search for life. You alone are Life, and you have become my life. I renounce all other gods, all idols, and I give you the place in my heart and in my life that you truly deserve. I confess here and now that it is all about you, God, and not about me. You are the Hero of this story, and I belong to you. Forgive me for my every sin. Search me and know me and reveal to me any aspect of my life that is not pleasing to you, expose any agreements I have made with my Enemy, and grant me the grace of a deep and true repentance.

Heavenly Father, thank you for loving me and choosing me before you made the world. You are my true Father—my Creator, my Redeemer, my Sustainer, and the true end of all things, including my life. I love you; I trust you; I worship you. Thank you for proving your love for me by sending your only Son, Jesus, to be my sacrifice and my new life. I receive him and all his life and all his work, which you ordained for me. Thank you for including me in Christ, for forgiving me my sins, for granting me his righteousness, for making me complete in him. Thank you for making me alive with Christ, raising me with him, seating me with him at your right hand, granting me his authority, and anointing me with your Holy Spirit. I receive it all with thanks and give it total claim to my life.

Jesus, thank you for coming for me, for ransoming me with your own life. I honor you as my Lord; I love you, worship you, trust you. I sincerely receive you as my redemption, and I receive all the work and triumph of your crucifixion, whereby I am cleansed from all my sin through your shed blood, my old nature is removed, my heart is circumcised unto God, and every claim being made against me is disarmed. I take my place in your cross and death, whereby I have died with you to sin and to my flesh, to the world, and to the Evil One. I am crucified with Christ. I now take up my cross and crucify my flesh with all its pride, unbelief, and idolatry. I put off the old man. I now bring the cross of Christ between me and all people, all spirits, all things. Holy Spirit, apply to me the fullness of the work of the crucifixion of Jesus Christ for me. I receive it with thanks and give it total claim to my life.

Jesus, I also sincerely receive you as my new life, my holiness and sanctification, and I receive all the work and triumph of your resurrection, whereby I have been raised with you to a new life, to walk in newness of life, dead to sin and alive to God. I am crucified with Christ, and it is no longer I who live but Christ who lives in me. I now take my place in your resurrection, whereby I have been made alive with you, I reign in life through you. I put on the new person in all holiness and humility, in all righteousness and purity and truth. Christ is now my life, the one who strengthens me. Holy

Spirit, apply to me the fullness of the resurrection of Jesus Christ for me. I receive it with thanks and give it total claim to my life.

Jesus, I also sincerely receive you as my authority and rule, my everlasting victory over Satan and his kingdom, and I receive all the work and triumph of your ascension, whereby Satan has been judged and cast down, his rulers and authorities disarmed, all authority in heaven and on earth given to you, Jesus, and I have been given fullness in you, the Head over all. I take my place in your ascension, whereby I have been raised with you to the right hand of the Father and established with you in all authority.

I bring your authority and your kingdom rule over my life, my family, my household, and my domain. And now I bring the fullness of your work—your cross, resurrection, and ascension—against Satan, against his kingdom, and against all his emissaries and all their work warring against me and my domain. Greater is he who is in me than he who is in the world. Christ has given me authority to overcome all the power of the Evil One, and I claim that authority now over and against every enemy, and I banish them in the name of Jesus Christ. Holy Spirit, apply to me the fullness of the work of the ascension of Jesus Christ for me. I receive it with thanks and give it total claim to my life.

Holy Spirit, I sincerely receive you as my Counselor, my Comforter, my Strength, and my Guide. Thank you for sealing me in Christ. I honor you as my Lord, and I ask you to lead me into all truth, to anoint me for all of my life and walk and calling, and to lead me deeper into Jesus today. I fully open my life to you in every dimension and aspect—my body, my soul, and my spirit—choosing to be filled with you, to walk in step with you in all things. Apply to me, blessed Holy Spirit, all of the work and all of the gifts in pentecost. Fill me afresh, blessed Holy Spirit. I receive you with thanks and give you total claim to my life.

Heavenly Father, thank you for granting to me every spiritual blessing in the heavenlies in Christ Jesus. I receive those blessings into my life today, and I ask the Holy Spirit to bring all those blessings into my life this day. Thank you for the blood of Jesus. Wash me once more with his blood from every sin and stain and evil device. I put on your armor—the belt of truth, the breastplate of righteousness, the shoes of the readiness of the gospel of peace, the helmet of salvation. I take up the shield of faith and the sword of the Spirit, the Word of God, and I wield these weapons against the Evil One in the power of God. I choose to pray at all times in the Spirit, to be strong in you, Lord, and in your might.

Father, thank you for your angels. I summon them in the authority of Jesus Christ and release them to war for me and my household. May they guard me at all times this day. Thank you for those who pray for me; I confess I need their prayers, and I ask you to send forth your Spirit and rouse them, unite them, raising up the full canopy of prayer and intercession for me. I call forth the kingdom of the Lord Jesus Christ this day throughout my home, my family, my life, and my domain. I pray all of this in the name of Jesus Christ, with all glory and honor and thanks to him.

About the Authors

John Eldredge is the founder and director of Ransomed Heart™ Ministries in Colorado Springs, Colorado, a fellowship devoted to helping people recover and live from their heart. John is the author of numerous books, including *Epic, Waking the Dead, Wild at Heart, Desire, The Way of the Wild Heart* and coauthor of *The Sacred Romance.* John lives in Colorado with his wife, Stasi, and their three sons, Samuel, Blaine, and Luke. He loves living in the Rocky Mountains so he can pursue his other passions, including fly-fishing, mountain climbing, and exploring the waters of the West in his canoe.

Stasi Eldredge is the coleader of the women's ministry of Ransomed Heart and is passionate about women discovering their identity as the Beloved of Christ. Stasi is drawn to the beauty of the West and would more likely be found outside adventuring than inside tending her home. She loves her family, bubble baths, deep conversations, the wind, her dog Scout, someone else doing the dishes, a good movie, a good cry, a horse named Cora, and "most of all, how God loves and surprises me by continuing to come for my heart in amazing and intimate ways."

To learn more about John and Stasi's ministry,
visit www.ransomedheart.com.

AVAILABLE NOW

*J*oin Stasi Eldredge and an intimate group of women as they journey together deep into the feminine heart. Come along as they gather to talk about their stories and how God is transforming their lives. Share in the laughter and the tears, and discover for yourself the healing power of the love of God to restore your heart as a woman and set you free.

A wonderful resource for women's groups and studies.

This kit includes:

‣ 5 DVDs
‣ CD-ROM
‣ Best-selling *Captivating* book
‣ *Captivating Heart to Heart Study Guide*
‣ *Captivating Guided Journal*
‣ *Captivating Leader's Guide*
‣ Quick Start Guide to launch the program at your church, women's retreat, or small groups!

THOMAS NELSON
Since 1798

WHERE DO I GO FROM HERE?

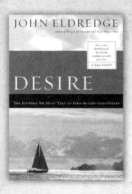

DESIRE

In *Desire*, formerly titled *The Journey of Desire*, John Eldredge writes of the journey people must take to find the life they prize. And the guide that has been given to all is the desire set deep within, the desire often overlooked or mistaken for something else or even ignored. In this groundbreaking book, Eldredge invites readers to acknowledge the significance of desire, abandon resignation, and embark on an adventure he calls "our heart's most important journey."

Trade Paper—ISBN 0-7852-8842-2 | $14.99
Study Guide—ISBN 1-4185-2857-9 | $7.99

EPIC

In *Epic*, a retelling of the gospel in four acts, John Eldredge invites us to revisit the drama of life, viewing God not only as the author but also as the lead actor, exploring His motives and His heart. Eldredge examines the power of story, the universal longing for a "plot" that makes sense deep inside us, our desire for a meaningful role to play, our love of books and movies, and how all of this points us to the gospel itself.

ISBN 0-7852-8878-3 | $9.99

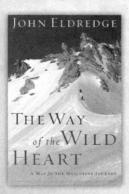

THE WAY OF THE WILD HEART

There is a journey every man must take to become a man. And there is a Father waiting to take him there. *The Way of the Wild Heart* gives men a map for their journey to true masculinity, and shows them how God offers the validation and initiation they need in order to live as truly confident men. It also lays out a plan for raising boys and young men into full manhood. A book that will give you direction and hope.

Hardcover—ISBN 0-7852-0677-9 | $22.99
Manual—ISBN 1-4185-1413-6 | $17.99

CALLING

Why can't we find the life we were created to live, if it is simply a matter of discovering our personality type and spiritual gifts and then matching them to the needs of the church or world? And if you have done that, why does it feel so life-less or life-taking?

God has already given you a map to your particular place in this Larger Story. Building off the message of *The Sacred Romance* and *Desire*, Gary Barkalow sheds light on interpreting the mysterious code written on our hearts, leading us to our place in The Story.

THE GOOD HEART

Is your heart good or bad? Can you trust that God will speak to you in your heart? Scripture teaches that the heart is central to our lives. Yet, many Christians find it hard to even talk about matters of the heart; they know the verse in Jeremiah 17:9 that says the heart is "desperately wicked."

How can we talk about loving God with all our heart? About living "from the heart"? The Gospel teaches that the work of Jesus Christ reaches even to the human heart.

Discover what God meant when he promised to set a new heart within us (Ezekiel 36:26) . . . and what Jesus offered when he talked about the "good and noble heart" (Luke 8:15).

THE HOPE OF PRAYER

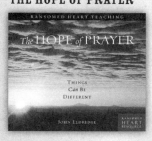

Everyone can point to things in our lives that we'd like to see change. Relationships, health issues, a need for direction, financial woes. To help us bring about change, God has given us prayer. The Scriptures talk a lot about prayer, but we're not really sure what to do with it, or, more importantly, how to do it in a way that works and actually brings about change.

But prayer is supposed to bring about change. When Jesus teaches us to pray "Thy Kingdom come, thy will be done," he means precisely that our prayers somehow enable the Kingdom of God to come and his will to be done "on earth as it is in heaven."

In this series, John Eldredge shows how to pray with hope and confidence, how to apply prayer to the various dilemmas of life with the most hopeful thought that things can be different.

Lots more great resources from John Eldredge at www.ransomedheart.com